# Normal Aging

To P. L. P. and J. M. P., models of normal aging

# Normal Aging

Reports from the Duke Longitudinal Study, 1955–1969,
edited by Erdman Palmore
Duke University Press, Durham, N.C.    1970

© 1970, Duke University Press
Third printing, 1974
L.C.C. card no. 74-132028
I.S.B.N. 0-8223-0238-1
Printed in the U.S.A.

# Foreword

The Longitudinal Study of Aging has been the central research project of the Duke Center for the Study of Aging since its beginning in 1954. This was the first interdisciplinary longitudinal study of aging in our nation. Over 100 articles have been published reporting its findings, but this is the first monograph to assemble and summarize these findings. By selecting the original research reports and by deleting duplicating paragraphs, Dr. Palmore has managed to include most of the basic findings within this one volume. In addition to these findings there have been many reports from "satellite" studies which are not included here because of space limitations. Other studies as well as additional analysis of these basic findings may be published in future monographs from the center.

In 1965 the center was renamed the Duke University Center for the Study of Aging and Human Development in order to reflect its broadened interest in the aging process during the early and middle years. At present the center is beginning a new longitudinal study of aging which includes persons in the middle as well as later ages (45–70). These longitudinal studies are now part of a comprehensive program of research in the center which includes eight other studies. The center has also instituted two specialized training programs: a two-year program for pre- or post-Ph.D. or M.D. fellows who desire to pursue research training in some aspect of the behavioral sciences or psychophysiology related to aging and human development, and a two-year geropsychiatry training program for fellows with two or three years of psychiatric residency training. Another recent development is the Information and Counseling Service for Older Persons which offers comprehensive evaluations, referral, and counseling for older persons in the Durham area. Full information on these and other programs of the center may be obtained from the address below.

Ewald W. Busse, *Director*
Center for the Study of Aging and Human Development
Duke University Medical Center
Durham, North Carolina 27706

*Ewald W. Busse*

# Preface

This is more than a book of readings, although it is made up of published articles or papers presented at professional meetings. When brought together and summarized, these articles combine to form a basic report on normal aging from the Duke Longitudinal Study of Aging. This study is a complex interdisciplinary project with a 13-year history, and it is impossible to report within one volume all of the findings, problems, and perspectives that have developed. However, we believe this book includes most of the study's findings related to normal aging to date.

"Normal" aging may have two meanings: healthy aging and typical aging. This volume deals with normal aging in both senses: (a) The aged persons studied were normal in that they were noninstitutionalized community residents who were willing and able to come to the Duke Medical Center for two days of tests and examinations. (b) The more common or typical patterns and problems of aging are focused upon rather than the unusual abnormalities. The reports deal with common medical problems, common mental health problems, normal patterns of intellectual functioning, patterns of family and sexual behavior, the normal association of activities with life satisfaction, and typical attitudes toward aging, health, and death.

Investigations of normal aging are of crucial importance in advancing the science of gerontology and in helping aged persons develop and enjoy a richer and longer life. When we can distinguish normal and inevitable processes of aging from those which may accompany aging simply because of accident, stress, maladjustment, or disuse, we can better focus our attention and efforts on those factors which can be changed and corrected. The attainment of a richer and more satisfying old age is of obvious interest to every living person, regardless of age.

One might raise the question why longitudinal and interdisciplinary methods were used to study normal aging. The answers are related to the nature of gerontology itself. *Webster's Seventh New Collegiate Dictionary* defines gerontology simply as "a branch of knowledge dealing with aging and the problems of the aged." There seem to be three implications for the study of normal aging that stem from this basic definition.

First, since aging is a process of change over time, it would seem that the best way to study aging is longitudinally, by repeated observations over time. There are, of course, many technical and methodological problems connected with a longitudinal study as illustrated by the problems discussed in Chapter I. Foremost among these problems are selective panel dropout and the length of time required between initial and final observations. Yet there are many more advantages to the longitudinal method:

1. Each panel member can be used as his own control so that background factors can be held fairly constant and the effects of aging can be measured more directly than in cross-sectional studies.

2. Observations made at three or more points in time allow the investigator to distinguish between consistent trends and temporary fluctuations due to chance or error in his measuring instrument.

3. Errors due to retrospective distortion or forgetting are minimized.

4. Early warning signs (antecedent events) of disease or death can be studied. Theories of contributory factors can be tested by prediction.

5. Cohort differences can be distinguished from age changes; for example, differences between 60- and 70-year-olds in 1968 due to different experiences between the two groups can be distinguished from changes in one group between 1958 and 1968.

6. The effects of one kind of change on another kind of change at a later time period can be studied (time-lag analysis).

Second, since aging affects many types of behavior and functioning, a comprehensive study of normal aging must involve several different disciplines. When the specialists from different disciplines work together on an interdisciplinary team, the mutual stimulation, correction, and combination of perspectives can result in more accurate, thorough, and comprehensive understanding of the aging process.

Third, the distinction between "aging and the problems of the aged" implies a distinction between normal aging and the diseases or trauma that may accompany aging. In order to study this difference, it is necessary to study a normal group of aging persons, such as healthy, functioning residents in the community, as well as those suffering from disease and trauma, such as residents of hospitals or nursing homes.

To summarize, these three implications suggest that comprehensive gerontological research would be longitudinal and interdisciplinary and would deal with normal as well as abnormal subjects. The Duke Longitudinal Study of Aging comes close to meeting all of these criteria. It has been going on for over 13 years, and five sets of observations have been recorded for most measures. Longitudinal analysis is used in about one-third of the reports in this book. The others use cross-sectional analysis, usually because they were published before sufficient longitudinal data were available. Most of the reports are interdisciplinary in the sense that they use data collected and interpreted by specialists in disciplines other than that of the primary author. All of the reports deal with normal subjects in the sense that all panel members were functioning mobile residents of the community. Some of the reports compare these normal subjects with residents of hospitals and nursing homes.

The original reports are usually presented with no deletions except for duplicate passages such as those that summarize previous reports or those that repeat the description of the panelists. A number of the articles are reprinted by permission from various journals. Deletions of a sentence or more in these articles are indicated by ellipses, and minor changes have been made for uniformity. Since most of the reports are interdisciplinary, the placement of some reports in one chapter rather than another was somewhat arbitrary, but an attempt was made to group reports by the type of central variable under investigation. After an introductory chapter discussing the goals and methods of the study, the book moves from reports on medical and mental problems through those on brain waves, reaction time, intelligence, perception, and affect. Two chapters contain the more sociological reports dealing with marriage, family, and social activities. The last chapters analyze attitudes toward health, age, death, and factors in longevity. The book concludes with a chapter summarizing the main themes of the reports.

We appreciate the cooperation of 31 authors and 24 journals or publishers for granting permission to reprint their articles. Special thanks are due to Mrs. Elizabeth Giles, Mrs. Nancy Glenn, Mrs. Janice Hall, Miss Helen Gill, and Mrs. Elizabeth Dickinson for their assistance in preparing the manuscript. The research reported in this book was supported in part by Public Health Service Grants AF-49(638)–354, CH-3582, GM-05385, H-3582, HD-00668, HD-0-325, M-900, M-2061, M-2109, MH-08244, MN-10096-03, PHS research career award 5153, PHS Fellowship MSP 18, 193, the National Science Foundation's support of the Duke Computing Laboratory, the Procter and Gamble Company, the Life Insurance Medical Research Fund, and the John and Mary Markle Foundation and its Fund for Research in Psychiatry.

*Erdman Palmore*

# Contents

# Figures

# Tables

# Contributors

Robert H. Barnes, M.D., Professor of Psychiatry, University of Texas School of Medicine, South Texas, San Antonio, Texas.

Jack Botwinick, Ph.D., Professor of Psychology, Washington University, St. Louis, Missouri.

Robert G. Brown, Ph.D., Professor of Sociology, George Washington University, Washington, D.C.

Ewald W. Busse, M.D., Sc.D., J. P. Gibbons Professor of Psychiatry and Chairman of the Department, Director of the Center for the Study of Aging and Human Development, Duke University Medical Center, Durham, North Carolina.

Louis D. Cohen, Ph.D., Professor and Chairman of the Department of Clinical Psychology, University of Florida, Gainesville, Florida.

Sanford I. Cohen, M.D., Professor and Chairman of the Department of Psychiatry, Biobehavioral Sciences, Louisiana State University Medical School, New Orleans, Louisiana.

Robert H. Dovenmuehle, M.D., Dallas County Mental Health and Mental Retardation Center, Dallas, Texas.

Carl Eisdorfer, Ph.D., M.D., Professor of Psychiatry and Medical Psychology, Duke University Medical Center, Durham, North Carolina.

E. Harvey Estes, M.D., Professor of Community Health Sciences and Chairman of the Department, Professor of Medicine, Duke University Medical Center, Durham, North Carolina.

K. Regina Frayser, Ph.D., Associate Professor of Medicine and Physiology, Indiana University Medical School, Indianapolis, Indiana.

Dorothy K. Heyman, M.S.W., Research Social Worker in Psychiatry, Duke University Medical Center, Durham, North Carolina.

Frances C. Jeffers, M.A., Research Associate in Psychiatry, Duke University Medical Center, Durham, North Carolina.

R. W. Kleemeier, Ph.D. (deceased), Professor of Psychology, Washington University, St. Louis, Missouri.

William H. Knisely, Ph.D., Director of the Institute of Biology and Medicine, College of Human Medicine, Michigan State University, East Lansing, Michigan.

Martin Lakin, Ph.D., Professor of Medical Psychology, Duke University Medical Center, Durham, North Carolina.

George L. Maddox, Ph.D., Professor of Medical Sociology, Duke University Medical Center, Durham, North Carolina.

W. Edward McGough, M.D., Associate Professor of Psychiatry, Rutgers Medical School, New Brunswick, New Jersey.

E. Gustave Newman, Jr., M.D., Assistant Professor of Psychiatry, College of Medicine, University of Florida, Gainesville, Florida.

Claude R. Nichols, M.D., Associate Professor of Psychiatry, University of Texas, Southwestern Medical School at Dallas, Dallas, Texas.

Walter D. Obrist, Ph.D., Professor of Medical Psychology, Duke University Medical Center, Durham, North Carolina.

Erdman Palmore, Ph.D., Associate Professor of Medical Sociology, Duke University Medical Center, Durham, North Carolina.

Eric A. Pfeiffer, M.D., Associate Professor of Psychiatry, Duke University Medical Center, Durham, North Carolina.

John B. Reckless, M.D., Associate Professor of Psychomatic Medicine, Duke University Medical Center, Durham, North Carolina.

William M. Satterwhite, Jr., M.D., The Forsyth Medical Park, Winston-Salem, North Carolina.

Barry M. Shmavonian, Ph.D., Professor of Psychology, Department of Behavioral Sciences, Temple University, Philadelphia, Pennsylvania.

Albert J. Silverman, M.D., Professor and Chairman of the Department of Psychiatry, Rutgers Medical School, New Brunswick, New Jersey.

J. Graham Smith, Jr., M.D., Professor and Chairman of the Department of Dermatology, Medical College of Georgia, Augusta, Georgia.

Larry W. Thompson, Ph.D., Associate Professor of Medical Psychology, Duke University Medical Center, Durham, North Carolina.

John P. Tindall, M.D., Assistant Professor of Dermatology, Duke University Medical Center, Durham, North Carolina.

Adriaan Verwoerdt, M.D., Associate Professor of Psychiatry, Duke University Medical Center, Durham, North Carolina.

Hsioh-Shan Wang, M.D., Assistant Professor of Psychiatry, Duke University Medical Center, Durham, North Carolina.

Stuart Wilson, Ph.D., Chief Psychologist, Southcoast Child Guidance Clinic, Newport Beach, California.

# Normal Aging

# Chapter 1. Goals and Methods

In order to evaluate the validity and generality for a set of findings, one must understand the goals of a project and the methods used in pursuit of those goals. The type of sample used, methods of examination and interviewing, research staff, types of analysis and inference are all critical factors in such an evaluation.

This chapter describes and discusses the general methodological problems and procedures of the Duke Longitudinal Study of Aging, while the subsequent chapters include descriptions of the specific techniques peculiar to the subject of each chapter. The first selection describes the goal of studying aging among normal community residents, the sampling techniques, the tests and examinations, and the interdisciplinary staff. The second presents some administrative principles for such an interdisciplinary research team. The chapter concludes with a discussion of the problems posed by the use of volunteers and by selective dropout of panelists.

## A Physiological, Psychological, and Sociological Study of Aging   *Ewald W. Busse*

### Goals

Awareness of the elderly and problems associated with aging in our society was becoming acute in the 1950's. Research, however, had been confined primarily to the institutionalized elderly, an estimated 6 percent of the total population 60 years of age and older, and research findings were consequently not adequately descriptive of older people living more or less adequately in various communities. Moreover, available studies were characteristically deficient methodologically; they were not adequate for the study of aging as a process nor adequate to take into account a wide range of theoretically relevant variables.

The Duke Longitudinal Study of Aging was initiated to investigate processes of aging among a panel of noninstitutionalized males and females 60 years of age and over from the time of initial observation to death. The study was conceived as exploratory and multidisciplinary. Its organization was intended to facilitate the accumulation of the widest possible range of observations from investigators with a variety of theoretical perspectives on a common panel of subjects. Medical, psychiatric, psychological, and sociological perspectives have been represented among project investigators over the first decade of the project's existence.

No single theory of aging informed the development of the study. The focus has been on the generation of hypotheses as much as the testing of hypotheses of interest to a variety of investigators who have brought quite different theoretical perspectives to bear on the analysis of data. The project has therefore offered each investigator an opportunity for contact with colleagues with different theoretical interests and perspectives and an opportunity for the use of the data of other investigators as control variables in his own research on panel members.

## Design and Sample

The centrality of detailed information on medical and psychological functioning which required precise measurements and laboratory evaluation presented a special problem in the development of a panel of older subjects. Two days of examination in the Duke Medical Center were required. The reported experience of survey research indicated that subjects' refusal to participate was a function of age in the later years. Since the proposed examination of panelists was costly and continued participation in the panel was vital, the Duke investigators chose to recruit volunteers rather than attempt to involve a randomly drawn sample of noninstitutionalized subjects.

A snowball technique was used to create a pool of volunteers 60 years of age and older. Initially, the median age of panelists was 70, and they ranged in age from 60 to 94. From this pool a panel was created that reflected the age, sex, ethnic, and socioeconomic characteristics of the older population in Durham, North Carolina. The purpose of this procedure was to maximize the variety of controls which might be introduced subsequently, not to give the appearance of random sampling without its substance. The primary inducement originally offered was a free annual physical examination. Four years were required to accumulate the basic panel of 256 subjects on whom baseline determinations were made. The mean time between the initial and the first longitudinal observation was 33 months with a standard deviation of approximately 6 months. The second, third, and fourth observations were completed in 20, 14, and 12 months, respectively. A description of the timing of these observations and panel attrition are summarized in Table 1–1.

Most panelists seem to have been motivated by the medical examination and have in fact been examined between longitudinal observations. In

Table 1–1. *Panel attrition during four longitudinal observations.*

| Observation | Dates | Subjects with complete records | Percentage of 256 who returned | Percentage of nonreturnees who: were | | | |
|---|---|---|---|---|---|---|---|
| | | | | died | ill | refused | other |
| I | 5/55–5/59 | 256 | — | — | — | — | — |
| II | 9/59–5/61 | 192 (10 added) | 71 | 43 | 23 | 20 | 14 |
| III | 1/64–3/65 | 139 ( 1 added) | 52 | 63 | 26 | 2 | 9 |
| IV | 10/66–7/67 | 110 | 41 | 68 | 18 | 1 | 13 |

the experience of project social workers, an equally important factor in maintaining the panel has been the opportunity for participants to obtain satisfying social recognition regularly. This recognition takes the form of greeting cards on special occasions, occasional contact by telephone with the social workers, and a solicitious attention on those days when the panelists are brought to the medical center for observation.

The degree of identification with the project is reflected in a relatively low rate of attrition for reasons other than by death or serious illness through four observations over the past decade. After the second longitudinal series, in which 20 percent of the 74 nonparticipants refused, refusals were minimal.

Several methodological problems associated with this design are immediately obvious. Generalizations from the data necessarily are limited to statements concerning the relationship among factors in the aging process under specified conditions. Statements based on data from this panel about the distribution of characteristics or configurations of characteristics among older people generally are not warranted. Statements about certain aging processes with each panelist used as his own control are warranted. Moreover, the length of time between observations is not identical for all panelists. Where this factor may be relevant, precise information about intervals between observations is available for each panelist.

For each panelist, approximately 788 pieces of information were coded in each series of observations for each subject. Of these, 336 were medical; 109, psychiatric or neurological; 109, psychological; and 234, social. A summary of observations is found in Table 1–2. Medical determinations included history and current status of systems, with special attention being given to cardiovascular ratings, serology, ophthalmology, and audiology. A summary rating of physical functioning was developed for estimating the presence or absence of pathology and associated degree of disability. An index estimating cardiovascular functioning has also been developed.

The psychiatric or neurological variables focus on aspects of mental

Table 1–2. *A summary of longitudinal observations.*

| | |
|---|---|
| Medical history (original and interim) | Laboratory studies |
| Physical examination | Urinalysis |
| Neurological examination | Blood morphology |
| Mental status | Blood chemistry |
| Depression and hypochondriasis | Serologic test for syphilis |
| Dermatological examination | Cholesterol |
| Ophthalmological examination | Urea nitrogen |
|   Visual fields | Medical summary |
|   Acuity | Psychological data |
|   Color perception |   Rorschach |
|   Depth perception |   Aspiration level (TAT) |
|   Color photographs |   Wechsler Adult Intelligence Scale |
| Audiometry |   Reaction time |
|   Pure tone | Social history and information |
|   Speech threshold | Retirement data |
| Electroencephalogram |   Activities |
| Chest x-ray |   Attitudes |

status and functioning, both current and historical, among panelists. Detailed electroencephalograph (EEG) evaluations supplement the findings of neurological examination.

Psychological variables include Wechsler Adult Intelligence Scale (WAIS) scores, assessment of reaction time in a variety of learning experiments, and summaries of Rorschach responses.

Sociological variables include life style indicators, work status and history, family relationships, and level of activity and of life satisfaction, including an adaptation on Cavan Activities and Attitudes scales.

### Staff

Core project investigators have included internists, ophthalmologists, psychiatrists, neurologists, psychologists, sociologists, and social workers. Usually examinations and observations were made by project investigators, although some routine examinations have been done by medical and psychiatric residents and fellows. Laboratory tests and x-rays have been done on a contractual basis with appropriate hospital service units. The project employs a computer programmer who presides over the records and is available to all investigators. Four core investigators have been with the project essentially since its inception, and three others have at least seven years of experience with the panel data.

# Administration of the Interdisciplinary Research Team*
## *Ewald W. Busse*

This paper will present some administrative principles and policies which appear basic to the development, maintenance, and satisfactory termination of research by an interdisciplinary team. It will not be concerned with research designs or the techniques which can be utilized by an interdisciplinary team. No attempt will be made to justify the team approach.

The empirical operating principles that are presented are the result of participation in and close association with interdisciplinary studies for over 15 years. The majority of the policies and guidelines evolved rapidly during the first few years of this experience and consequently have been in use for a number of years. This time interval has permitted the testing of the usefulness of these principles and policies and has led to certain modifications.

The formation of an effective interdisciplinary team requires considerable time and effort (Luzski, 1958a). Therefore, the cost in time and money of the so-called tooling-up period must be justified by and in proportion to the importance of the research, the duration of the project, and the possibility of maintaining the team at the conclusion of a project and shifting it to an appropriate but new investigation. For this reason mention will be made of the peculiarities of longitudinal studies, as such investigations frequently are based upon an interdisciplinary approach.

## Definitions

Although some persons become bored and annoyed by an insistence upon the definition of terms, an avoidance of definitions can lead to serious confusion, omissions, and false conclusions. Such clarification is not only important for delineating the proposed research during conception but also is of considerable value in preparing applications for research support and will later be needed to describe accurately the research methodology when the material is published. The following definitions may not be universally acceptable but are believed necessary for this discussion.

* Reprinted by permission from the *Journal of Medical Education*, 40:832–839, 1965. The author wishes to express appreciation to Dr. Margaret Thaler Singer, Adult Psychiatry Branch, National Institute of Mental Health, for her assistance in the preparation of this publication.

When more than one person is involved in a research task, the relations between them are either of a team or of a group nature.

### Group Research

This term describes an assemblage of two or more persons of the same or different disciplines who have some areas of similar interests in their research approaches. It is assumed that they are working in a close proximity to one another, which permits some degree of scientific communication. However, there are no formal and specified working relationships. Often large groups of researchers are brought together with the hope that there will be cross-fertilization of ideas from one worker to another and that enthusiasms will cause teams to form spontaneously within the larger group because of such communication and proximity.

### Team Research

The participants may be of the same or different disciplines, and it is assumed that they are in close proximity, but the working relationship is an explicit and formal one. These people are working together to achieve a goal by following a predetermined plan. Each member of the research team has an assigned task of data collection and integration and analysis. The team is highly dependent upon all members' centering their major efforts around the team goals and keeping their individual work timed according to the team's overall plans. In addition to being responsible for his assigned task, each member of a team must communicate the cross-correlate data. The team is highly dependent upon these fundamentals if it is to achieve the prescribed goal.

### Multidisciplinary (Group) Research*

Multidisciplinary research is a type of group research involving several distinct group scientific disciplines. The investigators are identified as a group because they are working in proximity and have interests in a common research topic. It is hoped and assumed that there is a maximum of communication between the investigators and, therefore, that the potential of their work is increased.

* These words are not defined in *Dorland's Illustrated Medical Dictionary*, 23rd ed., Philadelphia: W. B. Saunders, 1961, or *A Comprehensive Dictionary of Psychological and Psychoanalytic Terms,* New York: David McKay, 1964. *Webster's Seventh New Collegiate Dictionary* (1963) gives the following definition for "interdisciplinary": "adj. involving 2 or more academic disciplines." "Multidisciplinary" is not listed in *Webster's.*

## Interdisciplinary (Team) Research*

Interdisciplinary research is a team effort. The team is composed of two or more individuals representing distinct scientific disciplines who, because of their particular skills and interest, will accept certain responsibilities and will cooperate and collaborate with other members of the team to achieve their goal. The meaning of the prefix "inter" is "mutual" rather than just "among" or "between."

## Individual Research

For completeness, individual research needs to be mentioned. In this instance a single scientist, by his own efforts or by directing the efforts of others, is solely responsible for the research. Coinvestigation implies that the research activity is being conducted by equally responsible partners—a team. Their job responsibilities may not be identical, but they are balanced with each man having clear responsibility for certain tasks.

## Development

It appears unwise, if not impossible, to develop an effective interdisciplinary team without going through a careful process of selection and indoctrination. Not all professional persons are suited to, experienced at, nor genuinely interested in, interdisciplinary research. There are a substantial number of competent scientists who have never participated in a genuine interdisciplinary effort. It is not unusual to find reputable scientists who are very resistant to the concept of interdiscplinary research and are openly opposed to it as a research approach. Their views are often, at least in part, an expression of an unconscious prejudice; and, consequently, they exert a disrupting influence as site visitors. Fortunately, there are increasing numbers of scientific leaders who have appreciation of the scientific efforts of other disciplines and who understand the values as well as the limitations of an interdisciplinary approach.

There are parallels between developing and maintaining an effective interdisciplinary research team and developing a professional athletic team. The mere term "team" implies that members are selected because of demonstrated individual skill, but the ultimate success of a team is related to keeping the goals in focus and maintaining balance, motivation, and morale among members. In addition a team must have methods for successfully coping with the loss of members and replacing them as needed.

Selection of Investigators

During the process of selection for an interdisciplinary team, special attention should be given to the candidate's attitude toward his own profession and the satisfactions he receives from his work. It is important that he be content with his professional choice and that he believe that his interest, place, and future in his own profession are relatively secure. An individual who has more than realistic doubts about his professional choice does not possess sufficient security and identity to function within an interdisciplinary group. Such a person encounters difficulty making sustained and constructive contributions, as he is extremely vulnerable to the criticism of other disciplines (Kubie, 1953). Immature, seriously insecure, or markedly disorganized persons have little or no place on an interdisciplinary team, although it is agreed that such persons as individuals can be creative, productive researchers.

Disciplinary Influence and Interactions

The qualifications and professional characteristics of scholars and scientists can differ greatly. Such variation results from basic differences in interests which originally determine vocational choices. Additionally, there are selection processes within each discipline—attributes valued in an anthropology department may not be those sought by a committee choosing candidates for degrees in experimental psychology; further, these criteria change from time to time. Finally, within established disciplines, members learn both specific research techniques and approaches as well as patterns of thinking and various values and standards. These differences, some which have a positive influence and some a negative influence on the interdisciplinary approach to research, are significantly influenced by the overall graduate program producing the various doctor of philosophy and doctor of medicine specialists and by the particular periods of time during which they receive their education.

In the development of a research team it is evident that at the outset there is a status hierarchy (Luzski, 1958b). This hierarchy as perceived by the various members of the team is not a consistent one but is related to the current status system which exists within the academic structure and within society as a whole. As a team works together, the hierarchy undergoes considerable change. The skillful, creative, and industrious investigator assumes a higher place in the group. A special hierarchy is developed within the team, and shifts occur that are related to many factors. This is not appreciated or understood by the outsider. In fact, a visitor can be upset to find his discipline is not the highest in the "pecking order." The leadership in an interdisciplinary effort must make certain that team meetings are not utilized as a dueling ground or as a forum for debating the conflicts and power struggles between scientific disciplines. The work of an interdisciplinary team should be sufficiently challenging and exciting so that attention of the team members can be easily maintained upon the project itself. It is the author's observation, however, that the respect and understanding which develop between disciplines within such a team often promote good will and contribute to the solution of rivalries which exist outside the project. This experience of developing tolerance for divergent techniques and appreciation of the training and capacities of others is one of the major positive side effects that results from projects that are well conceived and well carried out.

An individual whose sole research activity is participation in an interdisciplinary team is likely to encounter certain difficulties that reduce his effectiveness as a team member. The clinical or services professions tend to restrict research to a team effort but this should be discouraged. A physician may take the position that he is heavily burdened with clinical obligations, and, therefore, he can do only team research because he must carefully allocate his research time. This decision may also be influenced by other motivations, such as the belief that the team will provide an exciting interchange with other disciplines or that it is a safer way to conduct research since the physician will receive the help of members with more knowledge of investigational procedures. Such a decision to participate in team activity and not to pursue individual but related research may appear to be based upon good reasons. Unfortunately, such team members are more vulnerable to loss of self-esteem than those who have both team and individual research interests. If the contribution of such an investigator to the team is criticized or doubted, this source of maintaining self-esteem is disrupted. He may feel uncomfortable, yet he is too dependent on the team for research prestige and publications to deal effectively with the situation. Some of these persons will terminate their relationship with the team, and others will attempt to hold on. Either pathway is marked by hostility which sooner or later causes difficulty for the individual and the team. Obviously, one should not adhere to strict rules, but the leader of an interdisciplinary team must be alert to this type of complication, for it is probable that in a team of three or more there will be at least one member whose research interests are confined to that team effort. A balance should be sought between the team commitment and individual work.

Rules

*Hypotheses, Questions, and Research Methods*

It is evident that the formulation of hypotheses and the statement of questions to be answered are the prerequisites of well-planned research. The responsible investigators in an interdisciplinary study will want to contribute to the development of both hypotheses and questions, and they should do so. This requires a prolonged period of development, and it is time-consuming and costly. Therefore, it follows that sound interdisciplinary research projects will be proposed by groups who are willing to make the necessary sacrifices and have resources for covering the planning period. It should also be anticipated that new members of an interdisciplinary team who are not present at the origin of the project usually are to varying degrees dissatisfied with the original aims and design of the project. New members include both those who are hired when the project is first funded but who do not participate in the original formulation and those later brought in as replacements. The degree of dissatisfaction affects the usefulness of the new member to the team. When it is minimal, even though it cannot be completely resolved, it can be converted to a strength by the promotion of satellite projects which have rational relationship to the main project.

It is important that the original team unanimously consent to and support the final aims of the project as well as the methods to be pursued. If a responsible member of the team wishes to change his methods of observation or procedures, it is essential that he have an opportunity to present his views to the team and have them agree to the change. If this is not done, it is on occasion found that a shift by one person completely invalidates the observations of other members of the team and hence makes a segment of the work useless.

*Central and Special Core Project Data and Satellite Projects*

One of the values of an interdisciplinary research effort is that time and effort are saved by having necessary central data, that is, control observations or identifying characteristics, which are usable by all members of the team. Such data collection must be carefully planned and without reservation be available to each member of the team. There are times when the individual investigator believes he needs control or identifying data not clearly useful to the entire group. When this occurs, the investigator must have the responsibility for programming it and properly fitting it into the entire procedure. It also must meet the criteria for acceptance which have been spelled out. Special data are those observations and procedures which are a fundamental part of the experimental design of the core project. These data are the result of ideas generated or accepted by the assigned investigator and reflect the area of his professional competency. In a previous section the desirability of combining team research with individual research was pointed out. However, within the design of the team, the investigator who confines his interest to the data resulting from his narrow field of professional interest will find that he is unlikely to remain a contented and effective member of the team.

Satellite projects are not the direct concern of the team but are very important for the continuing success and effectiveness of the individual investigator. Satellite projects, if encouraged, will easily develop from the team project. Research ideas are generated that cannot be carried out within the team framework. However, these relatively independent satellite projects often have tremendous feedback into the team project and provide a source of new stimuli.

Satellite projects when combined with interdisciplinary longitudinal study produce certain problems. Specifically, when the individual investigator wants to utilize the longitudinal subjects because of the advantage afforded by control or baseline data which have already been established, he cannot be permitted to do so without the permission of the interdisciplinary team. To be permitted free access to the subjects and the collected data without proper review could lose the subjects, invalidate the research, and destroy the morale of the team. For example, a satellite project that is painful physically or psychologically could result in the loss of volunteer subjects.

## Utilization Data for Publication

An interdisciplinary team frequently collects a large number of observations which require complex methods of cross-correlation and statistical analyses. The disputes over jurisdictional control and rights of publication can produce dissension in an interdisciplinary team; therefore, the possibility of such difficulties should be anticipated and reduced by establishment of ground rules. Central data must be available to every member of the team. Special data are the assigned responsibility of an individual investigator, so when his observations, analyses, or conclusions are utilized by another investigator for publication, the person whose work is incorporated should participate as a coauthor or a reviewer, and a footnote should mention his contribution to the article. Although at times there are reasons for deviating from the rule, in general it would appear that the individual who assumes major responsibility for writing the article should be the first author. With continuing proper communication there should be few problems that cannot be amiably resolved.

## Introduction of New Observations

Once a research procedure has been adopted, it undoubtedly will be under periodic review, and investigators will want to introduce new observations and new procedures. In an interdisciplinary team this must be accomplished by an established process. The investigator should present with an adequate explanation the work which he wishes to do. This frequently sharpens the proposal, and in the discussion there emerge stimulating thoughts and new ideas. This is an important ingredient in a scientific process and should not be minimized, as it is one of the great strengths in interdisciplinary research.

## Meetings and Minutes

Scheduled meetings are necessary to any team effort to insure communication, coordination, and cooperation. The frequency and the length of the meetings must be planned. The meeting provides an important opportunity for learning, for maintaining interest and motivation, and for generating new research ideas and opportunities for interdisciplinary work. Agendas for the meeting should be prepared and should include time for clarification of administrative procedures, budgetary explanation and reviews, review of research progress, clarification of research techniques, reports from the current literature, and an opportunity to present preliminary drafts of scientific papers resulting from the interdisciplinary research.

The administrative portion of the meeting is usually separated from the scholarly or research period. All decisions that relate to the functioning of the team must be carefully recorded and the reasons for arriving at that decision clearly elucidated. Perhaps the reason for this can best be understood by the use of an example. After the team has discussed alternative laboratory procedures and has selected one to be included in the central observations, the reason why procedure A was selected rather than procedure B should be recorded. Months later, the question arises, "How did it happen that we selected procedure A when procedure B seems to be just as good or better?" If a debate develops, it is often evident that group recall is incomplete and distorted, and the only reliable resource is the accurate minutes of the meeting when the original decision was made.

## Longitudinal Research

The study of the health and adjustment of humans can be approached by the cross-sectional method or by the longitudinal method. Both methods have advantages and disadvantages and for this reason when properly used often complement one another. If there were no urgency for action and if the perfect longitudinal study could be devised, it is possible that there would be no need for cross-sectional research. However, there is no doubt that the longitudinal studies of child development are extremely rewarding and provide information unobtainable through ordinary cross-sectional approaches. Longitudinal studies have the definite advantage of being more likely to identify events which precipitate or contribute to the appearance of changes or disease and, conversely, contribute to our understanding of what determinants prevent, reverse, or hold in check pathological progression. Longitudinal research is of considerable value because individual patterns of aging can be identified which cannot be recognized by cross-sectional studies. It is important to identify changes and to know which changes in an individual can be attributed to the passage of time and are not the result of a hostile environment or disease, and at what rate they transpire. When a longitudinal study is being organized, at least the following four major problem areas must be given attention: (*a*) the investigator or investigators, (*b*) the research methods, (*c*) the sample, and (*d*) financial support. Only those aspects of these areas relating to team efforts will be discussed here.

### *Personnel Losses and New Personnel*

In a longitudinal study of appreciable size and duration, it is impossible to maintain the same team throughout the life span of the study. Skillful investigators will be offered positions which are more attractive to them. In fact, the experience and reputation that they have developed while in a successful study are often vehicles for professional advancement. Consequently, there are rights and privileges that must be understood. When an individual divorces himself from a long-term study, he gives up the right to control the destiny of his contributions to the core study. He cannot take the data with him, and he cannot insist that because he was responsible for the collection of these data that he will remain a member of the team even though he is remotely located for the duration of the project. Obviously, he must be replaced, and an individual who replaces him must feel he is not a second-rate citizen. Although there are no absolute rules, a member who leaves the team should complete data analyses but not necessarily the writing of papers prior to departure. When he publishes the papers, he must adhere to all of the previously established rules and courtesies developed by the interdisciplinary team.

If the replacement of a resigned member causes a distortion in the data collection, the value of that particular effort can be destroyed. For this reason the new member should fully understand the methods, the observations, and the recording techniques. It is also essential that he appreciate why certain approaches were adopted so that he can comfortably work within that structure.

### Basic and Peripheral Studies

In another part of this article reference was made to the advisability of individual investigators participating in individual as well as interdisciplinary research. Longitudinal studies produce additional complications. A long-term study increases the period of data collection and is apt to slow down publications. In turn, interdisciplinary research can contribute to slowing of publications because papers are likely to be reviewed at the team meetings before they are read or submitted for publications; therefore, they may require greater time and effort. Investigators, particularly young ones who are in the process of establishing their scientific reputations cannot afford to wait a long period of time before they start to publish. Perhaps one can say that this is unfortunate and criticize this method of scientific or academic evaluation. However, it is a reality and must be given proper consideration. Therefore it is wise for the individual members of the team to participate in satellite or peripheral projects. The investigator is wise to plan such short-term studies so that they can be brought to a point where they are publishable and are not dependent on the end results of the longitudinal study.

### Comments

The policies, guidelines, and operating principles which are represented in this paper are not intended to be an exhaustive review of the subject of interdisciplinary research administration and are not, in fact, a complete listing of those which are now or have been utilized or considered. For example, the setting (Rioch, 1958) and the problem of cross-discipline communication are not covered in detail. It is possible that interdisciplinary research will flourish in one setting but die in another. If the factors presented in this paper are given consideration, the so-called problem of communication, that is, the languages employed by various groups, becomes the source of stimulation and learning for all (Luzski, 1958b). It is believed that particular types of team structure are needed to accommodate the specific demands and working environment of the research team. No attempt has been made in this paper to treat this subject.

The interdisciplinary research approach, particularly in the study of problems of aging and the aged, is likely to be involved with rather large numbers of subjects or patients and with methods and possible conclusions of a social, economic, and political nature that can produce adverse reactions and criticisms (Woolman, 1964). Again, no effort is made in this presentation to offer any helpful suggestions or specific solutions to this vexing complication. The research administrator and the members of an interdisciplinary team are urged to acquire knowledge of the source of their subjects and the impact of their work in the community and anticipate to the best of their ability the problems that could develop.

## Summary

This paper attempts to review practices and policies that should be included in the development of an interdisciplinary team and that are required for its successful functioning. Interdisciplinary research can be distinguished from multidisciplinary research. The selection of capable participants for interdisciplinary work is limited, as all competent scientists and scholars are not able to work effectively in such a setting. In order to maintain the morale and efficiency of an interdisciplinary team, it is necessary to provide a research climate that is exciting and rewarding. Such a favorable research climate must be planned and maintained. These factors and conditions are of utmost importance to the research administrator.

## References

Kubie, L. S. The problems of maturity in psychiatric research. *Journal of Medical Education,* 28:11–27, October, 1953.
Luzski, M. B. The challenge of the interdisciplinary team approach in research. In Jeffers, F. (Ed.), *Proceedings of seminars, Duke University Council on Gerontology.* Durham: Duke University, 1958. (a)
Luzski, M. B. *Interdisciplinary team research methods and problems.* New York: New York University Press, 1958. (b)
Rioch, D. K. Multidisciplinary methods in psychiatric research. *Journal of Orthopsychiatry,* 28:467–482, 1958.
Woolman, M. Bureaucratic structure and research restriction. Presented at the meeting of the American Orthopsychiatric Association, Chicago, Illinois, March, 1964. Special publication of the Institute of Education Research, Washington.

# Selected Methodological Issues*    *George L. Maddox*

Two characteristics of the research design are of special relevance for the issues to be discussed:

1. The subjects of the investigation are volunteers from among persons 60 years of age and over who were living in a community at the time they indicated a willingness to come to the medical center for two days of interviews and clinical evaluations.

2. The focus of the research is on the *processes* of change as well as on the changes commonly observed among elderly subjects. Continued observation of the same subjects over an extended period of time has been considered basic.

Sampling procedure and panel maintenance in longitudinal studies are not novel methodological issues. They are, however, persistent issues, and the method of handling them is fundamentally related to the analysis, interpretation, and generalization of research data. The purpose of this paper is to illustrate this relationship within the context of a specific research enterprise. . . .

### Selection of Subjects

The issue of sampling appropriate for the proposed research posed a basic problem. A review of the minutes of the seminar within which the research design was developed indicates that the discussion went something like this:

Persons engaged in a scientific enterprise can concern themselves with generalizations about the distribution of some characteristic or variable within a population; the epidemiologist, for example, is preoccupied with this type of generalization. But a scientist may also be interested in the relationship between or among characteristics or variables independent of their distribution in a population. The scientific experiment that seeks to relate variables X and Y under given conditions is a case in point. Generalizations of the first type require the investigation of some universe or of samples representative of that universe. Generalizations of the second type require, as a minimum, control of variables presumed to be relevant. While optimum research design should provide for both types of generalizations, practical considerations frequently make it necessary to choose one or the other type as an immediate goal.

* Reprinted by permission from the *Proceedings of the Social Statistics Section of the American Statistical Association*, 280–285, 1962.

With appropriate misgivings, the research group at Duke University decided to continue the practice of recruiting volunteers rather than attempting to involve a randomly drawn sample of elderly noninstitutionalized subjects in research that would require intensive clinical evaluation. In recruiting more volunteers from the community, however, an attempt was to be made to develop a panel of subjects 60 years of age and older whose age, sex, ethnic, and socioeconomic characteristics would reflect the range of these characteristics found among older persons in the locale. It was not the purpose of this procedure to provide the appearance of random sampling without its substance, but rather to maximize the variety of controls which could be introduced subsequently. In time, 256 subjects who met these criteria indicated a willingness to participate in the research and completed the initial two-day series of interviews and clinical examinations. The only inducements offered these volunteers were a free annual medical examination, a subscription to a magazine for elderly persons, and whatever satisfaction the subjects derived from their participation.

One consequence of the decision to use volunteer subjects was obvious. Generalizations from the data would necessarily be limited to statements concerning the relationship among factors in the aging process *under specified conditions*. Statements about elderly persons in general would not be warranted.

The deliberate decision of a research group to use volunteers and to accept the consequences of its decision does not have to be defended. But an interesting question is posed: Was there in fact a feasible alternative to their decision? When the research project is one which necessarily involves clinical evaluations and which must be carried out among noninstitutionalized subjects, the answer seems to be no. Attempts to involve randomly selected noninstitutionalized subjects in research requiring clinical evaluation have not proved rewarding. It is difficult to get subjects living in the community into a clinic for a single examination, much less for a series of different examinations; and the problem is intensified with the increasing age of the subjects. (Cobb, King, & Chen, 1957; Gordon, Moore, Shurtleff, & Dawber, 1959; Borsky & White, 1959; USNHS, 1960; Krueger, 1957).

The decision to use a panel of volunteers raises additional problems concerning subject selection which are not resolved by restraint in the generalization of findings. In addition to being a crucial condition of generalizing from a part to a whole, random selection procedure also has another function in research: it presumably minimizes the probability of introducing systematic bias from unrecognized or uncontrolled but potentially significant sources into the analysis of relationships among variables. For example, volunteers used as "normal controls" in clinical research may in fact neither be normal nor provide controls. In specific instances it has been demonstrated that volunteer subjects have introduced an uncontrolled but definitely biasing effect in clinical experiments (Esecover, Malitz, & Wilkins, 1961).[1] The fact that an individual is not institutionalized and not a patient does not necessarily make him a normal control within any frame of reference.

Subtle as well as gross biasing effects introduced by self-selection may also have a bearing on the analysis of relationships among variables. The Duke research project, for example, was designed to explore selected physiological, psychological, and sociological correlates of central nervous system aging. Each type of factor implies a number of universes within which subjects may be ordered in some fashion—say, in terms of relative health or illness, of higher or lower intelligence, of greater or lesser age, or of higher or lower socioeconomic status. Since a given individual is a member of each of these universes simultaneously, it is difficult to parcel out the effect of each factor in a given situation. If the subjects are volunteers, they may represent adequately the theoretically possible range of health and illness but include only those who are of higher intelligence and upper socioeconomic status; or they may run the gamut from high to low socioeconomic status but include only those who are relatively healthy and of high intelligence; or the subjects may be concentrated among those who are in good health, have high intelligence, and are in the upper range of status.

In the absence of probability sampling, the possibility of spurious relationships which are artifacts of the sampling procedure is increased. A cross-sectional analysis of project data, for example, indicated that activity, but not morale, decreased with age among these elderly subjects. That this finding is probably an artifact of the age distribution of antecedent or intervening variables known to affect the relationship between activity and morale will be illustrated later.

A number of studies involving noninstitutionalized elderly subjects have employed random sampling procedure. The nonparticipation rates in such studies have been high, especially when clinical evaluation of subjects has been involved. It is entirely possible that a high refusal rate in such instances produces a sample which is essentially the equivalent of a collection of volunteers. To investigate this possibility, the Duke panelists have

[1] This article presents a case in point and a convenient bibliography. It is pertinent that most discussions of volunteer "Normal controls" concern only younger subjects. Experience in the research reported here suggests that the usual characterization of the young volunteer as "not normal" cannot be extended uncritically to apply to elderly subjects.

been compared with samples of elderly persons used in other research projects.

Three types of comparisons have been made: (a) a comparison in terms of selected physical and mental health characteristics between the Duke panelists and samples presumed to be representative of local, regional, or national populations of older persons; (b) a comparison of the panel with itself at two points in time, on the assumption that selective dropout of subjects through time might provide a rough indication of the characteristics of subjects initially attracted to participate in the research; and (c) a comparison, in terms of selected characteristics, between some of the panelists and a probability sample of elderly white subjects drawn from the same community by another research group for a survey of community involvement and participation.

## Selected Comparisons with Randomly Drawn, Nonlocal Elderly Subjects

Physical health and associated degrees of disability are principal variables in any investigation of aging central nervous system. The Duke research excluded the minority of elderly persons totally confined to their home by physical disability. Whether, among the majority of mobile persons 60 years of age and over, those in poor or good health would be more likely to participate is problematical. A partial answer to this question is provided by a limited comparison with certain findings of the National Health Survey (USNHS, 1957).

The comparison is limited by the fact that the National Health Survey utilized the reports of respondents as the basis for assessing degrees of disability, while the comparable health evaluation of the Duke panelists was based on clinical examinations. Moreover, pathological conditions appear characteristically to be underreported in surveys (Krueger, 1957). One comparison which does seem warranted, however, involves the category of persons in each study rated as severely disabled. The probability of coincidence between self-reports and clinical evaluations should be maximum in the extreme cases. Thirty-three percent of the persons 65 years of age and older who were interviewed in the National Health Survey reported that they were either restricted in major life activities or totally confined to the home as a result of poor health. On the initial clinical examinations, 26 percent of the Duke panelists were assessed to be at least 60 percent disabled in carrying out normal life activities, and when the panelists were reevaluated approximately three years later 33 percent were so disabled.

The presence or absence of physical pathology is related to an individual's assessment of his health status but is not synonymous with it. Self-assessment of health status thus provides another basis for comparing the Duke panelists with a probability sample. Schnore and Cowhig (1959–1960) have reported the distribution of self-assessment of health status among a randomly drawn sample of persons living in several metropolitan centers. Among their respondents 60 years of age and over, 46 percent assessed their health as "excellent" or "good"; among Duke panelists, 52 percent made this assessment.

Neither of the foregoing comparisons shows a striking difference between the volunteer panelists and randomly selected subjects who were willing to participate in other studies.

A serious objection advanced against the use of volunteers in clinical research is the large proportion of persons with diagnosed or diagnosable psychiatric illness who tend to be attracted (Esecover et al., 1961). Among the panelists at Duke, however, 40 percent were found to be without significant signs or symptoms of psychiatric illness, and only 6 percent were classified as psychotic. This distribution between the extremes of mental health and illness is similar to comparable data based on mental health surveys utilizing random sampling techniques.

An example is Gruenberg's epidemiological study of mental illness among elderly subjects in selected census tracts in Syracuse (Hoch & Zubin, 1961). Approximately 4 percent of the respondents were classified by him as dangerous to themselves or unable to care for themselves. While the home survey sample of Srole and his associates in their study of mental illness in a metropolis (1962) does not include persons beyond the age of 59, only 38 percent of the subjects between 50 and 59 years of age were considered to be either "well" (unimpaired) or to exhibit only "mild" symptoms. Leighton (1956), in an epidemiological survey of mental health in a small town in Nova Scotia, also found that 14 percent of the respondents aged 18 and over were "asymptomatic" and another 21 percent were borderline "normals." Although she did not analyze her findings in terms of specific age categories, the Duke panelists obviously compare favorably.

Selected comparisons of the physical and psychiatric characteristics of the Duke volunteers with subjects selected by random procedures do not indicate striking differences. On the whole, the physical and mental health of the Duke subjects appear to be slightly better than that of the samples of elderly persons with whom they are compared. These similarities do not prove that the Duke subjects provide the equivalent of a randomly drawn sample of elderly subjects; rather, they indicate that the relatively high refusal rate among older persons asked to participate in surveys tends to make the participating respondents essentially the equivalent of volunteers.

*Selective Dropout among Panelists*

Of the 256 subjects for whom there was relatively complete information at the end of the first phase of the study, 182 (71 percent) repeated the two days of interviews and examinations approximately three years later. Of the 68 who failed to return, 66 percent had died in the interim or had been immobilized by illness, 14 percent had moved away, and the remaining 20 percent indicated in various ways a reluctance to continue participation.

Three characteristics were observed with significantly greater frequency in the subjects who refused to return for the second phase of the research than in those lost because of death or immobility. Refusals were concentrated among (a) females, (b) subjects with IQ (WAIS) scores below the median of the panel, and (c) those clinically assessed to be in relatively good health (less than 20 percent disability). In the case of this last factor, the voluntary dropouts were concentrated among subjects who were medically assessed to be in good health, but who assessed their own health status as poor. Subjects who refused to return also tended to be of lower socioeconomic status and relatively inactive socially, although these tendencies were not statistically significant.

When the 182 panelists who returned for the second evaluation are compared with the 256 original members of the panel, a significant increase is found in the proportion of subjects characterized as (a) active, (b) married and living with the spouse, (c) the head of a household, (d) in good health, (e) exhibiting high morale, and (f) intelligent (above median WAIS scores). The proportion of Negroes, females, and persons of higher social status among the panelists also increased, although these increases were not statistically significant.

Over the three years under consideration, the panelists as a group tended to become increasingly a physiological, psychological, and social elite. While part of this change reflects the effect of selective mortality, it is the impression of various members of the Duke research group that the volunteers initially represented a relatively elite category of elderly subjects, and only became more so through time. Supporting this impression are (a) the comparisons of the panelists, in terms of physical and mental health, with randomly drawn samples of elderly subjects who have "volunteered" by not refusing to cooperate in other studies; and (b) the observation that cooperation in a strenuous two-day sequence of interviews and examinations tends to exclude the physically disabled, the psychologically deteriorated, and the most socially deprived elderly persons in the community.

Analysis of changes in the composition of the panel through selective dropout does nothing more than suggest differences between the panelists and the population from which they came. The noted changes do, however, have important implications for data analysis in longitudinal research which will be discussed later.

### Comparison with a Random Sample of Elderly Subjects in the Same Locale

For a study of community participation among white persons of various ages, the Department of Sociology at Duke drew two area probability samples in Durham—one including persons through the age of 64, and another including persons 65 years of age and older. If the original panelists who are (a) Negro, (b) under 65, and (c) living outside the city limits are excluded, it is possible to compare those remaining (N = 108) with those persons 65 years of age and older in the probability sample (N = 139) in terms of age, sex, marital status, activity, and self-estimate of health.

In terms of age and self-estimate of health, the probability sample of persons 65 years of age and older and the comparable panelists are similar. The average age of the sample subjects was 72, and that of the panelists, 71; 14 percent of the former and 15 percent of the latter were 80 years of age or older. Sixty-two percent of the panelists being compared estimated their health to be good or excellent, while 56 percent of the sample subjects made this estimate.

In terms of reported activity, sex distribution, and marital status, however, these two groups of elderly subjects showed striking differences. The mean Activity Inventory score (Cavan, Burgess, Havighurst, & Gold-hamer, 1949) originally of the Duke panelists was 27.4, as compared with 20.4 for the subjects in the probability sample. Moreover, 54 percent (compare 36 percent) of the panelists were male, and 65 percent (compare 34 percent) were married and living with the spouse.

The high proportion of panelists who were married and living with their spouses can be explained by two factors: (a) the high proportion of males in the group and (b) the fact that there were 13 married couples participating. That even one couple would be drawn in a random sample of individuals is extremely unlikely. Since "married and living with spouse" is a factor positively associated with physical and mental health, the high proportion of persons in the panel who fall into this category helps to explain the favorable showing, in terms of health, made by the panelists in comparison with other groups.

Summing up, this comparison with a random sample of elderly subjects in the same community tends to support the inference that the Duke panelists represent an elite among the elderly. It is all the more interesting, therefore, that the panelists are so nearly similar, in selected health characteristics, to randomly drawn samples of elderly subjects in the instances noted.

## A Longitudinal Design

The initial conception of the Duke research project was to explore human aging as a complex process of interrelated changes. Selected physical, psychic, and social factors involved in this process were to be explored. A longitudinal design was proposed because it permitted intensive focus on individual subjects and also permitted each subject to be used as his own control.

Baselines for each subject were established in the first series of interviews and examinations. A cross-sectional analysis of the initial data explored the complex interrelationships among a wide range of variables and focused attention on those factors which would warrant the most attention in the longitudinal analysis. The second series of observations on the subjects who remained approximately three years later provided a basis for assessing individual changes and an additional check on the relationships initially observed.

The cross-sectional analysis proved to be a double temptation:

1. In addition to providing information about the relationship between factors under specified conditions, such an analysis also provides information about the distribution of these factors among the panelists and, in some cases, measures of central tendency.

Even though the temptation to draw unwarranted inferences about elderly persons from such distributions and statistics might be avoided by an investigator, there is little control over the inferences which others draw. By a conscious focus on processes of aging and their correlates among selected older persons rather than on the description of the population of elderly persons, the Duke investigators have kept such errors to a minimum.

2. A panel statistic based on observations at two different points in time understandably invites comparison. That such comparisons must be made with great caution when there is a selective dropout of panelists is suggested by the following illustration.

Both the initial and later cross-sectional analyses indicated a significant positive relationship between contact with the environment (activity) and morale among the panelists. It was hypothesized that, as activity tends to decrease with age, so should morale. When the age factor was controlled, however, both initial and later analyses showed an age-related decrease in activity, but not in morale. In the later analyses, moreover, the relationship between the activity and morale, while still significant, was less pronounced. A possible explanation for this observation is the "theory of disengagement" suggested by Cumming and Henry (1961) on the basis of their Kansas City data. These authors hypothesize that, with age, activity and morale become increasingly independent of each other.

Analysis of the Duke data suggested an alternative interpretation. The initial cross-sectional analysis disclosed three important factors in interpreting the relationship between activity and morale: (*a*) health, especially an individual's own assessment of his health status; (*b*) the presence or absence of clinical depression; and (*c*) the individual's reported sense of usefulness. Morale was likely to be higher in elderly panelists who were, or believed themselves to be, in good health, who were not depressed, and who felt useful than in those who reported an equal degree of activity but did not have these other characteristics. Moreover, the panelists who showed these characteristics were more likely than the others to have high morale, even though they reported low activity.

When the distribution of these modifying characteristics was checked against age, it was found that the proportion of subjects with one or more of these characteristics was slightly higher in the older age categories than among the younger panelists. This difference was even more noticeable when the later series of observations was made. In this instance, the finding that morale became increasingly independent of activity with age appears to have been an artifact of the particular characteristics of the subjects in the various age categories. The slight decrease in the mean activity score of the panel over approximately three years, concomitant with an increase in the mean morale score, can be explained in the same way. When individual subjects are used as their own controls, changes in activity scores tended to be related positively to changes in morale except in the presence of one or more of the factors known to modify the relationship (Maddox, 1962).

This illustration reemphasizes the soundness of the initial orientation of the research group to use each individual as his own control and, when comparisons of panelists in terms of group statistics seemed appropriate, to match the comparison groups with care. It also serves as a reminder that when summarizing measures are used in longitudinal studies an observed relationship may be an artifact of changes in the composition of the panel resulting from selective dropout.

*Summary*

Selected aspects of a research design have been described, and some consequences of this design for data interpretation have been discussed.

The research project involved a longitudinal multidisciplinary investigation of the aging process and its correlates among selected noninstitutionalized subjects 60 years of age and older. Of 256 elderly subjects who volunteered to participate initially in a two-day series of interviews and clinical examinations, 182 returned, approximately three years later, to complete a second series of investigations.

Two methodological issues discussed on the basis of experience in this investigation are (*a*) the use of volunteer subjects and (*b*) selective dropout of panelists in a longitudinal study. Regarding the first, it is argued that in spite of the limitations incurred, there is at present no feasible alternative to the use of volunteers in research requiring clinical examinations. Selective dropout of subjects imposes still further limitations on the use of group statistics in the analysis of longitudinal observations. Because of the changes in the characteristics of groups under investigation over a period of years, such statistics are dependable only if there is control for the effects of selective dropout of subjects.

## References

Borsky, P., and White, E. Factors affecting the decision to volunteer for a physical examination. *Public Opinion Quarterly,* 23:445–446, Fall, 1959.

Cavan, R. S., Burgess, E. W., Havighurst, R. J., and Goldhamer, H. *Personal adjustment in old age.* Chicago: Science Research Associates, 1949.

Cobb, S., King, S., and Chen, E. Differences between respondents and non-respondents in a morbidity survey involving clinical examination. *Journal of Chronic Diseases,* 6:95–108, 1957.

Cumming, E., and Henry, W. E. *Growing old.* New York: Basic Books, 1961.

Esecover, H., Malitz, S., and Wilkins, B. Clinical profiles of paid normal subjects volunteering for hallucinogen drug studies. *American Journal of Psychiatry,* 117:910–915, 1961.

Gordon, T., Moore, F. E., Shurtleff, D., and Dawber, T. R. Some methodological problems in the long-term study of cardiovascular disease: Observations on the Framingham study. *Journal of Chronic Diseases,* 10:186–206, 1959.

Hoch, P. H., and Zubin, J. A mental health survey of older persons. In Hoch and Zubin (Eds.), *Comparative epidemiology of mental disorders.* New York: Grune and Stratton, 1961.

Krueger, D. C. Measurement of prevalence of chronic disease by household interviews and clinical evaluation. *American Journal of Public Health,* 47:953–960, August, 1957.

Leighton, A. H. The distribution of psychiatric symptoms in a small town. *American Journal of Psychiatry,* 112:616–623, 1956.

Maddox, G. L. Activity and morale: A longitudinal study of selected elderly subjects. *Social Forces,* 42:195–204, 1963.

Schnore, L. F., and Cowhig, J. Some correlates of reported health in metropolitan areas. *Social Problems,* 7:218–225, Winter, 1959–1960.

Srole, L., Langner, T. S., Michael, S. T., Opler, M. Dk., and Rennie, T. A. C. *Mental health in the metropolis.* New York: McGraw-Hill, 1962.

*United States National Health Survey: Cooperation in health examination surveys,* Publication D-2, June, 1960.

*United States National Health Survey: Preliminary report on disability, United States,* Series B-4, July–September, 1957.

# Chapter 2. Physical Problems

A basic question in gerontology is the extent to which illness and disability are an inevitable part of normal aging. As is pointed out by Dovenmuehle in the "Aging versus Illness" report, there is much confusion between the "time-related, irreversible, and deleterious" manifestations of normal aging and the "reversible, deleterious" changes which represent illness. It is fairly well established that more of the aged suffer from various chronic illnesses and disabilities than do younger groups. This is shown by the cross-sectional and longitudinal analyses presented in this chapter as well as by other studies cited. Furthermore, these physical problems often are a basic cause of many other problems of aging, such as mental illness, decreases in intellectual functioning, slow reactions, reduced activity, and fewer satisfactions, as shown in other chapters.

On the other hand, most of the aged are healthy enough to carry on their major activity most of the time. Only 4 percent of people 65 and over are confined to hospitals, nursing homes, homes for the aged, or other such institutions (Epstein & Murray, 1967). The average aged person spends only 3 percent of his days in bed because of illness (National Center for Health Statistics, 1968). Only 15 percent of the aged are unable to carry on their major activity (NCHS, 1969). Also, illness and disability among the aged can often be cured. Some of the longitudinal analyses in this chapter show that some of the physical problems can be resolved over time. Follow-up examinations show that 44 to 58 percent (depending on time interval) of the returning panelists had no decline in physical functioning or had overall improvement in functioning.

Thus it is not true that serious crippling illness is normal for the majority of aged persons. Nor is it true that disabilities are an inevitable or irreversible part of aging. It is a goal of these studies to understand better the differences between the irreversible physical problems of normal aging and the reversible or even preventable illnesses now common among the aged.

The first two selections deal with the overall physical functioning of the panelists and changes in their functioning. The next selection describes the neurologic symptoms, and the third analyzes the relation of skin lesions to internal changes. The last two analyze the blood vessels and cholesterol of the panelists, both at the initial examinations and as they changed over time.

References

Epstein, L. A., and Murray, J. H. *The aged population of the United States.* Washington: Government Printing Office, 1967.

National Center for Health Statistics. *Disability days, July, 1965–June, 1966.* Series 10, No. 47, Vital and Health Statistics. Washington: Government Printing Office, 1968.

National Center for Health Statistics. *Chronic conditions causing activity limitations, July, 1963–June, 1965.* Series 10, No. 51, Vital and Health Statistics. Washington: Government Printing Office, 1969.

# Physical Problems of Older People* *Robert H. Dovenmuehle, Ewald W. Busse, and Gustave Newman*

There are many indications from statistical studies that there is an increase in the frequency and severity of chronic illnesses among the older people in our society.

In Leavell and Clark's textbook of preventive medicine (1953) it is indicated that host factors associated with aging result in a greatly increased prevalence rate of long-term illnesses involving circulatory impairments, metabolic dysfunctions, arthritides, and neoplasms. In referring to the National Health Survey published in 1940, it is stated that regarding chronic disease or impairment lasting three or more months, half of such cases occurred in persons over 45 years of age, consisting of less than one-third of the population. There were indications that the proportion increased with advancing age. This particular study showed that disability amounting to invalidism affected only 10.8 per 1,000 persons aged 30 to 44 years, 55 per 1,000 aged 65 to 74 years, and 101 per 1,000 aged 85 years and over.

Some of the major causes of disability and death from long-term illnesses become accentuated in the older age groups, according to Leavell and Clark (1953). The 10 leading causes of disability in persons aged 65 and over (Baltimore Survey) were heart disease (excluding rheumatic), arthritis, hypertensive vascular disease, nephritis, tuberculosis, diseases of bones and joints (except tuberculosis and arthritis), accidents, diabetes, cancer, and eye diseases. These data came from a five-year survey with monthly visits (1953).

* Reprinted by permission from the *Journal of the American Geriatrics Society,* 9:208–217, 1961.

The five leading causes of death in 1956 in persons aged 65 years and over indicate that many of the leading causes of disability also cause most of the deaths in this age group. Taken from Public Health Service statistics (Summary of Health and Vital Statistics, 1958), these were diseases of the heart, cerebral hemorrhage and other vascular lesions affecting central nervous system, cancer and other malignant neoplasms, general arteriosclerosis, and all accidents.

In the discussion on sickness surveys in Haven Emerson's textbook on administrative medicine (1951) it is pointed out that all types of surveys are limited either in the amount and accuracy of information available, or in terms of populations covered.

The present report concerns a limited group of older subjects who are active community members. Extensive medical, social, and psychologic data are available on all subjects.

## Definition of Group

As a part of a large study of the physiologic, psychologic, and sociologic interrelationships of the effect of aging upon the central nervous system (Dovenmuehle & Busse, 1956), we participated in the examination of 256 community volunteer subjects past the age of 60. This group, when impressionistically compared with a group of hospitalized and a group of institutionalized older people also examined for research purposes, seemed physically and psychologically much more intact.

Our total sample of 260[1] subjects was distributed as shown in Table

Table 2–1. *Distribution of 260 subjects on the basis of socioeconomic status, sex, race, and age.*

| | Lower socioeconomic group (Golden Age Club members, etc.) | | | Higher socioeconomic group (Top-level business and professional people) | |
|---|---|---|---|---|---|
| | Males | Females | | Males | Females |
| White | 44 | 47 | White | 42 | 42 |
| Negro | 31 | 34 | Negro | 9 | 11 |
| Age grouping | | | | | |
| Age range (years) | 61–64 | 65–69 | 70–74 | 75–79 | 80+ |
| Number of subjects | 47 | 72 | 69 | 39 | 33 |

[1] Includes 4 subjects with incomplete records.

2–1. It will be noted that more than half the subjects were in the 65–74-year age group—a factor which might affect the trends associated with aging in our study. In nine cases we did not have sufficient information on which to base a physical functional rating.

Physical Functioning Ratings

Because of the importance of physical health in the concerns of our older citizens, a method was developed for rating the functional physical status of each subject. This was based in part on an extensive medical history, physical and neurologic examinations, and laboratory studies included in the routine series of research investigations. The six possible ratings on this scale are shown in Table 2–2.

This scale is modified and adapted from those in use by the United States Army and Veteran's Administration for rating disability. For our purposes, social limitation is defined as any restriction upon activity or communication involved in usually possible social activities for the particular subject. Sometimes this is a hypothetical "normal" situation, but often is reinforced by specific information regarding daily activity. For example, a rating of 30–50 percent social incapacity would be given in the event of arthritic immobilization severe enough to prevent the subject from pursuing usual interests at church and at civil clubs but still permitting enjoyment of social intercourse with visiting friends. On the other hand, limitation of vision and hearing to the point that understandable social relationships with others were practically terminated would call for a rating of complete incapacitation.

Table 2–2. *Physical functioning ratings.*

| Condition | Rating |
|---|---|
| No pathology or limitation | 0 |
| Disease present, no limitation of social or industrial function | 1 |
| Limitation, 20 percent or less | 2 |
| Limitation, 21–50 percent | 3 |
| Limitation, 51–80 percent | 4 |
| Limitation, over 80 percent | 5 |

Industrial capacity included useful occupations, whether performed for pay or not, since most of our subjects were retired. For example, a person with arthritic limitation who could not possibly get to a place of work or of part-time hobby activity if located outside the home would be rated as seriously disabled. If in spite of this limitation the person was able to engage actively in productive work around the home, he would not be rated as completely disabled.

Psychiatric limitations on ability to perform were not considered in conjunction with this rating. Only the physical aspects of the individual's potentiality for social and industrial activity were assessed.

## The Problem

On the basis of physical functioning it was believed possible to demonstrate differences between sexes, races, socioeconomic groups, and age groups. If such differences could be demonstrated, it might be possible to determine whether or not higher and lower functioning groups are afflicted by similar illnesses, but of differing severity, or whether they are afflicted most severely by certain illnesses which have differential significance in terms of disability factors.

## Methods

In order to accomplish this objective, it was necessary to keep our sample carefully matched with regard to variables other than those under direct examination. This was done by keeping all of the factors, except the one under consideration, in the exact proportions in which they appeared in the total sample.

The process of matching on a proportionate basis reduced somewhat the total universe of subjects available for each consideration (Figures 2–1 through 2–4). Throughout the statistical work, attempts were made to include the maximal universe of subjects available to the particular consideration.

## Socioeconomic Comparison

In considering the socioeconomic differences in groups matched proportionately for age, sex, and race it was found that fewer limitations on physical functioning were present in persons of higher socioeconomic status (Figure 2–1). There were only 15 subjects with a physical functional rating of either 4 or 5 in this matched sample, whereas there were 22 with such a rating in the entire community group. Although this indicates some caution in accepting the significance of such a finding as applied to the upper range of disability, there is no question about the comparability in the lower ranges of the scale which indicate more adequate functioning. Forty-two of 47 subjects in the entire group who had no disease appeared in this particular sample. Of those who had disease without disability, 63 of 76 subjects appeared in this sample.

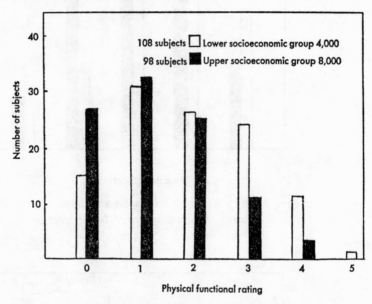

Figure 2–1. *PFR: Socioeconomic comparison. Subjects matched by proportion for sex, race, and age.*

## Comparison on the Basis of Age, Sex, and Race

When subjects younger than 70 and older than 70 were compared in a group matched for sex, race, and socioeconomic variables, the distribution was comparable to that in the larger group of subjects (Figure 2–2). Those under 70 were less likely to have limitation of capacity according to the physical functional rating.

A comparison of males and females in a group matched for race, age, and socioeconomic condition indicated no significant differences (Figure 2–3). Again this group was comparable to the entire sample of community subjects in terms of the distribution of physical functional ratings.

White subjects were compared with Negro subjects in a group matched proportionately for age, sex, and socioeconomic condition (Figure 2–4).

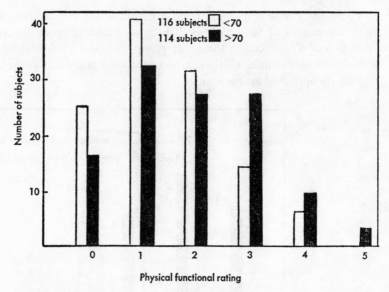

Figure 2–2. *PFR: Comparison on the basis of age (above or below 70 years). Subjects matched by proportion for sex, race, and socioeconomic level.*

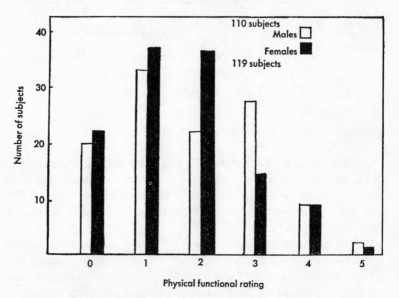

Figure 2–3. *PFR: Comparison on the basis of sex. Subjects matched by proportion for age, race, and socioeconomic level.*

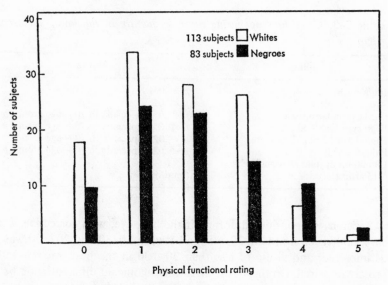

Figure 2–4. *PFR: Comparison on the basis of race. Subjects matched by proportion for sex, age, and socioeconomic level.*

The matched group contained only 28 subjects who had no disease and no disability, but otherwise it was quite comparable to the total community group.

## Incidence of Disease

Thus, there was a distinct difference between various socioeconomic and age groups regarding current physical capacity. It was decided to limit the initial study of disease incidence in these groups to conditions known to be highly prevalent in the older age group. Table 2–3 shows the conditions that appeared more frequently in our lower socioeconomic group. Some of these conditions also were more prominent in the older group than in the younger group.

Eisdorfer (see Chapter 7) found that combined impairment of hearing and vision had the greatest adverse effect on psychologic functioning, with a hearing defect alone having a pronounced effect. Since impairment of vision and hearing are common in elderly people, it was thought that the incidence of these disorders might be reflected in the characteristics of the groups. However, there was no significant difference on the basis of hearing impairment as judged from the medical interview.

Table 2–3. *Conditions appearing more frequently in the lower socioeconomic group.*

| Condition | *p* value |
| --- | --- |
| Impairment of vision | $p < .001$ |
| Arteriosclerosis | $p < .05$ |
| Cardiovascular disease | $p < .05$; especially in 70+ age group ($p < .05$) |
| High systolic blood pressure | $p < .05$; especially in 70+ age group ($p < .02$) |
| High diastolic blood pressure | $p < .02$; especially in 70+ age group ($p < .01$) |
| Pulmonary disease | $p < .02$; especially in 70+ age group ($p < .05$) |
| Limitation of joint movement due to arthritis | trend only |

Vision was considered normal if the best eye, with correction if necessary, had vision up to 20/30. Vision between 20/50 and 20/100 was rated as impaired, and vision of less than 20/100 in the best eye was rated as grossly impaired. On this basis, there was significant differentiation between various socioeconomic and age groups in our subjects.

Disorders of the vascular apparatus were common in our community group; 70 subjects had moderate or severe arteriosclerosis. The criteria for moderate arteriosclerosis were absence of pulsations in the pedal arteries and limitation of exercise because of symptoms due to vascular constriction in the legs and/or cardiac or pulmonary phenomena. Severe arteriosclerosis was indicated by a verified history of cardiac disease and strokes. Contrary to the findings of others in relation to the blood cholesterol level (Nichols & Obrist, 1958), we found no differentiation of age groups regarding the incidence of this condition, but there was a significant differentiation of socioeconomic groups on this basis. There was an association between arteriosclerosis and cardiovascular disease, including arteriosclerotic heart disease and hypertensive heart disease combined. The incidence of cardiovascular disease of all kinds was higher in the lower socioeconomic group, especially in persons past the age of 70.

This relationship, however, did not influence any relationship between cardiac status and group membership. Patients with a history of decompensated cardiac disease and/or clinical evidence of mild to severe cardiac failure were not statistically more frequent in either group. This may be attributable to the small number of cases, since only 23 subjects in the entire sample showed any evidence of decompensation either by history or by physical examination for the research study.

There was no distinct relationship with obesity. Although we had rough clinical ratings of obesity, it seemed more desirable to utilize an index of surface area calculated from the weight and height. On this basis, there was only a slight trend for persons past the age of 70 in the lower socioeconomic group to have larger surface areas. This was not considered a significant difference.

The clear relationship to arteriosclerosis indicated the possibility of characteristic group differences regarding both systolic and diastolic blood pressure. We chose a systolic blood pressure of 150 mm. Hg as the dividing line. The lower socioeconomic group clearly had a higher proportion of cases within the upper range of blood pressure. This was especially true for people over 70 in this group. A similar situation pertained with respect to diastolic blood pressure, with 90 mm. Hg as the dividing line. It is noteworthy that in the entire sample the diastolic blood pressure was between 90 and 100 mm. in 93 subjects, between 101 and 110 mm. in 39, and between 111 and 150 mm. in 39. There were 85 subjects in whom the systolic blood pressure was between 160 and 190 mm., and 48 in whom it was over 190 mm.

Electrocardiograms were available on 81 of the subjects from the community sample; in 55 there was some evidence of abnormality. For the purposes of this study no attempt was made to analyze these deviations. There was no significant relationship between electrocardiographic abnormalities and any of the other factors considered in this study.

Pulmonary disease, chiefly emphysema, is a relatively frequent accompaniment of aging. Among 40 subjects with some kind of pulmonary disease in the sample of 260 persons, 37 had emphysema regardless of what other pathologic lesion may have been involved. There was only 1 case of asthma uncomplicated by other disease. The occurrence of pulmonary disease was clearly related to socioeconomic status, and especially so in subjects aged 70 and over.

An outstanding cause of illness in elderly people is arthritis. In the sample of 260 subjects, 92 had some form of arthritis, excluding traumatic. Fifty-three of these had osteoarthritis, varying from mild to severe; 8 had rheumatoid arthritis, inactive or very mild; and 31 had undifferentiated arthropathy. There were no cases of gouty arthritis. No significant relationship could be found between arthritis and socioeconomic condition or age. However, there was a trend toward more severe limitation of joint motion in the lower socioeconomic group; the limitation included the joints of the upper extremity, lower extremity, hands, back, and neck. Mild limitation in one or more areas was present in 81 of the 260 subjects, and moderate to severe limitation in 71.

## Discussion

There are several possible explanations for the higher disease frequency invariably associated with the lower socioeconomic status.

The method of obtaining subjects by recruiting volunteers may have caused a bias in the sample with regard to the number of people with chronic illness from the lower socioeconomic group. However, it has been ascertained that there were essentially no differences between the two groups in their reasons for coming, especially as concerns the possibility of medical examination or treatment. In all likelihood there was randomization of factors influencing both groups, so that conclusions from data on these subjects have sufficient validity to be used in formulating hypotheses for further experimental study.

Socioeconomic classification involves many complex factors. Among them are education, occupational status, and income. In addition, there are differences in the degree of familism (see Chapter 8). Investigations are now in progress to determine which of these factors involved in socioeconomic rating could account for the greatest degree of variance in the results of this study. In general, the factors most heavily influencing the pattern of a person's living most likely influence his health status in old age.

The increase in incidence of many of these chronic illnesses with aging agrees with the findings of many previous studies. In view of the significantly different life expectancies of males and females, whites and Negroes, it is surprising that no significant differences in these respects were found in our study. Morbidity statistics do not necessarily relate directly to life expectancy, since illnesses may be of varying duration prior to the intervention of death. Since our sample is being followed longitudinally, mortality data will eventually be available.

Mayer and Hauser's (1950) study of life expectation in Chicago for the years 1880 to 1940 indicated that the highest economic groups had significantly greater life expectancy than the lowest economic groups. The difference was 7.5 years between upper-income and lower-income white males and females and 6 years between upper-income and lower-income Negro males and females in 1940. There was a spread of approximately 18 years between the highest-income whites and the lowest-income Negroes. However, the gap constantly narrowed from 1920 onward. Although life expectancy studies are not necessarily revealing concerning morbidity statistics as reported on our sample, it is possible that the lack of a significant difference between whites and Negroes regarding physical functional capacity indicates that the gap has closed to this extent. Woodbury (1936) quotes Children's Bureau statistics to the effect that infant mortality is related in inverse fashion to income or otherwise-determined economic status of the parents. Thus, it is also possible that the gap in life expectancy observed by Mayer and Hauser was largely on the basis of increased infant mortality in the lower socioeconomic groups. If true, one would not expect as great a difference in the older age groups.

## Summary

The factors of socioeconomic status, age, race, and sex have been examined in relation to physical functional capacity in a group of 260 community volunteers past the age of 60.

Differences in physical capacity were apparent in relation to socioeconomic status and age, but not in relation to sex or race.

Subjects, whether younger or older, or whether of high socioeconomic status or low, could not be differentiated on the basis of different patterns of illness. Rather, certain illnesses caused more disability in older subjects of lower socioeçonomic status.

Impairment of vision, arteriosclerosis and cardiovascular disease, elevated systolic and diastolic blood pressures, pulmonary disease, and arthritic limitation of joint motion were observed more frequently in the lower socioeconomic group.

## References

Dovenmuehle, R. H., and Busse, E. W. Studies of the processes of aging: A review of the findings of a multidisciplinary approach. *British Journal of Physical Medicine*, 1:100, May, 1956.

Eisdorfer, C. The effects of sensory decrement on Rorschach performance in an aged population. Doctoral dissertation, University Microfilms, Ann Arbor, Mich. (See Chapter 7.)

Emerson, H. (Ed.). *Administrative medicine*. New York: Thomas Nelson & Sons, 1951, p. 1007.

Leavell, R. H., and Clark, E. G. *Textbook of preventive medicine*. New York: McGraw-Hill, 1961, p. 629.

Mayer, A. J., and Hauser, P. Class differentials in expectation of life at birth. *Revue de l'Institut International de Statistique*, 18:200, 1950; reprinted in Bendix, R., and Lipset, S. M., *Class, status, and power*. Glencoe, Ill.: Free Press, 1953, pp. 281–284.

Nichols, C. R., and Obrist, W. D. Relation of serum cholesterol level to age, race, and sex in a community group of elderly people (abstract). *Journal of Gerontology*, 13:442, October, 1958.

Summary of Health and Vital Statistics. Washington: United States Department of Health, Education, and Welfare, Public Health Service, June, 1958.

Woodbury, R. M. Infant mortality in the United States. *Annals of the American Academy of Political and Social Science*, 188:94, November, 1936.

# Aging versus Illness    *Robert H. Dovenmuehle*

Immediately upon beginning the discussion of this subject, it becomes necessary to attempt a definition of terms in order to differentiate them properly. The most widely used current definition of aging stems from the biological sciences. Any biological processes which are time related, irreversible, and deleterious in nature are considered to be manifestations of aging. This definition serves quite well for the laboratory investigator concerned, for example, with the changes in connective tissue proteins during an animal's lifetime. These proteins change from a more soluble to a less soluble form. In the long run, however, even the biochemical investigator runs into difficulties with this definition. A good example is the change in mucopolysaccharide (a kind of protein) content in various body tissues. These tend to become of a less soluble form in older animals, but the type of mucopolysaccharide metabolic pattern and the content of the tissues has been changed to that of younger animals by the use of growth hormone in older animals.

Illness, on the other hand, is assumed to be time related, reversible, deleterious change in an organism. As shown above, the same definition may some day apply to all aging phenomena. Thus we seem to be left without completely satisfactory ways of differentiating these two phenomena.

Above and beyond the basic definition, however, we have many differences in the practical application of these terms. First, all medicine is concerned with illness and pathology. It is illness that we are trained to recognize and treat, and illness that we focus our attention upon when we examine people. Age changes per se depend on current definitions of disease. For example, not too many years ago arteriosclerosis was considered to be a manifestation of aging because the findings appeared more and more frequently in more and more people the older they became and also became more severe in particular individuals with advancing age. Today, however, this is recognized as a complex metabolic disturbance and is considered a disease.

The metabolic disturbance associated with arteriosclerosis can be modified to some extent by diet, exercise, and other measures. In this respect, arteriosclerosis does fit our definition of illness. However, if the condition has been present for very long in an unrecognized form, it has often left scars in the various body organs it afflicts which can never be removed. In this sense arteriosclerosis and all chronic illness to a certain extent represent irreversible deleterious change in the organism.

Second, with current knowledge of research findings, it is clear that removal of all chronic disease will not prevent changes with aging. It is true that all organ systems suffer a loss of cells with advancing age, which currently cannot be explained on the basis of disease conditions. As mentioned before, the nature of tissues changes, and in some cases these changes are visible, as in the skin. Decrease in muscle mass is measurable in terms of decreased strength. In other words, even though all disease conditions currently recognized were eliminated, people would still show changes of aging.

Since evidence of disease and disability due to disease can be appropriately classified in medical terminology, it is possible to look at older people and study the changes they show over a period of time to get a better delineation of the impact of chronic illness on the aged person. In a study of community volunteers over the age of 60 at Duke University, we have examined 182 people twice. The elapsed time between the initial examination and the subsequent examination varied from 22 to 65 months. This group included 62 Negroes and 120 whites. There were 92 males and 90 females. . . .

The most frequent disease conditions in this group were impairment of vision and hearing, arteriosclerosis, cardiovascular disease, high systolic or diastolic blood pressure, pulmonary disease (usually emphysema or asthma), and arthritis, often with joint limitation.

One of our particular interests in these people was to observe what changes took place in their physical condition as they became older. Figure 2–5 summarizes the changes in physical functional rating. As we can observe, there was a significant change from the original to the follow-up examination ($p < .01$ by $x^2$ test). Increases were especially noticed in the transition from disease without disability to disease with mild to moderate disability. Especially noticeable also are the few subjects remaining without a diagnosable disease condition.

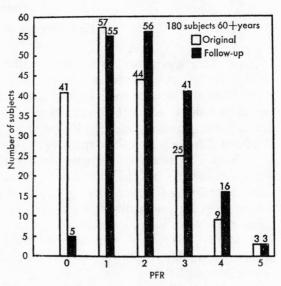

Figure 2–5. *PFR: Original and follow-up.*

It would be important to learn in more detail what the nature of these changes were. Figure 2–6 shows the physical functioning rating changes with time for the entire group. We note that 63 of the subjects changed one step upward in their PFR. This means they progressed to one further step of disability. Twenty-three subjects moved upward two steps, and so on. Thus we can see that 53 percent of the subjects suffered increased disability of one or more steps. A decreased rating of one or more steps was exhibited by 12 percent of the subjects. This means that for this 12 percent their health had improved during the intervening time. Thirty-five percent of the subjects remained in the same state they were in when initially examined.

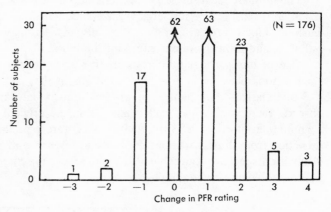

Figure 2–6. *PFR changes with time: Total group.*

Since there was an extensive range in the periods of time elapsed between the first examination and the second examination (22 months to 65 months) the subjects were broken down into three groups by time periods in order to see if the greater time period exhibited more change than a shorter period of time. The PFR changes by groups do not indicate significant differences over the elapsed time (Figure 2–7).

This may be accounted for partly by the racial distribution. In our original examination special effort had to be made toward the end of the study to obtain a sufficient number of Negro subjects to approximate their percentage in the community at large. For this reason there were significantly more Negro subjects seen at a lesser time interval ($p < .001$ by $x^2$ test). Many of the Negroes were from the lower socioeconomic level, and in our original study people from the lower socioeconomic level were found to have greater disability.

Another question of some importance is the kind of change to be

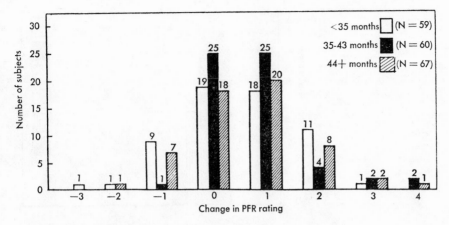

Figure 2–7. *PFR changes with time: Time groups.*

expected in health depending upon the original PFR level. Figures 2–8 and 2–9, showing the increase and decrease of PFR rating from the original, indicate that increase in PFR rating (increase in disease or disability) occurs chiefly in the groups which had no disease or only disease without disability. This, of course, is a reflection of the fact that these subjects have greater opportunity to suffer severe worsening of their condition compared to the following groups which already have some disability present.

It is interesting that only those subjects who initially had some rated disability showed any tendency to improve their health ratings. This may be a reflection of the fact that the occurrence of disease per se does not cause

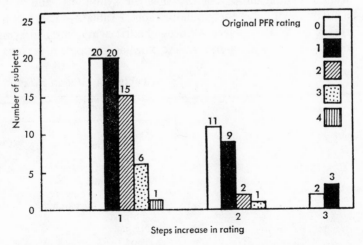

Figure 2–8. *Number of steps increase in PFR from original.*

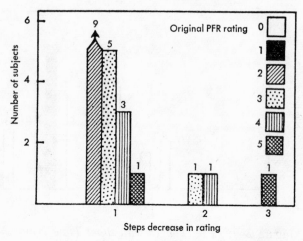

Figure 2–9. *Number of steps decrease in PFR from original.*

many of these subjects to seek out and stay with intensive medical care, whereas the subject with disability would be more apt to seek treatment persistently in order to obtain improvement.

What of the changes in the mental status of this group of people? The total group originally examined exceeded 256. Of these subjects, 222 were classified by a system which divided all psychiatric signs from the mental status into various categories considered to be neurotic, psychotic, functional, organic, and mixed in nature. Forty percent of the group were without significant psychiatric signs or symptoms, and 6 percent were actually classified in the psychotic range (Table 2–4). It will also be noted that many of the subjects with psychiatric symptoms had symptoms of an organic or mixed nature. In the normal group, 17 persons had recent

Table 2–4. *Mental status at initial study.*

| Status | | Number |
| --- | --- | --- |
| Psychotic | | 14 |
| Functional | 6 | |
| Organic | 7 | |
| Mixed | 1 | |
| Nonpsychotic | | 119 |
| Neurotic (25 severe) | 56 | |
| Organic, nonpsychotic | 21 | |
| Mixed | 42 | |
| Normal | | 89 |
| Total | | 222 |

memory loss, and 3 had some evidence of remote memory loss. They were not considered psychiatrically classifiable unless both such defects were present. Of the functional symptoms, bodily overconcern and depression were most prominent.

Following this initial study, it was felt that the standard psychiatric mental status was not a satisfactory instrument for measuring the degree of disability in a person's life from a psychiatric standpoint and especially not in a community group with relatively little psychiatric pathology. Scales were devised to indicate the amount of disability from behavioral pathology associated with brain syndrome symptoms, and a similar scale was drawn up for depressive symptoms (see Table 2–5).

Table 2–5. *Degree of behavioral impairment from organic brain syndrome.*

0  No signs of organic brain syndrome
1  Organic brain syndrome present, no disability
2  Mild disability (20 percent reduction of social
    and/or inductrial capacity)
3  Moderate disability (20–50 percent)
4  Severe disability (50–80 percent)
5  Total disability (over 80 percent)

The rating for disability due to behavioral pathology of everyday life probably associated with brain syndrome is identical to the scheme devised for the physical functional rating. This disability scale is used as an overall rating devised from six scales which deal with specific aspects of behavioral change.

Figure 2–10 shows that 52 percent of the subjects had no signs of such behavioral change or no disability from such change. Very few subjects were noted to have severe disability due to such change. Figure 2–11 shows that 65 percent of the group showed no signs of depressive symptoms whatever. Only 7 percent exhibited depressive symptoms severe enough to be classified as moderate in degree. These people had episodes of feeling worried, discouraged, troubled, and blue oftener than every two weeks and which lasted more than a day at a time and disabled them for up to half their usual life activity. The milder depressive symptoms were brief, less frequent, and only slightly disabling for daily activities.

In previous studies we have found the depressive symptoms in older people to be closely related to the presence of physical illness. Recent extensions of these studies would indicate that this is a firm finding. Subjects selected for current hospitalization for cardiac illness exhibited

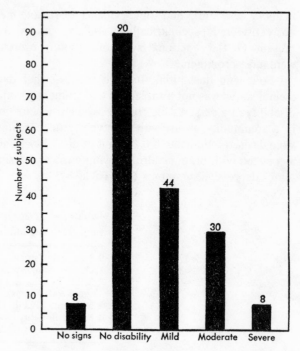

Figure 2–10. *Disability due to brain syndrome behavioral change.*

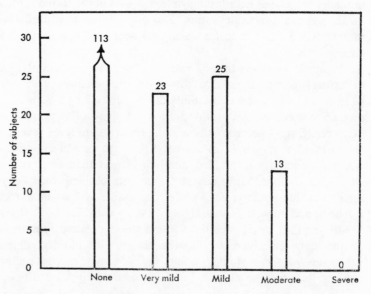

Figure 2–11. *Severity of depressive symptoms.*

much more frequent ratings of moderate and severe depressive symptoms concurrent with their cardiac disease.

In a sense we have now taken the long way around to demonstrate that many of the major psychological discomforts of aging are often associated with physical illness. We have also pointed out that most of these physical conditions are in the nature of chronic illnesses, a considerable number of which are partially reversible. . . .

Although disease and disability cannot be completely avoided with the passage of time, especially after the sixtieth year, there is good evidence to indicate that relative preservation of health and of ability to carry out one's life activities can be attained with adequate medical care. Much of this care has to be concentrated upon the physical aspects of illness and disability, but there is also room for considerably more effort toward improving the accompanying behavioral symptoms due to chronic brain syndrome and to depression associated with illness. As medical research adds to our knowledge of the common chronic illness associated with aging, we eventually may be able to shift our emphasis from better and more rehabilitative medicine to genuinely preventive measures.

# Alterations in Neurologic Status with Age* *Gustave Newman, Robert H. Dovenmuehle, and Ewald W. Busse*

Recent research in gerontology has included refined measurements of physiologic variables reflecting changes in the central nervous system in aging. Most such measurements are accurate and of general interest; however, they are of relatively little use to the clinician in his evaluation of the aged patient because of the elaborate equipment required. Standard reference works in medicine offer little help to the physician who attempts to evaluate the neurologic status of his aged patient. Information to be presented in this paper is based on data gathered from routine neurologic examination which has not involved the use of complicated electrical or mechanical equipment.

Materials and Methods

The 256 persons studied were volunteers who lived in the community in and around Durham, North Carolina. Their ages ranged from 60 to 93

* Reprinted by permission of the *Journal of the American Geriatrics Society*, 8:915–917, 1960.

years (average, 70 years). Males and females of both the white and Negro races were included. The neurologic examination was conducted using only the more common standard tools, such as a reflex hammer, a tuning fork, a straight pin, and some cotton. The findings were recorded in the usual clinical manner, that is, as indicating normal, moderately impaired function, or severely impaired function. Of 27 items from the neurologic examination, the 9 which presented the greatest number of deviations from normal were selected for closer scrutiny. These variables were gait, reflex activity, movements associated with gait, involuntary movements (tremor), vibratory sensibility (128 tuning fork), two-point discrimination, touch, pain, and olfaction. Variables such as palsies of the cranial nerves were of such infrequent occurrence as to be of no value in a statistical study. The foregoing 9 neurologic variables were cross-indexed against the 4 basic demographic variables of sex, race, age, and socioeconomic status, and tested for significance of variability by the chi-square test.

## Results

In the judgment of the clinical examiners, 33 percent of the subjects showed a deviation in the degree of reflex activity (either hypo-reflexia or hyper-reflexia); 15 percent had some abnormality of gait, most commonly a shortened stride or shuffling; 10 percent showed loss of the movement of the arms associated with gait; and 7 percent had involuntary movements, or tremor. Testing of the sensory modalities showed that 12 percent of the subjects had diminution or loss of vibratory sensibility, and 10 percent had diminution of two-point discrimination; only 5 percent exhibited alterations in touch or pain, including hypesthesia and hyperesthesia; and 26 percent had loss of olfactory function.

There was a significant difference between males and females with regard to the deep tendon reflexes; these reflexes tended to be exaggerated in the females. The difference however, was not great, being statistically significant at a $p$ value of .10. Alterations of reflex activity were much more highly correlated with race, the white subjects tending to be hyper-reflexic, whereas the Negroes were hypo-reflexic. This racial difference was statistically much more significant than the sex difference, and had a $p$ value of .001; that is, the probability was 1 in 1,000 that it was due to chance.

For simplicity in correlating the changes in neurologic variables with age, the approximate median age of 70 was used as a dividing line, and subjects were classified into two groups: (a) those less than 70 years old and (b) those 70 years of age or older. Since 70 was the approximate median age, this criterion divided the subjects into two roughly equal groups. Five of the nine neurologic variables were then found to be related to age as defined in this manner. The older group (those 70 and over) showed hypo-reflexia, reduced vibratory sensation, reduced two-point discrimination, and alterations in the sensibilities of pain and touch. However, the factor most highly correlated with age was the loss or marked diminution of the sense of smell.

Socioeconomic status in this study included only two categories, high and low. The socioeconomic status was determined by sociologists and social workers on the research team and was based on such factors as income, educational level, and occupation. For those acquainted with the socioeconomic separation of patients in a university hospital, our classifications of these community subjects might be approximated by thinking of the high-status persons as private patients and of the low-status persons as clinic or public patients.

Four neurologic variables were found to be significantly related to the socioeconomic status of the subjects. Three of these were associated with the motor system and bring to mind Parkinson's syndrome; the subjects in the low-status group showed more alterations of gait, greater loss of movements associated with gait, and a greater incidence of tremor. The fourth related variable was olfaction; the low-status group exhibited more reduction in olfactory sensibility than did the high-status group.

Discussion

Several other factors which have not been mentioned might conceivably have a bearing upon alterations of neurologic status in the elderly. Late manifestations of syphilis should be considered. In our study, we used the standard seriologic tests for syphilis; the findings were positive in 17 subjects. Of these, only 3 showed alterations in reflex activity—hyporeflexia. In no subject was the diagnosis of tabes made. Spinal fluid was not collected, so the more reliable diagnostic criteria using spinal fluid were not available.

Another possibility is a subacute form of pernicious anemia with spinal cord disease. We used the hemoglobin level as an index of hematologic status; no correlation was found with neurologic status. In only five persons was the hemoglobin level less than 12 Gm. per 100 ml., and in only one was it less than 10 Gm.

Six subjects had both glycosuria and a fasting blood glucose level of 200 mg. per 100 ml. or higher—presumptive evidence of diabetes mellitus. All of these subjects were hypo-reflexic. Three of the six were older than 70, and three were younger than 70; three were males and three were females; three were white and three were Negroes. Five of the six were of low socioeconomic status. The random distribution, however, did not obviate the correlation between neurologic status and demographic status.

## Summary

Statistically assessed observations on 256 elderly subjects living in a community environment indicate that, with aging, there are certain alterations in the neurologic status. In 33 percent of the subjects the degree of reflex activity was either above or below normal; in 15 percent there was some abnormality of gait; in 10 percent, loss of the arm movements associated with gait; in 7 percent, tremor; in 12 percent, diminution or loss of vibratory sensibility; in 10 percent, reduction of two-point discrimination; in 5 percent, alteration in touch or pain; and in 26 percent, loss of olfactory function.

# Skin Lesions of the Aged*   *John P. Tindall and J. Graham Smith, Jr.*

Constant increase in the number of individuals over 60 years of age has led to greater interest in diseases of the aged. Considerations of skin changes associated with aging and their management (Epstein, 1946; Palmer, 1946; Kierland & O'Leary, 1953; Thompson, 1953; Waisman, 1956) and comparisons of the presenting complaints of elderly patients with the incidences of a wide variety of skin lesions have been reported (Lane & Rockwood, 1949; Kennedy, 1950; Noojin & Osment, 1957; Young, 1958; Horne, 1959).

Elderly individuals have also been sought out in an effort to assess the occurrence of skin lesions in a sampling of an entire group of oldsters rather than just those persons specifically seeking dermatological aid (Zakon, 1952; Droller, 1955). As might have been expected, these studies revealed some differences in incidences.

This study was designed to carry the investigation a step further, and included information reflecting internal as well as external changes of the

* Reprinted by permission of the *Journal of the American Medical Association*, 186:1039–1042, 1963.

aging process. An attempt has been made to determine accurately the incidences of the geriatric dermatoses and to relate them with various internal aberrations.

Materials and Methods

One hundred and sixty-three community volunteers, aged 64 years and older, participated in a series of multidisciplinary examinations at the Duke University Regional Center for the Study of Aging. A complete dermatological history and a physical examination were administered, in addition to a medical, social, and psychiatric evaluation of the subjects. The data were analyzed for relationships within the dermatology examination, and between dermatological variables and the results of other examinations, through use of an IBM 7070 computer.

Evaluation of data fell into two large groupings: (a) incidence of skin lesions compared to the ranking of skin complaints from other studies in which elderly people sought the aid of dermatologists and also to the ranking of skin complaints for which individuals of all ages consulted dermatologists; and (b) statistical evaluation by chi-square ($x^2$) testing of variables available from all sources of examinations and tests performed on and by participants in the study.

Results

Incidence of the 16 physical findings most often observed in the group is presented in Table 2–6. Almost all the subjects (94 percent) had a loss of skin turgor and subcutaneous tissue of covered skin which gave the skin the "lax" appearance so often associated with aging. The most common new growth, seborrheic keratosis, occurred in 88 percent and cherry an-

Table 2–6. *Incidence of physical findings in 163 elderly individuals.*

| Rank | Percentage | Rank | Percentage |
|------|------------|------|------------|
| Lax skin | 94 | Lentigo | 51 |
| Seborrheic keratoses | 88 | Varicosities | 48 |
| Comedones | 81 | Seborrheic dermatitis | 31 |
| Dermatophytosis | 79 | Schamberg's disease | 31 |
| Asteatosis | 77 | Spider angiomas | 29 |
| Cherry angioma | 75 | Actinic keratoses | 28 |
| Nevi | 63 | Neurogenic excoriations | 12 |
| Skin tags | 56 | Rosacea | 12 |

giomas (ectasia) in 75 percent. These angiomas were seen in two and a half times as many patients as spider angiomas. Eighty-one percent had comedones, although only 4 percent had epidermoid cysts. In the dermatitis-dermatosis category, dermatophytosis and dry, scaly (asteatotic) skin were seen in more than three-fourths of the subjects. Clinically identified nevi, though seen in a lesser percentage of the group than seborrheic keratoses (63 percent versus 88 percent), were still frequently seen; 137 (84 percent) of the subjects had fewer than 10 nevi, and only 5 (3 percent) had more than 20. This was consistent with Stegmaier's report (1959) which showed the incidence of nevi in white individuals over 50 years of age to number about 4 per person, as determined by histological examination of all skin lesions suspected of being melanocytic nevi.

Several articles have been written concerning the incidences of geriatric dermatoses as seen in private practice (Lane, 1949; Horne, 1959). Zakon, Goldberg, and Forman (1952) examined 222 residents of an old peoples' home in Chicago and tabulated incidences. Droller (1955) visited 476 old people living at home in Sheffield, England, and listed incidences. Of the studies providing incidences, two of them (Noojin & Osment, 1957; Horne, 1959) were chosen to compare with this study because of their relative geographic proximity. There were 3 physical findings common to the top-ranking 16 found in this study: seborrheic keratoses, asteatosis, and actinic keratoses. The rankings of 2 of them, seborrheic keratoses and asteatosis, were fairly comparable between studies with seborrheic keratoses being fourth in frequency in Horne's group (1959), first in Noojin and Osment's (1959), and second in this study; asteatosis ranked seventh in Horne's, fifth in Noojin and Osment's, and fifth in this study. Dermatophytosis, fourth in our study, did not occur frequently in either of the other studies. Actinic keratoses, only fourteenth in this group, was third in Horne's and second in Noojin and Osment's, a presenting complaint frequent in the offices of private dermatologists compared to the actual incidence of physical findings in the present sampling. In a nationwide survey of presenting dermatological complaints of all age groups, dermatophytosis ranked sixth and seborrheic keratoses ninth (Welton & Greenberg, 1961). None of these three studies made racial distinction, a factor which may explain some of the discrepancy.

Less than 10 percent of the study group had ecchymoses (9 percent), eczematous dermatitis (8 percent), pruritus ani (7 percent), epidermoid cysts (4 percent), oral leukokeratoses (3 percent), purpura, xanthelasma, rhinophyma (2 percent each), and psoriasis (1 percent). In Lane and Rockwood's series (1949), eczema was the presenting complaint in 8.8 percent, and contact dermatitis in 6.5 percent, as compared with an incidence of 8 percent of all localized eczematous dermatitides in the present study. Rosacea occurred in their study in less than 2 percent as the presenting complaint, while it appeared much more frequently in the geriatric population of this study (12 percent). In all of the reports of geriatric skin lesions, the incidence of lesions commonly related to sun exposure was a prominent one among Caucasians. As presenting complaints in New Orleans, in Kennedy and colleague's study (1950), seborrheic and actinic keratoses occurred in a ratio of one of every three patients, and basal cell epitheliomas in a ratio of one in five patients over age 60. In the Noojin and Osment series (1957) from Birmingham, Alabama, actinic keratosis was the second most frequent presenting complaint, basal cell epithelioma was third, and squamous cell carcinoma was fourth; while in Horne's series (1959) in Rocky Mount, North Carolina, there was a reversal of ranking in that a combination of squamous cell carcinomas and basal cell epitheliomas ranked second in occurrence and actinic keratosis third. By comparison, a breakdown of four of the lesions associated with excessive actinic exposure showed lentigo occurred in almost three-fourths of the 104 white subjects seen. Hodgson (1963) found, in a home for aged, 90 percent of 124 white persons over 60 years of age had senile lentigines. Slightly over half (54 of 104) of this series had actinic keratosis. Twelve of the subjects had either a basal cell epithelioma or squamous cell carcinoma.

The only study in the literature dealing primarily with the Negro aged was by Wilson (1953) at Harlem Hospital in New York City and was concerned with the presenting complaints as seen by all services at that hospital. Pertaining particularly to the skin, the incidence of leg ulcers due to varicose veins, arteriosclerosis, diabetes, trauma, and sickle cell anemia ranked eleventh among all the Negro aged seen, and vitiligo ranked fourteenth. Table 2–7 presents a racial distribution of some of the common lesions in this study. The Negroes of both sexes had more seborrheic

Table 2–7. *Racial distribution of some common lesions (percentages).*

|  | White | | Negro | |
|---|---|---|---|---|
|  | Male | Female | Male | Female |
| Seborrheic keratoses | | | | |
| (10 or more) | 54 | 38 | 61 | 61 |
| Nevi (5 or more) | 37 | 23 | 46 | 27 |
| Cherry angiomas | | | | |
| (5 or more) | 77 | 77 | 11 | 45 |
| Varicosities | 56 | 58 | 29 | 39 |
| Totals (163) | 52 | 52 | 28 | 31 |

keratoses, while the males of both races tended to have more nevi. The numbers of cherry angiomas occurring in the whites were considerably more, but the differences in varicosities (though there were more in the whites) did not show the great difference in incidence that the cherry angiomas did.

One of the surprising features of the study was the incidence of clinical dermatophytosis. Of the 163 subjects, maceration and fissuring between the toes and/or hyperkeratotic crumbly toenails were seen in 129. Over the two-year period the patients were observed, 101 of them had material taken from the toewebs, the toenails, or both for potassium hydroxide examination and fungus culture. Almost half of these (43 of 101) had either a positive KOH preparation or culture. Fourteen patients had positive cultures of *Trichophyton rubrum*, eleven of *T. mentagrophytes*, and two of *Epidermophyton floccosum*. Of the 163 subjects, there were eight couples who had clinical evidence of dermatophytosis. Only one of the couples was infected with the same fungus, *T. rubrum*. However, in none of the other couples were both partners' cultures positive.

Chi-square $(x^2)$ testing was used to determine the relationships of the various physical findings, both dermatological and medical. Because seborrheic keratoses were extremely common, only those patients with 10 or more such lesions were used, and the diagnoses not relating significantly $(p > .05)$ with seborrheic keratoses were: history of acne, seborrheic dermatitis, asteatosis, nevi, obesity, cholesterol elevation, coronary artery disease, aortic calcification, and hypertensive retinopathy. It is particularly interesting to find no statistical relationship between the seborrheic keratoses and acne, seborrheic dermatitis, and cholesterol elevation. (Normal cholesterol 120 to 220 mg./100 cc., over 250 mg./100 cc. considered abnormal in this study.)

Changes in distribution of body hair have been a common and well-known observation related to the process of aging. Since all the patients were seen on only one occasion, it was necessary to ask the patients whether or not they had an increased, a decreased, or about the same amount of eyebrow, facial, axillary, pubic, and extremity hair as formerly. Almost the same number noted an increase in eyebrow hair as noted a decrease, so that for the average aging individual, this did not seem to be a consistent factor. However, in the three categories presented in Table 2–8 there was a consistent response in all those who admitted any change in the amount of hair, i.e., more facial hair, less axillary hair, and less pubic hair. Of the four criteria used in this study to reflect internal changes, only cholesterol elevation was consistently significant $(p < .05)$.

An attempt also was made to ascertain possible interrelationships among cutaneous and internal vascular lesions in the geriatric population

Table 2-8. *Relation of hair distribution to internal changes.*

| | | | |
|---|---|---|---|
| Elevated cholesterol | .02* | .01* | .05* |
| Arteriolarsclerotic retinopathy | ns** | ns | .05* |
| Coronary artery disease | .01* | Trend | ns |
| Aortic calcification | ns | ns | ns |

\* *p* values for chi-square tests.
\*\* ns—not significant.

examined. In Table 2–9, arteriolarsclerotic retinopathy (grade 11 or greater), aortic calcification seen on chest x-ray, and coronary artery disease as evidenced by electrocardiographic tracing were utilized to reflect the changes associated with aging as evidenced in different-sized internal blood vessels. Varicose veins, cherry angiomas, and scrotal angiomas, being more superficial vascular abnormalities, were compared among themselves and with diseased internal vessels. Among the cutaneous vascular lesions there was a significant relationship between cherry angiomas and scrotal angiomas ($p < .001$), and also between cherry angiomas and varicosities ($p < .05$). The presence of scrotal angiomas seemed to be associated with an increased incidence of both aortic calcification and arteriolarsclerotic changes. Bean (1956) states that cherry angiomas were almost universal in all individuals over 70 years of age, the universal incidence achieved earlier in females (75 percent of this group had them). He compared cherry angiomas, venous stars (varicosities), and caviar tongue lesions, and in his patients found that 50 percent of all females over 70 had all three of these types of lesions, while 30 percent of all males over 70 had evidence of all three.

The interrelationships between the manifestations of atopy and eye color were evaluated. The category "atopy" included asthma, hay fever, and atopic dermatitis, but for the purposes of this study urticaria was put

Table 2-9. *Interrelationships of vascular lesions.*

| | Scrotal angiomas | Varicosities | Cherry angiomas |
|---|---|---|---|
| Arteriolarsclerotic retinopathy | .02* | ns** | Trend |
| Aortic calcification | .05* | ns | ns |
| Coronary artery disease | ns | .05* | ns |
| Scrotal angiomas | | ns | .001* |
| Varicosities | | | .05* |

\* *p* values for chi-square tests.
\*\* ns—not significant.

into a separate category. Drug reactions, as defined here, reflected all reactions to medications, both local and systemic. In this study there appeared to be a highly significant relationship between atopic individuals and those who had drug reactions of various sorts ($p < .001$), and a significant relationship of individuals with blue eyes having manifestations of atopy ($p < .01$) and urticaria ($p < .001$). For this small group, this latter interrelationship was contrary to the study reported by Carney (1962). Baer and Schwarzschild (1955) felt that allergic skin disease in older people was not at all uncommon; the three most common allergic eruptions in persons over 50 years being allergic eczematous contact dermatitis, allergic drug eruption, and allergic urticaria. Thompson (1953) reported that "eczema is the most common lesion, often contact in type, to be found in the geriatric patient." Smith and Kiem (1961) confirmed the decreased incidence of sensitivity to Rhus antigen (3 pentadecylcatechol) in an elderly group and were unable to induce sensitivity to a significant degree by reexposure to the antigen. However, the elderly group members developed allergic contact sensitivity, as frequently as did youthful controls, to potent sensitizers not previously encountered. Lane and Rockwood (1949) had only 13 cases of dermatitis medicamentosa in the 2,000 records reviewed.

Finally, an attempt was made to compare cutaneous viral infections by chi-square ($x^2$) evaluation. This type of comparison, which relied solely on history from the patients, must necessarily be viewed with some reservation. However, three of the most common of the cutaneous viral infections (chicken pox, warts, and herpes simplex) interrelated with each other and also with apthae in all cases by at least a trend ($p = .05$ to $.1$) and in most instances with lower $p$ values. Though difficult to assess, this degree of consistent and significant relationship could not be ignored.

## References

Baer, R. L., and Schwarzschild, L. Selected allergic skin diseases in older persons. *Geriatrics*, 10:265, 1955.

Bean, W. B. Changing incidence of certain vascular lesions of skin with aging. *Geriatrics*, 11:97, 1956.

Carney, R. G. Eye color in atopic dermatitis. *Archives of Dermatology* (Chicago), 85:17, 1962.

Droller, H. Dermatologic findings in random sample of old persons. *Geriatrics*, 10:421, 1955.

Epstein, S. Dermatitis in aged. *Geriatrics*, 1:369, 1946.

Hodgson, C. Senile lentigo. *Archives of Dermatology* (Chicago), 87:197, 1963.

Horne, S. F. Common geriatric dermatoses. *North Carolina Medical Journal*, 20:177, 1959.

Kennedy, C. B., et al. Geriatric dermatology. *Southern Medical Journal*, 43:128, 1950.

Kierland, R. R., and O'Leary, P. A. Aging skin. *Journal of the American Geriatric Society*, 1:676, 1953.

Lane, C. G., and Rockwood, E. M. Geriatric dermatoses. *New England Journal of Medicine*, 241:772, 1949.

Noojin, R. O., and Osment, I. S. Common geriatric dermatoses. *Southern Medical Journal*, 50:237, 1957.

Palmer, A. E. Common disorders of aging skin. *Clinics*, 4:1211–1229, 1946.

Smith, J. G., Jr., and Kiem, I. Allergic contact sensitivity in aged. *Journal of Gerontology*, 16:118, 1961.

Stegmaier, O. C. Natural regression of melanocytic nevus. *Journal of Investigative Dermatology*, 32:413, 1959.

Thompson, R. C. Dermatologic problems of geriatric patients. *Journal of the Tennessee Medical Association*, 46:316, 1953.

Waisman, M. Problems of skin associated with aging. *Journal of the Florida Medical Association*, 43:452, 1956.

Welton, D. G., and Greenberg, B. G. Trends in office practice of dermatology. *Archives of Dermatology* (Chicago), 83:355, 1961.

Wilson, J. L. Geriatric experiences with Negro aged. *Geriatrics*, 8:88, 1953.

Young, A. W., Jr. Dermatologic complaints presented by 330 geriatric patients. *Geriatrics*, 13:428, 1958.

Zakon, S. J., Goldberg, A. I., and Forman, I. Geriatric dermatoses. *Illinois Medical Journal*, 101:37, 1952.

# Conjunctival Blood Vessels in the Aged*   *Regina Frayser, William H. Knisely, Robert Barnes, and William M. Satterwhite, Jr.*

Aging is a many-faceted problem which will be solved only by contributions from many sources. Alterations in the vasculature which might interfere with the normal transfer of oxygen and metabolic products at the tissue level are factors which should be considered. The bulbar conjunctiva (front of eyeball) offers a naturally exposed area in which the microcirculation may be clearly visualized by direct microscopy. These vessels contain a statistically valid sample of all the circulating arterial blood (Knisely, Stratman-Thomas, Eliot, & Bloch, 1945). There is, beneath a transparent epithelial coat, a vascular bed complete with arterioles, capillaries, and collecting venules. This vascular bed has been studied in health and disease for many years. As early as 1852, Coccius is reported by Luedde (1913) to have demonstrated the conjunctival circulation microscopically. Luedde

* From *"In Vivo* Observations on the Conjunctival Circulation in Elderly Subjects," reprinted by permission from the *Journal of Gerontology*, 19:494–500, 1964.

made a comprehensive clinical pathological study of the conjunctival vessels.

These early observations have been expanded through the years by such investigators as Zeller (1921); Ruedemann (1933); Knisely, Bloch, Eliot, and Warner (1947, 1950); Grafflin and Bagley (1953); Grafflin and Corddry (1953a, 1953b); and Bloch (1953, 1954, 1956). The early techniques were extended, and the conjunctival vessels were characterized with regard to morphology, function, and alterations in the characteristics of blood flow, changes in vessel permeability, and vascular morphology in a wide variety of conditions.

The alterations which have been found in the conjunctival vessels by various investigators were reviewed recently by Labram and Lestradet (1961). Descriptions of alteration considered to be characteristic of diabetes (Ditzel & Uffe, 1954; Ditzel, 1956), rheumatic heart disease (Laine & Zilliacus, 1950), arteriosclerosis (Davis & Landau, 1960), and hypertension (Lack, Adolph, Ralston, Leiby, Winson, & Griffith, 1949; Lee & Holze, 1950, 1951) have been reported. Changes attributable to age alone have been described (Ditzel, 1956; Ditzel & Uffe, 1954; Labram & Lestradet, 1961).

Materials and Methods

*Subjects*

Observations were made on the vasculature of the bulbar conjunctiva and the hemodynamic characteristics in these vessels in 209 subjects ranging in age from 60 to 93 years. These subjects represent a segment of the elderly population which is physically and mentally able and willing to undergo a two-day period of extensive medical and psychological testing. Institutionalized persons or those socially isolated were not included. Of this group 100 were male, 109 female; 135 were white and 74 Negro. Because of the reports in the literature on the alterations produced by hypertension and arteriosclerosis these 209 subjects were divided into two groups: (*a*) a hypertensive group having systolic blood pressure over 150 mm. Hg or diastolic pressure over 100 mm. Hg and (*b*) normotensive subjects with blood pressure less than 150 mm. Hg systolic and 100 mm. Hg diastolic. The subjects were divided into three age ranges, 60–70 years, 71–80 years, and 81–93 years, in order to evaluate the effect of increasing age.

*Methods*

All subjects were studied in the supine position. A Leitz binocular biobjective microscope of the Greenough type was used in the vertical position to examine the lateral aspect of the bulbar conjunctiva of each eye. Magnification was 50 to 100 times. The subject held his eye in the desired position by fixing his gaze on a distant object. The conjunctiva was obliquely illuminated by means of a Shahan ophthalmic lamp, which provided adequate illumination with minimum production of heat. Photographs were taken with an Exakta camera equipped with a 50 mm. lens and a ring strobe light.

The characteristic picture as seen in the vessels of the bulbar conjunctiva of normotensive young people has been well documented (Knisely et al., 1947; Bloch, 1956; Lee & Holze, 1950; Grafflin & Bagley, 1953; Grafflin & Corddry, 1953a, 1953b; Jackson, 1958).

From these observations in the literature and from previous observations in our own laboratory, the conjunctival vasculature in the healthy young individual may be briefly characterized as follows: blood flow is rapid and cellular detail usually cannot be made out in the arterioles at a magnification of 50–100 X. The flow of unagglutinated blood is laminar or streamlined with no evidence of red cell aggregation, no masses of red cells in the arterioles, and no edema in the perivascular tissue. There is no sign of white cells sticking together or sticking to the sides of the vessel wall. In persons with completely unagglutinated red blood cells, small differences in flow rate in the venules have no noticeable effect on the red cell suspension. There is no significant alteration in vessel permeability. This is evidenced by lack of edema, leaking plasma or whole blood, and the absence of hemosiderin in the perivascular tissue.

The blood vessels in the conjunctiva are in two layers—a deep one on the episclera and a superficial one just below the mucosa with anastomoses between the two layers. In the young, the conjunctival vessels are delicate, have an even caliber, and the venules follow a straight path, which is paralleled by the thinner arterioles. The capillaries arise from the end arterioles, follow a smooth course, and form a network of vessels, which join to form the collecting venules. The arteries may terminate in main arterio-venous channels, which communicate directly with the venular tree. In addition to these A–V communications there may be both arterial-to-arterial and venule-to-venule anastomoses. These channels may be open only intermittently.

The conjunctival vessels in the elderly subjects were evaluated against the criteria described above. Morphologic vascular changes were assessed subjectively from the configuration of the arterioles, capillaries, and venules. Noted were the degree of vascularity (the numbers of vessels visible per unit of surface area and the diameters of individual vessels per unit of surface area); tortuosity (the amount of curving or kinking of the vessels); and any evidence of sacculation (a localized widening of a vessel exceeding twice the diameter of the vessel at the ends of the sacculation). Perivascular changes were indicated by the presence in the conjunctival tissue of edema, leaking plasma, leaking whole blood, or pigment from old hemorrhages. Evidence for intravascular changes was based on alterations in the hemodynamic characteristics in the different parts of the conjunctival vascular system. This included observations on venous "sludge," the presence of red cell masses in the arterioles, and occurrence of static blood or flow reversal in venules.

## Results

. . . Table 2–10 presents the data obtained on the elderly subjects. Table 2–11 summarizes the changes seen in the conjunctival vessels of 40 elderly subjects after a three- to five-year interval.

The changes seen in the conjunctival vascular bed in the elderly subjects were widespread and involved changes in the vessel wall, in the perivascular tissue, and in the characteristics of blood flow. Seventy-seven percent of the normotensive and 84 percent of the hypertensive elderly subjects showed increased tortuosity of the vessels as compared with the young age group, while venous sacculations occurred in 87 and 89 percent. In the nonhypertensive group, the venules were tortuous and dilated, while the arterioles and capillaries were not involved to the same extent. In contrast, in the hypertensive subjects, the terminal arterioles appeared narrow and the capillaries were coiled and tortuous. In both groups there was an increase in vascularity and many anastomotic channels were open and filled with slowly moving blood. Spontaneous vasomotion was seldom seen.

From the data in Table 2–10, it may be seen that 93 percent of all the normotensive and 89 percent of the hypertensive subjects had venous sludge and that arterial masses were present in 62 percent and 70 percent, respectively. Twenty-five percent of the normotensive persons, compared to 37 percent of the hypertensive group, showed evidence of vascular abnormalities which had allowed the vessel content to escape into the surrounding tissue as indicated by the presence of edema, leaking plasma, whole blood, or hemosiderin.

There was no significant change between the ages of 60 and 93 years in either group in any of the modalities studied. It was not possible to find a significant correlation with race or sex, nor were the extra- and intravascular findings correlated with cholesterol or hemoglobin levels.

In an effort to determine if the changes seen in the elderly subjects as compared with the younger age group were permanent or if these changes might become progressively worse with increasing age, 40 of the original

Table 2–10. *Observations on the conjunctival vessels of elderly subjects.*

| Age range | 60–70 years | | 71–80 years | | 81–93 years | | 60–93 years | | | |
|---|---|---|---|---|---|---|---|---|---|---|
| | Normo-tensive | Hyper-tensive | Normo-tensive | Hyper-tensive | Normo-tensive | Hyper-tensive | Normo-tensive | | Hyper-tensive | |
| Observation | N = 60 | N = 55 | N = 29 | N = 45 | N = 8 | N = 12 | N = 97 | % | N = 112 | % |
| Increased vascularity | 42 | 28 | 17 | 27 | 5 | 5 | 64 | 66 | 60 | 54 |
| Decreased vascularity | 5 | 1 | 1 | 7 | 2 | 2 | 8 | 8 | 10 | 9 |
| Increased tortuosity | 46 | 46 | 24 | 42 | 5 | 6 | 75 | 77 | 94 | 84 |
| Venous sacculation | 50 | 50 | 27 | 40 | 7 | 10 | 84 | 87 | 100 | 89 |
| Venous sludge | 57 | 47 | 27 | 40 | 6 | 12 | 90 | 93 | 100 | 89 |
| Arterial masses | 40 | 32 | 17 | 38 | 3 | 8 | 60 | 62 | 78 | 70 |
| Static venous blood | 21 | 11 | 8 | 12 | 5 | 4 | 34 | 35 | 27 | 24 |
| Arterial flow reversal | 0 | 2 | 0 | 0 | 0 | 1 | 0 | 0 | 3 | 3 |
| Venous flow reversal | 6 | 0 | 0 | 5 | 0 | 1 | 13 | 13 | 6 | 5 |
| Edema | 11 | 4 | 0 | 19 | 3 | 1 | 14 | 14 | 24 | 21 |
| Leaking plasma | 3 | 3 | 2 | 4 | 0 | 1 | 5 | 5 | 8 | 7 |
| Leaking whole blood | 3 | 0 | 0 | 1 | 0 | 0 | 3 | 3 | 1 | 1 |
| Hemosiderin | 0 | 1 | 1 | 8 | 1 | 0 | 2 | 2 | 8 | 7 |

Table 2–11. *Comparison of first and second observations on 40 normotensive subjects.*

| Observation | Change | Age 60–70 years N | 71–80 years N |
|---|---|---|---|
| Vascularity | 0 | 9 | 2 |
| | ↑ | 6 | 0 |
| | ↓ | 12 | 11 |
| Tortuosity | 0 | 13 | 4 |
| | ↑ | 3 | 1 |
| | ↓ | 11 | 8 |
| Venous sacculation | 0 | 9 | 6 |
| | ↑ | 6 | 1 |
| | ↓ | 12 | 6 |
| Venous sludge | 0 | 6 | 6 |
| | ↑ | 5 | 1 |
| | ↓ | 16 | 6 |
| Arterial masses | 0 | 10 | 5 |
| | ↑ | 0 | 0 |
| | ↓ | 17 | 8 |

subjects were studied again after a three- to five-year interval. The data from this study are presented in Table 2–11. It is interesting to note that in each of the parameters studied, many of the subjects showed a decrease in severity.

## Discussion

One of the difficulties in assessing the effect of age per se on any observation is the problem of ruling out the contributions made by other preexisting conditions. Factors such as emotion, chronic sinusitis, and many minor illnesses are known to alter the character of blood flow in the conjunctival vessels. Drugs and alcohol may also alter the suspension characteristics of the red cells (Knisely et al., 1947). The alterations seen in the conjunctival vessels of both the nonhypertensive and the hypertensive elderly subjects were widespread and involved both the vessels and the hemodynamic characteristics of the blood within the vessels.

The most striking findings in the aged were the high incidence of both venous sludge and arteriolar red cell masses throughout the age groups studied. Venous sludge has been reported to occur in a variety of conditions (Knisely et al., 1947), but arterial masses have not been reported in healthy young people, although Ditzel (1956) has reported arterial masses in 3 percent of healthy subjects 36–55 years of age and in 3 percent of those 56–75 years of age. Thirteen percent of the 36–55-year group and 30 percent of the 56–75-year group had consistent aggregations in the smaller venules with occasional aggregations in the larger venules and in the capillaries. These figures are in sharp contrast to the 93 percent of the normotensive and 89 percent of the hypertensive group found to have venous sludge and the 62 percent and 70 percent found with arterial masses.

Altered cell nutrition as a result of inadequate flow and the formation of intravascular plugs may be of significance in explaining many of the vague manifestations of poor health so often complained of by the elderly person. It has been pointed out by Fowler and Fowler (1950) that vascular changes seen in the bulbar conjunctiva may also occur in other parts of the body and may be the cause of other signs and symptoms. Certainly, it has been demonstrated that tissue destruction anywhere in the body usually results in the production of erythrocyte aggregates in the arterioles of the bulbar conjunctiva (Knisely et al., 1947). Venous sludge has been observed in the conjunctival vessels with certain types of tinnitus (Fowler & Fowler, 1950) and vascular headache (Lee & Holze, 1950). With relief of the headache, the sludging disappeared or was markedly reduced.

It has not been possible to formulate a vascular pattern typical only of increasing age. The changes in the vessels seem to be random and do not fall into a pattern, such as has been described for hypertension, arteriosclerosis (Davis & Landau, 1960), or diabetes. The venous side of the vascular system is affected more than the arterioles or capillaries.

In a repeat study of 40 elderly individuals following a three- to five-year interval, it was found that a number of individuals had a decrease in the severity of abnormal findings. However, neither the abnormal vascular nor intravascular findings completely regressed. It is interesting to find that even in this age group venous sacculations can be spontaneously repaired and that the degree of intravascular aggregation can be modified.

## Summary

Observation were made on the vasculature of the bulbar conjunctiva and the hemodynamic characteristics of the vessels in a study of 209 subjects ranging in age from 60 to 93 years. The changes seen in the conjunctival vascular bed were widespread and involved changes in the vessel wall, in the perivascular tissue, and in the characteristics of blood flow. There was markedly increased tortuosity, primarily on the venous side, and numerous venous sacculations were seen. There was a high incidence of red cell masses and venous sludge. It was not possible to formulate a vascular pattern typical only of increasing age. Repeat observations on 40 subjects after a three- to five-year interval suggested that the changes in the vessel wall are reversible as are the intravascular aggregations.

## References

Bloch, E. H. The *in vivo* intravascular and vascular reactions in acute poliomyelitis. *American Journal of Medical Science*, 226:24–37, 1953.

Bloch, E. H. The bulbar conjuctiva of man as a site for the microscopic study of the circulation. *Anatomical Record*, 120:349–358, 1954.

Bloch, E. H. Microscopic observations of the circulating blood of the bulbar conjunctiva in man in health and disease. *Ergebnisse der Anatomie und Entwicklungsgeschichte*, 35:1–98, 1956.

Davis, E., and Landau, J. The small blood vessels of the conjunctiva and nail bed in arteriosclerosis. *Angiology*, 11:173–179, 1960.

Ditzel, J. Angioscopic changes in the smaller blood vessels in diabetes mellitus and their relationship to aging. *Circulation*, 14:386–397, 1956.

Ditzel, J., and Uffe, S. Morphologic and hemodynamic changes in the smaller blood vessels in diabetes mellitus: II. The degenerative and hemodynamic changes in the bulbar conjunctiva in normotensive diabetic patients. *New England Journal of Medicine*, 25:587–594, 1954.

Fowler, E. P., and Fowler, E. P., Jr. An explanation of tinnitus and deafness. *Laryngoscope* (St. Louis), 60:919–930, 1950.

Grafflin, A. L., and Bagley, E. H. Studies of peripheral blood vascular beds. *Johns Hopkins Hospital Bulletin*, 92:47–73, 1953.

Grafflin, A. L., and Corddry, E. G. A note on peripheral blood vascular beds in the bulbar conjunctiva of man. *Johns Hopkins Hospital Bulletin*, 92:423–425, 1953. (a)

Grafflin, A. L., and Corddry, E. G. Studies of peripheral vascular beds in the bulbar conjunctiva of man. *Johns Hopkins Hospital Bulletin*, 93:275–289, 1953. (b)

Jackson, W. B. The functional activity of the human conjunctival capillary bed in hypertensive and normotensive subjects. *American Heart Journal*, 56:222–235, 1958.

Knisely, M. H., Bloch, E. H., Eliot, T. S., and Warner, L. Sludged blood. *Science*, 106:431–440, 1947.

Knisely, M. H., Bloch, E. H., Eliot, T. S., and Warner, L. Blood circulating methods and apparatus. In Glaser, O. (Ed.), *Medical Physics*. Vol. II. Chicago: Year Book Publishers, 1950.

Knisely, M. H., Stratman-Thomas, W. K., Eliot, T. S., and Bloch, E. H. *Knowlesi* malaria in monkeys. I. Microscopic pathological circulatory physiology of rhesus monkeys during acute *Plasmodium knowlesi* malaria. *Journal of the National Malaria Society*, 4:285–300, 1945.

Labram, C., and Lestradet, H. La auto aglomeration des globules rouges observée *in vivo.* Interet de l'examen biomicroscopique des vaisseaux de la conjonctive bulbaire. *Presse Médicale,* 69:187–190, 1961.

Lack, A., Adolph, W., Ralston, W., Leiby, G., Winson, T., and Griffith, G. Biomicroscopy of conjunctival vessels in hypertension. *American Heart Journal,* 38:654–664, 1949.

Laine, V., and Zilliacus, H. Intravascular aggregation of the erythrocytes in rheumatoid arthritis. *Acta Medical Scandinavica,* 137:87–96, 1950.

Lee, R. E., and Holze, E. A. The peripheral vascular system in the bulbar conjunctiva of young normotensive adults at rest. *Journal of Clinical Investigation,* 29:146–150, 1950.

Lee, R. E., and Holze, E. A. Peripheral vascular hemodynamics in the conjunctiva of subjects with hypertensive vascular disease. *Journal of Clinical Investigation,* 30:539–546, 1951.

Luedde, W. H. A microscopic study of the conjunctival vessels. *American Journal of Ophthalmology,* 30:129–142, 1913.

Ruedemann, A. D. Conjunctival vessels. *Transactions of the American Medical Association Section on Ophthalmology,* 84:114–125, 1933.

Zeller, K. Studien an Bindehautgefässen. *Klinische Monatsblaetter fur Augenheilkunde und fur Augenaerztliche Fortbildung,* 66:609–622, 1921.

# Relation of Serum Cholesterol to Age, Sex, and Race*

*Larry W. Thompson, Claude R. Nichols, and Walter D. Obrist*

In recent years both age and sex differences in serum cholesterol levels have been reported (Adlersberg, 1957; Barker, 1939; Keys, 1952, 1963; Kornerup, 1950; Kountz, Sonnenberg, Hofstatter, & Wolff, 1945; McMahon, Allen, Weber, & Missey, 1951; Schilling, Christakis, Bennett, & Coyle, 1964; Sperry & Webb, 1950; Swanson, Leverton, Gram, Roberts, & Pesek, 1955). Although there is no complete agreement among the various studies, a consistent curvilinear relationship between age and cholesterol level has been observed in clinically healthy people. In general, cholesterol values begin to rise gradually after age 18. Peak values are observed in men in the middle fifties and in women as late as the sixties. A relatively small number of cholesterol determinations, however, have been made on people in the elderly age ranges. The present investigation was concerned with the relationship between serum cholesterol level and age, sex, and racial factors in a group of community volunteers over 60 years of age. Assessments of change within individuals over a three-year period were also made. Longitudinal measurements have not been reported in most previous studies.

* Reprinted by permission from the *Journal of Gerontology,* 20:160–164, 1965.

Materials and Methods

*Subjects*

The subject group was composed of elderly persons (60–93 years of age) living in or around Durham, North Carolina, who volunteered to participate in an extensive aging research program. White and Negro individuals of both sexes and a variety of educational and occupational levels were included in an attempt to approximate the sex, racial, and socioeconomic distributions of the local community (Heyman & Jeffers, 1964). All subjects were ambulatory, and approximately 75 percent showed little or no limitation in social or industrial function caused by impairments (Dovenmuehle, Busse, & Newman, 1961).

*Examination Procedures*

As part of this research program, the subjects were periodically evaluated by a physical examination and laboratory procedures, including an electrocardiogram and chest x-ray. The presence or absence of cardiovascular disease was clinically assessed from EKG interpretations, estimates of heart size, the extent of aortic calcification, and evidence of peripheral arteriosclerosis, hypertension, or cardiac decompensation. Total serum cholesterol determinations were made on blood drawn between 8 and 9 A.M. under fasting conditions. Analyses were made according to Bloor's (1922) method adapted to the photoelectric colorimeter. The Liebermann-Burchard reaction was used.

In the initial phase of the study, blood cholesterol determinations were made on 198 subjects, who were seen once during a two-year testing period. In the three-year follow-up study, cholesterol measurements were discontinued during one year of testing. Repeat determinations were limited to 74 of the remaining 100 potential subjects. Of the 26 individuals in this group who were not evaluated, 5 failed to fast, 5 refused to return, 14 died, 1 moved, and 1 was ill. The mean time interval between the first and second testing was 33 months, and the standard deviation was 6.2 months.

*Results*

Table 2–12 lists the means and standard deviation for subjects grouped according to age, sex, and race. An overall comparison of the three age groups (last line of the table) suggests a gradual decline in serum cholesterol over time. An analysis of variance, however, indicated that there was no significant age effect for the combined sample.

Figure 2–12 shows the mean cholesterol levels for males and females in

Table 2-12. *Means and standard deviations for serum cholesterol (mg. percentage) in elderly subjects grouped according to age, sex, and race.*

|  | 60–69 years | | | 70–79 years | | | 80–93 years | | |
|---|---|---|---|---|---|---|---|---|---|
|  | N | Mean | SD | N | Mean | SD | N | Mean | SD |
| White | | | | | | | | | |
| Male | 18 | 211 | 34 | 31 | 222 | 35 | 14 | 216 | 42 |
| Female | 20 | 266 | 49 | 31 | 261 | 48 | 11 | 255 | 32 |
| Total | 38 | 240 | 43 | 62 | 241 | 42 | 25 | 232 | 38 |
| Negro | | | | | | | | | |
| Male | 14 | 247 | 44 | 19 | 247 | 50 | 3 | 260 | 72 |
| Female | 17 | 277 | 58 | 14 | 271 | 48 | 6 | 233 | 71 |
| Total | 31 | 263 | 52 | 33 | 257 | 49 | 9 | 242 | 71 |
| Combined sample | 69 | 250 | 53 | 95 | 247 | 48 | 34 | 235 | 49 |

the three age groups. It is apparent that the female values were higher than the male values in each age range. The overall difference between sexes was significant beyond the .001 level. These curves also raise the question of a sex difference in age trend; it seems that males underwent little change with

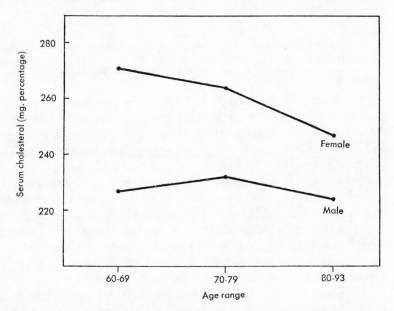

Figure 2–12. *Mean serum cholesterol of males and females at three age levels (total N = 98).*

time, while females showed a gradual decline in cholesterol level. Although the interaction only approached a statistical level of significance, the possibility of a different trend for males and females is supported to some extent by longitudinal data to be presented later.

It is evident from Table 2–12 that Negroes tended to have higher cholesterol levels than whites in the sixties and seventies ($p < .01$ level). A similar trend is apparent in the oldest age range (80–93), but the values for the Negro group are not reliable because of the small number of cases.

The analysis of variance also yielded a significant interaction ($p < .05$ level) between sex and race, illustrated in Table 2–13. This is attributable to the fact that Negro males had higher cholesterol levels than white males, while the difference between white and Negro females was minimal. In an attempt to explain the observed racial differences, an analysis was made of the relationship between serum cholesterol and occupational level. No significant differences were obtained between manual and nonmanual workers in any of the sex-race groups.

Table 2–13. *Means and standard deviations for serum cholesterol (mg. percentage) in relation to sex and race.*

|  | Male | | | Female | | | Total | | |
|---|---|---|---|---|---|---|---|---|---|
|  | N | Mean | SD | N | Mean | SD | N | Mean | SD |
| White | 63 | 218 | 36 | 62 | 261 | 45 | 125 | 239 | 46 |
| Negro | 36 | 248 | 48 | 37 | 268 | 57 | 73 | 258 | 54 |
| Total | 99 | 229 | 43 | 99 | 264 | 50 | 198 | 246 | 50 |

The means and standard deviations for subjects who had repeat cholesterol measurements after a three-year time lapse are given in Table 2–14. As in the previous analysis, subjects were divided according to age, sex, and race. Although racial differences are evident, both white and Negro groups were combined for purposes of statistical analysis, since both groups demonstrated a similar pattern of change in cholesterol over time. This is apparent from the differences between the first and second cholesterol measures listed in Table 2–14. A Type I analysis of variance (Lindquist, 1953) of these data yielded a significant interaction between age group and change from the first to the second measurement ($p < .05$ level).

The interaction between age and cholesterol change can be seen in Figure 2–13. In general, during the sixties, there tends to be an overall rise in cholesterol from first to second measurements, whereas a definite decline is evident for subjects in their seventies. However, a comparison of the sexes indicated that the principal portion of this interaction could be attributed to changes within the female group. In the sixties the cholesterol

Table 2–14. *Changes in mean serum cholesterol (mg. percentage) over time according to age, sex, and race.*[a]

|  | N | First measure | | Second measure | | Difference |
|---|---|---|---|---|---|---|
|  |  | Mean | SD | Mean | SD |  |
| White male |  |  |  |  |  |  |
| 60–69 | 6 | 205 | 34 | 205 | 33 | 0 |
| 70–79 | 10 | 213 | 35 | 212 | 28 | − 1 |
| White female |  |  |  |  |  |  |
| 60–69 | 5 | 248 | 57 | 276 | 58 | +28 |
| 70–79 | 10 | 272 | 36 | 256 | 45 | −16 |
| Negro male |  |  |  |  |  |  |
| 60–69 | 9 | 243 | 51 | 241 | 31 | − 2 |
| 70–79 | 12 | 248 | 40 | 237 | 48 | −11 |
| Negro female |  |  |  |  |  |  |
| 60–69 | 11 | 282 | 60 | 290 | 37 | + 8 |
| 70–79 | 11 | 273 | 51 | 258 | 50 | −15 |

[a] Mean time interval between measurements = 33 months; SD = 6.2 months.

level of males tended to remain constant from first to second measurements. The mean of the first measurements was 228.0 and that of the second was 226.7 mg. percent. The females showed an average increase in cholesterol over a three-year interval, from 271.2 to 285.6 mg. percent. In the seventies, the males revealed a slight drop in cholesterol from first to second measurements (from 231.8 to 225.5), but the females showed a greater decline (from 272.9 to 257.1). This difference approached the .05 level of significance.

Table 2–15 presents an analysis of cholesterol level in relation to the presence or the absence of coronary artery disease as indicated by the electrocardiogram and radiologic evidence of aortic calcification. It is evident that there were no significant differences between subjects who had definite EKG or x-ray findings and those with minimal or no evidence of pathology. A further breakdown of the data according to age, sex, and race was undertaken, but no consistent trends were apparent. Particular attention was given to the relative proportion of Negroes and whites classified according to the presence or absence of coronary artery disease and aortic calcification. Since Negroes tend to have higher average cholesterols than whites, the question was asked whether the lack of relationship between cholesterol and these signs might be caused by a higher proportion of Negroes than whites with negative findings. A closer inspection of the data, however, revealed a comparable proportion of Negroes and whites in the various subgroups.

A comparison of cholesterol change was also made in longitudinal subjects divided according to the same EKG or x-ray criteria. No significant change over time was observed for any of the groups, and there were

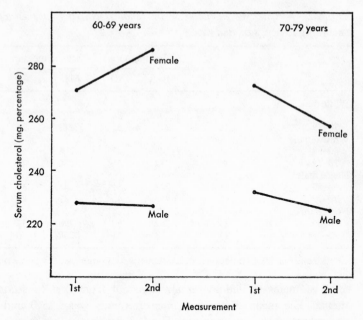

Figure 2–13. *Mean serum cholesterol changes of males and females over a three-year period at two age levels: 60–69 years and 70–79 years (total N = 74).*

no reliable differences between the groups for either measure. The number of the longitudinal subjects was not sufficiently large to examine these variables in relation to age, sex, and race.

A final comparison was made between subjects with and without clinical evidence of cardiovascular disease, based on one or more of the

Table 2–15. *Means and standard deviations for serum cholesterol (mg percentage) in elderly subjects with and without signs of cardiovascular disease.*

|  | N | Mean | SD |
|---|---|---|---|
| Electrocardiographic findings |  |  |  |
| No coronary artery disease | 94 | 251 | 46 |
| Coronary artery disease | 48 | 246 | 50 |
| Radiologic findings |  |  |  |
| None or mild aortic calcification | 173 | 246 | 50 |
| Moderate to severe aortic calcification[a] | 18 | 249 | 53 |
| Clinical evidence of cardiovascular disease |  |  |  |
| Absent | 45 | 245 | 42 |
| Present | 119 | 249 | 53 |

[a] Visualized along a quarter or more of the aortic arch on a P-A film.

following objective criteria: (*a*) systolic blood pressure above 190 mm.; (*b*) diastolic blood pressure above 100 mm.; (*c*) heart size increased by 55 percent; (*d*) EKG interpretation of infarction, injury, and/or ischemia; (*e*) moderate to severe aortic calcification; (*f*) moderate to severe arteriosclerosis or hypertension; (*g*) heart decompensation noted on physical examination. As shown in Table 2–15, the means and standard deviations were quite similar for the two diagnostic groups. Not all subjects are represented in this table, because insufficient technical personnel or scheduling difficulties made it impossible, at times, to complete all the procedures.

## Discussion

The cross-sectional data presented in Table 2–12 reveal an absence of the expected downward trend in cholesterol level of elderly males, which is not in complete agreement with previously reported observations (Barker, 1939; Keys, Mickelsen, Miller, Hayes, & Todd, 1950; Kountz et al., 1945; McMahon et al., 1951). However, there is some indication of a decline in cholesterol over time in the female groups, which suggests an age by sex interaction. This is further supported by a statistical comparison of men and women at three different age levels. *T* tests of the mean differences indicate that cholesterol values for females were significantly higher than values for males only in the 60–69 and 70–79 age ranges ($p < .01$). In the oldest age group (80–93), the sex differences were not statistically significant.

The minimal change in blood cholesterol levels of males over time shown in Figure 2–12 lends itself to the conclusion that males reach a peak value sometime before the youngest age range (60–69). The more marked decline in the female groups, however, suggests that their highest cholesterol levels may occur in the sixties, or at least at an older age than the males. This age by sex interaction is consistent with previous findings (Keys, 1963; Kountz et al., 1955; Schilling et al., 1964), and is in general agreement with the sex differences occurring over time reported by Adlersberg, Schaefer, Steinberg, and Wang (1956).

The repeat determinations on the same individuals over a three-year period resulted in trends, shown in Figure 2–13, that provide some agreement with the measurements made on different subjects at varying age levels. The absence of change in males, for example, from the first to second measures is in line with the lack of an age effect seen in the cross-sectional data, and together they invite the speculation that male cholesterol levels tend to become stabilized in these older age ranges, with a further change being unlikely. Sufficient longitudinal data, however, have not been collected on elderly subjects, particularly above 80 years of age, to substantiate this.

The female trends depicted in Figure 2–13 are in accord with the hypothesis that the highest cholesterol values are reached in the sixties, followed by a gradual decline in the seventies. Repeated determinations on females in the 60–69 age range indicate that a majority undergo an increase in cholesterol over a three-year period (mean change $= + 14.37$ mg. percent), in contrast to women in the 70–79 age range, who show a tendency to decline (mean change $= -15.72$ mg. percent). In some respects the foregoing trends are reminiscent of the cholesterol peak reported in men at age 45–55 (Keys, 1952) and suggest that the decrease in cholesterol seen in elderly female groups is not necessarily a result of selective mortality but reflects a general ontogenetic pattern.

A comparison of racial differences in Table 2–14 reveals that Negro cholesterol levels are consistently higher than white. The significant sex by race interaction is due to the fact that the racial difference between males is larger than the difference between females. Since previous studies (Keys, 1963; Walker & Arvidsson, 1954) cast doubt on the relevance of racial factors to serum cholesterol level, and emphasize dietary factors, the question is raised as to the importance of diet in the present sample. The finding of a greater racial difference for males than for females suggests the possibility of sex differences in either dietary habits or metabolic processes at this age level. Unfortunately, dietary information on these subjects was not available, which precludes further investigation of such questions at the present time.

The failure to demonstrate differences in serum cholesterol between subjects with and without evidence of cardiovascular disease is in agreement with the results of Kountz et al. (1945), who reported that cholesterol values of patients with "coronary sclerosis," calcification of peripheral arteries, or cardiac decompensation are similar or slightly lower than the values of elderly people without these signs. Such findings are interesting in view of the well-established relationship between hypercholesteremia and both atherosclerosis (Friedman, Roseman, & Byers, 1955) and coronary heart disease (Kannel, Dawber, Kagan, Revotskie, & Stokes, 1961) in younger subjects. The present data give little indication that increased cholesterol levels are related to disorders of the cardiovascular system in the elderly and raise the question that hypercholesteremia may play a different role in old age with respect to pathological processes.

## Summary

Total serum cholesterol determinations were made on 198 elderly persons (60–93 years) as part of a comprehensive study of human aging.

Repeat determinations were obtained on 74 of these people after a three-year interval. White and Negro community volunteers of both sexes and a wide range of socioeconomic levels were included.

No overall age effect was observed. Females in their seventh and eighth decades had significantly higher serum cholesterols than males, but sex differences were less pronounced in the oldest group (80–93 years). The data suggest that females reach a peak value in their sixties followed by a gradual decline, while males above 60 undergo little change with time. A sex by race interaction was also apparent, with the Negro males having significantly higher levels than the white males; the difference between white and Negro female groups was minimal. A comparison of subjects with and without clinical evidence of cardiovascular disease revealed no differences, which suggests that cholesterol level may play a less significant role in the development of pathological processes in senescence than in middle age.

References

Adlersberg, D. Hormonal influence on the serum lipids. *American Journal of Medicine*, 23:769–789, 1957.

Adlersberg, D., Schaefer, L. E., Steinberg, A. G., and Wang, C. I. Age, sex, serum lipids and coronary artherosclerosis. *Journal of the American Medical Association*, 162:619–622, 1956.

Barker, N. W. Plasma lipoids in arteriosclerosis obliterans. *Annals of Internal Medicine*, 13:685–692, 1939.

Bloor, W. R., Pelkan, K. F., and Allen, D. M. Determination of fatty acids (and cholesterol) in small amounts of blood plasma. *Journal of Biological Chemistry*, 52:191–205, 1922.

Dovenmuehle, R. H., Busse, E. W., and Newman, E. G. Physical problems of older people. *Journal of the American Geriatric Society*, 9:208–217, 1961.

Friedman, M., Roseman, R. H., and Byers, S. O. Deranged cholesterol metabolism and its possible relationship to human atherosclerosis: A review. *Journal of Gerontology*, 10:60–85, 1955.

Heyman, D. K., and Jeffers, F. C. Study of relative influences of race and socio-economic status upon the activities and attitudes of a southern aged population. *Journal of Gerontology*, 19:225–229, 1964.

Kannel, W. B., Dawber, T. R., Kagan, A., Revotskie, and Stokes, J. Factors of risk in the development of coronary heart disease: Six-year follow-up experience. *Annals of Internal Medicine*, 55:33–50, 1961.

Keys, A. The age trend of serum concentrations of cholesterol and of $S_f$ 10–20 ("G") substances in adults. *Journal of Gerontology*, 7:201–206, 1952.

Keys, A. Relationship of blood lipids to age and the diet (abstract). *Sixth International Congress of Gerontology*. International Congress Series No. 57. Amsterdam: Excerpta Medica Foundation, 1963, p. 113.

Keys, A., Mickelsen, O., Miller, E. v. O., Hayes, E. R., and Todd, R. L. The concentration of cholesterol in the blood serum of normal man and its relation to age. *Journal of Clinical Investigation*, 29:1347–1353, 1950.

Kornerup, V. Concentrations of cholesterol, total fat and phospholipid in serum of normal man. *Archive of Internal Medicine*, 85:398–415, 1950.

Kountz, W. B., Sonnenberg, A., Hofstatter, and Wolff, G. Blood cholesterol levels in elderly patients: I. Relationship of age, sex, basal metabolic rate, cardiac decompensation and coronary and peripheral sclerosis to blood cholesterol levels in the aged. *Biology Symposia*, 11:79–86, 1945.

Lindquist, E. F. *Design and analysis of experiments in psychology and education.* Boston: Houghton Mifflin, 1953.

McMahon, A., Allen, H. N., Weber, C. J., and Missey, W. C., Jr. Hypercholesterolemia. *Southern Medical Journal* (Birmingham), 44:993–1002, 1951.

Schilling, F. J., Christakis, G. J., Bennett, N. J., and Coyle, J. F. Studies of serum cholesterol in 4,244 men and women: An epidemiological and pathogenic interpretation. *American Journal of Public Health*, 54:461–476, 1964.

Sperry, W. M., and Webb, M. The effect of increasing age on serum cholesterol concentration. *Journal of Biological Chemistry*, 187:107–110, 1950.

Swanson, P., Leverton, R., Gram, M. R., Roberts, H., and Pesek, I. Blood values of women: Cholesterol. *Journal of Gerontology*, 10:41–47, 1955.

Walker, A. R. P., and Arvidsson, U. B. Fat intake, serum cholesterol concentration in the South African Bantu: I. Low fat intake and the age trend of serum cholesterol concentration in the South African Bantu. *Journal of Clinical Investigation*, 33:1358–1365, 1954.

# Chapter 3. Mental Illness

While mental illness is not "normal" in the sense of "healthy," some degree of mental or emotional difficulty is fairly common among the aged. Both hospitalization rates and community surveys usually show that the older age groups have substantially more mental illness than younger groups. These higher rates among the aged, coupled with the fact that more than half of the hospital beds in the United States are psychiatric beds, underline the seriousness of this problem for the aged. Again, the reports are concerned with better understanding of the nature and causes of these mental problems as well as what could be done to prevent or eliminate them.

The first two reports discuss the incidence, characteristics, and treatment of psychoneurotic reactions of the aged. The next two articles focus specifically on depression among the aged, and the last deals primarily with brain syndromes.

Perhaps it should be pointed out, lest it be overlooked in this emphasis on mental illness, that 40 percent of the panel were free of psychologic problems and that another 54 percent were functioning well enough to be classified as nonpsychotic even though they had various psychoneurotic symptoms. One implication of these reports is that improved treatment and prevention measures could substantially reduce the prevalence of mental illness among the aged.

## Psychoneurotic Reactions of the Aged*  *Ewald W. Busse, Robert H. Dovenmuehle, and Robert G. Brown*

The large and apparently increasing number of elderly patients being admitted to mental institutions is a justifiable concern and has received some attention from the medical profession. However, the elderly person who remains in the community and maintains an acceptable level of adjustment to his family and to society has been given little attention.

* Reprinted by permission from *Geriatrics*, 15:97–105, 1960. The authors wish to acknowledge the contributions of their colleagues to this interdisciplinary research effort, particularly Dr. Claude Nichols, Dr. Walter Obrist, Dr. Carl Eisdorfer, and Miss Frances Jeffers.

Psychoneurotic reactions do occur in such elderly people and do interfere with their health and happiness. If the medical profession is to develop preventive and therapeutic measures for the emotional reactions which are present in the declining years, a better understanding of such disorders is necessary.

To study the frequency and the types of mental reactions is a complicated and difficult research effort. To classify reactions properly requires a specific definition based upon the characteristic signs and symptoms. Normal defense mechanisms must be differentiated from pathologic manifestations, and this requires a rating scale which will permit quantification of symptoms and psychic processes. The usual clinical definition of psychoneurosis is far from satisfactory for investigation and study. A review of the literature has failed to provide a definition of psychoneurosis which is sufficiently concise and precise to fit our needs and our investigational approach. The *Diagnostic and Statistical Manual of Mental Disorders* (1954) of the American Psychiatric Association is probably the most widely accepted diagnostic standard utilized by clinical psychiatrists. This manual indicates that the chief characteristic of a psychoneurotic disorder is anxiety, which is either directly felt or expressed or may be unconsciously or automatically controlled by defense mechanisms but without the serious distortion or falsification of external reality which is seen in patients with psychosis. In addition, the psychoneurotic person does not represent a gross distortion of personality. Such generalization, although useful for clinical purposes, are unsatisfactory from a research viewpoint, because they permit such variation in independent judgments that uniform classification by independent observers is practically impossible.

The second problem—to distinguish on a quantitative basis when a psychic process or defense mechanism can be accepted as within normal limits—is complicated by the recognition that certain psychic processes which are clearly detrimental to a younger adult are necessary to maintain a satisfactory adjustment in the aged. For instance, denial is used by elderly persons who are maintaining a successful social adjustment to control the anxiety resulting from realistic threats. A younger person using denial in a similar manner would be considered by most psychiatrists to be poorly adjusted.

Method

. . . The data which we will present in this paper are primarily taken from a study of 222 volunteers who are maintaining a satisfactory social adjustment in the city of Durham and in the surrounding area. Utilizing the psychiatric evaluations, the subjects were divided into nine categories. Signs and symptoms have been selected which are believed to be characteristic of each category or are most likely to appear in such a category. Probably, in most instances, the reason for the assignment to a category is self-evident and consistent with clinical experience. Unfortunately, to explain fully how this differentiation was decided upon would require a thorough familiarization with our entire research effort, including the serious problems of quantification and consistency of recording data. The system we employed, as well as the cutoff levels which separate normal from disturbed functioning, is shown in the accompanying list.

A. Neurotic, nonorganic signs:
1. Mood
 calm
 _____

 depressed
 anxious
 confused
 **perplexed**
 scared
2. Affect
 normally composed
 _____

 wildly elated
 euphoric
 moderately depressed
 deeply depressed
3. Anxiety
 slight situational anxiety
 no apparent anxiety
 _____

 panic
 acutely anxious
 chronically anxious
 apathetic
4. Obsessions
 none
 mild
 _____

 moderate
 severe
5. Compulsions
 none
 **mild**
 _____

 moderate
 severe
6. Hypochondriasis
 none
 mild
 _____

moderate
severe
7. Self-condemnatory trends
 absent
 _____

 present
8. Expansive trends
 absent
 _____

 present

B. Functional psychotic signs:
1. Delusions
 none
 _____

 grandiose beliefs
 nihilistic ideas
 political delusions
 religious delusions
 other
2. Persecutory trends
 none
 mild
 _____

 actively discriminated against
 severe persecutory feelings, unspe-
 cific
 severe, circumscribed
 severe, generalized
 severe, systematized
3. Somatic delusions
 absent
 _____

 present

C. Organic psychotic signs:
1. Illusions
 none
 _____

shadows
voices
noises
movements
odors
other

2. Perception
hyperalert
alert
_____

mildly confused
grossly confused
illusions
grossly variable

3. Intellectual function
very superior
superior
normal
borderline
_____

mildly defective, spotty
mildly defective, generalized
grossly defective
completely incapacitated

4. Form of talk
_____

neologisms
confabulations
echolalia

D. Mixed functional and organic signs:

Combines groups B and C above.

E. Probable organic, nonpsychotic
signs:

1. Motor activity
normal
_____

hyperactive
retarded

2. Form of talk
_____

scattered
circumstantial
repetition

3. speed of reaction
normal
_____

increased
decreased

4. Appropriate to ideas
yes
_____

no

5. Insight into defects: (a) physical;
(b) mental
both physical and mental, yes
yes mental, physical not applicable
yes physical, mental not applicable
_____

both physical and mental, no
no mental, physical not applicable
no physical, mental not applicable
physical, no mental
mental, no physical

6. Judgment concerning: (a) general
activities; (b) future plans
good on general activities, nothing
noted on future plans
good on future plans, general activities not noted
good on both future plans and
general activities
_____

poor on general activities, nothing
noted on future plans
poor on future plans, nothing
noted on general activities
good on general activities but not
on future plans
good on future plans but not on
general activities
poor on both future plans and
general activities

F. Mixed neurotic and probable organic, nonpsychotic signs:

Combine groups A and E above.

G. Normal group:

None of above signs in groups A
through F.

In order to differentiate further the neurotic group, a further subdivi-
sion was made into mild and severe neurosis. Criteria for severe neurosis
were as follows: (a) two or more of the symptoms previously required for
inclusion, or (b) one severe symptom from one of the following: (1) affect
deeply depressed, (2) severe obsessions, (3) severe compulsions, or (4)
severe hypochondriasis.

Results

This method of distinguishing various groups of mental disorders re-sulted in our finding that only 89 of the 222 could be considered normal. The group of 89 normal persons would be further reduced if we removed all those with any evidence of memory impairment. A recent memory defect appeared to be part of the aging process and could not be considered a discriminating variable which would separate normal elderly persons from the emotionally disturbed. In the normal group, 17 persons had recent memory loss, and 3 had some evidence of remote memory loss. When both recent and remote losses were present, the subjects were classified as having organic mental signs. They were not necessarily consid-ered psychotic, but recent and remote memory defects were present in all subjects who were thought to have an organic psychosis.

One hundred and nineteen persons had a nonpsychotic mental disorder (Table 2–4). Fifty-six were considered neurotic. This number included 25 with severe neurotic reactions. Twenty-one had relatively minor organic changes which impaired function, and 42 subjects demonstrated evidence of both neurotic and organic pathology. Surprisingly, 14 of this community group of subjects were psychotic. Of these psychotic persons, the psychosis was considered to be predominantly functional in origin in 6, organic in 7, and a mixture of organic and functional in 1. It is probable that all persons with organic disturbances have some functional overlay or concomitants, but this system of dividing various subjects appears to point to the primary etiologic factor in the psychosis.

Although a single cause for a disease is scientifically convenient, it is evident that the cause of the majority of mental disorders cannot be attributed to a single factor. In most instances, there is a complicated interaction between physiologic functioning as influenced by genetic and environmental forces, previous learning and life experiences, and socioeco-nomic forces. Consequently, it is necessary to look for possible interrela-tionships between current and past factors and the presence or absence of psychic aberrations.

Intellectual capacity was not significantly different within the various community groups with the exception of the psychotic group. The psy-chotic group, including those with a functional disorder, contained no person with better than average intellectual function. In regard to age, a previous finding was confirmed in this study—that is, that many neurotic persons, particularly those with hypochondriac symptoms, are found in the younger subjects (Busse & Dovenmuehle, 1958). This inverse relationship between age and mental disorders suggests either a negative survival factor or the possibility that with advancing years a better adjustment is attained. The psychotic group also tended to be younger than the normal group; but, in this instance, because of the possibility of organic complications, the negative survival factor is perhaps more acceptable as an explanation.

Although psychologic projective tests have proved to be reliable measures for distinguishing certain features of our subjects, in this study, we were unable to correlate Rorschach indexes, the Fisher Maladjustment and Rigidity Scores, and the Index of Primitive Thought with psychiatric evidence of psychoneurosis (Friedman, 1956). This phase of our work will receive considerable attention, and it is possible that other methods of comparison will prove to be of value.

In order to ascertain any possible relationship between the efficiency of physical function and psychologic processes, it was necessary to devise a rating scale of the physical status. This scale is a composite of a number of other ratings. It is as follows:

1. No disease or illness
2. Diagnosis of pathology but no disability
3. Up to 20 percent disability
4. Up to 50 percent disability
5. Up to 80 percent disability
6. Up to 100 percent disability

Utilizing this scale, it was found that neurotics and "normals" are not significantly different. However, the psychotic group was much more disabled than the normal group, and the mixed or pure nonpsychotic, organic group was very much like the "normals." In a previous study, it was found that depressed subjects had significantly more physical pathology but not more current physical disability than the normals (Busse & Dovenmuehle, 1959). This suggests that the impending decline in physical function increases the likelihood of depression. The hypochondriac subjects, although free of pathology, had many more symptoms than the normal group. However, their ability to perform physically, as would be expected, was similar to that of the normal group.

To determine the correlation of psychiatric evaluations with social adjustment, a series of social adjustment scales was examined. Utilizing a master rating scale, social adjustment was found to be significantly lower in those who were severely neurotic. The mildly neurotic group, although somewhat impaired socially, was not strikingly different from the normal individuals. A social activity score derived from the overall scoring of the Chicago Activity Inventory indicated that the severely neurotic group was markedly less active in a social sense. However, when these rating scales are carefully examined, it is understandable that this correlation would be present, since the overall rating is a social diagnosis which has a number of features in common with the psychiatric evaluation. In order to reduce as far as possible this overlapping, specific ratings contributing to the master rating are given attention, which include attitudes toward health, friends, work, security, religion, and so forth.

In regard to health attitudes, the psychoneurotic group differed markedly from the normal group. This scale includes the subject's own rating of his health and his feelings about it and the number of days spent in bed in the previous year. Interestingly, those who were severely psychoneurotic were worse than the psychotic subjects who were continuing to live in the community. The better health attitude on the part of psychotic persons may be a contributing factor to their ability to remain in the community. The individuals with severe psychoneuroses showed strong differences in regard to their evaluation of their overall happiness in life and in the number of friends they have and their attitudes toward their friends. There are two major points which should be made in regard to the psychoneurotic group. One is the fact that a majority of those with severe neuroses are hypochondriacs. The other point is that they are not significantly different as far as their physical functions are concerned. For these reasons, the differences in health attitudes as seen on a social adjustment scale are the result of a neurotic overconcern with body functions. Of interest is the fact that there is no discernible difference between the neurotic and normal groups in regard to attitudes toward work. It is conceivable that this is an important finding, since a socially accepted attitude toward work may be one of the major factors in maintaining an individual in a community in spite of neurotic processes. Undoubtedly, there are other influences, some of which are culturally determined. It is our impression that in the geographic area in which we are working, tolerance of neurotic symptoms is very high, with the result that people continue to pursue many of their usual activities in spite of feelings of discomfort and anxiety.

Our research data provide several systems whereby the subjects are placed in various socioeconomic levels. In this regard, one wonders if retirement increases the psychoneurotic features. Retirement or continued employment does not distinguish the neurotic from the normal group. An index of status characteristics, a score derived from combined ratings of current or past occupations, sources of income, and areas of residence, shows no difference between the neurotic and normal groups. This is another frustrating finding, as it does not agree with some of our previous work in which we studied elderly people in another geographic area. This and many other discrepancies that we have found in studying elderly persons in widely separated and different cultural settings reenforce our belief that generalizations regarding the cause and effect of psychic disturbances must be made with considerable caution (Busse, Barnes, & Silverman, 1954; Busse et al., 1955).

No attempt was made to distinguish further psychoneurotic reactions into types, but it is evident that certain manifestations were quite prevalent. Two of these have been recognized for some time as being common to the aged person. Hypochondriasis, or intense body concern, was found in 16 of the 25 persons with severe neuroses, and depressive features were seen in 12. Thirty-three percent of all community subjects had mild to severe hypochondriasis. This condition, as usually defined by the practicing physician, does not only include excessive or unwarranted overconcern with body functions but also the pattern of prolonged and repeated medical contacts. It is the latter part of this definition which breaks down when neurotic individuals are considered, since these persons have not attempted to relate to the medical profession. Although they expressed great concern over their body functions and presented many symptoms, they did not seek medical consultation or advice. Perhaps this is because they have a limited amount of insight, since the basis of hypochondriasis appears to be quite similar to that encountered in psychiatric practice. The condition is a defense against loss of self-esteem and prestige, an excuse for failure, and a guilt-reducing masochistic phenomenon. However, hypochondriasis does not appear to be a very effective defense, because, in such subjects, depressions have a high likelihood of being present. Statistically, the interrelationship is highly significant. Hypochondriasis also relates to the presence of overt signs of fear and anxiety. Persecutory trends—expressed feelings of neglect—were not found in the chronic complainers in the community, but they were very evident in those requiring hospitalization. Here, one can speculate that this complicating symptom interferes with social adjustment, and hospitalization is apt to result.

Summary and Conclusion

The primary concern of this report is to determine the prevalence and significance of so-called psychoneurotic manifestations in a group of persons over the age of 60 who are reasonably well adjusted and living in the community. All of the subjects were volunteers, and an attempt has been made to control the selection system so that the sample is reasonably representative. In order to understand the results of this investigation, it is important to remember that this sample is quite different from a hospitalized or clinical population or from an elderly group drawn from homes for the aged.

The psychoneurotic subjects and other diagnostic groups were separated by utilizing specific signs and symptoms. Positive findings in many instances required a quantitative scale with a cutoff point differentiating "normal" from pathologic. Of a total of 222 aged people, 89 were considered normal; 56 were psychoneurotic, of whom 25 had severe neurotic reactions; 21 demonstrated relatively mild, nonpsychotic organic changes; 42 had combined nonpsychotic and neurotic symptoms; and 14 presented evidence of psychosis. The psychoneurotic subjects were compared to normal individuals in regard to a number of parameters, including physical, psychologic, and social measurements. Those who are psychoneurotic were decidedly less social than were those of the normal group, and they were very apt to be hypochondriacal and depressed. Although their attitude toward friends was distorted, their attitude toward work was not strikingly different from the normal group. This acceptable attitude toward work may be one of the determinants that prevents emotionally disturbed people from becoming patients. Subjects in the community who were extremely concerned with their health did not have feelings of neglect and persecution. This factor distinguished them from the hospitalized hypochondriac patients who felt strongly that they were being mistreated. This work presents evidence of the fact that a number of elderly people with psychoneurotic reactions of varying degrees are still able to maintain a reasonably acceptable adjustment in society. To recognize the elements which permit a person to maintain a satisfactory role in the community requires much further investigation.

## References

Busse, E. W., Barnes, R. H., and Silverman, A. J. Studies of processes of aging: VI. Factors that influence the psyche of elderly persons. *American Journal of Psychiatry,* 110:897, 1954.
Busse, E. W., Barnes, R. H., Silverman, A. J., Thaler, M., and Frost, L. L. Studies of processes of aging: X. Strengths and weaknesses of psychic functioning in the aged. *American Journal of Psychiatry,* 111:896, 1955.
Busse, E. W., and Dovenmuehle, R. H. Patterns of successful aging. Paper read at the Annual Gerontological Meeting, Philadelphia, November, 1958.
Busse, E. W., and Dovenmuehle, R. H. Neurotic symptoms and predisposition in aging people. Paper read at the annual Orthopsychiatric Meeting, San Francisco, April, 1959.
*Diagnostic and statistical manual of mental disorders.* Washington: American Psychiatric Association, 1954.
Friedman, E. L. Level of aspiration and some criteria of adjustment in an aged population. Doctoral dissertation, Duke University, 1956.

# Psychoneurotic Reactions and Defense Mechanisms in the Aged*    *Ewald W. Busse*

Psychologic defense mechanisms are the habitual modes or patterns of thinking and behavior that an individual utilizes as means of meeting his needs and satisfying his drives in a manner acceptable to himself.

Physiologic drives clearly alter throughout the life span, as do the ways which are open to individuals for expressing feelings, reducing drives, and maintaining self-esteem. Social environmental forces, past experiences, and efficiency of physical functioning all interact to alter mental processes and behavior. . . .

### "Isolation" as a Factor in Adjustment

Almost everyone who is interested in the problems of our aged population—particularly episodes of depression, feelings of neglect, hypochondriasis, and so forth—has expressed the opinion that many such problems can be attributed to "isolation." Although speakers on the subject are rarely specific about the type of isolation, they usually imply separation from children and other members of the family. Certainly the person who no longer has an opportunity to interact with those whom he loves and with whom he feels secure suffers some degree of isolation. On a much broader basis, however, isolation could be interpreted as separation from an opportunity to work productively and to be associated with large groups of people. Another type of isolation results from a reduction in perceptual stimuli as a result of decreases in visual and auditory acuity. These and many other forms of isolation, occurring alone or in combination, can produce considerable emotional stress.

Robert Brown, a medical sociologist at Duke University, has explored the relationship between the changing family organization and so-called social isolation (Brown, 1960). In recent years the American family has become increasingly mobile, and families are often separated when the growing children depart for distant places. The interdependency of parent and child has been reduced, and there is some degree of cultural difference between successive generations. Brown's studies, however, suggest that the degree of social isolation resulting from disintegration of the family struc-

* Reprinted by permission of Grune and Stratton, from *Psychopathology of Aging*, ed. Hoch, P. H., and Zubin, Joseph, 1961.

ture—that is, diminished contact with children and other members of the family—cannot be a fixed measure, but is related to the expectations of the elderly person. He found that feelings of isolation and neglect were expressed only by elderly persons belonging to the upper classes. Apparently, older people at this social level have high expectations which are not met by their children. I cannot help but speculate that speakers who emphasize the role of social isolation in the problems of the aged may be influenced by the attitude of their social class, and that this factor may not be of great importance to the majority of elderly people.

Hypochondriasis

Since hypochondriasis or depression was a major factor in all of the severe psychoneuroses, these two problems warrant more attention. It is generally accepted that hypochondriasis is not a disease entity but is a syndrome consisting of an anxious preoccupation with the body or a portion of the body which the patient believes is either diseased or not functioning properly. Hypochondriasis may be part of the symptom pattern in a neurosis, a psychosis, a psychophysiologic reaction, or a personality disturbance. In our group of elderly subjects in the community, 33 percent were found to have hypochondriacal tendencies. A much greater number showed what we call "high bodily concern," although in many of these cases the degree of concern was probably reality-determined—that is, consistent with the amount of organic disease—rather than neurotic in origin.

Three major components are recognized in the psychodynamics of hypochondriasis: (*a*) The patient's interests may be withdrawn from other persons or objects around him and centered upon himself, his body, and its functioning. (*b*) The restrictions and discomforts produced by this psychic illness may be utilized by the patient as punishment and partial atonement for guilt resulting from feelings of hostility and a desire for revenge. (*c*) The syndrome can be caused by a shift of anxiety from some specific area of psychic conflict to a less threatening concern with bodily functioning. Although the guilt mechanism is found in young hypochondriacs, it is rarely encountered in older patients. The older person's high bodily concern is more likely to result from a withdrawal of his interests in other persons or objects, or to develop as a displacement of his anxiety.

In a separate study of elderly hypochondriacs, we found that 74 percent had a wide variety of other neurotic manifestations (Busse, Barnes, & Dovenmuehle, 1956). Information obtained from the medical histories showed that 53 percent of the hypochondriacal persons had had neurotic symptoms for many years, while only 4 percent of the control group were clearly neurotic in their younger years. Although more than half of the hypochondriacs had had previous neurotic tendencies, the symptoms had altered considerably with the passing years. It is my belief that many individuals have a persistent core conflict of a neurotic nature, but that the manifestations of this conflict alter with the socioeconomic situation and with the passage of time. Consequently, several types of psychoneuroses may have been recognized in such individuals at different periods during their lives when they came to the attention of a clinician.

My colleagues and I have invested considerable time and effort in developing principles of psychiatric treatment specifically designed to deal with the peculiarities of the chronic complainer. I do not feel that I should review them again at this time, however, as they have been presented at a number of meetings and are available in the medical literature (Busse, 1959, 1960).

## Depression

I have elected to focus upon the problem of depression, a psychiatric disorder which is poorly understood. The complexity of the depressive states was skillfully reviewed by H. E. Lehmann in an article published in 1959 (Lehmann, 1959).

Depression, according to a definition accepted by the American Psychiatric Association, is "a morbid sadness, dejection, or melancholy; to be differentiated from grief which is realistic and proportionate to what has been lost. A depression may vary in depth from a neurosis to a psychosis." This definition correctly indicates that normal individuals experience grief. A normal person knows why he is sad, and can identify what he has lost. He does not permit the loss to overwhelm him because he deals with each specific memory or reminder of the loss as it occurs; and his self-esteem is such that he knows he can eventually make up for the loss, at least in part.

To put it in other terms a normal person experiences grief when he loses someone he loves and in effect says to himself: "I have lost something very important. Now I have very little, but I will make up for it." The morbidly depressed person reacts somewhat differently after a loss. He experiences a loss of narcissistic gratifications without restorative measures, and he says: "I have lost everything. Now I have nothing." This mechanism is referred to as depression from loss of narcissistic supplies.

Depression may also result from another mental mechanism—introjection. This term means that the patient turns against himself the hostile impulses which are a part of his feelings toward someone else—usually a person whom he both needs and hates. In effect, the patient is saying: "I do not hate him; I hate myself. I am a terrible person. I am not liked, and I do not deserve attention or affection."

These two pathologic mechanisms are the basic processes encountered in depressions, although it is obvious that modifications and mixtures of these two mechanisms can and do occur. For instance, a patient may react as if he is saying: "I have lost everything. I do not deserve more, because I have not tried hard enough." The extent to which one mechanism or the other predominates in producing the depression determines the therapeutic techniques which are most likely to succeed.

Our research has led us to the conclusion that introjection, or the turning inward of unconscious hostile impulses which are unacceptable to the superego, is the common mechanism in the depression of younger adults, but is seldom present to the same degree in elderly people (Busse et al., 1954). Instead, the depressions of old age are primarily related to the loss of self-esteem which results from the aged individual's inability to supply his needs or drives (loss of narcissistic supplies) or to defend himself against threats to his security. This inability may be caused by decreased efficiency of the bodily functions, loss of an adequate social role, financial insecurity, or a combination of several of these factors.

Evidence indicates that depressive episodes increase in frequency and depth in the advanced years of life. In one of our early investigations of "normal" community volunteers over the age of 60 years (Busse et al., 1955), my colleagues and I found that elderly subjects were aware of more frequent and more annoying depressive periods than they had experienced earlier in life. The subjects reported that during such episodes they felt so discouraged, worried, and troubled that they often saw no reason to continue their existence. Only a small number admitted entertaining suicidal ideas, but a larger percentage stated that during such depressive periods they would welcome a painless death.

Approximately 85 percent of the subjects were able to trace the onset of most of these depressive episodes to specific stimuli. Such "reactive" depressions resemble the grief reactions of younger people in that the loss can be identified. The fundamental difference lies in the increased frequency of these episodes and in the fact that the normal grief reaction gradually assumes a neurotic pattern. It is not easy to trace the development of this pattern, but it is clear that there are two important pathways that could be followed: (*a*) The elderly person who tends to blame himself for his failures may lose more and more of his self-esteem as these depressive episodes recur repeatedly. (*b*) The person who tends to blame others for his failures will overemphasize the features of neglect and rejection by those around him.

We found that the number of depressive episodes in elderly subjects bears some relation to the individual's socioeconomic level and continuing employment. Depressive episodes were experienced by about 45 percent of the unemployed or retired group, as compared with 25 percent of elderly subjects who continued to work. One should be cautious, however, in concluding that work alone plays some vital role in preventing or decreasing the number of depressive episodes. It is possible that the same personality factor which permits some persons to remain at work past the usual retirement age also makes them relatively immune to depressive episodes.

Almost as effective as continued employment in maintaining emotional stability is planned creative and recreational activity. Experience has shown, however, that so-called hobbies are of little value to elderly people unless they result in something which is appreciated by others. A hobby which contributes nothing to others but merely occupies the time of an elderly person is an unsatisfactory defense against depressive episodes. The life histories of those subjects who were engaged in adequately planned creative activity revealed that this was not a newly developed pattern but one that had existed for many years. Although it is possible that elderly patients can develop a new interest in planning some worthwhile activity for themselves, they are not likely to do so without the help of persons in their environment.

## Treatment

Treatment of the elderly person who is depressed is a real challenge to the true physician. As I have already indicated, the onset of many of these depressive episodes is based on reality. The elderly person does actually lose a great deal of the attention he has been accustomed to receive from others. Often he has few activities which make him feel useful, and the possibility of rewards for accomplishment is minimal. A physician can, with some justification, take the stand that since society is primarily responsible for the elderly patient's problem, society should take the lead in relieving his unhappiness. Fortunately, society has recognized this responsibility, and many attempts are being made to provide adequate substitutes for the work and personal relationships that many elderly people have lost. Many of these old people, however, do not take advantage of the opportunities which are provided for them; and as their depression increases and symptoms of insomnia, irritability, crying spells, and constipation develop, they are apt to come to a physician for help. The primary goal of the physician at this point is to restore the patient to a level of functioning where he can take advantage of the substitute sources of gratification that are available to him.

The treatment program which I will describe is based upon some of our research findings and is primarily applicable to the elderly person who is living in the community, who is not financially destitute, and whose depression is not severe enough to require hospitalization. The first step in the therapeutic process is to restore the "appreciation of self." If the physician listens attentively to the patient's complaints, he will feel that someone "does appreciate my difficulties and wants to help me; so I must be worthwhile." The second step is to encourage the patient to develop interests outside himself—to maintain or develop work or activity which maintains his self-esteem and as much independence as possible. A third step is the restoration of rewards for accomplishments. The physician should take every opportunity to recognize the patient's willingness to try —for example, his efforts to follow a treatment regimen—or on any display of interest in others. For instance, the physician may say, "I am very glad to hear that you are walking for at least two hours every afternoon." At a later time, the patient may report that another older person has joined him in his afternoon walks, but may complain that the other person talks about himself too much. To this the physician can reply, "I am sure that is true; but if Mr. X likes you enough to tell you all these things, he certainly needs you."

During the initial phase of treatment, many depressed elderly people do not react well to other old folks who may be waiting to see the physician. They may discourage one another, and tend to compete for the attention of the physician and his assistants. If the physician succeeds in turning his patients' interests outward, the problem will soon solve itself.

If the physician does not encourage the patient to seek sources of gratification outside the doctor-patient relationship, the patient will become extremely dependent upon him and eventually will demand much more time than he is able to give. In such cases, the physician can encourage his office personnel to give the elderly patient the attention he needs. An office secretary or nurse who knows how to deal with older patients can often relieve the doctor of much of the burden of their treatment.

## References

Brown, R. G. Family structure and social isolation of older persons. *Journal of Gerontology*, 15:170–174, 1960.

Busse, E. W., Barnes, R. H., and Dovenmuehle, R. H. Incidence and origins of hypochondriacal patterns and psychophysiological reactions in elderly persons.

Paper read at the First Pan American Congress on Gerontology, Mexico City, September, 1956.

Busse, E. W. On or off your rocker. *Southern Medical Journal*, 52:1575–1582, 1959.

Busse, E. W. Mental disorders of the aging. In Johnson, W. (Ed.), *The older patient.* New York: Paul B. Hoeber, 1960.

Busse, E. W., Barnes, R. H., and Silverman, A. J. Studies of the processes of aging: Factors that influence the psyche of elderly persons. *American Journal of Psychiatry*, 110:897–903, 1954.

Busse, E. W., Barnes, R. H., Silverman, A. J., Thaler, M., and Frost, L. L. Studies of the processes of aging: X. The strengths and weaknesses of psychic functioning in the aged. *American Journal of Psychiatry*, 111:896–901, 1955.

Lehmann, H. E. Psychiatric concepts of depression, nomenclature and classification. *Canadian Psychiatric Association Journal*, 4, special supplement: 1–10, March, 1959.

# Depressive Reactions in the Elderly   Robert H. Dovenmuehle, John B. Reckless, and Gustave Newman

Previous studies of large groups of both hospitalized and normally functioning elderly citizens in two widely separated geographical areas of the United States have indicated a high incidence of depressive symptoms.

In the first study depressive feelings occurring as often as once a month were noted in 48 and 44 percent of two retired community groups over the age of 60, and 25 percent of a similar group continuing to work. Most of these depressive episodes were in the nature of "reactive" depression since the subjects were aware of specific preceding events (Dovenmuehle & Busse, 1956).

In a group of 256 volunteers from the community of Durham, North Carolina, all over the age of 60, 54 percent experienced similar depressive feelings (Busse & Dovenmuehle, 1958). Depressive reactions were also responsible for the majority of subjects in the neurotic sumptoms category in this same population (Busse, Dovenmuehle, & Brown, 1960; Busse & Dovenmuehle, 1960). During the collection of interview data from subjects, it has been noted that these reactions are not typical of the usual depressive picture in younger individuals. The subjects themselves often state that these symptoms are not like any they had experienced in years past. In the second place, there seems to be a marked absence of guilt feelings, self-condemnation, and other evidence of inwardly turned hostility.

The present study is based on data specifically designed to clarify further the nature of these depressive states.

Subjects

Following collection of the initial data on community subjects, a program of longitudinal study was developed. Included was a more detailed examination of the nature of symptomatology, associated symptoms, etc., of depression and obtained from all of the 89 subjects seen during the course of the first-year follow-up study. These subjects were all over the age of 60 when initially seen for research examination. All were "normally functioning" community citizens and had volunteered for the two-and-one-half-day program.

In addition to these subjects, all persons over the age of 60 admitted to the John Umstead State Hospital with a staff diagnosis of depressive reaction were examined beginning in March, 1960. Because of the low admission rate of this age group and the small percentage (25 percent) of "functional" diagnoses only 14 subjects have been examined to date. None of these subjects had accompanying organic syndromes as severe as some of the depressed patients admitted did.

Of the community subjects, 27 (31 percent) were found to be suffering some degree of depression at the time of examination. When subjects with depression in the recent past were included, a total of 34 subjects was involved (38 percent).

Results

A preliminary examination of the two groups in regard to primary symptoms, associated symptoms, and physiological concomitants of depression was made. It can be seen from Table 3–1 that with one exception the subjects in the community group had depressions rated by the examiner as very mild or mild in nature. Without exception the hospital group had either moderate or severe depression, with the majority of them being rated as severe ($p < .001$). (chi-square analysis of all data was used throughout.)

Although the examiner was not limited to these factors in judging the severity of the depression, the following were some of the guidelines imposed by defining hypothetical "typical" cases. The very mild depressive episodes occurred less than once a month and were brief, nondisabling, and the subject was easily distractible from the unpleasant state. Mild depression may occur as often as once every two weeks but should last only a few hours to a day; the discomfort should not be accompanied by wishes for death or by physiological concomitants; there should also be no more than 20 percent disablement for life activities caused by the depression, and the

Table 3–1. *Primary symptoms of the community group and the hospital group with depressive reactions.*

|  | Community group (N = 27) | Hospital group (N = 14) |
|---|---|---|
| Severity of depression | | |
| Very mild | 12 | 0 |
| Mild | 14 | 0 |
| Moderate | 1 | 4 |
| Severe | 0 | 10 |
| Guilt | | |
| None | 19 | 2 |
| Mild | 7 | 5 |
| Moderate | 1 | 5 |
| Severe | 0 | 1 |
| Tenacity self-determined | | |
| Fairly distracted | 22 | 0 |
| Distracted with difficulty | 5 | 10 |
| Undistractible | 0 | 4 |
| Tenacity other determined | | |
| Easily distracted | 19 | 0 |
| Distracted with difficulty | 5 | 9 |
| Undistractible | 0 | 5 |
| Death wishes | | |
| None | 21 | 3 |
| Death wishes | 6 | 6 |
| Suicide thoughts | 0 | 4 |
| Suicide attempts | 0 | 1 |
| Sleep | | |
| No change | 16 | 0 |
| Mild decrease | 7 | 8 |
| Moderate to severe decrease | 4 | 6 |
| Appetite and weight change | | |
| No change | 25 | 3 |
| Increase | 2 | 1 |
| Moderate decrease | 0 | 5 |
| Severe decrease | 0 | 5 |
| Variation during day | | |
| None | 19 | 4 |
| Morning depression | 6 | 6 |
| Evening depression | 2 | 4 |
| Sex drive | | |
| No change | 27 | 9 |
| Decrease | 0 | 5 |
| Irritability | | |
| None | 15 | 3 |
| Mild | 11 | 8 |
| Moderate to severe | 1 | 3 |
| Anxiety | | |
| None | 6 | 0 |
| Mild | 13 | 3 |
| Moderate | 7 | 9 |
| Severe | 1 | 2 |

subject should be easily distracted from the state. Moderate depressions may occur more often than every two weeks and last more than one day; there may be wishes for death and minimal physiological concomitants; disability may be as much as 50 percent; the subjects may be distracted only with effort from the painful state. Severe depressions are those in which the suffering is intense, may be almost constant, and the feeling state is a nondistractable one; there may be active suicidal ruminations and prominent physiological concomitants; there may also be greater than 50 percent disablement for life activities.

The table also indicates the presence and degree of guilt. Again it will be noted that few of the community group had moderate or severe evidence of guilt feelings and that the majority had none ($p < .001$).

Guilt feelings were generally defined as self-condemnation. This includes generalized feelings of lack of worth or a consciously experienced responsibility for failure in direct relation to what is felt as a precipitated loss where love objects are involved. When the feelings are mild in degree, the individual considers himself still worthwhile in the general sense but grieves over his failure, especially during periods of depression. In moderate guilt, self-accusation is more painful, more constant, and more likely to interfere or alter present life activity in human relationships. Severe guilt feelings involve an almost total condemnation of self which interferes deeply with usual activities and relationships. Although it was anticipated that some cases may exhibit behavior indicative of guilty feelings and defensive handling of them, though without conscious recognition, none were found.

Another characteristic aspect of depressive affect is the tenacity of the unpleasant feeling. Most of the community subjects were easily distractible from the unpleasant affect. Tenacity of affect can be measured only by the degree to which a person can be distracted from it. It was felt that it would be hypothetically possible for some individuals to distract themselves more easily by willful action and for others to find it easier to distract themselves by willful shift of thought. A third possibility considered was that some subjects might be easily distracted by either method ($p < .001$).

A similar pattern in the distractibility by others can be seen. Again the community subjects were easily distracted by other people's suggestions, and the hospital subjects were distractible either with difficulty or not at all ($p < .001$).

Under death wishes were considered those wishes for painless death that occur in subjects who think only of the cessation of life and cannot tolerate the thought of the process of dying, which is usually physically or mentally painful. Some subjects, on the other hand, experience wishes for death by a specific illness, often associated with a particular illness that the subject suffers from, or perhaps indicating a hostile identification with someone with whom the subject is or has been closely associated, for example, "I wish I could get a stroke and die like mother did."

Suicidal thinking can be isolated or ruminative in nature, and it can be either generalized or quite specific as to method. Suicidal attempts are usually preceded by a period of suicidal thinking. Table 3–1 shows that community subjects suffer very infrequently from these phenomena and never suffer from active suicidal thinking. In the hospitalized subjects, however, one finds very few who have not had some form of death wish.

Physiological concomitants frequently characterize depressions of younger people. Among these are disturbances in sleep. Of community subjects who experience change in sleep patterns with depressive episodes, many of them show an increase, usually lengthened night sleep, not associated with daytime sleeping. All of the hospitalized subjects show a decrease in normal sleep. Included were restlessness, dreaming, and shortened night sleep in the mild cases, with restlessness and early morning waking in various degrees in the moderate to severe cases ($p < .01$).

Appetite and weight change also characterize depressions. Here it will be noted that the majority of community subjects had no change, whereas the majority of hospital subjects had moderate to severe decrease. Considered as increases in appetite were only those cases indicating definite evidence of eating to satisfy emotional need for feeling of security, love, and comfort during a depressive episode. If the subjects experienced a gain of five to ten pounds, this was rated as a moderate increase; if they gained more than ten pounds, it was rated as a marked increase. A similar scale was used for decrease ($p < .001$).

Diurnal variation has also been noted as being characteristically associated with depression, and it was found that the majority of community subjects did not experience either morning or evening variation ($p < .05$).

Changes in sexual drive were rated only when they occurred in definite association with depressive episodes. Community subjects noted no such changes and only a small number of the hospitalized subjects noted such ($p < .01$).

Because of the frequency of changes in bowel habits with age, none of the subjects was able specifically to associate change in bowel habits with the occurrence of depression, although many suffered from constipation.

Symptoms often associated with depression are anxiety and irritability. Irritability was considered to be an irrational, angry intolerance for activity on the part of others, especially when frustration is involved for the individual. This was not rated if it occurred as a character trait. Irritability in association with depression was found to occur quite commonly in both community and hospitalized subjects. This was rated as mild when outbursts occurred only occasionally, were short-lived and easily controlled regardless of how much inward resentment the subject might feel. A moderate degree consists of severe outbursts or constant grumbling sufficient to give rise to many unpleasant interpersonal encounters during the depressive episode. Severe irritability consisted of grumblings and outbursts of serious nature throughout the period of depression sufficient to interfere with more than half of the subject's interpersonal relationships during the particular episode.

Anxiety associated with depression usually takes the form of a morbid fearfulness of further loss and leads to indecisiveness and ineffectiveness of action for fear that such will come about. Occasionally it has the nameless quality of a more free floating kind of anxiety. Sometimes anxiety is not felt as such but expressed in terms of physiological components of it, such as tachycardia or "butterflies in the stomach" ($p < .01$).

Associated symptoms occurred frequently in both groups of subjects. Mild degrees of anxiety were considered those relatively predisabling episodes of restlessness and fearfulness, with mild psychophysiological components, if at all present. Severe anxiety consisted of constant agitation and restlessness, which might be more marked at night, with strong psychophysiological components.

## Discussion

Noyes and Kolb (1958), in discussing involutional depressive reactions, highlight the symptoms of irritability, peevishness, pessimism, insomnia, retardation, and easy weeping as prominent aspects of the prepsychotic syndrome. In the development of more or less typical cases they emphasize the conspicuousness of profound depression, anxiety, agitation, hypochondriasis, delusions of sin, unworthiness, disease, and impending death.

The same authors, in discussing the depressive phase of manic depressive psychoses, emphasize difficulties in detecting mild depression because of the absence of striking disturbances. Periods of fatigue, staleness, and inertia, or physical complaints without organic basis along with mild downheartedness, often represent the total range of symptoms. Severe depressions, the authors state, pass into profound affective distress with posture, muscle tensions, and various physical signs and symptoms presenting a composite picture of depression. Loss of weight, decrease in muscle tone, constipation, decrease in sexual desire, and poor sleep with early waking are common. Helplessness and despondency are also emphasized. Patients occasionally make statements such as, "I have no feelings," and some manifest hostile bitterness. Efforts at reassurance make no impression.

Noyes and Kolb emphasize the reactive nature of psychotic depressive reaction and indicate that the reaction is one of a definitely pathological depression associated with gross misinterpretation of reality in the form of delusions (frequently, but not always somatic), suicidal ruminations or attempts, intense feelings of guilt, and retardation of thought and of psychomotor activity.

In our groups the hospitalized cases conform much more closely to typical pictures of pathological depression than do the community subjects. It must be emphasized here that although 60 percent of our community subjects suffered some type of psychiatric symptomatology (Busse et al., 1960) none were coming to us for psychiatric help. They were also functioning as independent individuals in the community. This in itself may account for the small number of occurrences of guilt feelings, the easy distractibility, and the lack of occurrence of suicidal thoughts, since such symptoms are those most apt to precipitate hospitalization. It is apparent, however, that sleep disturbance occurs fairly frequently but is the only physiological concomitant of depression that does so. Associated symptoms of irritability and anxiety also occur relatively more frequently than other symptoms.

It may be that these mild depressive states of elderly people in the community are precursors of more typical depressive episodes which can lead to hospital admission. Our longitudinal follow-up should answer this question.

Emil Gutheil (1959) indicates that reactive depression can be physiologic or neurotic. A physiological depression is a reaction to life's acute difficulties, such as loss of a job, loss of a sex object, or the like. The dysphoria is transient and ends with a spontaneous remission without causing deep-rooted change in the patient's life adjustments. It may be that the mild depression seen in our community subjects is of this nature. In a previous study (Busse & Dovenmuehle, 1958) depressive feelings related significantly ($p < .001$) to presence of disease.

Neurotic depressive symptoms, according to Gutheil, can be (a) a pure form of neurosis, (b) a first noticeable sign of oncoming or concurrent somatic or psychic disease, or (c) hidden behind other somatic and psychic symptoms. These reactions are noted by the patient's inability to overcome them by his own efforts. Gutheil considers elderly patients to have a lowered threshold for depressive response to stress, especially in chronic form. He indicates that depressions in the elderly often have an added element of anxiety.

Gutheil also says that patients usually know they are sick and do not blame themselves for being bad, lazy, or unworthy but try to get well. He considers especially significant the absence of physiological concomitance in this type of reaction. He emphasizes also the easy response to a therapeutic approach by other people. Many of Gutheil's statements in relation to reactive depression are also clearly reflected in our community subjects. This may mean that "physiologic" depressions may become chronic neuroses in elderly subjects, and further investigation is underway to examine this possibility.

## Summary

A group of normally functioning community volunteers and a group of hospitalized subjects were considered from the standpoint of symptomatology occurring in depressive episodes. Depressions occurring in the 27 community volunteers, as opposed to the hospitalized group, were less severe, with less exhibition of guilt and with much less tenacity of unpleasant affect. Suicidal thoughts were absent. The absence of most physiological concomitants except the occasional occurrence of sleep disturbance was prominent. Anxiety and irritability as associated symptoms of depression occurred quite frequently. These may represent a "physiological" depression or a common neurosis. The hospitalized subjects, on the other hand, exhibited more severe symptomatology, likely to be associated with evidence of psychotic depressive reactions.

## References

Busse, E. W., and Dovenmuehle, R. H. Patterns of successful aging. Paper presented at the Symposium on Patterns of Successful Aging at the 1958 Annual Meeting of the Gerontological Society.

Busse, E. W., Dovenmuehle, R. H., and Brown, R. G. Psychoneurotic reactions of the aged. *Geriatrics*, 15:97–105, 1960.

Busse, E. W., and Dovenmuehle, R. H. Neurotic symptoms and predisposition in aging people. *Journal of the American Geriatrics Society*, 8:328–336, May, 1960.

Dovenmuehle, R. H., and Busse, E. W. Studies of the processes of aging: A review of a multidisciplinary approach. *British Journal of Physical Medicine*, 100–103, May, 1956.

Gutheil, E. Reactive depressions. In Arieti, S. (Ed.), *American handbook of psychiatry*. New York: Basic Books, 1959.

Noyes, A. P., and Kolb, L. C. *Modern clinical psychiatry*. Philadelphia: W. B. Saunders, 1958.

# Aging, Culture, and Affect: Predisposing Factors*
## Robert H. Dovenmuehle and W. Edward McGough

There is a recent resurgence of interest in examining the role of racial and socioeconomic factors in producing or coloring psychiatric symptoms. Studies concerned with relative incidences of schizophrenia and manic-depressive illnesses among hospitalized patient populations have been reported (Babcock, 1895; Bevis, 1921; Faris & Dunham, 1939; Green, 1917; Nolan, 1918; O'Malley, 1914; Stern, 1913; Tietze, Lemkau, & Cooper, 1941), as have studies in out-patient facilities emphasizing socioeconomic differences (Hollingshead & Redlich, 1958; Srole, Langner, Michael, Opler, & Rennie, 1962). There is a paucity of reports concerned with depressive syndromes in the Negro population (Sainsbury, 1963; Vitols, 1961).

Hypotheses obtained from the study of hospitalized and treated individuals exhibiting depressive affect were applied to a group of volunteer subjects from the Piedmont area of North Carolina. Subjects were psychiatrically examined as a part of an on-going interdisciplinary study of aged persons and rated on a scale which separates groups in an ordinal fashion as to the amount of experience with depressive affect and degree of limitation in usual activities thus produced.

It is important to emphasize at this point that the subject group was not rated according to diagnosis of depression, but only to presence and degree of depressive affect. The majority of subjects moderately or severely disabled because of this experience would probably be diagnosed as neurotic or psychotic depressives, with few, if any, in the latter category.

Based on the assumption that the conclusions drawn from statistical studies of large samples would apply to this small group, the hypotheses of the study were formulated as follows:

1. The incidence of depressive experience will be higher among whites than among Negroes (Babcock, 1895; Bevis, 1921; O'Malley, 1914; Prange & Vitols, 1962; Vitols, 1961).

2. The incidence of depressive experience will be higher in upper socioeconomic classes than in lower socioeconomic classes (Faris & Dunham, 1937; Hollingshead & Redlich, 1958; Nolan, 1918; Noyes, 1954; Stern, 1913; Tietze et al., 1941); in both Negro and white subjects the

* Reprinted by permission from the *International Journal of Social Psychiatry*, 11, 1965.

socioeconomic differences may obliterate the racial differences when proper control is exercised for these variables.

3. The incidence of depression will be higher than in studies reporting younger groups, but characteristic racial and social class differences will have freedom to exert their effects (Sainsbury, 1963; Stromgren, 1963; Srole et al., 1962).

## Method

The subject group was composed of 180 community residents being followed longitudinally for the duration of their lives: there were a total of 61 Negroes and 119 whites. Of the Negroes, 32 were male and 29 female. Of the whites, 60 were male and 59 female. Many of the subjects were currently married and living with spouse (57 percent of the Negroes and 64 percent of the whites).

### Social Class

All of the subjects were classified in terms of the principal lifetime employment of the head of the household. Married women who also worked were classified according to the occupation of the husband, to emphasize the family status and style of life which is typically established by the male. Single women were treated as head of household. The classification is as follows:

Primarily nonmanual:

1. Professionals, both free and salaried, but not technicians.
2. Managers and proprietors, with minimum income or value of business in range of $5,000 to $14,000. Some types of salesmen belong here and some types of salespeople with supervisory responsibility.
3. Farmers who qualify as proprietors or managers and own or manage a minimum of 100 acres.
4. Clerical, sales, technicians, proprietors or managers of small businesses with income or sale value below $5,000.

Primarily manual:

5. Skilled craftsmen, foremen.
6. Operatives, semiskilled workers.
7. Service workers including household workers when female is treated as head of household.
8. Unskilled.
9. Farm labor, tenant, or owner of less than 100 acres with unmechanized farming.

Nonmanual occupations are considered evidence of higher social class, and manual occupations evidence of lower social class for the purposes of this study.

3. Mental Illness   100

*Depression*

All subjects were rated with respect to current experience with depressive affect. The scale is as follows:

Not disabled:

1. No depressive experience in current daily life.
2. Regular occurrences of mild depression less than once a month and nondisabling for usual activities when it occurs.

Disabled:

3. Depressive episodes occurring as often as two weeks to one month and disabling up to half of the individual's usual daily activities when they occur.
4. Depressive reactions occurring oftener than two weeks and seriously disabling life activity when present.
5. Very frequent and depressive experience with almost total alteration of daily activity because of it.

Only the last two categories would be considered psychiatric illness. Depression of lesser significance is of common occurrence in community subjects. From previous experience with this rating, only the last three categories are used to indicate currently significant depressive feeling, i.e., disabling depression.

Results

For the purposes of clarity and brevity, all of the contingency tables necessary to the statistical work have been condensed with relationship expressed in percentages and statistical results displayed. In each case the direction and degree of association has been expressed by the Coefficient of Association (Q), which measures the degree of association and varies from minus one, when there is complete negative association, to zero, when there is no association, to plus one, when there is complete positive association. Its range of values and meaning are comparable to Pearson's $r$, the coeffi-

Table 3–2. *Distribution of ratings: predisposing factors.*

| Depression rating | Negro | White | Total |
|---|---|---|---|
| 1 | 36 | 82 | 118 |
| 2 | 6 | 18 | 24 |
| 3 | 12 | 13 | 25 |
| 4 | 7 | 6 | 13 |
| 5 | 0 | 0 | 0 |
| Total | 61 | 119 | 180 |

cient of correlation, but it is not identical with *r* nor equivalent to it
(Hagood & Price, 1957).

Table 3–2 is the distribution of ratings on the scale among Negro and
white races. A total of 62 subjects had some experience with depression at
the time of examination, comprising 34 percent of the sample. Only 38
subjects exhibited any disability from these affective symptoms, making the
incidence of disabling depression 21 percent for the entire group. The
incidence of disabling depression in Negroes is nearly twice that of whites
and results in a moderately high degree of association which is statistically
significant.

Table 3–3. *Race differences in depression in the total sample.*

| White (N = 119) | Negro (N = 61) | Q = .408 |
|---|---|---|
| 16 percent | 31 percent | $x^2 = 4.66$ ($p < .05$) |

Lower social class, expressed by manual occupational category, is
associated with almost twice the incidence of disabling depression as is
higher social class expressed by nonmanual occupational status. The degree
of association is moderate and statistically significant.

Table 3–4. *Class and race differences in disabling depression.*

|  | Lower class | | Higher class | | | | |
|---|---|---|---|---|---|---|---|
|  | Number | Percentage | Number | Percentage | Q | $x^2$ | p |
| Total subjects | 81 | 28 | 99 | 15 | −.379 | 3.93 | < .05 |
| White | 38 | 24 | 81 | 12 | −.375 | 1.65 | < .20 |
| Negro | 43 | 32 | 18 | 28 | −.113 | 0.00 | < .99 |

When the distribution of depressive incidence is considered in relation
to social class in each race separately, the large nonmanual occupational
group of white subjects, with an unusually low incidence of depression,
accounts for the major portion of the degree of association found previously. The Negro subjects show an incidence of depression in both classes
which has a low degree of association and high probability that this is

Table 3–5. *Race differences in lower social class in the total sample.*

| White (N = 110) | Negro (N = 61) | Q = .671 |
|---|---|---|
| 32 percent | 70 percent | $x^2 = 22.54$ ($p < .001$) |

chance occurrence. The entire group of Negro subjects approximates quite closely the lower-social-class white, as represented by subjects of manual occupational status.

Table 3–4 indicates the marked discrepancy in incidence of lower social class among whites and Negroes. The Negro sample has twice the proportion of lower-class subjects with a high level of association which reaches statistical significance. In the lower social class the incidence of disabling depression is very similar in Negro and white subjects. In the higher social class disabling depression appears more frequently in Negro subjects, though not statistically significant.

Table 3–6. *Age, race, and class differences in disabling depression.*

|  | Age under 73 | | Age 73+ | | $Q$ | $x^2$ | $p$ |
|---|---|---|---|---|---|---|---|
|  | Number | Percentage | Number | Percentage |  |  |  |
| Total subjects | 90 | 24 | 90 | 18 | −.198 | 0.84 | < .50 |
| White | 56 | 21 | 63 | 11 | −.371 | 1.70 | < .20 |
| Negro | 34 | 29 | 27 | 33 | .090 | 0.00 | < .98 |
| Lower class | 38 | 32 | 43 | 26 | −.146 | 0.12 | < .80 |
| Upper class | 50 | 20 | 49 | 10 | −.375 | 1.13 | < .30 |

There is a slightly higher incidence of disabling depression in the younger age group which is not significant statistically. When the incidence of depression in the two age groups is examined in the separate races it is found that the distribution is almost identical in the Negro race, with the statistical likelihood that the younger and older Negroes are identical populations with respect to depressive incidence.

In the white subjects the incidence in the young group is almost twice that of the older group, although not statistically significant. Therefore, small overall differences in incidence with age seem to be determined by the low incidence in older whites.

The older upper-class subject has the least incidence, followed by the younger upper-class, older lower-class, and younger lower-class subjects, respectively.

In summary, the findings of this study would lead to the conclusion that Negroes and lower-social-class subjects experience more disabling depression than their white and higher-social-class cohorts. These results are consistent, though not statistically significant, when the two variables are partialled. The most deviant group is the upper-class white subject, who has a lower incidence of depression than any other group. Age does not seem to significantly affect the frequency of depression in either racial group in this sample. The older white group has the smallest incidence of depression, as does the older upper-class subject.

## Discussion

### *General Cultural Differences*

The comparative rarity of depression and near absence of suicidal tendencies among the Negro insane were reported in 1895 by Babcock. In 1914, O'Malley reported from the Government Hospital for the Insane, Washington, D.C., that manic-depressive psychosis was not as prevalent among Negroes as among white patients. Also, the excited phase of psychosis was more frequently observed in Negro patients, and depressive types were not common. Further, involutional melancholia and depressions of various forms were rare among Negroes.

One differing report is that of Green (1917) at the Georgia State Sanitarium. This report indicates that manic-depressive psychosis was by no means rare in institutions with large Negro populations and formed one of the larger classifications. Bevis (1921) collected from various Southern State hospitals 2,732 admissions and concluded that the incidence of manic-depressive psychosis was higher than that given by Green (17 percent) and agreed that the manic phase is the one usually seen. He states that the Southern Negro has certain psychological traits that are reflected in his psychoses, noting that sadness and depression have little part in the Southern Negro psychological makeup. He noted that suicide was almost absent in Negro patients, the ratio being 1 to 3,000 in state hospitals at that time.

Vitols (1961) observed that only 1 percent of first admissions to the State Hospital for Negroes in North Carolina were for psychotic depressive reactions, whereas 4.3 percent of first admissions to state hospitals for white patients were diagnosed as such. Prange and Vitols (1962), in commenting on this low admission rate of severely depressed Negroes, state that although the syndrome of depression defined by criteria evoked from the white population does occur, it is rare in the state hospital studied. They state that depression appears to be much less common in Southern Negroes than in Southern whites (Vitols, 1961) and predict that the occurrence of depression will be more frequent among Southern Negroes as they come to share more fully the white man's culture. Our findings are in line with this prediction. The two samples are not directly comparable; one sample is from a hospitalized population and the other an ambulatory population of voluntary subjects without overt psychiatric illness. All that can be said is that the incidence of depressive affect is greater in this latter sample than the study of the former sample (Vitols, 1961) would lead one to expect, and that this higher incidence is in line with Prange and Vitol's (1962) prediction.

In summary, there is much evidence in the literature to support the hypothesis that incidence of disabling depressive affect is higher among whites than among Negroes. The data reported indicate that in this sample of community residents the hypothesis is not substantiated. It was the higher-social-class white subjects that had a distinctly lower incidence than the other groups in the study.

Since the subjects were volunteers for research study one can assume that the lower-class persons were motivated, at least in this respect, more in accord with upper-class values. If this assumption is extended to include a generalized high level of aspiration in this particular group, the data should indicate that they experience high rates of depression, which were found. For this reason, it is quite possible that the nature of the sample accounts for the findings.

Until a study of depression in a sample randomly drawn from the general population of Southern Negroes is undertaken, no statements about the prevalence of depression in this population can be made; however, we feel that the actual prevalence of depression has been previously underestimated from samples available in the past. A current study of Negro and white hospital admissions to recently integrated Southern State hospitals (McGough & Blackley) show little differences in incidence of depressive syndromes among first admissions.

It would seem that hypotheses about racial and cultural differences in mental illness patterns based on hospital admission rates do not hold up when applied to community populations. Although it is difficult to reconcile these disparate findings, perhaps a cultural factor, as well as a sampling factor, does account for the variance. The doctor who examines populations for psychiatric symptoms, by virtue of intensive professional training, is subject to a more rigid and explicit cultural tradition than is his patient group. Not only conceptions of health and disease are determined by this tradition, but also the avenues through which patients are received. These avenues require very specific behavior on the part of the patient, and if a doctor is approached through unfamiliar channels the symptoms may not cause the person to be recognized as a patient. Not only does the recognition of illness depend on the avenue by which the doctor is approached, but also the treatment itself. Treatment, of course, does vary according to the skill of the doctor and current medical knowledge, but the manner in which it is applied is determined by medical tradition and channels of approach. From this point of view, the findings of Hollingshead and Redlich (1958) that type of diagnosis and therapy varies with social status of patients could be interpreted as meaning that medical treatment is provided to and sought by persons of differing social status through different channels.

The evidence that there are differences in the incidence of treated depressive syndromes between different racial groups does not necessarily imply that these differences are the direct result of constitution, culture, personality, or family patterns and child rearing practices. The results indicating low incidence of depressive psychoses in hospitalized Negroes may simply reflect the fact that Negroes with depression do not present themselves at hospitals nor to their physicians in a manner which allows them to be recognized as patients.

What in effect happens is the cultural determinants of a given group of patients determine the sample in which they are found. For example, in Vitols's report the hospital sampled is a great distance from the homes of many of its patients and is traditionally dreaded and sometimes avoided by patients who might otherwise utilize it. Depressed patients can more easily avoid hospitalization than excited patients or schizophrenics. The recently integrated hospital population being studied by one of the authors (McGough & Blackley) is geographically more accessible, has a better reputation among patients, and draws a somewhat peculiar Negro population which will not reflect the incidence of illness in the general Negro population.

### Social Class Differences

Many studies indicate a higher incidence of depression in upper socioeconomic classes in both Negro and white subjects. Tietze, Lemkau, and Cooper (1941) have demonstrated that more manic-depressive psychosis is found in upper socioeconomic groups. Among the manic-depressive patients, depression was noted to be more frequent than elation in the entire sample. Stern (1913) in Germany and Nolan (1918) in America had reported essentially the same findings Lemkau reports. The incidence of manic-depressive illness placed German farmers more closely to factory workers and in New York more closely to business and professional groups. Faris and Dunham (1937) note a tendency, not clearly defined, for manic cases to come from higher cultural and economic levels in Chicago. Hollingshead and Redlich (1958) note that in New Haven neurotic depressive reactions are scattered through their five-class socioeconomic status scale and that Classes I and II, the two highest, have 50 percent more depressives than Class V, the lowest in the scale. All affective psychoses were linked directly to class position. The higher the class, the larger proportion of patients with affective psychoses.

Noyes (1954) cites Luxemberger indicating three times the frequency of manic-depressive psychoses reported in the highest social class and four times in professional classes as in the general population. He also cites the studies of manic-depressive psychoses during World War II in which officers were afflicted three times as often as enlisted men. In summary, there is much to support the hypothesis that a high incidence of depressive affective disorder is associated with high social status.

When the hypothesis is particularized to this community group the findings do not support the hypothesis, the lower class showing consistently higher incidence. The same sampling problems cited earlier could account for this. In addition, the age status of the sample introduces complications. If one assumes that suicide rates, in part, reflect prevalence of depression, Sainsbury's (1963) study is pertinent. He indicates that suicide tends to decrease after 65 in higher social classes and increase in the lower ones. His index of social class was an occupational classification very similar to the one described in this study.

Age also seems to be a factor with respect to depression. Stromgren (1963) reports increasing percentages of depressive illnesses through age 74, with a decrease thereafter in patients in Danish psychiatric hospitals. Sainsbury (1963), in reviewing worldwide suicide statistics, indicates increasing rates with increasing age, with preservation of national and socio-economic difference throughout. Srole, Langner, Michael, Opler, and Rennie (1962) document large increases in rates of hospitalization for persons above 60 and decrease in out-patient status for the same group. In the Midtown Home Survey sample, which was limited to ages 20 to 59, there is a decrease in the well group with increasing age and a corresponding increase in the psychiatrically impaired groups. It can be assumed that depressive conditions would be among the conditions noted in this significant increase with age.

In this study, the 21 percent incidence of depression in the group would certainly indicate an unusually high frequency of this finding. The incidence of disabling depression is slightly higher than this in our younger subjects and slightly lower in the older subjects.

The fact that occurrence of depression varies with age, race, and social class also raises the question how this happens. Psychodynamic theory postulates a close relationship between loss of valued relationships or personal possessions or prestige and the experience of depressive affect. The aged, the Negro, and the lower social class have been found to suffer more losses with respect to income, access to prestigeful occupation, and health than younger, white and upper-class groups. (Dovenmuehle, Busse, & Newman, 1961). In this regard age, race, and social class may influence the frequency of precipitating factors in depression, serving as active predisposing factors. The sample under study will not permit generalization, but an examination of precipitating factors is being prepared for future reports.

## Summary

Generalizations concerning the relative frequency of depression in upper-class and white groups, obtained from the literature, were applied to a group of 180 older volunteer longitudinal research subjects from Piedmont North Carolina.

Both Negroes and lower-class subjects were found to have higher incidence of disabling depression than expected. Age made no significant difference in this older group, although the incidence was higher than would be expected in younger individuals.

## References

Babcock, J. W. *Alienist and Neurologist*, 16:423, 1895.
Bevis, W. M. *American Journal of Psychiatry*, 1:69, 1921.
Dovenmuehle, R. H., Busse, E. W., and Newman, E. G. Physical problems of older people. *Journal of American Geriatrics Society*, 9:208–217, March, 1961.
Dunham, H. W. The ecology of the functional psychoses in Chicago. *American Sociological Review*, 2:467–479, 1937.
Faris, R. E. L., and Dunham, H. W. *Mental disorders in urban areas*. Chicago: University of Chicago Press, 1939.
Green, E. M. *Journal of Insanity*, 73:619, 1917.
Hagood, M. J., and Price, D. C. *Statistics for sociologists*. (Rev. ed.) New York: Holt, 1957.
Hollingshead, A. B., and Redlich, F. C. *Social class and mental illness*. New York: Wiley, 1957.
McGough, W. E., and Blackley, R. J. Personal communication.
Nolan, W. J. *State Hospital Quarterly*, 4:75, 1918.
Noyes, A. P. *Modern clinical psychiatry*. Philadelphia: W. B. Saunders, 1954.
O'Malley, M. *Journal of Insanity*, 71:309, 1914.
Prange, A. J., Jr., and Vitols, M. M. *International Journal of Psychiatry*, 8:104, 1962.
Sainsbury, P. In Williams, R. H., Tibbitts, C., and Donahue, W. (Eds.), *Processes of aging.* Vol. 2. New York: Atherton, 1963.
Srole, L., Langer, T. S., Michael, S. T., Opler, M. Dk., and Rennie, T. A. C., *Mental health in the metropolis.* New York: McGraw-Hill, 1962, chap. 9.
Stern, L. *Kulturkreis und From der Geistugen Erkandung*. Halle: Carl Marhold, 1913.
Stromgren, E. In Williams, R. H., Tibbetts, C., and Donahue, W. (Eds.), *Processes of aging.* Vol. 2. New York: Atherton, 1963.
Tietze, C., Lemkau, P., and Cooper, M. Schizophrenia, manic-depressive psychosis and social-economic status. *American Journal of Sociology*, 47:167–175, 1941.
Vitols, M. M. The significance of the higher incidence of schizophrenia in the Negro race in North Carolina. *North Carolina Medical Journal*, 22:147–158, April, 1961.

## Geriatric Psychiatry*  *Robert H. Dovenmuehle*

The mental problems specific to older individuals are defined on the basis of their frequency of occurrence in the later years of life. An arbitrary landmark for senescence in most statistical studies is the age of 65.

Mental illness generally is now the third-ranked cause of chronic illness in the country. The evidence seems conclusive that there is a genuine increase in the rate of first admissions of mental patients to hospitals (Malzberg, 1959). With specific reference to psychosis with cerebral arteriosclerosis, one of the chief illnesses of older people, there has been a rate of increase five times the amount for mental disease in general. Senile psychosis, another frequent affliction of the elderly, increased at a somewhat lesser rate.

The rates for mental illness are at a maximum in the older age groups, and it has been suggested that one explanation would be that there is currently less selection of people living to middle age and beyond (because of the lesser incidence of disease in early years) and that this allows more people to develop degenerative diseases with accompanying psychiatric disorder. Another factor in the mental illnesses of the older age group is that the organic psychoses predominate and rates of discharge are very low compared to other mental illnesses. A study by the American Psychiatric Association of patients over 65 in public hospitals would indicate that 30 percent of state hospital residents are currently over 65 and that 27 percent of all first admissions are in this age group (American Psychiatric Association, 1959). A significant proportion of the resident patients over the age of 65 were admitted, of course, for other illnesses and remain in the hospital to grow old there. There is a much higher death rate for organic psychoses relatively soon after admission to the hospital than for any other kind of condition. For this reason newly admitted patients do not tend to form the majority of residents over 65.

Since more than half of the total hospital beds in the United States are psychiatric beds, there can be no doubt about the sizable proportion of the problem presented by mental illness in this age group. Eighty-two percent of first admissions over 65 are senile arteriosclerotic brain syndromes. Other chronic and acute brain syndromes form another 6 percent of

* Reprinted by permission from *Law and Contemporary Problems*, 27:133–141, 1962.

admissions with functional psychotic disorders, and all other mental disorders constitute about 12 percent of total admissions in this age group (American Psychiatric Association, 1959). In order to clarify the nature of these serious disturbances, a discussion of brain syndrome is in order.

## Brain Syndrome

"Brain syndrome" is a name given to a group of symptoms which occur in the presence of impairment of brain tissue function. The disorders are all characterized by impairment of orientation, memory, all intellectual functions, judgment, and by liability and shallowness of affect.

Orientation is the ability to recognize one's own location in time, space, and situation. Disorientation is spoken of also as confusion. This is commonly seen in older people.

Memory impairment can affect either recent memory or remote memory. Many elderly people constantly revive memories of long ago but are unable to remember such simple things as where they put their glasses down last or where the bathroom might be. Careful study of such individuals reveals large gaps even in their remote memory, and the areas that stand out clearly in their memory are usually quite meaningful to them emotionally.

Impairment of intellectual functions reduces the person's ability to comprehend any sort of abstract situation, the ability to calculate, the ability to retain previous knowledge, and the ability to learn new things.

Largely because of failure to marshal accurate facts on which to base decisions regarding behavior, a lack of judgment is often quite apparent. Frequently such persons are easily provoked to tears or laughter, and sometimes spontaneously shift as the mood of the moment shifts. Although this may appear to be a quite lively affect, it usually has little consistent effect on their behavior. For example, one moment an elderly person with brain syndrome may be weeping about the loss of a mate, but if a joke is told the sadness immediately gives place to laughter. This is what is meant by shallowness of affect (American Psychiatric Association, 1952).

Brain syndrome disorders are classified into acute and chronic. In the acute brain disorders the disturbance is usually sudden in onset, and recovery is implied in the sense that physiological brain functioning returns relatively to normal. Nevertheless, certain specific defects may remain in the case of people with strokes. The severity of the changes in behavior with brain syndrome is thought to parallel the severity of organic impairment of brain tissue function. However, some studies have shed considerable doubt on this, especially in the more chronic syndromes.

*Acute Brain Disorders*

These are usually precipitated suddenly, and inevitably involve various degrees of impairment of the sensorium. The clinical syndrome of delirium is largely limited to these temporary disturbances of brain function. Confusion appears early. This may be periodic and occur only at night or during other periods when the patient is cut off from external sensory stimuli. There may be restlessness, rambling talk, and marked emotional changes during delirium. Fright, hallucinations and delusions, irritability, and even violence may occur.

Recent studies at the Langley Porter Clinic indicate that acute brain syndrome frequently ends in death, usually because of the underlying acute disease process. The nature of the syndrome is determined to some extent by the kind of causative agent involved.

Infections in the brain are not specific to older people but sometimes occur. Acute brain syndromes with delirium are often associated with systemic infections. In the elderly persons this is a most likely result of pneumonia.

All kinds of intoxicating agents are apt to provoke acute brain syndrome in elderly people. People with cardiorespiratory disorders who are receiving medication (and especially so if they have been confined to bed) are very susceptible. Such reactions to barbiturates and bromide drugs are very common, and alcoholic intoxication must also be considered. Trauma to the head associated with unconsciousness can precipitate delirium in older people as well as younger. Head trauma may also activate an underlying chronic brain syndrome in an elderly person.

In addition to the development of delirium with medication for cardiorespiratory disease, cardiorespiratory failure itself is a common cause of this condition. Localized disturbances in the brain due to strokes are often followed by a short period of coma followed by confusion or a delirious period, and may result in lasting irritability and personality changes with chronic brain syndrome.

It can be seen that in the acute brain syndromes medical problems of an acute nature are often present. Nevertheless, the disturbed behavior of individuals with this disturbance is sometimes a cause of legal commitment to a psychiatric hospital. This is especially the case in areas where adequate psychiatric management is not available locally and the hospital is unable to cope with both the medical illness and the acutely disturbed behavior.

Seldom, however, are such acute disturbances the cause for other types of legal action affecting elderly people.

### Chronic Brain Syndrome

With these syndromes, delirium may usher in the first appearance of symptoms, but the impairment of memory, intellectual functioning, and judgment is far more characteristic. Acute confusion may occur periodically. Personality changes are frequently seen and may become very marked. In many cases, the accompanying behavioral reaction (personality change), psychotic reaction (hallucinations, delusions, marked paranoid trends, etc.), or accompanying neurotic reactions overshadow the basic symptoms.

Circulatory diseases such as arterial hypertension, cardiorenal disease, and cardiac decompensation sometimes give rise to chronic brain syndrome, as already mentioned. Delirium with acute cardiac decompensation is common. However, even in the absence of delirium, disorders of judgment, memory, and orientation are frequently seen. Irritability, moodiness, and emotional instability are common (Noyes, 1953).

Cerebral arteriosclerosis may cause chronic brain syndrome in people as young as 45 but is more frequent after the age of 65. Symptoms are usually reported as having an abrupt onset in spite of the fact that the pathological process is clearly a slowly progressive one. Mental and physical stresses do often precipitate an apparently abrupt appearance of symptoms. Oftentimes the onset is associated with the occlusion of blood vessels cutting off blood supply in a local area and is then accompanied by localizing neurological signs. It is of course rare to find vascular change existing only in the brain, and these changes are usually widespread throughout the body (Young, Gofman, Malamund, Simon, & Waters, 1956). The initial symptom in these cases again is often a delirium followed by the chronic syndrome.

Senile brain disease is accompanied by other evidence of exaggerated aging affecting the entire body. There is wasting of muscles, shrinking of soft tissue, loss of elasticity of the skin, thinning and graying of hair, and muscular weakness. The gait is unsteady and speech disturbance is quite common. The condition is a chronic one, lasting from a year to eleven or more years. Mild cases may manifest only self-centeredness, difficulty in assimilating new experience, and mild disturbances of emotional equilibrium. Again, accompanying psychotic, neurotic, or behavioral disturbances are not unusual. Eventually severe deterioration of mental faculties occurs. The condition is more common in women by a ratio of two to one. In this condition symptoms usually do not appear until after the age of 60. Fifty percent of these cases follow a pattern of simple deterioration of mental function. Others show marked symptoms of depression, agitation, paranoia, and schizophrenic-like symptoms. In the latter types of cases, long-standing personality conflicts and difficult patterns of adjustment have often been present. Paranoid reactions are the most common, and constitute from 15 to 25 percent of the diagnostic category. In milder cases this can lead to suspicions of family, the changing of wills, and so on.

In all cases of chronic brain syndrome legal problems relative to competence of the individual can occur. The eventual decline in these conditions is such that those affected inevitably become dependent upon relatives or upon society for management of all aspects of their daily living. In obviously deteriorated cases it would not be expected that difficult legal problems would arise, but in the earlier stages, when emotional changes may be more prominent than the underlying deterioration, such problems can be quite difficult to settle.

Among the variables influencing the appearance of organic syndromes in the elderly are psychogenic factors. In all cases showing impairment of memory and intellectual function the impairment is worsened by the appearance of anxiety. Depression is felt to underlie some cases of what clinically appears to be simple organic deterioration (Ehrentheil, 1957; Holman). Active treatment for depression has produced remission of psychosis in some individuals, with a return to more normal functioning of memory and intellectual capacity.

Some studies indicate that there is a high association between organic psychoses of the elderly and residence in poor neighborhoods (Dunham, 1955; Gruenberg, 1954). The meaning of these sociological variables in mental illness is not clear. . . .

### Brain Syndrome Symptoms

In the original Duke study it was found impossible to differentiate satisfactorily degrees of severity of symptoms due to organic brain syndrome by using the standard mental status. A series of scales rating the subject on decrements in personal behavior related to various aspects of brain syndrome were devised, and an overall rating based on the combined results of these scales was made. Of 180 subjects, only eight were rated as having no signs of behavioral change possibly associated with organic brain syndrome. Ninety of these subjects had symptoms of behavioral change but no disability for ordinary activities of living. This high proportion was a result of frequent admission of memory impairment or intellectual decline. Forty-four of the subjects had signs of behavioral change due to organic factors, with 20 percent or less decline in previous capacity from these symptoms. Thirty were judged to have between 20 and 50 percent disability, and eight showed very serious disability with up to 80 percent disablement for previous behavioral function.

In examining the component parts of this overall rating scale it was found that changes in sensorium were relatively infrequent. One hundred and twenty-five of the subjects had never experienced any "confusion," getting "mixed up," or being "turned around." Only twenty-three persons became confused in unfamiliar neighborhoods or completely unfamiliar circumstances. Six of the subjects had occasional confusion on awaking at night in the dark.

With regard to memory the situation was quite different, only sixteen subjects having no impairment whatsoever. Eighty-four subjects forgot at times names, dates, places, and articles that had given them no problem earlier in life. Sixty-nine subjects had this difficulty severely enough to require corrective action, either by reliance upon other persons or through the use of notes, etc. Only eleven persons were unable to compensate adequately for a memory difficulty by some kind of corrective action on their parts.

Only thirteen subjects had no impairment in intellectual function. Forty-eight of them had very mild declines in previous intellectual activity but no real disablement for daily activity. Seventy-one subjects had mild intellectual impairment, exemplified by giving up teaching Sunday School classes because of difficulty in exerting the proper thinking effort required. Forty-seven subjects had sufficient difficulty to make it difficult to read newspapers or magazines with comprehension and meaning, and two had difficulty in dealing with simple concrete tasks.

As expected, very few of the subjects showed impairment of judgment. Fourteen persons no longer made major decisions by themselves without extensive help from others, and only two needed the daily presence of another person in their life to assist them in managing daily affairs. Similar low rates of disability were found in these subjects' affective life.

Preliminary examination of the relationships between these findings and other medical examinations of the same subjects conducted at the same time would indicate a close relationship between the occurrence of these psychiatric problems and the person's physical condition. There was a significant relationship between decrement in behavior due to possible brain syndrome effects and the degree of physical disability which the person had. Interestingly enough, it was specifically the mild deterioration in sensory and other neurologic functions that seemed to be most important in determining this relationship. . . .

## Conclusion

Many times psychiatric symptoms are related to physical problems which are greatly increased in incidence in the elderly. Hospitalization for psychiatric illness shows a major upswing, at least in public hospitals, in elderly people and again with diseases closely related to the occurrence of physical illness, especially those illnesses which interfere with the function of the nervous system.

## References

American Psychiatric Association, *Diagnostic and statistical manual of mental disorders.* Washington: American Psychiatric Association, Mental Hospital Service, 1952.

American Psychiatric Association. *Report on patients over 65 in public mental hospitals.* Washington: American Psychiatric Association, Mental Hospital Service, 1959.

Dunham, H. W. Current status of ecological research in mental disorder. In Rose, A. (Ed.), *Mental health and mental disorders.* New York: W. W. Norton, 1955.

Ehrentheil, O. F. Differential diagnosis of organic dementias and affective disorders in aged patients. *Geriatrics*, 12:426–432, 1957.

Gruenberg, E. M. Community conditions in psychoses of the elderly. *American Journal of Psychiatry*, 110:888–896, 1954.

Holman, L. B. Personal communication.

Malzberg, B. Important statistical data about mental illness. *American Handbook of Psychiatry*, 1:161–174, 1959.

Noyes, A. P. *Modern clinical psychiatry.* (4th ed.) Philadelphia: W. B. Saunders, 1953.

Young, W., Gofman, J. W., Malamund, N., Simon, A., and Waters, E. S. The interrelationship between cerebral and coronary atherosclerosis. *Geriatrics*, 11:413–418, 1956.

# Chapter 4. Electroencephalograph Patterns

Several types of electroencephalographic (EEG) abnormality often accompany aging. About half of the panelists showed some EEG abnormality. The first report, however, warns that the occurrence of focal EEG abnormalities has little or no prognosis or diagnostic value among the aged, even though such abnormalities have serious clinical implications among younger adults. On the other hand, the second report shows that diffuse EEG slowing is associated with diminished intellectual functioning, and the third report shows that increased fast activity is associated with learning ability. The last selection links the pattern of diffuse EEG slowing with insufficient cerebral blood flow associated with arteriosclerosis, ischemia, or low blood pressure. Such findings suggest that EEG patterns may eventually be used to detect incipient cerebral circulatory disturbances and incipient declines in intellectual function among the aged.

## Significance of Focal Electroencephalographic Changes in the Elderly*    *Ewald W. Busse and Walter D. Obrist*

In attempting to evaluate an elderly patient who shows beginning signs of neurologic deficit, intellectual impairment, or emotional instability, the medical practitioner frequently requests an electroencephalogram (EEG) as a diagnostic aid. The examination report often includes a description of focal abnormality. These disturbances are present in approximately one-third of the waking EEGs made of persons more than 60 years old and are usually limited to or maximal over the temporal area. Similar findings in a young adult would have serious clinical implications; for example, a space-occupying lesion might be considered. In order to assess the clinical significance of such foci, it is necessary to view them in the light of observations on average, relatively healthy old people.

Busse, Barnes, Silverman, Shy, Thaler, and Frost (1954) first reported the presence of focal EEG deviations in a significant proportion of elderly

* Reprinted by permission from *Postgraduate Medicine*, 34:179–182, 1963.

persons. Since that time numerous investigators have described focal disturbances in the aged, including both hospitalized patients (Barnes, Busse, & Friedman, 1956; Harvald, 1958; Obrist & Henry, 1958; Frey & Sjogren, 1959) and normal control subjects (Silverman, Busse, & Barnes, 1955; Busse, Barnes, Friedman, & Kelty, 1956; Mundy-Castle, 1962). The present paper summarizes our recent findings on focal EEG signs among apparently healthy, well-adjusted people and confirms earlier work.

## Method

Electroencephalograms were made of 266 (10 added in the second wave) community volunteers who participated in an interdisciplinary study on social, psychologic, and medical aspects of aging. . . .

Recordings were made on a Grass electroencephalograph from 15 electrodes; standard monopolar and bipolar technics were used. Particular attention was given to the location of the anterior temporal leads, placed

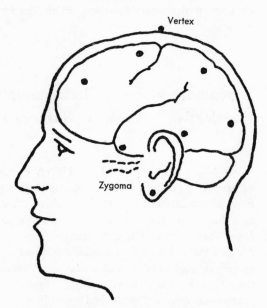

Figure 4–1. *Electrode placement. The anterior temporal lead is advantageously placed above the zygomatic arch to maximize the detection of focal discharges common in elderly persons.*

1.5 cm. above the zygomatic arch at a point one-third of the distance between the auditory meatus and external canthus of the eye (Figure 4–1). A sufficient length of tracing was obtained to insure an adequate evaluation of the waking state; when possible, drowsiness and natural sleep were also recorded. The possible effects of medication taken by a few of the subjects were considered in EEG interpretations.

## Results

### Incidence of Abnormality

Fifty-one percent of the group studied had normal EEGs when judged according to young adult standards (Gibbs & Gibbs, 1950; Hill & Parr, 1950). These tracings were dominated by an alpha rhythm or low-voltage fast activity, or both. Although alpha activity was within normal limits of 8 to 12 cycles per second, it should be noted that the frequencies were about 1 cycle slower on the average than those found in young adults. Similar observations had been made previously (Obrist, 1954; Mundy-Castle, Hurst, Beerstecher, & Prinsloo, 1954; Friedlander, 1958).

Forty-nine percent of the subjects had abnormal EEGs according to young adult standards. A focal disturbance was the most common deviation, occurring in 37 percent of the total group. This type of abnormality is described in detail below. The remaining deviations consisted of diffuse slow activity—less than 7 cycles per second, widely distributed over the head (11 percent of the group)—and excess fast activity—usually 20 to 30 cycles per second, maximal over the frontal region (12 percent of the group). As evident from the percentages, a number of individuals had more than one type of abnormality.

The focal disturbances may be described as follows. Slow theta or delta waves are most common, appearing in 85 percent of the subjects with foci. Approximately four-fifths of these slow dysrhythmias occur exclusively or predominantly on the left side of the brain. In 77 percent of the cases, the amplitude and abundance of the focal slow waves are maximal over the anterior temporal area (Figure 4–2). The distribution is wider in 20 percent of the dysrhythmias, in which there is an equal involvement of the anterior and posterior temporal leads. A slow-wave focus over the occipital area accounts for the remaining small percentage. Focal spikes or sharp waves are found in approximately one-quarter of the patients with focal disturbances. When present, the same distribution occurs; that is, they are usually maximal in the anterior temporal lead and have a left-sided emphasis.

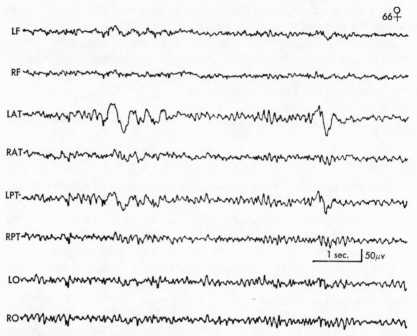

Figure 4–2. *Focal EEG abnormalities. Over 30 percent of elderly people have focal EEG abnormalities. This tracing is from an apparently normal, well-adjusted 66-year-old woman. Note the maximal slowing in the left anterior temporal lead, spreading to the left posterior temporal and frontal areas, with only minor reflection on the right. Key: L = left, R = right, F = frontal, AT = anterior temporal, PT = posterior temporal, O = occipital. All leads are referred to the vertex.*

### Changes during Drowsiness and Sleep

Although sleep records were desired and encouraged, drug-induced sleep was not utilized in this study of normal aged community subjects. Drowsiness and sleep were classified according to the criteria of Gibbs and Gibbs (1950). Of the 266 subjects, 171 displayed EEG evidence of drowsiness or sleep; 74 subjects remained in the drowsy stage, whereas an additional 97 progressed to sleep. Drowsiness is associated with a greater incidence of focal abnormality over the temporal area. This is primarily due to the appearance of focal sharp waves and amplitude asymmetries that are not evident during the waking state. Preexisting slow waves, however, tend to increase in abundance. The overall occurrence of focal disturbances increases from approximately 30 to 40 percent during drowsiness. Sleep, on the other hand, is accompanied by a marked reduction in focal patterns of all types, dropping to 7 percent of the cases.

## Relation of EEG Findings to Mental and Physical Status

For many years investigators have attempted to establish definitive relations between EEG activity and psychologic functioning. Studies on normal children and young adults have failed to establish any clear relationship between EEG characteristics and efficiency of intellectual activity. In contrast, sick or mentally disturbed children and adults show a high incidence of EEG abnormality; as might be expected, this is particularly common in patients with demonstrable organic brain disease. There is ample evidence that clinically recognizable senile mental deterioration is associated with slowing of the EEG (Obrist & Henry, 1958; Frey & Sjogren, 1959; Silverman et al., 1955; Mundy-Castle et al., 1954; McAdam & Robinson, 1956). It might be speculated that early or mild mental deterioration can also be detected by EEG deviations. When such a correlation is reported, it appears to depend greatly on the source and health status of the sample studied (Obrist, Busse, Eisdorfer, & Kleemeier, 1962). Elderly people who are living in the community show no significant relationship between EEG findings and intellectual functioning (Busse et al., 1956; Mundy-Castle, 1962). In contrast, institutionalized aged show a definite relationship, based primarily on diffuse slow-wave changes (Barnes, et al., 1956; Obrist, et al., 1962). To date no intellectual impairment has been found in association with focal temporal lobe disturbances. Our studies fail to reveal any correlation between left-sided EEG abnormalities and cerebral dominance.

Relationships have been sought between senescent EEG patterns and physical signs and symptoms. Several investigators have observed a relationship between EEG abnormalities and clinical evidence of arteriosclerosis (Harvald, 1958; Obrist & Bissel, 1955; Gaches, 1960). Among aged psychiatric patients, blood pressure influences the EEG; an elevated pressure is associated with normal EEGs, whereas reduced pressure is correlated with diffuse slow-wave abnormalities (Obrist, Busse, & Henry, 1961). It seems likely that vascular pathologic conditions and low blood pressure contribute to impaired cerebral blood flow and EEG disturbances. The presence of focal slowing alone, however, is unrelated to the blood pressure level, suggesting an ischemia of primarily local origin. The possibility that temporal lobe discharges are the result of cerebral ischemia is consistent with the well-known fact that the sylvian area of the brain is quite vulnerable to ischemic changes. It has been reported that focal temporal slowing can be activated by inhalation of low oxygen mixtures or compression of the carotid artery (Bruens et al., 1960). The same investigators suggest that the appearance of a focal disturbance may be a useful indicator of impending decompensation of the cerebral circulation. The term "impending" could be interpreted as meaning that decompensation can be expected shortly. Our serial recordings over a four-year period do not support this contention. However, it is hoped that longitudinal studies now in progress will contribute to a better understanding of this problem.

## Comment

The anterior temporal abnormality frequently encountered in elderly persons is probably, but not proved to be, of ischemic origin. The presence or absence of this focal pattern has little or no clearly demonstrated prognostic or diagnostic value. It does not appear to be related to alterations in psychologic functioning, and it is not related to convulsive disorders. The wave form and frequency of focal disturbance are not specific in nature, and they do not constitute a reliable basis for a differential diagnosis, particularly from an expanding intracranial lesion (Van der Drift & Magnus, 1962). If an intracranial mass is considered, serial EEGs must be relied on to determine if the dysrhythmia is progressing.

## References

Barnes, R. H., Busse, E. W., and Friedman, E. L. The psychological functioning of aged individuals with normal and abnormal electroencephalograms: II. A study of hospitalized individuals. *Journal of Nervous and Mental Disorders*, 124:585–593, 1956.

Bruens, J. H., Gastaut, H., and Giove, G. Electroencephalographic study of the signs of chronic vascular insufficiency of the Sylvian region in aged people. *Electroencephalography and Clinical Neurophysiology*, 12:283–295, 1960.

Busse, E. W., Barnes, R. H., Silverman, A. J., Shy, M. G., Thaler, M., and Frost, L. L. Studies of the process of aging: Factors that influence the psyche of elderly persons. *American Journal of Psychiatry*, 110:897–903, 1954.

Busse, E. W., Barnes, R. H., Friedman, E. L., and Kelty, E. J. Psychological functioning of aged individuals with normal and abnormal electroencephalograms: I. A study of non-hospitalized community volunteers. *Electroencephalography and Clinical Neurophysiology*, 7:135–141, 1956.

Frey, T. S., and Sjogren, H. The electroencephalogram in elderly persons suffering from neuropsychiatric disorders. *Acta Psychiatrica and Neurologica Scandinavica*, 34:438–450, 1959.

Friedlander, W. J. Electroencephalographic alpha rate in adults as a function of age. *Geriatrics*, 13:29–31, 1958.

Gaches, J. Etude statistique sur les traces "alpha largement developpe" en fonction de l'age. *Presse Médicale*, 68:1620–1622, 1960.

Gibbs, F. A., and Gibbs, E. L. *Atlas of electroencephalography: Methodology and controls.* (2nd ed.) Vol. I. Cambridge, Mass.: Addison-Wesley, 1950.

Harvald, B. EEG in old age. *Acta Psychiatrica and Neurologica Scandinavica,* 33:193–196, 1958.

Hill, D., and Parr, G. (Eds.). *Electroencephalography.* London: MacDonald, 1950.

McAdam, W., and Robinson, R. A. Senile intellectual deterioration and the electroencephalogram: A quantitative correlation. *Journal of Mental Science,* 102:819–825, 1956.

Mundy-Castle, A. C. Central excitability in the aged. In Blumenthal, H. T. (Ed.), *Medical and clinical aspects of aging.* New York: Columbia University Press, 1962.

Mundy-Castle, A. C., Hurst, L. A., Beerstecher, D. M., and Prinsloo, T. The electroencephalogram in the senile psychoses. *Electroencephalography and Clinical Neurophysiology,* 6:245–252, 1954.

Obrist, W. D. The electroencephalogram of normal aged adults. *Electroencephalography and Clinical Neurophysiology,* 6:235–244, 1954.

Obrist, W. D., and Bissel, L. F. The electroencephalogram of aged patients with cardiac and cerebral vascular disease. *Journal of Gerontology,* 10:315–330, 1955.

Obrist, W. D., and Henry, C. E. Electroencephalographic findings in aged psychiatric patients. *Journal of Nervous and Mental Disease,* 126:254–267, 1958.

Obrist, W. D., Busse, E. W., and Henry, C. E. Relation of electroencephalogram to blood pressure in elderly persons. *Neurology,* 11:151–158, 1961.

Obrist, W. D., Busse, E. W., Eisdorfer, C., and Kleemeier, R. W. Relation of the electroencephalogram to intellectual function in senescence. *Journal of Gerontology,* 17:197–206, 1962.

Silverman, A. J., Busse, E. W., and Barnes, R. H. Studies in the processes of aging: Electroencephalographic findings in 400 elderly subjects. *Electroencephalography and Clinical Neurophysiology,* 7:67–74, 1955.

Van der Drift, J. H. A., and Magnus, O. The EEG with space-occupying intracranial lesions in old patients. *Electroencephalography and Clinical Neurophysiology,* 14:664–673, 1962.

# Relation of the Electroencephalogram to Intellectual Function in Senescence* *Walter D. Obrist, Ewald W. Busse, Carl Eisdorfer, and Robert W. Kleemeier*

Cross-sectional studies reveal that the electroencephalogram undergoes certain changes in later life (Obrist, 1954; Mundy-Castle, Hurst, Beerstecher, & Prinsloo, 1954; Silverman, Busse, & Barnes, 1955). The degree to which the EEG differs from young adult standards, however, varies among individuals. Some people of advanced age show normal patterns, whereas others have tracings that are clearly deviant. The question is frequently asked whether such EEG deviations are associated with changes in intellectual function.

* Reprinted by permission from the *Journal of Gerontology,* 17:197–206, 1962.

Reduced speed and accuracy of performance have been observed on a wide variety of cognitive tasks (Jones, 1959), including standard intelligence tests (Doppelt & Wallace, 1955; Eisdorfer & Cohen, 1961; Kleemeier, Justiss, Rich, & Jones, 1961). The possibility arises that these intellectual changes are influenced by the same neurologic mechanism responsible for alterations in the senescent EEG. A certain degree of concomitance might therefore be expected between the two variables.

The present study attempts to correlate EEG characteristics with intellectual function during senescence. The hypothesis was posed that subjects with age-related EEG deviations would perform more poorly on intelligence tests than those with normal young adult patterns. Higher correlations were predicted for nonverbal as opposed to verbal tests, because of the greater decline of nonverbal skills with age (Fox & Birren, 1950; Eisdorfer, Busse, & Cohen, 1959).

Previous reports indicate little or no relationship between EEG and intellectual ability in healthy children and young adults (Knott, Friedman, & Bardsley, 1942; Henry, 1944; Shagass, 1945; Ellingson, Wilcott, Sineps, & Dudek, 1957). Patients with organic cerebral disease, however, show a definite association between EEG abnormalities and intellectual impairment (Hoch & Kubis, 1941; Stroller, 1949; Kooi & Hovery, 1957; Klove, 1959). This suggests that the correlation in elderly people might depend on alterations of the cerebral cortex and its physiology.

Among psychiatric patients, there is ample evidence that senile mental deterioration is associated with EEG changes. Aged patients with chronic brain syndrome have significantly more diffuse slow waves in the theta (4–7 cps) and delta (1–3 cps) bands than do control subjects (Barnes, Busse, & Friedman, 1956; Obrist & Henry, 1958). A rough quantitative relationship has been found between the degree of EEG slowing and severity of intellectual impairment as assessed by psychiatric interview (McAdam & Robinson, 1956; Weiner & Schuster, 1956).

In less deteriorated old people given psychological tests, the correlation between EEG and intellectual function varies with the sample studied. Busse, Barnes, Friedman, and Kelty (1956) found no relationship between EEG and WAIS or Wechsler-Bellevue scores in a large group of elderly community volunteers. Similar negative results have been obtained by Obrist (1962) on a select group of healthy community subjects and by Mundy-Castle (1960) on residents of an old-age home. In contrast, Barnes et al. (1956) noted a tendency for aged psychiatric patients to show abnormal slowing in association with decreased performance on several WAIS and Wechsler-Bellevue subtests. Among elderly medical clinic patients, Thaler (1956) found significantly lower total Wechsler scores in cases with diffuse EEG abnormalities. A similar finding was obtained by

Silverman, Busse, Barnes, Frost, and Thaler (1953) on a heterogeneous group of hospitalized psychiatric and medical clinic patients. It should be noted that the highest correlations were reported in studies where clinically more severe EEG abnormalities appeared. While diffuse disturbances, especially abnormal slowing, were associated with intellectual impairment, focal patterns and deviant fast activity were not.

The above reports suggest that there is little or no relationship between EEG and intellectual ability in average, relatively healthy old people who show only minor electrocortical deviations. Significant trends are found, however, in aged medical and psychiatric patients who manifest more severe EEG abnormalities. It could be argued that the magnitude of the correlation is a function of the degree of pathology involved. Thus, the health status of the sample may be particularly relevant in explaining discrepancies among previous findings.

It is the purpose of the present paper to examine the relationship between EEG and intelligence test performance in three groups of elderly subjects: (*a*) community volunteers, (*b*) residents of a home for the aged, and (*c*) hospitalized psychiatric patients. Subgroups of patients with known cardiovascular disease are also included. Because the data were obtained from separate studies that varied in methodology, only a gross comparison of groups is possible. Nevertheless, it was hoped that tentative conclusions could be drawn concerning factors of subject selection and health as they influence the correlations.

## Methods

### Subjects

Three groups of subjects were tested as follows: 245 community volunteers living in Durham, North Carolina, ages 60 to 94; 115 residents of Moosehaven, a fraternal home for the aged in Orange Park, Florida, ages 66 to 91; and 37 psychiatric patients from the John Umstead State Hospital in Butner, North Carolina, ages 62 to 84. Table 4–1 gives the mean age and standard deviation for each group. It should be noted that the average Moosehaven resident is seven years older than the other subjects. The sexes were about equally present in the community and hospital samples, but only males were studied at Moosehaven. All subjects were of Caucasian extraction, except 78 Negroes in the community group.

No claim is made for the representativeness of these samples. Subjects from the community cover a wide range of socioeconomic and educational backgrounds. While some were laborers who did not finish grammar school, others were professional people with advanced degrees. Because of selective factors in admission, the two institutional groups were relatively more homogeneous in these respects, being drawn largely from lower-middle socioeconomic strata.

Except for exclusion of cases with gross sensory or motor defects that might interfere with intelligence testing, no attempt was made to select subjects on the basis of physical health or disease. In consequence, there existed a wide range of physical pathology, including many cases with cardiovascular and neurologic disorders.

The hospitalized group was necessarily limited to patients whose illness was mild enough to permit psychological testing. Thirty-seven out of 53 recent admissions were thus selected. Fifteen had a diagnosis of chronic brain syndrome; the remainder had a variety of functional disorders, predominantly depressive and paranoid reactions. None of the community or Moosehaven subjects was grossly psychotic, although a few manifested less severe mental disturbances. In contrast to the hospitalized patients, individuals in the latter groups were making adequate social adjustments.

A number of subjects were taking medications at the time of study, all of which were carefully noted. Although no attempt was made to exclude such cases, EEGs were interpreted with appropriate allowance for sedatives and other drugs known to have specific effects.

### Intelligence Testing

Results are based on two intelligence tests that have a high degree of comparability (Wechsler, 1958). The Moosehaven subjects were given Form I of the Wechsler-Bellevue test (W-B). Community and hospital subjects received the Wechsler Adult Intelligence Scale (WAIS). Table 4–1 gives the mean IQs for the several groups. IQs of the community and hospital cases were based on published WAIS norms for this age level (Wechsler, 1955). The Moosehaven IQs were derived by extrapolation of W-B normative curves for the young and middle-adult years (Wechsler, 1944).

Both the community and Moosehaven groups have mean IQs corresponding to average for the normal population. The larger standard deviation of the community sample probably reflects the greater heterogeneity of socioeconomic and educational status. The lower mean IQ of the hospital subjects may indicate more severe intellectual deterioration, although sampling differences cannot be ruled out. In order to evaluate the groups by young adult standards, full scale Efficiency Quotients were derived, the means of which are presented in Table 4–1. A low level of function is apparent in these elderly subjects, whose average performance lies in the borderline, dull-normal range for young adults.

Table 4–1. *Characteristics of three elderly groups.*

| Type of subject | Community: volunteers from Durham | Moosehaven: residents of fraternal home | Hospital: psychiatric patients |
|---|---|---|---|
| Number of cases | 245 | 115 | 37 |
| Age | | | |
| Mean | 70.7 | 77.0 | 69.8 |
| SD | 7.0 | 6.2 | 6.4 |
| Full Scale IQ | | | |
| Mean | 100 | 101 | 81 |
| SD | 19 | 10 | 17 |
| Efficiency quotient | | | |
| Mean | 83 | 77 | 66 |
| SD | 20 | 13 | 16 |
| Incidence of diffuse EEG slowing | 10% | 21% | 43% |
| EEG alpha frequency | | | |
| Mean | 9.4 | 9.0 | 8.7 |
| SD | 0.8 | 0.8 | 1.2 |

Since the present study is concerned with efficiency of intellectual function in the absolute sense, only weighted (scaled) scores were analyzed statistically. IQ was not considered a suitable measure because it involves an adjustment for age that has no parallel in the EEG procedure. Of particular interest is the relative magnitude or EEG correlations for the Verbal and Performance parts of the test. The present analysis is based on the sum of weighted scores from each of these parts, as well as from the Full Scale. Correlations between EEG and the 11 individual subtests will also be presented.

*Electroencephalograms*

Recordings were made on 8-channel Grass equipment while the subject was fully awake with his eyes closed. Ten to 15 electrodes were placed bilaterally over the major brain regions, from which both bipolar and scalp-to-ear runs were obtained. A low anterior temporal placement was utilized on all subjects except those in the Moosehaven sample. EEGs were evaluated according to young adult standards (Gibbs & Gibbs, 1950; Hill & Parr, 1950), with particular attention being given to age-related changes as reported in the literature. The EEGs were classified into four groups:

*Normal*, consisting of either a dominant alpha rhythm from 8 to 13 cps, or a low voltage fast tracing.

*Diffuse Slow*, defined as greater than normal amounts of delta or theta activity (1 to 7 cps), present bilaterally, and involving three or four cerebral areas: frontal, parietal, occipital, or temporal. Tracings with wide-spread alpha-like rhythms under 8 cps were also included in this category.

*Focal Slow*, characterized by delta or theta waves (1 to 7 cps) that are localizable to a particular brain region. Although often unilateral, the homologous area of the opposite hemisphere was sometimes involved.

*Excess Fast*, defined as rhythmic fast waves above alpha frequency, averaging 15 microvolts or greater, and persisting in one or more leads. Such activity was usually maximum in the frontal and precentral derivations.

EEGs with more than one abnormality were classified according to the clinically more severe type. Thus, tracings with both diffuse and focal disturbances were assigned to the former category, while slow waves took precedence over fast activity. A few records revealed spikelike potentials in association with slow waves, but only the latter was used as a basis for classification.

The frequency of the alpha rhythm was determined for all individuals in whom it was present more than 10 percent of the time. Alpha rhythm was defined as a sequence of 3 or more waves between 7 and 13 cps, originating from the posterior region of the head and blocking with visual stimulation. Since there is a definite tendency for such activity to become slower with age (Obrist. 1954; Friedlander, 1958), a lower limit of 7 cps was established instead of the usual value of 8 cps applied to young people. Frequency measurements were made throughout the monopolar occipital record on a minimum of 300 waves.

EEG differences between subject groups were most pronounced with respect to diffuse slow activity. Table 4–1 shows the incidence of such tracings in each of the three samples. Whereas only 10 percent of community cases had diffuse slow waves, 21 and 43 percent, respectively, of the Moosehaven and hospital subjects showed this type of abnormality. The latter values are considerably in excess of those reported for young adults (Gibbs & Gibbs, 1950).

Also shown in Table 4–1 are the mean alpha frequencies for the three elderly groups. These vary between 8.7 and 9.4 cps, with the institution-alized cases having lower frequencies. All of the means are significantly below previous values of 10.2 and 10.5 cps obtained on young control subjects (Lindsley, 1938; Brazier & Finesinger, 1944).

## Results

### Relation of Intelligence Scores to EEG Classifications

No significant differences were found between the mean weighted scores of subjects with normal EEGs and those with *focal slow* or *excess fast* tracings. The small differences observed did not occur consistently in one direction, nor was there a tendency for a particular sample to show a greater degree of relationship.

Individuals with *diffuse slow* activity, on the other hand, revealed consistently poorer test performance than those with normal EEGs. Table 4–2 permits a comparison of subjects with such tracings in each of the three samples. Mean weighted scores for Verbal, Performance, and Full Scales are given, along with the standard deviations. In all instances, the

Table 4–2. *Means and standard deviations of intelligence scores in subjects with normal and diffuse slow EEGs.*

|  | Community (WAIS) | | Moosehaven (W-B) | | Hospital (WAIS) | |
|---|---|---|---|---|---|---|
|  | Normal | Diffuse slow | Normal | Diffuse slow | Normal | Diffuse slow |
| Number of cases | 134 | 25 | 71 | 24 | 17 | 16 |
| Mean age | 70.5 | 75.8 | 76.2 | 80.7 | 69.0 | 72.4 |
| Verbal weighted score | | | | | | |
| Mean | 55.0 | 51.7 | 38.1 | 32.8 | 40.8 | 32.4 |
| SD | 21.4 | 20.0 | 11.3 | 10.8 | 19.3 | 15.9 |
| Performance weighted score | | | | | | |
| Mean | 26.9 | 23.2 | 28.5 | 22.0 | 18.8 | 10.3 |
| SD | 12.7 | 13.6 | 9.8 | 9.4 | 12.4 | 8.1 |
| Full Scale weighted score | | | | | | |
| Mean | 82.5 | 74.6 | 67.3 | 54.8 | 59.6 | 42.7 |
| SD | 32.9 | 33.4 | 19.2 | 18.5 | 30.1 | 21.8 |

mean for subjects with diffuse slow activity falls below that of the corresponding group with normal EEGs.

Figure 4–3 illustrates these two types of EEG. The upper record, which is considered normal, shows 9 cps alpha waves mixed with traces of faster activity. The lower one was classified as diffusely slow on the basis of a slow alpha rhythm (7 cps) and scattered theta waves (5–6 cps).

The relationship between intellectual function and diffuse slow activity was evaluated by means of biserial correlation. Weighted intelligence test scores served as the continuous variable; two EEG categories, normal and diffuse slow, constituted the dichotomous variable. Such a procedure has the advantage of indicating degree of relationship. Its validity is open to question, however, because of the omission of subjects with focal and fast tracings. Each biserial correlation was therefore checked by a *t* test of difference between mean intelligence scores. In every case, a significant biserial coefficient was associated with a reliable difference between the normal and diffusely slow EEG groups.

Table 4–3 presents the biserial correlations for total Verbal, Performance, and Full Scale weighted scores, as well as for the individual subtests. All of the coefficients are positive, indicating that subjects with normal EEGs have consistently higher mean scores. None of the correlations for the community sample deviate significantly from zero. In contrast, a number of the Moosehaven and hospital values are statistically reliable. Corre-

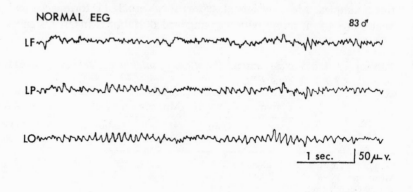

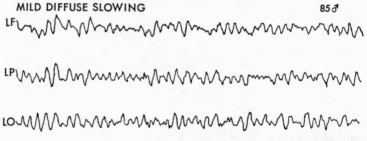

Figure 4–3. *Two types of EEG commonly found in elderly people. Upper tracing: normal by young adult standards. Lower tracing: diffuse slow activity (mild). Key: L = left, F = frontal, P = parietal, O = occipital. All leads are referred to the left ear.*

lations for the Performance Scale are generally larger and more significant than those for the Verbal Scale.

It is interesting to observe that the magnitude of the correlations parallels the incidence of diffuse slow activity in the three samples. The larger coefficients are found in the institutionalized groups, where there is a higher proportion of records with such slowing (see Table 4–1).

In interpreting these results, it should be noted that the average age of subjects with diffuse slow activity is greater than that of the normal EEG group in each of the samples (see Table 4–2). This age difference is statistically reliable (.01 level) for the community and Moosehaven sub-

Table 4–3. *Biserial correlations between intelligence scores and type of EEG: normal versus diffuse slow.*

|  | Community (WAIS) | Moosehaven (W-B) | Hospital (WAIS) |
|---|---|---|---|
| Verbal weighted score | .09 | .27* | .30 |
|   Information | .03 | .24 | .35 |
|   Comprehension | .07 | .18 | .11 |
|   Arithmetic | .10 | .05 | .45* |
|   Similarities | .06 | .25 | .13 |
|   Digit Span | .21 | .38** | .26 |
|   Vocabulary | .03 | .22 | .26 |
| Performance weighted score | .16 | .38** | .48* |
|   Digit Symbol | .23 | .27* | .44* |
|   Picture Completion | .08 | .45** | .49* |
|   Block Design | .09 | .35* | .52* |
|   Picture Arrangement | .21 | .10 | .24 |
|   Object Assembly | .03 | .26 | .44* |
| Full Scale weighted score | .12 | .37** | .39 |

\* Significant at the .05 level.
\*\* Significant at the .01 level.

jects and approaches significance for the hospital patients. Thus the intelligence test results could be attributed to variations in age, independent of EEG type.

## Relation of Intelligence Scores to Alpha Frequency

Table 4–4 presents the product-moment correlations between occipital alpha frequency and weighted intelligence scores. None of the correlations for the community sample are significantly different from zero, and several are in the negative direction. On the other hand, all of the Moosehaven values are positive, with 10 out of 14 being statistically reliable. The hospital group yields correlations of comparable size, although fewer are significant because of the small number of cases.

These findings agree with those based on the EEG classification, in that a low intelligence test score is associated with slower brain potentials. In accord with the earlier results, correlations for institutionalized subjects are higher than those for community volunteers. However, the previous tendency for Performance subtests to give larger coefficients than Verbal items applies only to the hospital sample.

Again, the magnitude of the correlations tends to parallel the EEG findings. As shown in Table 4–1, the institutionalized groups have a lower mean alpha frequency. Thus, larger coefficients are obtained in samples where the alpha frequency deviates more from young adult norms.

Table 4-4. *Product-moment correlations between intelligence scores and alpha frequency.*

|  | Community (WAIS) | Moosehaven (W-B) | Hospital (WAIS) |
|---|---|---|---|
| Verbal weighted score | .01 | .25* | .16 |
| Information | −.07 | .21* | .25 |
| Comprehension | .03 | .07 | .05 |
| Arithmetic | −.06 | .14 | .23 |
| Similarities | .07 | .27** | .12 |
| Digit Span | .10 | .24* | −.01 |
| Vocabulary | −.01 | .20* | .12 |
| Performance weighted score | .06 | .26** | .45* |
| Digit Symbol | .07 | .20* | .36 |
| Picture Completion | .02 | .19 | .37* |
| Block Design | .04 | .39** | .43* |
| Picture Arrangement | .04 | .09 | .18 |
| Object Assembly | .09 | .22* | .39 |
| Full Scale weighted score | .03 | .27** | .29 |

* Significant at the .05 level.
** Significant at the .01 level.

The possibility arises that variations in age among subjects may account for the significant relationships observed. Partial correlations were therefore computed for the Moosehaven and hospital groups between alpha frequency and total weighted score, holding age constant. The results are as follows: Moosehaven, .18, .13, .16; hospital, .17, .39, .27, for Verbal, Performance, and Full Scales, respectively. Only the highest value, .39, is reliably different from zero. Although all six of the partial correlations are positive, five of them are lower than the corresponding zero-order coefficients, indicating that variations in age have some influence on the degree of relationship.

Mundy-Castle (1958) has recently obtained significant correlations between alpha frequency and intelligence scores on an intellectually homogeneous sample of young adults, which he attributes to factors of temperament. An attempt was made to verify this finding on a homogeneous subsample of 68 upper-class white subjects from the present community group. The results were entirely negative.

*Magnitude of Correlation as a Function of Arteriosclerosis*

The tendency for EEG–intelligence test correlations to be higher in institutionalized than in community subjects suggests that factors of health (i.e., pathology) may contribute to the relationship. Recent studies have demonstrated an association between EEG abnormalities and cardiovascular disease (Obrist & Bissell, 1955; Gastaut & Meyer, 1961), including arteriosclerosis (Harvald, 1958). There is also some evidence that intelligence scores may be lower in arteriosclerotic disorders (Inglis, 1958). A separate analysis was therefore undertaken of Moosehaven and hospital subjects who had sufficient data to permit an evaluation of cardiovascular status.

Two subgroups were formed from each institution: (*a*) individuals in whom there was unequivocal evidence of arteriosclerosis in any part of the cardiovascular system, regardless of severity; and (*b*) subjects who showed no evidence of arteriosclerotic disease on routine clinical or laboratory tests.

Details of the cardiovascular examination have been described elsewhere (Obrist & Bissel, 1955). Arteriosclerosis was judged to be "present" when any of the following conditions existed; palpable evidence of sclerosis in peripheral vessels, x-ray signs of calcified peripheral or systemic arteries, grade III or IV arteriosclerotic retinal changes, physical findings and electrocardiographic abnormalities suggestive of arteriosclerotic heart disease, a clear-cut history of coronary thrombosis or insufficiency, definite neurologic manifestations of cerebral thrombosis or vascular insufficiency. Arteriosclerosis was judged to be "absent" when all of the above signs were either negative or equivocal.

In order to rule out factors of aging not associated with cardiovascular disease, the two subgroups in each sample were matched for age. Thirty-two Moosehaven and 30 hospital cases were thus selected. As shown in Table 4–5, the mean age and standard deviation of the arteriosclerotic

Table 4–5. *Description of subjects classified according to clinical evidence of arteriosclerosis.*

| Arteriosclerosis | Moosehaven | | Hospital | |
|---|---|---|---|---|
| | Absent | Present | Absent | Present |
| Number of cases | 14 | 18 | 14 | 16 |
| Age | | | | |
|   Mean | 76.8 | 77.2 | 70.7 | 70.2 |
|   SD | 7.0 | 6.8 | 6.0 | 6.1 |
| Efficiency quotient | | | | |
|   Mean | 83 | 74* | 66 | 66 |
|   SD | 12 | 11 | 17 | 15 |
| EEG alpha frequency | | | | |
|   Mean | 9.2 | 8.3** | 8.7 | 8.7 |
|   SD | 0.7 | 0.5 | 1.1 | 1.3 |

* Significantly lower than "absent" group at the .05 level ($t = 2.05$).
** Significantly lower than "absent" group at the .001 level ($t = 4.18$).

Table 4-6. *Product-moment correlations between intelligence scores and alpha frequency in subjects with and without arteriosclerosis.*

| | Arteriosclerosis | | Combined groups |
|---|---|---|---|
| | Absent | Present | |
| Moosehaven | | | |
| Verbal | −.16 | .20 | .18 |
| Performance | .03 | .58** | .44** |
| Full Scale | −.08 | .41 | .34 |
| Hospital | | | |
| Verbal | −.15 | .43 | .16 |
| Performance | .23 | .61** | .45** |
| Full Scale | −.01 | .56* | .29 |

\* Significant at the .05 level.
\*\* Significant at the .02 level.

subjects approximate those of the corresponding subgroup with no pathology. It is interesting to note that Moosehaven subjects with arteriosclerosis "present" have a significantly lower mean Efficiency Quotient and a slower alpha frequency than those with arteriosclerosis "absent." Comparable differences between diagnostic subgroups were not found among the hospital patients. Possible reasons for this discrepancy will be discussed below.

Table 4–6 presents the product-moment correlations between occipital alpha frequency and weighted intelligence test scores for subjects classified according to the absence or presence of arteriosclerosis. Separate coefficients are given for the Verbal, Performance, and Full Scales in each of the two institutionalized samples. The last column shows the results of combining clinical subgroups.

Several points are brought out by the statistics in Table 4–6. Subjects with clinical evidence of arteriosclerosis reveal consistently higher correlations than those without signs of arteriosclerosis. Not a single correlation in either of the "absent" subgroups is reliably different from zero. Indeed, four of the six coefficients have negative signs, which is contrary to the expectation of a slow alpha rhythm associated with lower test scores. On the other hand, all of the correlations in the "present" subgroups are in the predicted positive direction, with three of the six reaching statistical significance. In accordance with the earlier results, the correlations are larger for the Performance than Verbal Scale.

Discussion

The present results confirm previous findings of little or no relationship between EEG and intelligence test performance in elderly community subjects leading relatively normal lives (Busse et al., 1956; Obrist, 1963). They also agree with earlier reports of small but significant correlations in aged patients with medical and psychiatric disorders (Thaler, 1956; Barnes et al., 1956). In the latter case, low intelligence scores are associated with EEGs that deviate from young adult norms.

Not all types of EEG deviation, however, are related to test performance. About a fourth of all subjects revealed focal slow activity, predominantly over the temporal lobe. Although such abnormalities show a definite increase with age (Silverman et al., 1955), they were entirely unrelated to intelligence scores, thus confirming previous work (Mundy-Castle, 1960). A similar lack of correlation was obtained for excess fast activity, which is also age-related (Gibbs & Gibbs, 1950) and found in approximately 12 percent of the subjects.

Only diffuse slow activity and its frequent accompaniment, a slow alpha rhythm, were significantly related to impairment of intellectual function. Both of these patterns increase with age (Obrist, 1954; Busse et al., 1956), reaching their highest incidence and degree of severity in elderly psychiatric patients with chronic brain syndrome (Luce & Rothschild, 1953; Obrist & Henry, 1958).

As expected, there was a tendency for certain intelligence subtests to correlate more highly with EEG than others, particularly on the Performance Scale. Among institutionalized subjects, Block Design, Picture Completion, Object Assembly, and Digit Symbol gave predominantly significant results. Coefficients for the Verbal items tended to be lower and more variable. This pattern of correlations parallels the differential decline of subtest scores with age (Fox & Birren, 1950; Eisdorfer et al., 1959).

The results suggest that age, per se, is not a crucial factor influencing the magnitude of EEG–intelligence test correlations. This is supported by the general absence of relationship in the community subjects, where age variation was greatest. Rather, it would appear that health status is the critical determinant of the degree of relationship. Sampling factors, such as institution admission policies and method of recruiting community volunteers, are relevant in this regard. Whereas 26 percent of the Moosehaven residents were convalescent because of some acute or chronic illness, only 9 percent of the community subjects could be so classified. As reported elsewhere (Dovenmuehle, Newman, & Busse, 1960), the hospital subjects also had a greater incidence of chronic physical disease than the community volunteers. Thus, higher correlations were obtained in those samples where physical pathology was more evident.

The findings indicate that cardiovascular disease contributes to the degree of relationship between EEG and intelligence scores. When arteriosclerosis is clinically absent, institutionalized subjects show the same lack of correlation as community volunteers. In the presence of arteriosclerosis,

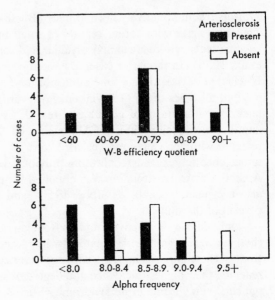

Figure 4–4. *Comparison of intelligence scores and EEG findings of Moosehaven subjects with and without arteriosclerosis (N = 18 and 14, respectively). The two groups are of comparable age, but differ significantly in both efficiency quotient and alpha frequency. See Table 4–5 for means and standard deviations.*

however, subjects of comparable age yield significant correlations (see Table 4–6). It might be speculated that variations in cardiovascular pathology, more than any other factor, are responsible for the results obtained here, as well as those reported in the literature. This is consistent with recent evidence that cerebral circulatory and metabolic variables have a direct effect on both brain potentials and intellectual function (Gastaut & Meyer, 1961; Doust, Schneider, Talland, Walsh, & Barker, 1953; Lassen, Feinberg, & Lane, 1960).

The occurrence of significant correlations in groups with cardiovascular disease raises a question concerning the influence of this factor on each of the variables under study. In the Moosehaven sample, subjects with arteriosclerosis yield reliably lower means for intelligence test performance and alpha frequency than those without such pathology. Figure 4–4 compares the distributions of the two diagnostic subgroups. It is apparent that arteriosclerosis is associated with a reduction of scores in both variables.

In the hospital sample, on the other hand, the diagnostic subgroups do not differ with respect to either intelligence test performance or alpha frequency (see Table 4–5). It might be inferred from this that arteriosclerosis has no effect on the scores of psychiatric patients. Such an interpretation is open to question, however, because of the lack of an appropriate control group. Both diagnostic subgroups deviate appreciably from community volunteers on each of the variables (compare Tables 4–1 and 4–5). Presumably other pathological factors, i.e., those related to psychiatric illness, are operating to reduce the scores of patients without arteriosclerosis. Whether the equally low scores of the arteriosclerotic group are attributable to cardiovascular disease or to some other factor is difficult to evaluate.

An unexpected finding of this and earlier studies is the very low set of correlations obtained on community volunteers. Both EEG and intelligence test performance undergo certain "normal" changes with age, even in relatively healthy subjects (Obrist, 1963; Botwinick & Birren, 1962). As seen in Table 4–1, the mean Efficiency Quotient for the community group lies a full standard deviation below young adult norms, with alpha frequency showing a comparable deviation. Changes of this magnitude might be expected to result in some degree of concomitance between the two measures. The observed lack of correlation implies that factors responsible for "normal" age changes in one variable are quite independent of those affecting the other.

Previous authors have disagreed on the magnitude and significance of correlations between EEG and intellectual function in old age. Turton and Warren (1960) claim that only the more severe forms of EEG abnormality and organic dementia are related. McAdam and Robinson (1958, 1960), on the other hand, report an association between minor EEG deviations and mild intellectual deficit. The present results suggest that slight to moderate degrees of relationship may occur, depending upon the type of subject selected and the particular EEG variables analyzed. Thus, only groups with appreciable physical pathology, notably cardiovascular disease, would be expected to show significant correlations, and these would be confined to variations in alpha frequency or diffuse slow activity. If valid, the restricted nature of this generalization seriously limits the usefulness of EEG in predicting intellectual impairment among elderly people.

## Summary

The present study concerns the relation of EEG characteristics to intellectual function in senescence. The hypothesis was made that EEGs deviating from young adult norms would be associated with poor performance on standard intelligence tests. EEGs and either WAIS or Wechsler-

Bellevue examinations were administered to three groups of subjects over 60 years of age: 245 community volunteers, 115 residents of a fraternal home, and 37 hospitalized psychiatric patients.

No significant relationships were observed between EEG and intelligence scores in community volunteers. In contrast, hospital subjects and residents from the old-age home showed small but significant correlations. There was a tendency in these cases for low intelligence scores to be associated with diffuse slowing of the EEG and a slow alpha rhythm. Focal slow waves and excess fast activity, however, were not related to intelligence test performance in any of the groups. Scores from the Performance part of the test gave generally higher correlations with EEG than those from the Verbal portion.

Differences in the degree of relationship among the several groups were attributed to variations in health status of the subjects. This interpretation was supported by a comparison of age-matched subgroups classified according to the absence or presence of clinically diagnosed cardiovascular disease. Correlations for subjects with arteriosclerosis were consistently higher and more significant than those without such pathology.

## References

Barnes, R. H., Busse, E. W., and Friedman, E. L. The psychological functioning of aged individuals with normal and abnormal electrocardiograms: II. A study of hospitalized individuals. *Journal of Nervous and Mental Disease*, 124:585–593, 1956.

Botwinick, J., and Birren, J. R. Cognitive processes: Mental abilities and psychomotor responses in aged men. In Birren, J. E., Butler, R. N., Greenhouse, S. W., Sokoloff, L., and Yarrow, M. R. (Eds.), *Human aging: A biological and behavioral study*. Washington: Government Printing Office, 1963, pp. 143–156.

Brazier, Mary A. B., and Finesinger, J. E. Characteristics of the normal electroencephalogram: I. A study of the occipital cortical potentials in 500 normal adults. *Journal of Clinical Investigation*, 23:303–311, 1944.

Busse, E. W., Barnes, R. H., Friedman, E. L., and Kelty, E. J. Psychological functioning of aged individuals with normal and abnormal electroencephalograms: I. A study of non-hospitalized community volunteers. *Journal of Nervous and Mental Disease*, 124:135–141, 1956.

Doppelt, J. E., and Wallace, W. L. Standardization of the Wechsler Adult Intelligence Scale for older persons. *Journal of Abnormal and Social Psychology*, 51:312–330, 1955.

Doust, J. W. L., Schneider, R. A., Talland, G. A., Walsh, M. A., and Barker, G. B. Studies on the physiology of awareness: The correlation between intelligence and anoxemia in senile dementia. *Journal of Nervous and Mental Disease*, 117:383–398, 1953.

Dovenmuehle, R. H., Newman, E. G., and Busse, E. W. Physical problems of psychiatrically hospitalized elderly persons. *Journal of the American Geriatric Society*, 8:838–846, 1960.

Eisdorfer, C., Busse, E. W., and Cohen, L. D. The WAIS performance of an aged sample: The relationship between verbal and performance IQs. *Journal of Gerontology*, 14:197–201, 1959.

Eisdorfer, C., and Cohen, L. The generality of the WAIS standardization for the aged: A regional comparison. *Journal of Abnormal and Social Psychology*, 62:520–527, 1961.

Ellingson, R. J., Wilcott, R. C., Sineps, J. G., and Dudek, F. J. EEG frequency-pattern variation and intelligence. *EEG Clinical Neurophysiology*, 9:657–660, 1957.

Fox, Charlotte, and Birren, J. E. The differential decline of subtest scores of the Wechsler-Bellevue Intelligence Scale in 60–69 year old individuals. *Journal of General Psychology*, 77:313–317, 1950.

Friedlander, W. J. Electroencephalographic alpha rate in adults as a function of age. *Geriatrics*, 13:29–31, 1958.

Gastaut, H., and Meyer, J. S. (Eds.). *Cerebral anoxia and electroencephalogram.* Springfield, Ill.: Charles C. Thomas, 1961.

Gibbs, F. A., and Gibbs, E. L. *Atlas of electroencephalography.* Vol. I. *Methodology and Controls.* (2nd ed.) Cambridge, Mass.: Addison-Wesley, 1950.

Harvald, B. EEG in old age. *Acta Psychiatrica and Neurologica Scandinavica*, 33:193–196, 1958.

Henry, C. L. Electroencephalograms of normal children. *Monographs on Social Research in Child Development*, 9, No. 3, 71 pp., 1944.

Hill, D., and Parr, G. (Eds.). *Electroencephalography.* London: Macdonald, 1950.

Hoch, P. H., and Kubis, J. Electroencephalographic studies in organic psychoses. *American Journal of Psychiatry*, 98:404–408, 1941.

Inglis, J. Psychological investigations of cognitive deficit in elderly psychiatric patients. *Psychology Bulletin*, 54:197–214, 1958.

Jones, H. E. Intelligence and problem-solving. In Birren, J. E. (Ed.), *Handbook of aging and the individual.* Chicago: University of Chicago Press, 1959.

Kleemeier, R. W., Justiss, W. A., Rich, T. A., and Jones, A. L. Intellectual changes in the senium: Death and the IQ. Paper presented at the American Psychological Association, New York, September, 1961.

Klove, H. Relationship of differential electroencephalographic patterns to distribution of Wechsler-Bellevue scores. *Neurology*, 9:871–876, 1959.

Knott, J. R., Friedman, H., and Bardsley, R. Some electroencephalographic correlates of intelligence in eight-year and twelve-year-old children. *Journal of Experimental Psychology*, 30:380–391, 1942.

Kooi, K. A., and Hovey, B. Alterations in mental function and paroxysmal cerebral activity. *American Medical Association Archives of Neurology and Psychiatry*, 78:264–271, 1957.

Lassen, N. A., Feinberg, I., and Lane, M. H. Bilateral studies of cerebral oxygen uptake in young and aged normal subjects and in patients with organic dementia. *Journal of Clinical Investigation*, 39:491–500, 1960.

Lindsley, D. B. Electrical potentials of the brain in children and adults. *Journal of Genetic Psychology*, 19:285–306, 1938.

Luce, R. A., Jr., and Rothschild, D. The correlation of electroencephalographic and clinical observations in psychiatric patients over 65. *Journal of Gerontology*, 8:167–172, 1953.

McAdam, W., and Robinson, R. A. Senile intellectual deterioration and the electroencephalogram: A quantitative correlation. *Journal of Mental Science*, 102:819–825, 1956.

McAdam, W., and Robinson, R. A. Psychiatric and electroencephalographic studies in socially adjusted old people. *Journal of Mental Science*, 104:840–843, 1958.

McAdam, W., and Robinson, R. A. Diagnostic and prognostic value of the EEG in geriatric psychiatry. Paper presented at the Fifth Congressional International Association on Gerontology, San Francisco, August, 1960.

Mundy-Castle, A. C. Electrophysiological correlates of intelligence. *Journal of Personality*, 26:184–199, 1958.

Mundy-Castle, A. C. Central excitability in the aged. Paper presented at the Fifth Congressional International Association on Gerontology, San Francisco, August, 1960.

Mundy-Castle, A. C., Hurst, L. A., Beerstecher, D. M., and Prinsloo, T. The electroencephalogram in the senile psychoses. *EEG Clinical Neurophysiology*, 6:245–252, 1954.

Obrist, W. D. The electroencephalogram of normal aged adults. *EEG Clinical Neurophysiology*, 6:235–244, 1954.

Obrist, W. D. The electroencephalogram of healthy aged males. In NIMH Research Report, *Human aging: A biological and behavioral study*. Washington: Government Printing Office, 1963.

Obrist, W. D., and Bissell, L. F. The electroencephalogram of aged patients with cardiac and cerebral vascular disease. *Journal of Gerontology*, 10:315–330, 1955.

Obrist, W. D., and Henry, C. E. Electroencephalographic findings in aged psychiatric patients. *Journal of Nervous and Mental Disease*, 126:254–267, 1958.

Shagass, C. An attempt to correlate the occipital alpha frequency of the electroencephalogram with performance on a mental ability test. *Journal of Experimental Psychology*, 36:88–92, 1945.

Silverman, A. J., Busse, E. W., and Barnes, R. H. Studies in the process of aging: Electroencephalographic findings in 400 elderly subjects. *EEG Clinical Neurophysiology*, 7:67–74, 1955.

Silverman, A. J., Busse, E. W., Barnes, R. H., Frost, L. L., and Thaler, M. B. Studies on the processes of aging: 4. Physiologic influences on psychic functioning in elderly people. *Geriatrics*, 3:370–376, 1953.

Stoller, A. Slowing of the alpha rhythm of the electroencephalogram and its association with mental deterioration and epilepsy. *Journal of Mental Science*, 95:972–984, 1949.

Thaler, M. B. Relationships among Wechsler, Weigl, Rorschach, EEG findings, and abstract-concrete behavior in a group of normal aged subjects. *Journal of Gerontology*, 11:404–409, 1956.

Turton, E. C., and Warren, P. K. G. Dementia: A clinical and EEG study of 274 patients over the age of 60. *Journal of Mental Science*, 106:1493–1500, 1960.

Wechsler, D. *The measurement of adult intelligence*. (2nd. ed.) Baltimore: Williams and Wilkins, 1944.

Wechsler, D. *Manual for the Wechsler Adult Intelligence Scale*. New York: Psychological Corporation, 1955.

Wechsler, D. *The measurement and appraisal of adult intelligence*. (4th ed.) Baltimore: Williams and Wilkins, 1958.

Weiner, H., and Schuster, D. B. The electroencephalogram in dementia: Some preliminary observations and correlations. *EEG Clinical Neurophysiology*, 8:479–488, 1956.

# Electrocortical Reactivity and Learning in the Elderly*
## Larry W. Thompson and Stuart Wilson

It has been well established that various behavioral capacities undergo progressive decline with the onset of senescence. This is particularly apparent in tasks involving psychomotor skills (Gerard, 1959; Welford, 1959), the development of new associations or problem-solving techniques (Je-

* Reprinted by permission from the *Journal of Gerontology*, 21:45–51, 1966.

rome, 1959; Jones, 1959), and the utilization of "adaptive abilities" as contrasted to tasks measuring principally "stored information" (Reed & Reitan, 1963a).

Progressive changes in the EEG from young adulthood to senescence have also been repeatedly reported and are discussed fully in a recent review (Obrist & Busse, 1965). Briefly, the most common finding in normal elderly persons is a general slowing of the alpha rhythm. The incidence of fast activity, however, is also found in greater preponderance. Focal disturbances, particularly in the temporal lobe region, are apparent in 30 to 40 percent of community volunteers over age 60. Diffuse slowing is seen principally in hospitalized patients and community subjects above 80 years. The extent of these EEG changes reflects increased individual differences among elderly individuals, such that some individuals of advanced age have tracings comparable to young adults, while others in early senescence may have considerable age-related changes in their EEG.

In keeping with the notion that observed behavioral deficits seen in the elderly can be attributed to central nervous system (CNS) changes (Gerard, 1959; Reed & Reitan, 1963b; Reitan, 1955; Welford, 1959), the question of a relationship between EEG variations and intellectual impairment is often posed. Such relationships have been consistently found in elderly persons who have undergone considerable deterioration (Hoch & Kubis, 1941; Jaffe & Reisman, 1960; Liberson & Seguin, 1945; McAdam & McClatchey, 1952; McAdam & Robinson, 1956; Mundy-Castle, Hurst, Beerstecher, & Prinsloo, 1954). Comparable findings, however, have not been as convincingly demonstrated in community subjects or mentally normal persons living in residential homes (Barnes, Busse, & Friedman, 1956; Busse, Barnes, Friedman, & Kelty, 1956; Mundy-Castle, 1962; Obrist, Busse, Eisdorfer, & Kleemeier, 1962). This may be due in part to the limitations of the measures generally used. The standard clinical evaluation of the EEG does not lend itself to quantification and therefore may not reflect subtle changes in CNS functioning. Similarly, the standardized indices of intellectual function typically employed may not be sufficiently refined to provide a reliable estimate of the minimal, albeit substantial, impairment in normal community subjects.

In line with these limitations, the possibility that decreased cortical reactivity, as measured by the EEG, may be associated with intellectual changes in the elderly has been overlooked. Cortical reactivity refers to the effect of a stimulus on the spontaneous electrocortical activity in the EEG. The presentation of a novel stimulus during eye closure frequently results in desynchronization of alpha activity with an increase in low voltage fast waves, and this effect varies for different individuals. The concept that this response may provide a useful index of cerebral dysfunction was introduced by Liberson (1944). Wells (1962, 1963) has further reported that

brain-damaged persons evidenced less EEG reactivity and became habit-
uated more quickly than normal controls. Decreased EEG reactivity has
also been reported in elderly subjects (Andermann & Stoller, 1961; Verdeaux, Verdeaux, & Turmel, 1961). A comparison of arousal responses to
photic stimulation in healthy young and old community volunteers of
superior intelligence also revealed decreased EEG reactivity in the old
(Obrist, 1965; Wilson, 1962).

The findings in the preceding studies suggest that a decreased electrocortical response to sensory input, as reflected in the "reactive EEG," could
conceivably be associated with a decline in behavioral functioning and that
such a relationship may be apparent in the absence of substantial deterioration. The present study was designed specifically to investigate the relationship between changes in the EEG frequency spectrum during photic stimulation and performance on a paired-associates learning task in elderly
persons. The hypothesis was made that subjects with decreased learning
ability would demonstrate lower cortical reactivity responses (i.e., less
desynchronization and low voltage fast waves apparent following stimulation) than subjects with more adequate learning ability.


Materials and Methods

### EEG Procedure

Subjects were comfortably seated in a dimly illuminated sound chamber
during the entire procedure. A Grass electroencephalograph was used to
obtain bipolar tracings from the prefrontal, precentral, anterior temporal
and parieto-occipital regions. Recordings were made at increased paper
speed (6 cm. per second) and augmented gain (1 mm. = 10 v) during the
following three conditions:
1. *A rest control condition* of 200-second duration. One hundred seconds
of EEG were recorded at the beginning and end of the procedures, while
the subject was relaxed with eyes closed.
2. *An eyes open period* lasting 100 seconds. Following the rest control, the
subject was requested to open his eyes and look at a red cross on the
chamber wall, five feet in front of him. He was asked to continue looking at
the cross and blink normally until told to stop.
3. *Repetitive stimulation.* A 75-watt DC light in a white reflector was
placed 24 inches from the subject at eye level. The subject was informed
that the light would come on from time to time and that he was to keep his
eyes closed. Ten seconds after eye closure, the light was turned on. It
remained on for 3 seconds and off for 9, for a total of 20 trials. The
duration of the light stimulus and interstimulus interval was controlled

automatically by a Lafayette timer. A marker channel on the EEG recorded the onset and termination of each stimulus presentation.

Manual frequency analysis, reported in this study, was confined to the parieto-occipital leads. The frequency of each wave which had a rising surface of 2 mm. or more, and which returned at least half the distance to baseline was measured. Measurements were made on six 3-second segments of tracing, randomly selected from the rest control condition. During the eyes open condition six 3-second sections were selected at 15-second intervals. Each of the twenty 3-second stimulus segments in the repetitive stimulation condition was also analyzed. A split half reliability check of this method of analysis yielded a correlation coefficient of .85.

## Behavioral Testing

Following the EEG, subjects were administered an abbreviated WAIS including three verbal and two performance subtests. These were: information, similarities, vocabulary, digit symbol, and picture completion. These subtests were selected because of their reported high correlation with the full scale score in a 70 or 74 age sample (Eisdorfer & Cohen, 1961).

At a later date, each subject returned to the laboratory and participated in a paired-associates learning task. He was required to learn a list of eight pairs of words selected from recent norms compiled by Russel and Jenkins (1954). Four pairs were selected for high association value and four for low association value. The pairs were presented at 3-second intervals on a Gerbrand memory drum. Four different arrangements of the pairs were used sequaciously to prevent a position effect in the learning. The learning task was continued to a criterion of two errorless trials. The data are reported in terms of number of trials taken to learn the list to criterion level. Subjects were divided into subgroups of good and poor learners depending upon their performance.

## Subjects

Fifteen men (63 to 85 years) were selected from a group of community volunteers, living in or around Durham, North Carolina, who are seen regularly in a longitudinal research program. An attempt was made to select high-level persons, homogeneous with respect to age, socioeconomic class, intellectual level, and occupational classification, but different with regard to learning ability. All except one subject had at least three years of college; the sample included retired professors, engineers, ministers, business executives, and one diplomat. Table 4–7 lists the means and standard deviations for WAIS IQ scores, age, and education for the good and poor learner subgroups. Although good health was not included in the criteria for selection, all subjects were relatively healthy with only mild complaints of the usual chronic illnesses. None was acutely ill, and none was taking any prescribed medications at the time of testing.

Results

Table 4–8 shows the results of good and poor learner groups on the paired-associates learning task. These data are in agreement with the concept that learning ability declines differentially in the elderly. It can be seen that the fastest learner in the poor group took twice as long as the slowest learner in the good group. The marked discrepancy between the two groups cannot be explained readily in terms of intellectual, educational, or age variables. Table 4–7 indicates that there are no significant differences between good and poor learners on any of these measures.

Figure 4–5 shows the distribution of select frequencies between 5 (or less) and 30 cps for the rest control condition. The percentage number of waves in each frequency is reported for both good and poor learner groups. Although there were no statistically significant differences, these data suggest a general shift to the slower frequencies in the resting record of the poor learners. The peak frequency was 10 cps for the good learners and 9 cps for the poor. There was also some indication that the good learners had a greater abundance of waves above 14 cps.

Figure 4–6 illustrates the EEG activity in three different frequency bands (beta > 12 cps, alpha 8–12 cps; slow waves < 8 cps) during the resting control, eyes open, and photic stimulation conditions. The data are reported as the mean number of waves per second. It is evident that overall, the number of beta waves increased as a result of stimulation

Table 4–7. *Comparison of good and poor learners on WAIS IQ scores, age, and education.*

|  | Good learners (N = 7) | | Poor learners (N = 8) | | |
|---|---|---|---|---|---|
|  | Mean | SD | Mean | SD | t ratio |
| Verbal IQ | 147.14 | 9.51 | 140.75 | 9.77 | 1.28 |
| Performance IQ | 124.28 | 7.37 | 122.12 | 6.01 | 0.18 |
| Full Scale IQ | 139.71 | 9.06 | 134.50 | 6.02 | 1.20 |
| Age | 77.41 | 7.94 | 75.70 | 6.65 | 0.40 |
| Education[a] | 16.00 | 2.38 | 16.75 | 1.77 | 0.70 |

[a] Reported as number of academic years in school.

Table 4–8. *Total trials to criterion in the paired-associate words task for the good and poor learners.*

| Good learners | Poor learners |
|---|---|
| 6 | 28 |
| 8 | 44 |
| 5 | 30[a] |
| 8 | 19 |
| 9 | 26 |
| 9 | 36[b] |
| 6 | 25 |
|  | 18 |

[a] Subject learned 6 pairs and refused to continue.
[b] Subject learned 7 pairs before stopping.

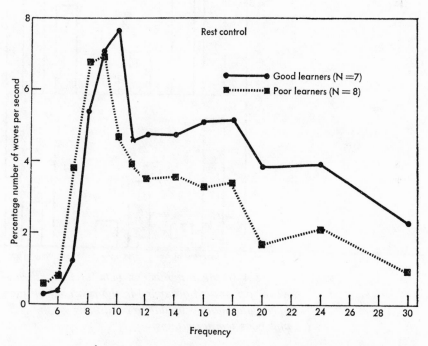

Figure 4–5. *Comparison of EEG frequency distributions for good and poor learners during the rest control condition. The curves represent the percentage number of waves between 5 (or less) and 30 cps which appeared in the parieto-occipital area.*

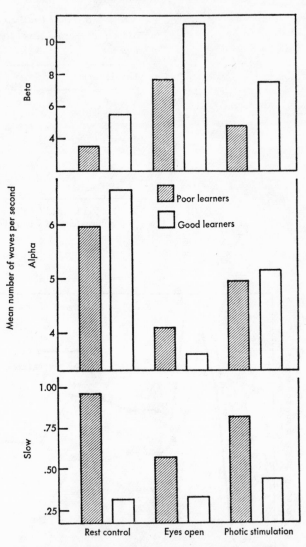

Figure 4–6. *Mean number of beta, alpha, and slow waves per second occurring in the rest control, eyes open, and photic stimulation conditions for the good and poor learner groups.*

($F = 13.45$, $df = 2/26$, $p < .001$) while the number of alpha waves decreased ($F = 21.26$, $df = 2/26$, $p < .001$) for both good and poor learners. The greatest increase in beta activity occurred during the eyes open condition, but the difference between the rest control and photic stimulation was also significant at the 0.001 level. Similarly, the greatest reduction of alpha occurred during eyes open, but both the eyes open and the photic stimulation conditions showed significantly less alpha waves than the rest control ($p < .001$ level for both). The overall difference in number of slow waves for the three conditions was significant at the 0.05 level ($F = 3.60$, $df = 2/26$). This was due principally to the decrease in slow waves during eyes open for the poor learner group.

A differential effect of stimulation for the two learning groups was also

Table 4–9. *Mean number of beta, alpha, and slow waves per second during rest control, eyes open, and photic stimulation conditions for both good and poor learners.*

|  | Good learners | Poor learners | $F$[a] ratio |
|---|---|---|---|
| Rest control |  |  |  |
| Beta waves | 5.49 | 3.67 | 2.86 |
| Alpha waves | 6.76 | 5.92 | 1.20 |
| Slow waves | 0.31 | 0.98 | 5.20* |
| Eyes open |  |  |  |
| Beta waves | 10.83 | 7.46 | 6.05* |
| Alpha waves | 3.49 | 4.08 | 1.75 |
| Slow waves | 0.33 | 0.56 | 1.08 |
| Photic stimulation |  |  |  |
| Beta waves | 7.37 | 4.67 | 4.95* |
| Alpha waves | 5.16 | 4.93 | 1.63 |
| Slow waves | 0.43 | 0.81 | 2.21 |

[a] Mean differences were tested by analysis of covariance using WAIS Full Scale IQ as the uncontrolled variable.
 * $p < .05$ ($df = 1/12$).

indicated by the data reported in Figure 4–6 and Table 4–9. A comparison of differences by $t$ tests revealed that the good learners had significantly more beta waves during the eyes open and photic stimulation conditions. Regarding the alpha waves, there were no significant differences between good and poor learners during any of the conditions. More slow waves were apparent in the poor learner group during all three conditions, but this difference also was not statistically significant. Since it was possible that the differences in fast activity might have been a function of IQ variations rather than differences in learning ability, an analysis of covariance was performed for the three different wave bands in each condition, by using intelligence as the predictor variable. The $F$ ratios between the adjusted mean squares for within and between groups are reported in Table 4–9. It can be seen that the good learners still have significantly more fast waves during the eyes open and photic stimulation conditions than the poor

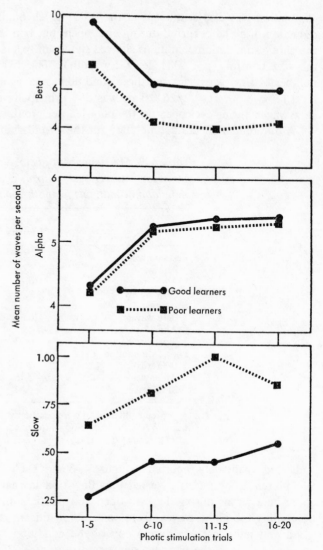

Figure 4–7. *Variations in EEG activity during repetitive photic stimulation. Mean number of beta, alpha, and slow waves per second during four blocks of five stimulations each are reported for both good and poor learners.*

learners. It is also of interest that, when the effects of intelligence are controlled, the poor learners have significantly more slow waves during the rest control than the good learners.

During photic stimulation, the rate of adaptation was comparable for both learning groups. Figure 4–7 illustrates the mean number of beta, alpha, and slow waves per second for good and poor learners during photic stimulation. The 20 photic stimulations have been grouped into four blocks of 5 stimulations each. Although the good learners have more fast waves, the rate of change as a function of stimulation was similar for both groups. An analysis of variance revealed that the interaction between learning groups and decrease in beta with continued stimulation was not significant ($F = 1.03$, $df = 3/39$). Similarly, the interaction effect between learning groups and alpha changes with stimulation was not significant ($F = 1.65$, $df = 3/39$). For the slow waves, however, the poor learners showed a marked decrease during the early trials and a greater increase with repeated stimulations than was seen in the good learner group ($F = 8.17$, $df = 3/39$, $p < .001$).

## Discussion

The results demonstrate an overall increase in beta activity and decrease in alpha activity during eye opening and photic stimulation. Such variations in EEG activity due to stimulation are somewhat comparable to EEG arousal responses produced by sensory stimuli (Lindsley, 1958; Sharpless & Jasper, 1956) or by direct stimulation of the reticular system (Moruzzi & Magoun, 1949). There was also evidence of a differential effect in the EEG activity of the good and poor learner groups. In the rest control records the poor learners tended to have more slow waves than the good learners, accompanied by a suggested shift to a slower alpha frequency as well as the appearance of decreased beta activity. During eye opening and photic stimulation, the good learners had significantly more beta waves than the poor learners. Alpha changes resulting from the stimulation conditions were comparable for both groups.

The significant differences between good and poor learners in the beta activity raises the question of a relationship between cortical arousal and learning ability, such that the good learners appear to be more reactive to sensory input than the poor learners. This finding is in accord with recent theoretical speculations concerning the functional significance of the reticular system (Lindsley, 1958; Jasper, 1958; Magoun, 1958). Cortical arousal via the reticular activating system is believed to facilitate the "integration" or "elaboration" of information being transmitted from sensory-end-organs or other cortical areas, by influencing the excitability level of the cortex. That such a system may underlie complex psychological processes like sustained attention or learning ability is understandable. There is even some suggestion that these excitatory influences must reach a relatively high level before associative bonds can be developed (Thompson & Obrist, 1964). All things considered, one might expect that subjects who have larger arousal responses to stimulation may achieve a more optimal cortical excitability level, which in turn produces increased attentive processes and a more rapid development of learned connections.

While the significant increase in fast activity in the good learner group was in the expected direction, the similarity in alpha activity between the two groups is not consistent with the above interpretation. Failure to find alpha differences may be partially a function of the method of analysis, which reflects primarily the number of waves within specific frequencies independent of amplitude changes.

Since alpha and beta activity tend to vary inversely, it might be argued that the greater change in fast activity seen in the good learners may be due to a masking effect of the alpha rhythm. The good learners may have had significantly more fast waves in their EEGs even during the rest control, but this difference became apparent only when alpha was attenuated by stimulation. The considerably, although not significantly, larger amount of beta in the good learner group even during the rest control in combination with an absence of an interaction effect between learning ability and alpha blocking offers support for this argument. The present system of analysis, however, was not sufficiently refined to measure fast waves which may have been superimposed on the higher amplitude alpha rhythms. Nevertheless, the possibility of differences in beta during the rest control is interesting in view of studies reporting an absence or significant decrease of fast rhythms in elderly persons who show signs of deterioration (Noel, 1952; Mengoli, 1952; Mundy-Castle et al., 1954; Barnes et al., 1956; Obrist & Henry, 1958; Frey & Sjögren, 1959). To the extent one considers poor learning ability as an indication of impairment, the present data are consistent with these findings and offer some support to the concept advanced by Obrist and Busse (1965) that the presence of fast activity is a favorable sign in the elderly EEG.

The tendency for increased slow waves in the poor learner group during rest control may be accounted for in large part by variations in alpha frequency. The trend toward a general slowing of alpha frequency in the poor learners may result in a situation where a greater number of waves on the slow end of the alpha distribution fall within the slow wave band ($< 8$ cps). If such were the case, presentation of any stimulus which blocks alpha would most likely affect slow activity as defined in this study. A comparison of alpha and slow waves in Figures 4–6 and 4–7 indicates parallel variations of these measures in the poor learner group. Furthermore, a decrease in slow activity during stimulation was not apparent in the good learner group.

The EEG differences which emerge between the two groups as a function of stimulation are in agreement with Liberson's (1944) position, in that the "dynamic" aspects of the EEG increased its association with measures of behavioral decrement in the elderly. This procedure may be particularly applicable where the so-called age-related changes are yet minimal, with little discernible deficit upon confrontation by gross measures. The subjects in this study were all high-level professional-type people who were active in community affairs and showed no evidence of severe impairment on psychological tests. That there were differences, however, became readily apparent in the learning task. A somewhat parallel observation indicated that the resting EEGs of these two groups were comparable on gross inspection; the more quantitative analysis yielded differences which were suggestive but not significant. Introduction of stimulation techniques, however, enhanced the relationship between EEG variables and a complex behavioral task. The fact that both the behavioral and electrophysiological differences show up only under special circumstances suggests that the present measures may be more sensitive to the subtle changes occurring in the early stages of a deteriorative process.

Although the present study reports significant findings, these data are merely suggestive and should be considered with caution. In view of the limited number of subjects as well as the homogeneous nature of the group, it does not seem feasible to make generalizations based on the obtained relationships at the present time. Additional studies involving other socioeconomic and intellectual levels and utilizing more refined methods of analysis are essential before any final conclusions can be made.

## Summary

The relationship between cortical reactivity and verbal learning was studied in 15 elderly subjects of superior intelligence. Bipolar tracings from the parieto-occipital region were recorded, and a manual frequency analysis was completed on the tracing during rest control, eyes open, and repetitive photic stimulation. In the last condition a light was turned on for 3 seconds and off for 9 seconds for 20 trials, during eye closure. Subjects also learned eight pairs of words by the paired-associates method and were divided into two groups according to the number of trials required to reach criterion. There was a significant increase in fast waves and decrease in alpha during eyes open and photic stimulation for both groups. A comparison of learning and EEG measures indicated that the good learners had significantly more fast waves during eyes open and photic stimulation than the poor learners. The number of alpha waves was comparable for both groups during all three conditions. The data suggested that cortical arousal level may be associated with learning ability in the elderly. Consideration of increased low-voltage fast waves as a favorable sign in the elderly EEG was also raised.

## References

Andermann, K., and Stoller, A. EEG patterns in hospitalized and non-hospitalized aged (abstract). *Electroencephalography and Clinical Neurophysiology*, 13:319, 1961.

Barnes, R. H., Busse, E. W., and Friedman, E. L. The psychological functioning of aged individuals with normal and abnormal electroencephalograms: II. A study of hospitalized individuals. *Journal of Nervous and Mental Disease*, 124:585–593, 1956.

Busse, E. W., Barnes, R. H., Friedman, E. L., and Kelty, E. J. Psychological functioning of aged individuals with normal and abnormal electroencephalograms: I. A study of non-hospitalized community volunteers. *Journal of Nervous and Mental Disease*, 124:135–141, 1956.

Eisdorfer, C., and Cohen, L. D. The generality of the WAIS standardization for the aged: A regional comparison. *Journal of Abnormal and Social Psychology*, 62:520–527, 1961.

Frey, T. S., and Sjögren, H. The electroencephalogram in elderly persons suffering from neuropsychiatric disorders. *Acta Psychiatrica and Neurologica Scandinavica*, 34:438–450, 1959.

Gerard, R. W. Aging and organization. In Birren, J. E. (Ed.), *Handbook of aging and the individual*. Chicago: University of Chicago Press, 1959.

Hoch, P., and Kubis, J. Electroencephalographic studies in organic psychoses. *American Journal of Psychiatry*, 98:404–408, 1941.

Jaffe, R., and Reisman, E. EEG and mental status: A correlative study in 100 aged subjects (abstract). *Electroencephalography and Clinical Neurophysiology*, 12:245, 1960.

Jasper, H. H. Reticular-cortical systems and theories of the integrative action of the brain. In Harlow, H. F., and Woolsey, C. N. (Eds.), *Biological and biochemical bases of behavior*. Madison, Wis.: University of Wisconsin Press, 1958.

Jerome, E. A. Age and learning: Experimental studies. In Birren, J. E. (Ed.), *Handbook of aging and the individual*. Chicago: University of Chicago Press, 1959.

Jones, H. E. Intelligence and problem-solving. In Birren, J. E. (Ed.), *Handbook of aging and the individual*. Chicago: University of Chicago Press, 1959.

Liberson, W. T. Functional electroencephalography in mental disorders. *Disorders of the Nervous System*, 5:357–364, 1944.

Liberson, W. T., and Seguin, C. A. Brain waves and clinical features in arteriosclerotic and senile mental patients. *Psychosomatic Medicine*, 7:30–35, 1945.

Lindsley, D. B. Psychophysiology and perception. In *Current trends in the description and analysis of behavior*. Pittsburgh: University of Pittsburgh Press, 1958.

McAdam, W., and McClatchey, W. T. The electroencephalogram in aged patients of a mental hospital. *Journal of Mental Science*, 98:711–715, 1952.

McAdam, W., and Robinson, R. A. Senile intellectual deterioration and the electroencephalogram: A quantitative correlation. *Journal of Mental Science,* 102:819–825, 1956.

Magoun, H. W. *The waking brain.* Springfield, Ill.: Charles C Thomas, 1958.

Mengoli, G. L'elettroencefalogramma nei vecchi. *Review of Neurology,* 22:166–193, 1952.

Moruzzi, G., and Magoun, H. W. Brain stem reticular formation and activation of the EEG. *Electroencephalography and Clinical Neurophysiology,* 1:455–473, 1949.

Mundy-Castle, A. C. Central excitability in the aged. In Blumenthal, H. T. (Ed.), *Aging around the world.* Vol. 4. *Medical and clinical aspects of aging.* New York: Columbia University Press, 1962.

Mundy-Castle, A. C., Hurst, L. A., Beerstecher, D. M., and Prinsloo, T. The electroencephalogram in the senile psychoses. *Electroencephalography and Clinical Neurophysiology,* 6:245–252, 1954.

Noel, M. G. L'EEG dans Parteriosclerose cerebrale. *Review of Neurology,* 87:198–199, 1952.

Obrist, W. D. Electroencephalographic approach to age changes in response speed. In Welford, A. T., and Birren, J. E. (Eds.), *Behavior, aging and the nervous system.* Springfield, Ill.: Charles C Thomas, 1965.

Obrist, W. D., and Busse, E. W. The electroencephalogram and old age. In Wilson, W. P. (Ed.), *Applications of electroencephalography in psychiatry.* Durham, N.C.: Duke University Press, 1965.

Obrist, W. D., Busse, E. W., Eisdorfer, C., and Kleemeier, R. W. Relation of the electroencephalogram to intellectual function in senescence. *Journal of Gerontology,* 17:197–206, 1962.

Obrist, W. D., and Henry, C. E. Electroencephalographic frequency analysis of aged psychiatric patients. *Electroencephalography and Clinical Neurophysiology,* 10:621–632, 1958.

Reed, H. B. C., Jr., and Reitan, R. M. Changes in psychological test performance associated with the normal aging process. *Journal of Gerontology,* 18:271–274, 1963. (a)

Reed, H. B. C., Jr., and Reitan, R. M. A comparison of the effects of the normal aging process with the effects of organic brain damage on adaptive abilities. *Journal of Gerontology,* 18:177–179, 1963. (b)

Reitan, R. M. The distribution according to age of a psychologic measure dependent upon organic brain functions. *Journal of Gerontology,* 10:338–340, 1955.

Russel, W. A., and Jenkins, J. J. The complete Minnesota norms for responses to one hundred words from the Kent-Rosanoff word association test. In *Studies on the role of language and behavior.* Technical Report No. 11. Minneapolis: University of Minnesota Press, 1954.

Sharpless, S., and Jasper, H. H. Habituation of the arousal reaction. *Brain,* 79:655–680, 1956.

Thompson, L. W., and Obrist, W. D. EEG correlates of verbal learning and overlearning. *Electroencephalography and Clinical Neurophysiology,* 16:332–342, 1964.

Verdeaux, G., Verdeaux, J., and Turmel, J. Etude statistique de la fréquence et de la réactivité des electroencephalogrammes chez les sujets agés. *Journal of the Canadian Psychiatric Association,* 6:28–36, 1961.

Welford, A. T. Psychomotor performance. In Birren, J. R. (Ed.), *Handbook of aging and the individual.* Chicago: University of Chicago Press, 1959.

Wells, C. E. Response of alpha waves to light in neurologic disease. *Archives of Neurology,* 6:478–491, 1962.

Wells, C. E. Alpha wave responsiveness to light in man. In Glaser, G. H. (Ed.), *EEG and behavior.* New York: Basic Books, 1963.

Wilson, S. Electrocortical reactivity in young and aged adults. Doctoral dissertation, George Peabody College, 1962.

# Cerebral Ischemia and the Senescent Electroencephalogram*  *Walter D. Obrist*

There is considerable evidence that the electroencephalogram undergoes changes in later life, notably a shift to slower frequencies. It is also well established that cerebral anoxia (reduction of oxygen) and ischemia (blood deficiency) are associated with a slowing down of electrocortical activity, which in many respects resembles the EEG alterations commonly found in old age.

The wide occurrence of cerebral vascular disease among elderly people has been described by Dr. Simonson in introducing this symposium. The high metabolic rate of the brain and its dependence on a constant supply of oxygen have been emphasized by Dr. Schmidt. Given these facts, plus the known effect of anoxia on electrocortical activity, it is not unreasonable to expect that EEG alterations in old people are related to cerebral ischemia. The purpose of the present paper is to discuss the possible role of ischemia in producing senescent brain wave changes and to evaluate the extent to which the EEG might be useful in detecting cerebral vascular insufficiency in this age group. . . .

## The Senescent Electroencephalogram

In 1941, Pauline Davis reported the presence of a slow alpha rhythm and delta waves in the EEGs of elderly psychiatric patients. She suggested that the senescent EEG undergoes a shift toward the slow end of the frequency spectrum relative to young adult standards. Berger (1933) had previously noted similar changes in patients with senile dementia, but regarded them as purely pathological, denying the existence of an age trend. Subsequent research has confirmed Davis's hypothesis that the EEG becomes slower in old age, while at the same time supporting the view of Berger that mental deterioration is an important correlate of such changes.

Slowing of the dominant alpha rhythm is perhaps the most common finding in senescence, where it occurs as a function of both age and mental

---

* Reprinted by permission from *Cerebral Ischemia*, compiled and edited by Simonson, E., and McGavack, T. H., Springfield, Ill.: Charles C Thomas, 1964, pp. 71–98. Parts of this article reviewing other research have been deleted.—*Editor.*

status. In comparison with the young adult average of 10.0 to 10.5 cps, the mean alpha rate of mentally normal old subjects is significantly lower, reaching 9.0 cps around age 70 and 8.5 cps after age 80 (Obrist, 1954; Mundy-Castle, Hurst, Beerstecher, & Prinsloo, 1954; Friedlander, 1958). The decline is even greater among aged psychiatric patients where the frequency may be as slow as 7 cps (Sheridan, Yeager, Oliver, & Simon, 1955; Obrist & Henry, 1958b; Frey & Sjögren, 1959). Such slow alpha rhythms are often interrupted by theta waves, which give the tracing an irregular appearance. In very old or deteriorated individuals, the alpha rhythm may drop out completely, being replaced by diffuse theta (4–7 cps) or delta (1–3 cps) activity. These cross-sectional findings have been sub-stantiated by longitudinal observations (Obrist, Henry, & Justiss, 1961).

Individuals differ widely in the degree to which their EEGs manifest senescent changes, so that some subjects over age 80 have tracings indistin-guishable from young adults, whereas others only 60 years old show pronounced deviations. . . .

Although small but definite EEG changes have been observed among relatively healthy old subjects living in the community, such alterations do not appear to be correlated with mental function (Busse, Barnes, Fried-man, & Kelty, 1956; Obrist, 1963). In contrast, institutionalized subjects residing in hospitals or old-age homes show greater EEG deviations that are significantly related to intellectual impairment (Barnes, Busse, & Fried-man, 1956; Obrist, Busse, Eisdorfer, & Kleemeier, 1962). Both a slow alpha rhythm and the occurrence of diffuse theta or delta waves are associated with intellectual deterioration, as measured by standard psycho-logical tests or psychiatric ratings. In aged psychiatric patients, there is a high correlation between the amount of diffuse slow activity and severity of organic dementia (Mundy-Castle et al., 1954; McAdam & Robinson, 1956; Weiner & Schuster, 1956), which may be helpful in differentiating chronic brain syndrome from functional disorders (Liberson & Seguin, 1945; Luce & Rothschild, 1953; Obrist & Henry, 1958a). Both prognosis and longevity are also correlated with EEG findings in mental hospital patients (Pampig-lione & Post, 1958; McAdam & Robinson, 1962).

Fast beta rhythms of 20–30 cps are present to a variable degree in about half of all elderly subjects, where they are usually maximum over the frontal region. Such activity is clearly a development of middle life that persists into early senescence but gradually drops out in advanced old age (Gibbs & Gibbs, 1950; Silverman, Busse, & Barnes, 1955; Maggs & Turton, 1956). Beta rhythms are inversely related to intellectual impair-ment, in that they are less common in deteriorated seniles, tending to disappear as the frequency spectrum shifts to the slow side (Mundy-Castle et al., 1954; Obrist & Henry, 1958b; Frey & Sjögren, 1959). . . .

Focal slow activity is found in approximately one-third of normal control subjects after age 60 (Busse, Barnes, Silverman, Shy, Thaler, & Frost, 1954; Busse, Barnes, Friedman, & Kelty, 1956; Mundy-Castle, 1962). It occurs most commonly over the anterior temporal area but may extend to the adjacent posterior temporal and/or frontal regions. Temporal slow waves have also been observed in aged psychiatric patients (Barnes et al., 1956; Obrist & Henry, 1958a; Frey & Sjögren, 1959), although the incidence is somewhat lower due to the prevalence of more diffuse types of slow activity. About 40 percent of the foci are strictly left-sided, while another 30 to 40 percent are bilateral with a left-sided emphasis. Only a quarter of the cases have slow waves that are confined to, or maximum over, the right hemisphere. . . .

In contrast to diffuse slow wave abnormalities that bear a significant relation to intellectual impairment, focal disturbances over the temporal lobe tend to be clinically silent. No definitive correlations have been obtained with routine psychological or psychiatric assessments, even in severe cases with high amplitude delta waves (Silverman et al., 1955; Obrist et al., 1962; Mundy-Castle, 1962). Temporal slowing does not appear to be related to cerebral dominance, aphasia, or seizures. It is associated with intellectual deterioration only when the focus extends widely into adjacent areas, suggesting a mass action effect. The possibility of a highly specific psychological correlate remains an intriguing prospect for future research.


Relation of EEG to Circulatory Disorders in Old Age

Because of the prevalence of cardiovascular disease among elderly people, many of the studies on EEG and circulatory disorders cited above include subjects over 60 years of age. These reports, however, are based almost exclusively on clinic or hospital patients who have a specific neuro-logic or cardiovascular complaint. With few exceptions, the EEG examinations were conducted for the purpose of solving a particular diagnostic problem and were not intended to answer broader questions concerning age-related changes. Although such studies have clearly demonstrated a relationship between cerebral ischemia and EEG in patients with severe vascular disease, they shed very little light on the extent to which circulatory factors affect the EEG in "normal" old age or in patients whose primary complaint is mental deterioration. In spite of a growing literature on the descriptive aspects of geriatric EEG, there are surprisingly few papers dealing with the interrelationship of brain waves and circulatory variables as they relate to aging. The present discussion will touch upon some of the studies that have been concerned with this problem.

Several investigators have reported a relationship between alpha frequency and the presence or absence of arteriosclerosis. Although a slow alpha rhythm is a common finding among patients with cerebral vascular disease (Frantzen & Lennox-Buchthal, 1961), it also occurs in subjects who manifest arteriosclerosis in regions other than the brain. Obrist and Bissell (1955) noted that elderly people with arteriosclerotic heart disease were just as likely to show alpha slowing as individuals who had a history of stroke, and that both types of disorder gave significantly slower rhythms than healthy control subjects of the same age. The upper graph in Figure 4–8 (Group A) presents some findings from this study, based on residents of an old-age home. Arteriosclerosis was considered present when there were definite signs and symptoms of arterio- or atherosclerosis anywhere in the body, including vessels of the periphery, heart, or brain. Arteriosclerosis was considered absent on the basis of negative physical, neurologic, x-ray, and electrocardiographic data. It is apparent from the graph that more than half of the arteriosclerotics had occipital alpha frequencies below 8.5 cps, the lower limit for normal young adults, while none of the control subjects gave values this deviant.

The bottom graph in Figure 4–8 (Group B) shows the results from a later study by Obrist and co-workers (1963), in which a similar comparison was made of elderly people with and without arteriosclerosis. This group differs from the previous one in that the subjects were community volunteers who had been carefully selected for their apparent good health. When arteriosclerosis occurred, it was usually asymptomatic or subclinical, being detected only by extensive laboratory tests. In spite of a minimal degree of pathology, the arteriosclerotics had significantly lower alpha frequencies than the age-matched controls, although the difference is not as striking as in Group A. Interestingly, both Groups A and B yielded a significant correlation between alpha frequency and heart size, while Group A gave reliably lower frequencies for subjects with abnormal electrocardiograms. A relationship between EKG findings and brain waves in elderly people has been reported elsewhere (Morpurgo, Serra, & Mars, 1955). Funduscopic findings, however, are not consistently related to EEG (Mars, Morpurgo, & Serra, 1955).

The results in Figure 4–8 were interpreted as supporting the notion that very mild degrees of vascular disease may influence brain potentials. A certain correlation probably exists between the occurrence of extracranial and cerebral arteriosclerosis (Young, Gofman, Malamud, Simon, & Waters, 1956; Giongo & Mononi, 1959), so that cases with coronary or

peripheral vascular disease are more likely to develop cerebral hemodynamic alterations. This was suggested in Group B by nitrous oxide studies
of the cerebral circulation (Dastur, Lane, Hansen, Kety, Butler, Perlin, &
Sokoloff, 1963), which yielded a lower mean blood flow and higher
vascular resistance for the arteriosclerotic subgroup than for the healthy
controls. If it is true that asymptomatic degrees of arteriosclerosis are
capable of altering gross measures of cerebral blood flow (Sokoloff, 1966),
then it is not unreasonable to believe that they might also affect the EEG. It
should be pointed out, however, that only part of the age deviation in alpha
frequency is accounted for by the presence of diagnosable arteriosclerosis.

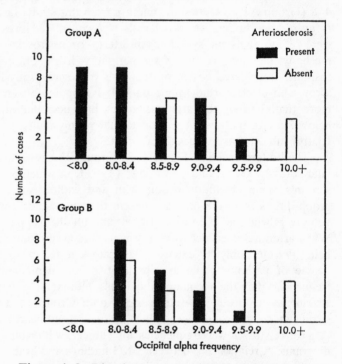

Figure 4–8. *Distributions of occipital alpha frequency
in subjects with and without clinical or laboratory evidence of arteriosclerosis. Group A: residents of an old-
age home (mean age, 77 years). Group B: healthy
community volunteers (mean age, 72 years). Subjects
with arteriosclerosis "present" and "absent" are approximately the same age within each group, but differ significantly with respect to alpha frequency (p <
.01 for both comparisons).*

The healthy control subjects in both Groups A and B have a mean frequency that is 0.5 to 1.0 cps below the young adult average. It is probable that factors other than cardiovascular disease are operating to produce these EEG changes.

Frequency is not the only characteristic of the alpha rhythm that may be related to circulatory disorders and aging. Gaches (1960) has shown that the spatial distribution and degree of synchronization of alpha activity increases with age and is uniformly higher in patients with various cardio-vascular diseases. He relates this finding to a tendency for greater synchronization in the early stages of anoxia and suggests that disturbances in cerebral blood flow may be a contributing factor. This interesting hypothesis deserves further investigation.

The high incidence of temporal lobe slow wave abnormalities in senescence has stimulated interest in their possible etiology. Bruens, Gastaut, and Giove (1960) studied a group of clinic patients with moderately severe temporal foci and found that 89 percent had neurologic findings suggestive of cerebral vascular disease. Hyperventilation, compression of the carotid artery, or inhalation of low oxygen exacerbated the slowing, while breathing $CO_2$ tended to reduce it. This was considered support for the hypothesis that "chronic" circulatory insufficiency is responsible for temporal lobe slowing in old age. The same authors noted that activation techniques sometimes uncover a previously unsuspected focus, which was regarded as a sign of "latent" circulatory insufficiency. They suggested that temporal foci in elderly people may be useful indicators of impending decompensation of the cerebral circulation. Although this study makes an important contribution, its applicability to the average old person is open to question due to the highly select nature of the sample. As noted earlier, approximately one-third of elderly community volunteers have temporal foci, but very few of them reveal neurologic impairment. Further investigation of "normal" aged subjects seems definitely indicated.

In line with these results are several studies pointing to the sensitivity of the elderly person's EEG to procedures that embarrass the cerebral circulation. Weiss and Froelich (1958) reported that 40 percent of elderly control subjects gave a positive slow wave response to combined tilting and carotid artery compression, compared with a general absence of response in young adults. A higher incidence of ischemic EEG responses in old age has also been observed by McBeath, Winston, and Friedlander (1961), who applied carotid compression to patients lacking clinical signs of vascular insufficiency. Loeb (1961) investigated carotid compression in "apparently normal" old people and found unilateral slowing in 25 percent of the cases. These studies would seem to indicate that latent cerebral vascular insufficiency is present in a fair proportion of elderly people who do not have specific neurologic complaints. In the case of low oxygen inhalation, however, Rossen, Simonson, and Baker (1961) obtained fewer EEG changes in healthy 60-year-old men than in normal young adults. They suggested that the healthy old brain may be less sensitive to anoxia but raised the possibility that their results might be due to uncontrolled variations in hypocapnia. The pronounced EEG changes evoked in patients with cerebral vascular disease (Meyer & Waltz, 1961; Gastaut, Bostem, Fernandez-Guardiola, Naquet, & Ribson, 1961) points to the need for more information on the average old person's response to low oxygen.

Because blood pressure is one of the major variables influencing cerebral blood flow, it is not surprising that several investigators have commented on its relationship to EEG. Harvald (1958) noted that severe diffuse slow activity was common among patients with cerebral arteriosclerosis but quite rare in elderly cases with hypertension. He regarded such slowing as a sign of diffuse ischemia and argued that its low incidence in hypertension indicated a good cerebral blood flow. Turton (1958) observed a tendency for aged psychiatric patients with low blood pressure to have abnormal EEGs, a finding that he attributed to cerebral circulatory disturbances.

A more thorough study of the relationship between blood pressure and EEG was undertaken by Obrist, Busse, and Henry (1961), who performed a statistical analysis on 494 elderly cases. They found no correlation between these variables in mentally normal old people but a highly significant relationship in hospitalized psychiatric patients. The incidence of normal EEGs among patients rose steadily as blood pressure increased, while the number of tracings with diffuse slow activity declined, the latter being more prevalent at lower pressures. Figure 4–9 presents some of these findings. The normal and focal tracings were combined because they revealed similar blood pressure trends. As evident from the bottom graph, patients with the highest 25 percent of the pressures (Level IV) had almost three times as many normal and focal tracings as those with the lowest 25 percent (Level I). The reverse was true for diffuse slow activity (theta and delta waves), which occurred maximally at low blood pressure levels. The small number of diffusely slow EEGs among the mentally normal controls accounts for the lack of correlation in the upper graph.

These results might be explained by the hypothesis that aged psychiatric patients have increased cerebral vascular resistance due to arteriosclerosis, which necessitates an elevated blood pressure in order to maintain adequate cerebral circulation and a normal EEG. Thus it might be speculated that failure to develop a compensatory rise in blood pressure with arteriosclerosis is an etiologic factor in diffuse EEG slowing. The negative findings on mentally normal old people might be attributed to lower

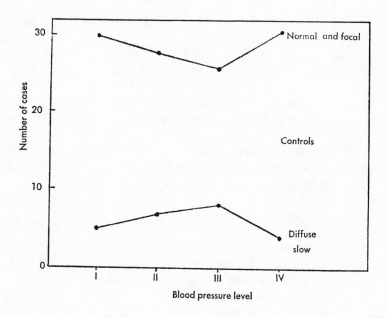

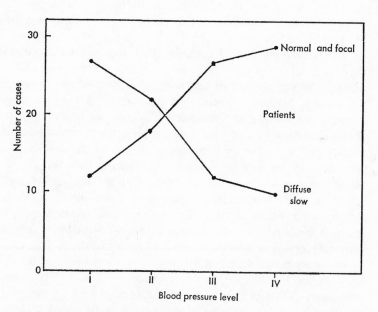

Figure 4–9. *Incidence of EEG findings as a function of blood pressure in elderly community volunteers (upper graph) and aged mental hospital patients (lower graph). Level I indicates the lowest 25 percent of the blood pressures; Level IV, the highest. Levels II and III represent intermediate quarters of the sample. The geometric mean of the systolic and diastolic values was used to determine blood pressure level.*

cerebral vascular resistance, where blood pressure is not as critical for the preservation of cerebral blood flow and EEG normality. It should be noted that the range of blood pressures in Figure 4–9 is not extreme; very few of the subjects would be regarded as having more than a mild hypo- or hypertension, with 90 percent of the systolic values lying between 110 and 200.

An attempt was made to assess the relative adequacy of cerebral blood flow in these subjects on the basis of information concerning blood pressure and vascular disease. Given the equation,

$$\text{Cerebral blood flow} = \frac{\text{Blood pressure}}{\text{Cerebral vascular resistance}},$$

the probability of a high or low cerebral blood flow might be inferred from (a) systemic blood pressure and (b) clinical evidence of peripheral, coronary, or cerebral vascular disease. The assumption was made that arteriosclerotic disease, regardless of its location in the body, is associated statistically with cerebral arteriosclerosis (Young et al., 1956) and increased cerebral vascular resistance (Sokoloff, 1966), so that higher blood pressures would be required, on the average, for the maintenance of adequate cerebral blood flow.

Approximately half of the subjects in this series showed unequivocal signs of arteriosclerosis based on x-ray, EKG, physical, and neurologic findings; the remaining half had minimal or no evidence of arteriosclerosis any place in the body. When blood pressure is plotted separately for each of these subgroups, an interesting difference is observed. Figure 4–10 shows that among control subjects the presence of arteriosclerosis is associated with a relative hypertension, and its absence with a low blood pressure level. In the case of psychiatric patients, however, the incidence of blood pressure among arteriosclerotics yields a bimodal distribution. Some arteriosclerotics have elevated pressures, while others have a tendency toward hypotension. It might be argued that individuals with low blood pressure in the presence of vascular disease are more likely to have reduced cerebral blood flow than patients with higher pressures. This interpretation is supported by the fact that 70 percent of the patients with both arteriosclerosis and low blood pressure have diffuse slow activity in their EEGs, while only 30 percent of the arteriosclerotics with an elevated pressure reveal such slowing. Because of the correlation between diffuse slow activity and chronic brain syndrome, these findings may have relevance for mental status. Patients with chronic brain syndrome in the present sample had significantly lower blood pressures than those with functional disorders. There is also some evidence that aged mental hospital patients have lower blood pressures than elderly people living in the community (Doven-

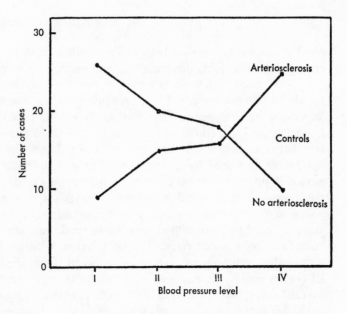

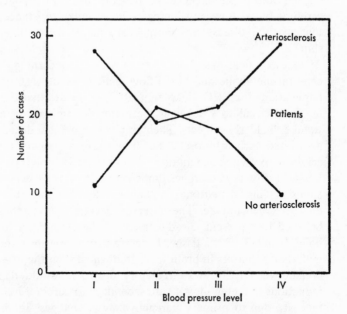

Figure 4–10. *Incidence of clinically diagnosed arterio-sclerosis as a function of blood pressure level in elderly community volunteers (upper graph) and aged mental hospital patients (lower graph). Note the more frequent occurrence of arteriosclerosis in association with low blood pressure among the patients as opposed to the controls.*

muehle, Newman, & Busse, 1960). The implication of these results for the etiology of senile EEG abnormalities and mental deterioration is obvious.

As Dr. Schmidt has already pointed out, both cerebral blood flow and metabolic rate decline in old age, particularly in patients with cardiovascular disease and/or mental deterioration (Sokoloff, 1966). Using an EEG frequency analysis, Obrist and co-workers (1963) determined the relationship between amount of slow activity under 7 cps and cerebral oxygen uptake, as measured by the nitrous oxide and radioactive krypton techniques. A product-moment correlation approaching zero was obtained for a select group of healthy old people whose oxygen uptake was in the normal young adult range. In contrast, a coeffiicent of $-.78$ was obtained for a group of aged patients with chronic brain syndrome whose cerebral metabolic function was depressed. The latter value, which is highly significant statistically, indicates an association between diminished $O_2$ uptake and EEG slow activity. It was concluded that brain waves bear little relation to overall cerebral metabolism in healthy old people but that the two variables are highly correlated in patients where pathological processes limit cerebral oxygen consumption. Since the patients also had significant reductions in cerebral blood flow and increases in vascular resistance, it was assumed that vascular disease was the primary factor responsible for the relationship.

A theoretical issue has arisen, however, concerning the etiology of the cerebral metabolic and blood flow changes in old age, which has definite implications for EEG. Sokoloff (1966) proposes that tissue anoxia resulting from circulatory deficit is the major determinant of a reduced oxygen uptake in elderly subjects. Their results suggest that decreases in blood flow associated with arteriosclerotic disease are a precursor of the decline in cerebral oxygen consumption. An alternative point of view is held by Lassen (1966), who argues that cortical atrophy associated with an endogenous decline in neuronal metabolic rate is mainly responsible for a reduced oxygen uptake. The observed decreases in cerebral blood flow are believed to represent an adjustment of the circulation to the lesser metabolic demands of the tissue. If cerebral metabolism is the critical variable underlying changes in brain wave frequency, then the extent of the correlation between EEG and circulatory disorders would depend on whether reductions in metabolic rate are secondary to cerebral ischemia, or whether they are due to primary parenchymatous changes. In the former case, a substantial relationship might be expected between EEG findings and the occurrence of cardiovascular disease, whereas a much smaller correlation would be anticipated if the latter were true. The evidence presented in this paper strongly suggests that circulatory variables are at least as important, if not more so, than noncirculatory factors in the production of senescent EEG changes. Needless to say, it is entirely conceivable that several types of pathological process exist,. even in the same individual. Postmortem pathological studies may provide some answers to these questions, but only a small beginning has been made to date in relating such variables to EEG (Sheridan et al., 1955).

Assuming that cerebral ischemia is an important determinant of senescent EEG changes, the question might be asked whether the observed slowing of brain waves is the direct result of concomitant tissue anoxia, or whether it is due to some degenerative neural process brought on by prolonged and repeated ischemic insults. Whereas most acute, reversible EEG alterations appear to be a direct manifestation of cerebral anoxia, the more permanent EEG changes probably require some kind of tissue damage—possibly a loss of neurons or a disturbance in intermediary metabolism that impairs the ability of cells to utilize oxygen. Only speculations can be offered at this time.

At least some of the issues raised by the present discussion are subject to investigation by methods currently available for the study of human cerebral metabolism, particularly the nitrous oxide technique of Kety and Schmidt (1946, 1948). It is curious, however, that three decades of EEG research on circulatory disorders have produced only a handful of papers on the quantitative relationship of brain potentials to cerebral hemodynamic and metabolic variables. This is especially surprising in view of the heavy emphasis placed on metabolic factors underlying the brain's electrical activity as early as the mid-thirties, and of the availability of techniques for measuring cerebral blood flow since the mid-forties. A few papers by Heine (1953), Lassen, Munck, and Tottey (1957), and Loeb (1961) have presented data on both cerebral blood flow and EEG in elderly people, without, however, attempting any precise quantitative analysis. A truly physiologic study comparable to those in electrocardiography remains to be done. The introduction of new radioisotopic techniques for the continuous determination of cerebral blood flow (Lewis, Sokoloff, Wechsler, Wentz, & Kety, 1960) and measurement of cerebral circulation time (Oldendorf, 1962) holds promise for future research in this area. It is hoped that such methods may eventually provide regional or hemispheral estimates of blood flow that can be correlated with focal EEG patterns.

## References

Barnes, R. H., Busse, E. W., and Friedman, E. L. The psychological functioning of aged individuals with normal and abnormal electroencephalograms: II. A study of hospitalized individuals. *Journal of Nervous and Mental Disease,* 124:585–593, 1956.

Berger, H. Uber das elektrenkephalogramm des menschen. Funfte mitteilung. *Archiv für Psychiatrie und Nervenkrankheiten,* 98:231–254, 1933.

Bruens, J. H., Gastaut, H. and Giove, G. Electroencephalographic study of the signs of chronic vascular insufficiency of the Sylvian region in aged people. *Electroencephalography and Clinical Neurophysiology,* 12:283–295, 1960.

Busse, E. W., Barnes, R. H., Friedman, E. L. and Kelty, E. J. Psychological functioning of aged individuals with normal and abnormal electroencephalograms: I. A study of non-hospitalized community volunteers. *Journal of Nervous and Mental Disease,* 124:135–141, 1956.

Busse, E. W., Barnes, R. H., Silverman, A. J., Shy, G. M., Thaler, M., and Frost, L. L. Studies of the process of aging: Factors that influence the psyche of elderly persons. *American Journal of Psychiatry,* 110:897–903, 1954.

Dastur, D. K., Lane, M. H., Hansen, D. B., Kety, S. S., Butler, R. N., Perlin, S., and Sokoloff, L. Effects of aging on cerebral circulation and metabolism in man. In NIMH Research Report, *Human aging: A biological and behavioral study.* Washington: Government Printing Office, 1963.

Davis, P. A. The electroencephalogram in old age. *Diseases of the Nervous System,* 2:77, 1941.

Dovenmuehle, R. H., Newman, E. G., and Busse, E. W. Physical problems of psychiatrically hospitalized elderly persons. *Journal of the American Geriatric Society,* 8:838–846, 1960.

Frantzen, E., and Lennox-Buchthal, M. Correlation of clinical electroencephalographic and arteriographic findings in patients with cerebral vascular accident. *Acta Psychiatrica and Neurologica Scandinavica,* 36, supplement 150:133–134, 1961.

Frey, T. A., and Sjögren, H. The electroencephalogram in elderly persons suffering from neuropsychiatric disorders. *Acta Psychiatrica and Neurologica Scandinavica,* 34:438–450, 1959.

Friedlander, W. J. Electroencephalographic alpha rate in adults as a function of age. *Geriatrics,* 13:29–31, 1958.

Gaches, J. Etude statistique sur les traces "alpha largement developpe" en fonction de l'age. *Presse Médicale,* 68:1620–1622, 1960.

Gastaut, H., Bostem, F., Fernandez-Guardiola, A., Naquet, R., and Ribson, W. Hypoxic activation of the EEG by nitrogen inhalation: III. Preliminary results in patients suffering from cerebrovascular disease. In Gastaut, H., and Myer, J. S. (Eds.), *Cerebral anoxia and the electroencephalogram.* Springfield, Ill.: Charles C Thomas, 1961.

Gibbs, F. A., and Gibbs, E. L. *Atlas of electroencephalography.* Vol. I. *Methodology and Controls.* (2nd ed.) Cambridge, Mass.: Addison-Wesley, 1950.

Giongo, F., and Mononi, G. Contributo clinico allo studio della sindrome cerebrocardiaca. *Ospedale Maggiore* (Milan), 47:393–401, 1959.

Harvald, B. EEG in old age. *Acta Psychiatrica and Neurologica Scandinavica,* 33:193–196, 1958.

Hass, W. K., and Goldensohn, E. S. Clinical and electroencephalographic considerations in the diagnosis of carotid artery occlusion. *Neurology,* 9:575–589, 1959.

Heine, G. Comparison of EEG, cerebral blood flow and cerebral $O_2$-consumption in 113 cases with heart, circulatory and vascular diseases. *Electroencephalography and Clinical Neurophysiology, Supplement,* 3:28, 1953.

Kety, S. S., and Schmidt, C. F. The effects of active and passive hyperventilation on cerebral blood flow, cerebral oxygen consumption, cardiac output, and blood pressure of normal young men. *Journal of Clinical Investigation,* 25:107–119, 1946.

Kety, S. S., and Schmidt, C. F. The effects of alterations in the arterial tensions of carbon dioxide and oxygen on cerebral blood flow and cerebral oxygen consumption of normal young men. *Journal of Clinical Investigation,* 27:484–492, 1948.

Lassen, N. A. Cerebral blood flow and cerebral metabolism in health and disease. *Research Publications, Association for Research in Nervous and Mental Disease,* 41:205–215, 1966.

Lassen, N. A., Munck, O., and Tottey, E. R. Mental function and cerebral oxygen consumption in organic dementia. *Archives of Neurology and Psychiatry,* 77:126–133, 1957.

Lewis, B. M., Sokoloff, L., Wechsler, R. L., Wentz, W. B., and Kety, S. S. A method for the continuous measurement of cerebral blood flow in man by means of radioactive krypton (Kr[79]). *Journal of Clinical Investigation,* 39:707–716, 1960.

Liberson, W. T., and Seguin, C. A. Brain waves and clinical features in arteriosclerotic and senile mental patients. *Psychosomatic Medicine,* 7:30–35, 1945.

Loeb, C. Effects of alternate carotid compression in aged and apparently normal subjects. In Gastaut, H., and Meher, J. R. (Eds.), *Cerebral anoxia and the electroencephalogram.* Springfield, Ill.: Charles C Thomas, 1961.

Luce, R. A., Jr., and Rothschild, D. The correlation of electroencephalographic and clinical observations in psychiatric patients over 65. *Journal of Gerontology,* 8:167–172, 1953.

McAdam, W., and Robinson, R. A. Senile intellectual deterioration and the electroencephalogram: A quantitative correlation. *Journal of Mental Science,* 102:819–825, 1956.

McAdam, W., and Robinson, R. A. Diagnostic and prognostic value of the electroencephalogram in geriatric psychiatry. In Blumenthal, H. T. (Ed.), *Medical and clinical aspects of aging.* New York: Columbia University Press, 1962.

McBeath, J., Winston, R., and Friedlander, W. J. Evaluation of controlled digital artery compression in cerebral vascular insufficiency. *Neurology,* 11:143–150, 1961.

McDowell, F., Wells, C. E., and Ehlers, C. The electroencephalogram in internal carotid artery occlusion. *Neurology,* 9:678–681, 1959.

Maggs, R., and Turton, E. C. Some EEG findings in old age and their relationship to affective disorder. *Journal of Mental Science,* 102:812–818, 1956.

Mars, G., Morpurgo, M., and Serra, C. Sul valore diagnostico dell'esame oftalmoangioscopico ed elettroencefalografico in soggetti di eta avanzata. *Progress in Medicine,* 11:193–197, 1955.

Meyer, J. S., and Waltz, A. G. Arterial oxygen saturation and alveolar carbon dioxide during electroencephalography: Comparison of hyperventilation and induced hypoxia in subjects with cerebral vascular disease. In Gastaut, H., and Meyer, J. S. (Eds.), *Cerebral anoxia and the electroencephalogram.* Springfield, Ill.: Charles C Thomas, 1961.

Morpurgo, M., Serra, C., and Mars, G. Sull'analisi comparativa dei dati elettroencefalografici ed elettrocardiografici in pazienti di eta senile. *Minerva Medica,* 46:361–372, 1955.

Mundy-Castle, A. C. Central excitability in the aged. In Blumenthal, H. T. (Ed.), *Medical and clinical aspects of aging.* New York: Columbia University Press, 1962.

Mundy-Castle, A. C., Hurst, L. A., Beerstecher, D. M., and Prinsloo, T. The electroencephalogram in the senile psychoses. *Electroencephalography and Clinical Neurophysiology,* 6:245–252, 1954.

Obrist, W. D. The electroencephalogram of normal aged adults. *Electroencephalography and Clinical Neurophysiology,* 6:235–244, 1954.

Obrist, W. D. The electroencephalogram of healthy aged males. In NIMH Research Report, *Human aging: A biological and behavioral study.* Washington: Government Printing Office, 1963, pp. 70–93.

Obrist, W. D., and Bissell, L. F. The electroencephalogram of aged patients with cardiac and cerebral vascular disease. *Journal of Gerontology,* 10:315–330, 1955.

Obrist, W. D., Busse, E. W., Eisdorfer, C., and Kleemeier, R. W. Relation of the electroencephalogram to intellectual function in senescence. *Journal of Gerontology,* 17:197–206, 1962.

Obrist, W. D., Busse, E. W., and Henry, C. E. Relation of electroencephalogram to blood pressure in elderly persons. *Neurology,* 11:151–158, 1961.

Obrist, W. D., and Henry, C. E. Electroencephalographic findings in aged psychiatric patients. *Journal of Nervous and Mental Disease*, 126:254–267, 1958. (a)

Obrist, W. D., and Henry, C. E. Electroencephalographic frequency analysis of aged psychiatric patients. *Electroencephalography and Clinical Neurophysiology*, 10:621–632, 1958. (b)

Obrist, W. D., Henry, C. E., and Justiss, W. A. Longitudinal study of EEG in old age. *Excerpta Medica*, International Congress Series No. 37:180–181, 1961.

Obrist, W. D., Sokoloff, L., Lassen, N. A., Lane, M. H., Butler, R. N., and Feinberg, I. Relation of EEG to cerebral blood flow and metabolism in old age. *Electroencephalography and Clinical Neurophysiology,* 15:610–619, 1963.

Oldendorf, W. H. Measurement of the mean transit time of cerebral circulation by external detection of an intravenously injected radioisotope. *Journal of Nuclear Medicine*, 3:382–398, 1962.

Pampiglione, G., and Post, F. The value of electroencephalographic examinations in psychiatric disorders of old age. *Geriatrics*, 13:725–732, 1958.

Rossen, R., Simonson, E., and Baker, J. Electroencephalograms during hypoxia in healthy men. *Archives of Neurology*, 5:648–654, 1961.

Sheridan, F. P., Yeager, C. L., Oliver, W. A., and Simon, A. Electroencephalography as a diagnostic and prognostic aid in studying the senescent individual: A preliminary report. *Journal of Gerontology*, 10:53–59, 1955.

Silverman, A. J., Busse, E. W., and Barnes, R. H. Studies in the processes of aging: Electroencephalographic findings in 400 elderly subjects. *Electroencephalography and Clinical Neurophysiology*, 7:67–74, 1955.

Sokoloff, L. Cerebral circulatory and metabolic changes associated with aging. *Research Publications, Association for Research in Nervous and Mental Disease*, 41:237–251, 1966.

Turton, E. C. The EEG as a diagnostic and prognostic aid in the differentiation of organic disorders in patients over 60. *Journal of Mental Science*, 104:461–465, 1958.

Weiner, H., and Schuster, D. B. The electroencephalogram in dementia: Some preliminary observations and correlations. *Electroencephalography and Clinical Neurophysiology*, 8:479–488, 1956.

Weiss, S., and Froelich, W. Tilt table electroencephalography in insufficiency syndromes. *Neurology*, 8:686–693, 1958.

Young, W., Gofman, J. W., Malamud, N., Simon, A., and Waters, E. S. G. The interrelationship between cerebral and coronary atherosclerosis. *Geriatrics*, 11:413–418, 1956.

# Chapter 5. Reaction Time

Most psychologists seem to agree that decreasing speed in responding to stimuli is a normal or typical part of aging. This is not to deny the substantial individual variation which shows that some aged persons respond even faster than some younger persons. Nor does it deny that there are substantial group differences due to sex, practice, and exercise, as shown in the reports that follow. But despite all these exceptions and specifications, this "fact of aging" still stands: older adults tend to have longer reaction times than younger adults.

Botwinick and Thompson carried out a series of studies comparing the reaction times of the panelists with those of younger subjects. The first report analyzes reaction time into two component parts, premotor time and motor time, and finds that the elderly were slower in both parts. The second shows that the elderly improved their reaction time with practice under certain conditions, while the younger subjects did not. The third shows that there are greater individual differences among the elderly than among the young, and the final report suggests that some of the slower reactions among the elderly may be related to their lack of exercise.

## Components of Reaction Time in Relation to Age and Sex* *Jack Botwinick and Larry W. Thompson*

In a recent examination of some of the antecedents of reaction time, especially as it related to the study of aging, three theories were explicated: nerve conduction theory, set theory, and bio-potential wave theory (Botwinick, 1965). The present study was concerned with nerve conduction and set theories, and in addition, specific questions regarding the interaction between age and sex in relation to reaction time were investigated. Nerve conduction theory focuses upon segmenting total reaction time into component parts, and set theory attempts to explain variations in reaction time as functions of set or attention factors which may be manipulated experimentally.

Two studies bear most directly on the present one. Weiss (1965)

* Reprinted by permission from the *Journal of Genetic Psychology*, 108:175–183, 1966.

segmented reaction time into motor and premotor components and examined these components in relation to age and to other variables. This will be discussed later in relation to the present study. The second study involved the finding that elderly female subjects were quicker (shorter reaction time) than elderly males, while with younger controls the reverse was the case; young men were quicker than young women (Botwinick & Brinley, 1962a). It may be speculated that if, as many at least imply (Birren & Wall, 1956; Hügin, Norris, & Shock, 1960; Weiss, 1965), reaction time is a reflection of central nervous system function, then the age-sex interaction in reaction time may have central nervous system implications. The finding that elderly women were quicker than elderly men was based upon subjects aged 61–80 years. It was indicated, however, that the elderly women were eight years younger than the men, and this may have contributed to the results (Botwinick & Brinley, 1962a). In the present study, ages of men and women were adequately equated for the test of an age-sex interaction in reaction time.

## Method

### Subjects

The subjects were 88 white men and women volunteers of two age groups. The elderly groups comprised 44 subjects of the Duke Longitudinal Study, the characteristics of whom were described by Busse (1962, pp. 680–681). The total sample of elderly subjects comprised community residents from a wide socioeconomic range. The present subsample was selected on the basis of having completed 12 or more years of formal education or the equivalent. There were 17 men aged 68 to 87 years (median = 78.0) and 27 women aged 69 to 84 years (median = 76.0). The respective median years of education were 17 and 15. The younger group comprised students, secretarial and clerical staff, housewives, and unemployed people recruited from the local employment agency. Subjects volunteered to receive a nominal fee, to fulfill the requirements of a first course in psychology, or simply for the reason of contributing their time for research purposes. There were 29 men aged 19 to 32 years (median = 20.0) and 15 women aged 18 to 35 years (median = 20.0). The median years of education were 14 and 13, respectively.

### Procedure

Reaction times were measured on each subject individually with both regular series and irregular series. (In regular series the foreperiod or preparatory interval is constant within a block of trials, and in irregular series the preparatory interval is varied within a block of trials.) Approximately twice as many subjects within each age and sex subgrouping experienced the irregular series first and the regular series second. In collecting the data, subjects were assigned to an equal counterbalanced arrangement of regular and irregular series; but afterward, when data were discarded in order to equate for age within the sex subgroupings, to maintain relatively homogeneous education levels among the subgroups, and to have records only of completed series, it worked out in the manner indicated. The appropriate data were discarded *before any* analyses were begun. The regular series were presented in quasi-counterbalanced arrangements of ascending and descending preparatory interval orders. (An ascending series is one in which the preparatory interval order is from a short duration of 0.5 seconds to a long duration of 15.0 seconds.)

The exact procedure may be found in a study by Botwinick and Thompson (1966) in which most of the data of young subjects of the present study were analyzed for a different purpose. The important features of the procedure involved a warning signal of 0.5-second duration which came on approximately 2 seconds after a telegraph response key was pressed. This was followed by the preparatory interval and then the stimulus, which was terminated by the finger lift response. The stimulus was a 1,000-cycle-per-second tone approximately 85 db measured at the subject's position 5–6 feet from the sound source speaker. The warning signal which preceded the tone stimulus was a 400-cycle-per-second tone of approximately 75 db. Four preparatory intervals—0.5, 3.0, 6.0, and 15.0 seconds—were used in both regular and irregular series.

Simultaneously with the reaction time measurements, electromyograms (EMGs) were recorded from the *extensor digitorum communis* of the responding forearm. The potentials were amplified and recorded with a Grass, Model III, eight-channel EEG. EMGs were recorded for the middle reaction time trials of each preparatory interval. There were 40 EMGs in regular series (10 of each preparatory) and 42 EMGs in irregular series (9–11 of each preparatory interval).

For each reaction time, the ink record was analyzed manually by measuring with a millimeter scale the distance between the point on the EMG tracing where the stimulus began and the point of first increased muscle firing. This was the premotor time. Reaction time was the measured distance between stimulus onset and finger lift response. The premotor time measurement was subtracted from the reaction time measurement to give the motor time. For each subject the medians of reaction time, premotor time, and motor time were computed independently for each preparatory interval within each of the two series.

Results

Variance analyses by the unweighted means approach for unequal cell frequencies (Winer, 1962, pp. 222–224) were carried out with the reaction time data, and with the data of premotor and motor components of reaction time. These analyses were of both regular and irregular series and were based upon the median values of the individual subjects. The means of these median reaction times, premotor times, and motor times may be seen in Figure 5–1. The means of motor time are of pooled sex groups within each of the two age groups. The reason for this was that group mean differences of motor time were so small that the figure would be unclear if the motor times were presented for each of the four subgroups. For example, the range of reaction times in Figure 5–1 was from .193 to .407 seconds, the range of premotor times was from .152 to .346 seconds, and the range of motor times from .032 to .059 seconds. The analyses of the data, however, were based on the subgroups unpooled.

The main effect variables in these analyses were age of subject, sex of subject, and the preparatory interval. In Table 5–1 the contribution of these variables and their interactions may be compared for reaction time and for components of reaction time in regular and in irregular series. In each of the six variance analyses, the two elderly age groups were statistically slower than their younger controls ($p < .01$). That is, motor time, premotor time, and reaction time were slowed with advanced age when subjects responded to stimuli in both regular and irregular series.

In each of the six analyses, except one, response time was related to the preparatory interval ($p < .01–.05$). The one exception was motor time in irregular series ($p > .05$). Statistically significant interactions were found only with regular series. Sex of subject interacted with preparatory interval in regard to reaction time and premotor time ($p < .05$), the nature of which may be seen in Figure 5–1. There was a statistically significant interaction between age and preparatory interval with motor time ($p < .05$). Elderly and young subjects were more similar in motor time with the 6.0-second preparatory interval than with preparatory intervals of longer and shorter duration.

It may be seen in Figure 5–1 that the premotor components constituted an appreciable percentage of total reaction time. This was the case for each age and sex group of both regular and irregular series. Percentages (ratios) of premotor to reaction time ranged from 79 to 90 when computed with the means of each of the four subgroups (two ages and two sexes) in relation to the four preparatory intervals within both the regular and irregular series. The mean of these 32 percentages was 84.4. The comparable

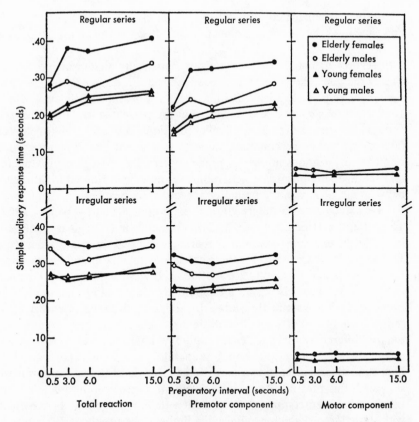

Figure 5–1. *Simple auditory reaction time as a function of the pre- paratory interval for four classes of subjects. Reaction time was segmented into two component parts: premotor time and motor time. Mean reaction time and mean components of reaction time are seen in relation to the preparatory interval within irregular and regular series. Mean motor times are of pooled male and female subgroups; other means are of male and female subjects separately within an age group.*

percentages of motor time to reaction time ranged from 12 to 21 with a mean of 15.5.

## Discussion

Elderly subjects were slower than young subjects in both premotor time and motor time, and, therefore, reaction time. In both age groups, the premotor component constituted approximately 84 percent of total reaction time, and the motor component constituted the remaining 16 percent. In the present study, the interactions between age and preparatory interval with respect to reaction time were not statistically significant ($p > .05$). These relations, however, have been shown in previous studies to be significant (e.g., Botwinick & Brinley, 1962a; Botwinick, Brinley, & Birren, 1957) and thus cannot be disregarded in the present study. Premotor time and reaction time were nearly parallel functions, related to the preparatory interval within every condition. Since variations in reaction time which result from variations in the preparatory interval are attributed to anticipatory set, age differences in reaction time set may be attributed to differences between age groups in the premotor aspects of the response.

This study was an outgrowth and extension of one by Weiss (1965). The extensions included use of both regular and irregular series and included the expanded range of preparatory interval durations from 0.5 to 15.0 seconds. The reasons for these extensions may be found in the studies by Botwinick and Brinley (1962a, 1962b). It was found that a preparatory interval of 0.5 seconds played a different role in reaction time than longer preparatory intervals in the series. In addition, the regular and irregular series with this short preparatory interval of 0.5 seconds appeared to require different abilities to respond quickly, abilities which were unrelated to an extent. Long 15.0-second preparatory intervals were considered important because reaction times of the aged tend to be extraordinarily slow with this preparatory interval duration. Therefore, an analysis of the relations between components of reaction time and age may best be made with those factors which maximize the limits of the problem.

The results with irregular series of the present study were similar to those of Weiss (1965). The preparatory interval played a role in premotor time and not motor time. With regular series, however, the preparatory interval played a role in motor time when both elderly and young subjects were considered together ($p < .05$), and when the data of only elderly subjects were analyzed ($p < .01$). When, however, the data of young subjects alone were examined, motor time differences due to the preparatory interval were not seen ($p > .05$). This explained the significant interaction between age and the preparatory interval with respect to motor time in regular series in Table 5–1 ($p < .05$). The interpretation of these results is not clear. If this is not a case of an error of accepting as statistically significant that which is not significant, then the elaboration and elucidation must await further study.

It does not seem likely, however, that these motor time results warrant serious attention. The actual magnitudes of the motor time differences were small, and the variations of the preparatory interval, and the interaction between age and the preparatory interval, were statistically significant only with .05 levels. With irregular series, neither the preparatory interval nor the interaction between age and the preparatory interval was statistically significant even with .05 levels.

Table 5–1. *Variance analyses of reaction time and components of reaction time of regular and irregular series.*

| | | F | | | | | |
|---|---|---|---|---|---|---|---|
| | | RT[a] | | PMT[a] | | MT[a] | |
| Source | df | Regular | Irregular | Regular | Irregular | Regular | Irregular |
| Between subjects | 87 | 9.52** | 19.49** | 9.42** | 19.09** | 8.10** | 19.78** |
| Age (A) | 1 | 22.21** | 14.25** | 15.42** | 10.13** | 12.76** | 13.72** |
| Sex (S) | 1 | 3.72 | 1.11 | 3.28 | 1.10 | 0.00 | 0.08 |
| A × S | 1 | 2.26 | 0.67 | 1.64 | 0.15 | 1.18 | 2.33 |
| Error (mean square)[b] | 84 | (31.72) | (30.80) | (32.65) | (31.91) | (1.14) | (0.90) |
| Within subjects (mean square)[b] | 264 | (4.30) | (1.82) | (4.16) | (1.83) | (0.16) | (0.05) |
| Preparatory interval (PI)[a] | 3 | 29.70** | 7.85** | 32.98** | 4.72** | 3.61* | 0.86 |
| A × PI | 3 | 2.08 | 1.12 | 1.53 | 1.29 | 3.26* | 0.77 |
| S × PI | 3 | 2.95* | 0.25 | 3.58* | 0.01 | 0.30 | 1.06 |
| A × S × PI | 3 | 2.59 | 1.82 | 2.47 | 0.33 | 1.11 | 0.98 |
| Error (mean square)[b] | 252 | (3.12) | (1.68) | (2.94) | (1.78) | (0.15) | (0.05) |
| Total | 351 | | | | | | |

Note.—The *F* ratio may not equal exactly the ratio of the respective mean square to the error terms, due to rounding off to two decimal places. Differences are only in the decimals.

[a] Reaction time (RT) was fractionated into two component parts: premotor time (PMT) and motor time (MT). RT was measured in relation to the variation of the preparatory interval (PI) which was the period of time between the warning signal and the stimulus.

[b] Analyses were carried out with reaction time, premotor time, and motor time in milliseconds. Thus mean squares were divided by 1,000 in this table.

* Significant at .05 level.

** Significant at .01 level.

Another extension of the study by Weiss (1965) was the testing of both male and female subjects. There were no statistically significant sex differences, and age and sex did not interact significantly with regard to reaction time and its components ($p > .05$). However, there were interactions between sex and preparatory interval in reaction time and premotor time of regular series ($p < .05$). Thus, in the present study, the finding that elderly female subjects were quicker than elderly male subjects (Botwinick & Brinley, 1962a) was not supported. In fact, Figure 5–1 suggests that the elderly men were faster than elderly women in reaction time and premotor time; but variance analyses of the data of each age group separately indicated that sex differences were not statistically significant for reaction time, premotor time, or motor time ($p > .05$). The data of Figure 5–1 also suggest an age-sex interaction, but the variance analyses (Table 5–1) did not indicate this ($p > .05$). Thus, if the status of the central nervous system is a correlate of speed of response, then the reaction time data of the present study did not suggest superior neural functioning of elderly women compared to elderly men.

## Summary

Reaction time was segmented into two component parts, premotor time and motor time. The reaction times and the components were analyzed in relation to four preparatory intervals within an irregular series and a regular series. These functions were then compared among subgroups comprising elderly males, elderly females, young adult males, and young adult females. The reaction times were segmented by the method of Weiss (1965). Electromyograms were recorded from the extensor muscle of the responding forearm during measurement of reaction time. The time between stimulus presentation and occurrence of increased muscle firing was the premotor time; the motor time was the reaction time minus the premotor time.

Premotor times, motor times, and, therefore, reaction times were found to be slowed in advanced age. Interactions between age and sex were not significant ($p > .05$), indicating that whatever the antecedent mechanisms of the slowing process with advanced age may be, they may be the same for men and women.

## References

Birren, J. E., and Wall, P. D. Age changes in conduction velocity, refractory period, number of fibers, connective tissue space and blood vessels in sciatic nerve of rats. *Journal of Comparative Neurology*, 104:1–16, 1956.

Botwinick, J. Theories of antecedent conditions of speed of response. In Welford, A. T., and Birren, J. E. (Eds.), *Behavior, aging, and the nervous system*. Springfield, Ill.: Charles C Thomas, 1965.

Botwinick, J., and Brinley, J. F. Aspects of RT set during brief intervals in relation to age and sex. *Journal of Gerontology*, 17:295–301, 1962. (a)

Botwinick, J., and Brinley, J. F. An analysis of set in relation to reaction time. *Journal of Experimental Psychology*, 63:568–574, 1962. (b)

Botwinick, J., and Thompson, L. W. Premotor and motor components of reaction time. *Journal of Experimental Psychology*, 1966.

Botwinick, J., Brinley, J. F., and Birren, J. E. Set in relation to age. *Journal of Gerontology*, 12:300–305, 1957.

Busse, E. W. Findings from the Duke geriatrics research project on the effects of aging upon the nervous system. In Tibbitts, C., and Donahue, W. (Eds.), *Social and psychological aspects of aging.* New York: Columbia University Press, 1962.

Hügin, F., Norris, A. H., and Shock, N. W. Skin reflex and voluntary reaction times in young and old males. *Journal of Gerontology,* 15:388–391, 1960.

Weiss, A. D. The locus of reaction time change with set, motivation, and age. *Journal of Gerontology,* 20:60–64, 1965.

Winer, B. J. *Statistical principles in experimental design.* New York: McGraw-Hill, 1962.

# Practice of Speeded Response in Relation to Age, Sex, and Set*    *Jack Botwinick and Larry W. Thompson*

The study of speed of response has been prominent in the effort to understand aging processes. Different theoretical positions have been taken regarding the significance of the loss of speed with advanced age, and many related studies have been carried out. Some of these have been summarized in recent reports (Botwinick, 1964, 1965). In spite of this, we do not know of any studies which have focused upon the problems of measurement of speed of response in relation to age. It would seem that understanding the significance of a behavior is limited by, and perhaps impossible without, knowledge about problems of measuring the behavior in question.

Part of the data of speed of response in the present study were collected for different purposes (Botwinick and Thompson, 1966b), but when reanalyzed to determine the role of practice or learning during the course of the experiment, an interesting measurement problem was elucidated. Speed of response, measured as simple auditory reaction time (RT), was examined as it changed with continued performance, and these changes were compared between two age groups of men and women. Furthermore, these relationships were investigated in the context of anticipatory or preparatory RT set.

## Materials and Methods

### Subjects

There were 112 men and women subjects, of which 52 were elderly and 60 were younger adults, aged 67 to 92 and 18 to 35 years, respectively.[1]

* Reprinted by permission from the *Journal of Gerontology,* 22:72–76, 1967.

[1] The ages of young men (YM) and young women (YW) were 19–24 and 19–35 years, respectively, with the 0.5-second regular PI (Figure 5–2A). With the 15.0-second regular PI (Figure 5–2B), the ages were 19–20 and 19–24, respectively. Old men

All subjects had 12 or more years of formal education or the equivalent. The elderly subjects were recruited from the pool of the Duke Longitudinal Study (Busse, 1962), and the younger subjects were students, secretarial and clerical staff members, housewives, and unemployed people referred by the local employment agency.

### Procedure

The procedure in great detail may be seen in the study by Botwinick and Thompson (1966a), and only the relevant features are indicated here. Elderly and young adult subjects were individually measured for RT in a situation which involved a warning signal of 0.5-second duration, a fore-period or preparatory interval (PI), and the stimulus which was terminated by a finger-lifting response from a telegraph key. The warning signal was a 400-cycle-per-second tone, approximately 75 db, and the stimulus was a 1,000-cycle-per-second tone, approximately 85 db, measured at subject's position of five to six feet from the sound source.

In the measurement of RT, one group of each of the two age categories experienced a regular 0.5-second PI, a second group experienced a regular 15.0-second PI, and a third group experienced an irregular series comprising PIs of 0.5, 3.0, 6.0, and 15.0 seconds. . . .

Elderly and younger subjects of both sexes made up the three groups. The regular 0.5-second PI group comprised 14 young adults (8 men and 6 women) and 12 elderly adults (6 men and 6 women). The regular 15.0-second PI group comprised 15 younger subjects (9 men and 6 women) and 10 elderly subjects (3 men and 7 women). The irregular series group comprised 31 younger and 30 elderly subjects. There were 20 men and 11 women in the younger group, and there were 12 men and 18 women in the older group.

### Data Analysis

There were 21 trials within each of the two regular PI conditions, and there were 85 RT trials within the irregular series. The two series of 21 regular RT trials were each divided into four blocks: three of five trials and the last of six trials. For each subject, the median of each of the four blocks was computed. The 85 irregular RT trials comprised 21 RTs with three of the PIs, and 22 RTs with the 3.0-second PI. Within each of these four PIs the RT trials were divided into four blocks: five trials within each of the

(OM) and old women (OW) were aged 68–87 and 68–78 years, respectively, with procedure 2A, and 70–86 and 67–78 2B. In irregular series the ages of YM, YW, OM, OW, respectively, were: 19–32, 18–28, 67–86, and 69–92 years.

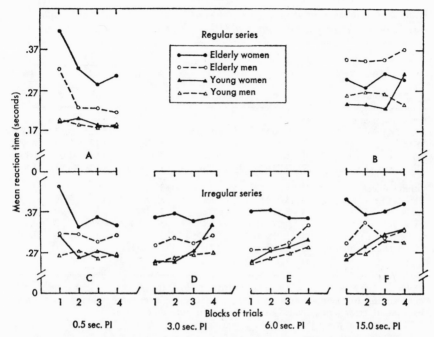

Figure 5–2. *Age and sex differences in mean reaction time as a function of practice trials for different preparatory intervals (PIs). There were five to seven RT trials within each block. Functions A and B are of PIs in regular series, and C through F are of PIs in irregular series. Functions A and C are of short, 0.5-second PIs, and functions B and F are of long, 15.0-second PIs.*

first three blocks, and the remaining trials of the last block. The median RT of each block of trials was computed for each subject. In addition, practice effects with irregular series were analyzed irrespective of the PI. The 85 irregular RT trials were divided into 17 blocks of five RTs each, and the 17 RT medians were computed for each subject.

These median data were subjected to a series of variance analyses.[2] The

[2] Plots of the means of RTs within blocks of training trials appeared similar to plots of the medians of these RTs. The means of regular series were subjected to variance analyses as a spot check of this apparent similarity. With one exception, when statistical significance was found with the means, it was also found with the medians. The one exception was the sex × trials interaction of the 15.0-second regular series. This interaction was not statistically significant with the median RTs but was significant at less than the .05 level with the means. In general medians of latency data are to be preferred to means because of skewing which can occur as a result of some very slow responses.

Table 5–2. *Variance analyses of the effects of practice trials on reaction time in relation to the preparatory interval (PI) of regular and irregular series.*

| | Regular PI (seconds) | | | | Irregular PI (seconds) | | | | |
|---|---|---|---|---|---|---|---|---|---|
| | 0.5 | | 15.0 | | | 0.5 | 3.0 | 6.0 | 15.0 |
| Source | df | F | df | F | df | F | F | F | F |
| Between subjects | 25 | | 24 | | 60 | | | | |
| Age (A) | 1 | 9.44** | 1 | 9.85** | 1 | 6.02* | 5.72* | 5.37* | 6.46* |
| Sex (S) | 1 | 1.83 | 1 | 1.55 | 1 | 1.44 | 2.12 | 2.32 | 2.58 |
| A × S | 1 | 1.36 | 1 | 1.45 | 1 | 0.53 | 0.61 | 1.07 | 1.13 |
| Error (mean square) | 22 | (2.84) | 21 | (1.08) | 57 | (4.35) | (3.83) | (3.87) | (3.32) |
| Within subjects | 78 | | 76 | | 183 | | | | |
| Trials (T) | 3 | 13.41** | 3 | 1.85 | 3 | 6.17** | 3.81* | 3.56* | 3.69* |
| A × T | 3 | 8.31** | 3 | 0.82 | 3 | 0.72 | 2.56 | 0.70 | 3.14* |
| S × T | 3 | 0.37 | 3 | 1.98 | 3 | 5.94** | 0.86 | 1.32 | 0.90 |
| A × S × T | 3 | 1.01 | 3 | 5.33** | 3 | 0.31 | 2.13 | 2.12 | 2.61 |
| Error (mean square) | 66 | (0.18) | 64 | (0.11) | 171 | (0.31) | (0.33) | (0.31) | (0.30) |
| Total | 103 | | 100 | | 243 | | | | |

Note.—The *F* ratio may not equal exactly the ratio of the respective mean square to the error term due to rounding off to two decimal places. Differences are only in the decimals. Mean square error terms divided by 10,000 for the purpose of this table.
  * Significant at $p < .05$.
  ** Significant at $p < .01$.

unweighted mean approach for unequal cell frequencies was used (Winer, 1962). The variance analyses had as the main effect variables age of subject, sex of subject, and the role of RT practice trials.

Results

In Figures 5–2 and 5–3 the group means of the individual medians are presented for young adult and elderly men and women in relation to the PIs. The mean RTs were investigated in relation to the blocks of RT trials, making the slopes of the functions reflective of the role of practice on RT. The slopes may be examined as the interaction between the main effect subject variables and practice trials.

Table 5–2 summarizes the variance analyses of the two regular series. In the short regular interval condition (Figure 5–2A), there was a practice effect for the older subjects that was not apparent for the younger controls (age × trials, $p < .01$). On the other hand, this was not the case with the 15.0-second regular PI (Figure 5–2B), although age and trials interacted in conjunction with sex of subject ($p < .01$). It was the data of young female subjects, however, which mainly contributed to this second order interaction. Figure 5–2B indicates that the young women became differentially slower than any of the other groups during the last six RT trials of the 15.0 regular PI.

In Figure 5–2 there are also RT practice functions with the four irregular PIs. The respective variance analyses are summarized in Table 5–2. These four analyses, one for each PI, were similar in the relationships indicated. In each case, the elderly were slower than the young ($p < .05$),

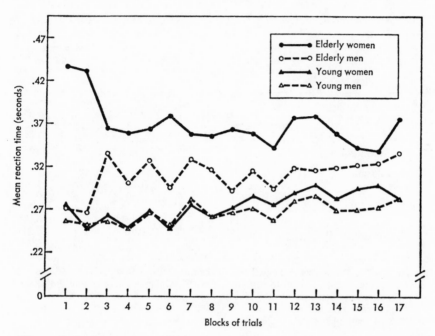

Figure 5–3. *Age and sex differences in mean reaction time as a function of practice trials. Each of the 17 blocks was composed of 5 RT trials.*

and changes in RT occurred with practice trials ($p < .01$–$.05$). In the shortest duration PI (Figure 5–2C), sex of subject interacted significantly with trials ($p < .01$), and in the longest PI (Figure 5–2F), age of subject interacted significantly with trials ($p < .05$). The specific nature of these results may be seen in Figure 5–2. With the brief 0.5-second irregular PI (Figure 5–2C), the women appeared to have required at least 5 RT experiences to reach asymptote within the 21 RT trials. With the long 15.0-second irregular PI (Figure 5–2F), elderly women required more experience before reaching optimum RT. They tended, however, as did the other subjects, to become slower, not faster, with further experience.

The data of irregular series in Figure 5–2 represent practice effects with specific PIs. It is to be understood that the first block of trials with a particular PI involved RTs which came later in the session than some RTs associated with other PIs. In Figure 5–3, the RT practice effects with irregular series were with mixed PIs within each practice block, representing a sequential analysis of consecutive RTs with irregular series.

Three related variance analyses were carried out with the data of

Table 5–3. *Variance analyses of the effects of blocks of practice trials on reaction time with irregular series.*

| | 17 blocks | | 5 blocks | | 4 blocks | |
|---|---|---|---|---|---|---|
| Source | df | F | df | F | df | F |
| Between subjects | 60 | | 60 | | 60 | |
| Age (A) | 1 | 7.52** | 1 | 7.10** | 1 | 7.07* |
| Sex (S) | 1 | 1.78 | 1 | 2.14 | 1 | 2.91 |
| A × S | 1 | 1.02 | 1 | 1.74 | 1 | 1.96 |
| Error (mean square) | 57 | (15.31) | 57 | (7.62) | 57 | (6.44) |
| Within subjects | 976 | | 244 | | 183 | |
| Trials (T) | 16 | 1.47 | 4 | 1.25 | 3 | 1.50 |
| A × T | 16 | 1.11 | 4 | 0.30 | 3 | 0.25 |
| S × T | 16 | 1.39 | 4 | 6.55** | 3 | 5.79** |
| A × S × T | 16 | 0.30 | 4 | 4.70** | 3 | 6.19** |
| Error (mean square) | 912 | (0.34) | 228 | (0.31) | 171 | (0.31) |
| Total | 1,036 | | 304 | | 243 | |

Note.—The *F* ratio may not equal exactly the ratio of the respective mean square to the error term due to rounding off to two decimal places. Differences are only in the decimals. Mean square error terms divided by 10,000 for the purpose of this table.
* Significant at $p < .05$.
** Significant at $p < .01$.

Figure 5–3, as may be seen in Table 5–3. The first analysis involved all 17 blocks of training trials. The second involved only the first 5 blocks, and the third involved the first 4 blocks. The latter two analyses were done because the greatest slope of improvement of elderly subjects was seen in the first 4 and 5 blocks of practice trials. This was considered a meaningful portion of the data to analyze since 20–25 RTs, as represented by the 4 and 5 blocks of practice trials, are as many RTs as are frequently given in a single experiment.

Table 5–3 indicates that the elderly were slower than the young in each analysis ($p < .01–.05$). This was the only statistically significant factor when all 17 blocks were considered. When only 4 and 5 blocks were considered, sex of subject interacted with the practice trials, as did the relationship between age and sex of subject ($p < .01$).

In order to understand these interactions better, four additional series of variance analyses were carried out, one for each group and one for each sex group. Each of the four series involved analyses of 17, 5, and 4 blocks of training trials.

Young men and women were not different in overall RT, nor were they different in practice effects ($p > .05$). On the other hand, elderly men and women, although not different in overall RT ($p > .05$), were different in the effects of practice trials (sex groups $\times$ practice trials, $p < .01-.05$). The interaction between age groups and practice trials was statistically significant for women with the 17 blocks ($p < .01$), but not with only the 4 or 5 blocks ($p > .05$). For men, there was a significant age $\times$ trials interaction with 4 and 5 blocks ($p < .01-.05$) but not when considering all 17 blocks ($p > .05$).

## Discussion

A generalized summary of the present data must include the concept that RT varies with continuous practice and that this variation is a function of preparatory set as defined by the PI duration and the context of the PI. Furthermore, age and sex of subject modify these relationships.

The RT measurement problem with regard to age of subject was most apparent with the 0.5-second regular PI. It is clear from Figure 5–2A that both elderly men and women would be found excessively slow to the extent that the first five RT trials are represented in a series of RT measurements with this PI. These data are very compatible with those of Brinley and Botwinick (1959), who measured simple and choice response times of elderly and younger men with four warning interval durations. They retested with nine additional trials on a 0.5-second interval and found that this practice reduced the mean age difference to a statistically significant extent. The magnitude of this reduction, although small, was greater than the original age differences measured at intervals of 1.0 and 4.0 seconds. It was concluded that "part of the increase in age differences at the 0.5-second interval reflects a learning difficulty" (p. 227).

There have been other data which suggest that age comparisons early in the practice periods are unrepresentative of overall age differences. Botwinick and Shock (1952) investigated performance decrement (not improvement) with continued work and found that age differences were greater to start with than later in the sessions.

It may be a mistake, however, to overemphasize this relationship between age and practice trials. It was only with the 0.5-second regular PI that this relationship was found, except when sex of subject contributed to the variance. This does not negate the importance of the relationship. In fact, it introduces the need to reevaluate in this context all the studies of set in relation to age when the focus is on the short duration PIs.

Perhaps more apparent in these data than the relationship between age and practice trials was the differential effect of sex of subject in practice or RT. With the regular 15.0-second PI (Figure 5–2B), the younger women subjects tended to become slower with the last block of trials, thus making for a significant interaction between age, sex, and practice. It is with the irregular series, however, that sex of subject contributed most. In Figure 5–2C it may be seen that it was again the 0.5-second PI which provided the occasion for significant interaction. Women improved with practice in a way that men did not. This was the case for both elderly and younger subjects, and indicated that women were not as adequate as men in responding quickly during a short uncertain time interval without some experience. Men, on the other hand, required little warm-up.

The role of sex of subject was more complicated in its contribution to the RT data of irregular series when PI was not involved in the analyses. In general, young men and women did not differ with respect to the role of practice in RT, but elderly men and women did differ. Therefore, the aging patterns of practice effects were different for each of the sexes.

The reason for these interactions is not understood. Nevertheless, to the extent that it is possible to generalize from these data, it is clear that if the measurement of RT is to be meaningful in its applicability, the role of practice, the age of subject, the sex of subject, and the condition of preparatory set must be specified as part of the operations of the measurement.

## Summary

Simple auditory reaction time (RT) was examined as it changed with continued performance, and these changes were compared between two age groups of adult men and women. Furthermore, these relationships were investigated in the context of preparatory RT set.

There were three conditions of preparatory set: a regular 0.5-second preparatory interval (PI), a regular 15.0-second PI, and an irregular series of four PIs (0.5, 3.0, 6.0, and 15.0 seconds). With the short regular interval condition, elderly people improved with practice, and younger people did not. With the long, 15.0-second regular PI, young women became differentially slower with continued practice. With irregular series, depending upon the specific method of analyzing the data, sex, and age × sex interactions were statistically significant with respect to the effects of practice.

It was concluded that for meaningful measurement of RT, and for meaningful theories of the loss of speed with age, the role of practice in relation to both age and sex of subject must be considered very carefully in the context of the condition of preparatory set.

## References

Botwinick, J. Research problems and concepts in the study of aging. *Gerontologist,* 4:121–129, 1964.

Botwinick, J. Theories of antecedent conditions of speed of response. In Welford, A. T., and Birren, J. E. (Eds.), *Behavior, aging, and the nervous system.* Springfield, Ill.: Charles C Thomas, 1965.

Botwinick, J., and Shock, N. W. Age differences in performance decrement with continuous work. *Journal of Gerontology,* 7:41–46, 1952.

Botwinick, J., and Thompson, L. W. Premotor and motor components of reaction time. *Journal of Experimental Psychology,* 71:9–15, 1966. (a)

Botwinick, J., and Thompson, L. W. Components of reaction time in relation to age and sex. *Journal of Genetic Psychology,* 108:175–183, 1966. (b)

Brinley, J. F., and Botwinick, J. Preparation time and choice in relation to age differences in response speed. *Journal of Gerontology,* 14:226–228, 1959.

Busse, E. W. Findings from the Duke geriatrics research project on the effects of aging upon the nervous system. In Tibbitts, C., and Donahue, W. (Eds.), *Social and psychological aspects of aging.* New York: Columbia University Press, 1962.

Winer, B. J. *Statistical principles in experimental design.* New York: McGraw-Hill, 1962.

# Individual Differences in Reaction Time in Relation to Age*    *Jack Botwinick and Larry W. Thompson*

When old and young adults are compared with respect to the extent of individual differences in biological and behavioral functioning, the older adults tend to be the more variable. This is so often the case that it constitutes one of the major generalizations in the field of aging.

In spite of this generalization, it is not advisable to assume its applicability in any specific situation, since exceptions to rules, while not proving them, are to be expected. Obrist (1953) confirmed the applicability of this generalization to reaction time (RT), demonstrating that both the inter- and intraindividual RT differences increased with advancing age.

Obrist (1953) measured RTs with preparatory intervals (PI) varying

* Reprinted by permission from the *Journal of Genetic Psychology,* 112:73–75, 1968.

from one to two seconds duration. . . . Since the time of Obrist's study it has been shown in a variety of investigations (Botwinick & Brinley, 1962) that RTs of older people vary more with respect to variations of the PI than do RTs of young adults. Thus, when Obrist examined RTs combining different PIs within the range of one to two seconds, his results with respect to age may have been due more to the role of the PI than to intrinsic changes with age in RT variability.

The present study tests the hypothesis that older adults are more variable in RT than are younger adults independent of the PI effect.

### Subjects and Procedures

The data of a previous study were used for the present analysis, and the important features of the procedure and subject descriptions may be seen in that study (Botwinick & Thompson, 1966). For the present it is essential to know that simple auditory RTs of young and elderly adults were measured with PIs of .5-, 3.0-, 6.0-, and 15.0-second durations in both regular and irregular series. . . .

Each of 88 subjects experienced both series; 44 men and women were aged 18–35 years, and an equal number of men and women were aged 60–87 years. In the older group there were 17 men and 27 women. The older group was significantly slower in RT than the younger group, but there were no statistically significant RT differences between men and women, nor with the interaction between age and sex.

### Results and Discussion

Within regular series and within irregular series, RT variances associated with each of the four PI conditions were computed for elderly and young subjects. In addition, these variances were computed for the four age and sex subgroups. The $F$ ratios associated with age (larger variances divided by the smaller variances) may be seen in Table 5–4. These ratios were examined for statistical significance, using the one-tailed probability levels given in the usual tables of $F$ distribution.

Table 5–4 presents the $F$ ratios for each of the eight PI conditions. In all instances the variances of the older groups were larger than the corresponding ones of the younger groups, and in all but one instance (indicated in Table 5–4), the $F$ ratios were statistically significant. With possibly one exception, inferences based upon one- and two-tailed tests of significance would be the same.

These overall results, then, demonstrate that the generalization regarding increased individual differences with increased age holds for RT even when there is a control for the PI condition. To the extent that there are important psychophysiological correlates of RT—as several investigations would indicate, e.g., Surwillo (1963)—and to the extent that we can assume that the increased heterogeneity of RTs with increased age is intrinsic to age and not due to "error" factors, such as sickness, unreliable measuring instruments, etc., then it should be easier to discover these correlates of RT by examining older subjects rather than by examining, as we usually do, young adults. Indices of correlation are proportional to the

Table 5–4. F *Ratio comparisons of reaction time variances among groups of elderly and young male and female adult subjects.*

| | Preparatory interval (seconds) | | | | | | | |
| | Regular series | | | | Irregular series | | | |
| F ratios[a] | 0.5 | 3.0 | 6.0 | 15.0 | 0.5 | 3.0 | 6.0 | 15.0 |
|---|---|---|---|---|---|---|---|---|
| Elderly/young | 12.89 | 14.69 | 7.22 | 6.39 | 8.08 | 10.10 | 7.53 | 5.10 |
| Elderly male/young male | 16.50 | 8.91 | 1.48* | 3.50 | 6.33 | 2.57** | 4.03 | 4.44 |
| Elderly female/young female | 8.68 | 15.61 | 9.20 | 6.61 | 11.10 | 16.53 | 8.01 | 7.09 |

[a] Degrees of freedom: elderly = 43, young = 43, elderly male = 16, young male = 28, elderly female = 26, and young female = 14.

\* $p > .05$.

\*\* $p < .05$; all other F ratios significant at less than the .01 level of confidence.

"true" variances which are involved and inversely proportional to the magnitude of the "error" variances.

## Summary

Typically, old adult subjects vary more among themselves with respect to reaction time (RT) than do young adult subjects, but it was argued that this may be due to the different preparatory intervals (PIs) in the RT series. Variations in PIs make for greater variations in RTs of older subjects than younger ones. To determine whether RT variances of the old are greater than those of the young, independent of PI durations in both regular and irregular series: .5, 3.0, 6.0, and 15.0 seconds. Holding PI constant in this manner, the RT variances were still greater for the old than for the young.

References

Botwinick, J., and Brinley, J. F. Aspects of RT set during brief intervals in relation to age and sex. *Journal of Gerontology*, 17:295–301, 1962.
Botwinick, J., and Thompson, L. W. Components of reaction time in relation to age and sex. *Journal of Genetic Psychology*, 108:175–183, 1966.
Obrist, W. D. Simple auditory reaction time in aged adults. *Journal of Psychology*, 35:259–266, 1953.
Surwillo, W. W. The relation of simple response time to brain-wave frequency and the effects of age. *Electroencephalography and Clinical Neurophysiology*, 15:105–114, 1963.

# Age Difference in Reaction Time: An Artifact?*    *Jack Botwinick and Larry W. Thompson*

A fact as solid as any in the psychological study of aging is that, as adults grow older, they become increasingly slow in responding to environmental events. It is not necessary here to refer to the substantial literature bearing on this fact except, perhaps, to indicate that the literature goes back to the earliest days of modern experimental psychology. Psychologists are interested in the slowing in older age, not only because of its importance in psychomotor skills, but also because of its presumed reflection of central nervous system (CNS) functioning (Botwinick, 1965).

We never doubted this fact of slowdown with age, having contributed to the literature establishing it. However, we wonder about it now. In carrying out a study that may be reported at some future date we made a chance observation which, while not refuting unequivocally the fact of age differences in reaction time (RT), challenges, or at least requires an elaboration of, theories relating to age deficits in CNS functioning.

### Young Athletes and Nonathletes

In the course of simultaneously recording heart rate (EKG) and RT[1] from both elderly men (68–86, M = 74.1 years) and young men (18–27,

* Reprinted by permission from the *Gerontologist*, 8:25–28, 1968.
[1] We were carrying out an experiment to determine whether RTs varied in relation to when in the cardiac cycle the stimulus calling for a response occurred. The apparatus was designed such that the subject's own R-wave (peak amplitude of the

M = 19.5), we thought we discerned that a succession of several young subjects had unusually slow heart rates and, perhaps, unusually quick RTs. When we inquired about these subjects, our assistants identified some of them as Duke University team athletes. We seemed to have had a run of these subjects and we wondered why. Upon questioning we learned that because we were collecting data toward the end of the school year when the athletic seasons were over, the athletes had more time to serve as subjects. They needed to do this in order to fulfill their requirements for their psychology courses.

Recognizing that this sampling bias may be important to control, we decided to call back all the subjects we had tested up to that time to question them about their habits of exercise. All subsequent young subjects were similarly questioned. On the basis of their reports, the young subjects were categorized into two groups: (*a*) those who were team athletes committed to continuous exercise, or those who were not team athletes but, who exercised or played ball regularly, four to five days of each week, (*b*) those who exercised irregularly or not at all. When subjects exercised as much as three times during some weeks but their exercise pattern was either not regular or not taken seriously, it was difficult to place them in one of the two categories. Almost always these subjects were placed in the nonathletic category rather than in the athletic category. The numbers for the athlete and nonathlete groups were 20 and 17, respectively.

## Age Differences and Similarities: Results

We compared the RTs of elderly subjects with those of the athletes and nonathletes, and the results were very clear, unequivocal, and—to us at least—surprising. While the older subjects were significantly slower than

---

cycle) triggered the stimulus (a 1,000-cycle/second, 85db tone, terminated by a finger lift response). The R-wave triggered the stimulus immediately (zero latency), 0.2 second, 0.4 second, or 0.6 second later, according to a prearranged schedule. For the purpose of the present study, these periods of stimulus occurrence were disregarded and all RT data were grouped; the subject had no idea that his own heart cycling was involved in the timing of the stimulus.

Each subject was comfortably seated in a soft lounge chair and pressed a telegraph key on a side table to initiate the RT sequence. The subject was forewarned of the stimulus by the occurrence of a tone (400 cycles/second, 65 db, lasting 0.5 seconds) preceding the stimulus tone. The time between the warning tone and the stimulus tone, i.e., the preparatory interval (PI), was a constant, set at just over 1.0 seconds. However, both the heart cycling and the apparatus contributed to some small variation of the PI. Small as it was, it was necessary to contend with it since it made for a group difference in mean PI, and thus, conceivably, in RT itself. More will be said about this in the text, in the concluding part of the section, "Age Differences and Similarities: Results."

the young athletes, they were not significantly slower than the young nonathletes. These results suggest that a reexamination, or at least an elaboration, of one of the basic "facts" of aging is in order.

The remainder of this section involves a more technical presentation of these results. Those who are not interested in the technical details may procede without loss of concept to the next section, "Fact or Artifact: Discussion."

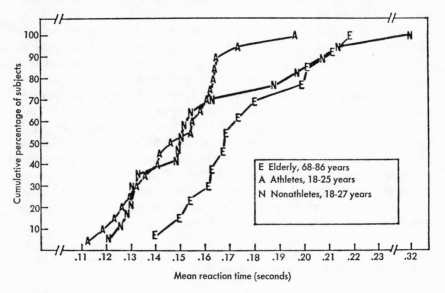

Figure 5–4. *Cumulative percentage of subjects in each of three groups who have mean reaction times indicated on the abscissa.*

Each subject had 120 RT trials. All these trials were with regular PIs during which there were 16 irregularly spaced catch trials (only a warning signal was presented, no stimulus). A short, 5–10 minute break was given at the half-way point of the 120 trials.

Each subject was characterized by his mean and median RT, and the group means of these are shown in Table 5–5. This table also shows the group standard deviations (SD), the number of subjects (N), and the results of *t*-test group comparisons of RT. The only place in Table 5–5 in which the results of individual mean and median RTs are different is with the combined samples of young subjects. A statistically significant age difference was found with the mean RTs, not with the medians.

The measures in which the individual subjects contributed to their respective groups may be seen in Figure 5–4. In Figure 5–4, each elderly subject and each young athletic and nonathletic subject is represented as a percentage of his group having a particular mean RT. These percentages are cumulated such that, for example, Figure 5–4 may be read as follows: approximately 7 percent of the elderly subjects had mean RTs of 0.14 seconds, 15 percent had RTs approximately 0.15 seconds or less, and 100 percent had mean RTs approximately 0.22 seconds or less. Similarly, 100 percent of the young athletes had RTs approximately 0.20 seconds or less, but only 82 percent of young nonathletes performed this well. In Figure 5–4 it may be seen that the nonathletes may really be composed of two

Table 5–5. *Mean and standard deviation (SD) of individual subject mean and median reaction time (RT).*

|  | Elderly (E) | Young athletes (A) | Young nonathletes (N) |
|---|---|---|---|
| Mean RT |  |  |  |
| Mean | 176.15 | 148.14 | 165.06 |
| Median | 157.00 | 137.45 | 155.76 |
| SD |  |  |  |
| Mean | 23.88 | 20.31 | 48.65 |
| Median | 24.50 | 18.91 | 51.45 |
| N | 13.00 | 20.00 | 17.00 |

$t$ test of mean difference of individual means.
E vs. A: $t = 3.37, p < .01$.
E vs. N: $t = .79, p > .05$.
E vs. (A + N): $t = 2.18, p < .05$.
A vs. N: $t = 1.30, p > .05$.
$t$ tests of mean difference of individual medians.
E vs. A: $t = 2.36, p < .05$.
E vs. N: $t = .08, p > .05$.
E vs. (A + N): $t = 1.16, p > .05$.
A vs. N: $t = 1.35, p > .05$.

subgroups: one similar to the athletes, and one different, being much slower and comparable to slower older people (5 of 17 subjects, nearly 30 percent). This idea is also reflected in the relatively large standard deviations of the nonathlete group, seen in Table 5–5. One young nonathlete had a mean and median RT of 0.32 and 0.33 seconds, respectively—so slow that he may belong in a category by himself. When the data of this subject were eliminated from the analysis, the overall results and conclusions were not changed in any important way.

The apparatus controlling the PI (interval between the warning signal and the stimulus) was set at approximately 1.0 second. In the usual RT experiment, this is considered sufficient to describe the PI, but since the original purpose of the investigation was to examine RT relationships with cardiac function while keeping the PI controlled, we had a more precise measurement of the PI than usual. For each subject, we measured 120 RTs. While the PIs were approximately 1.0 seconds in duration, there were differences among them due to variations in the functioning of the apparatus and in the cardiac cycle which triggered the stimuli.

Because we kept such a fine control and record of the PI, we were able to test for group differences in the PI. We know that RT is a function of the PI (e.g., Botwinick & Thompson, 1966), and, thus, if groups differ in the PI this can account for the extent of group differences in RT.

PIs were found significantly different between elderly and nonathletic young subjects—the PIs of the elderly subjects were longer. To adjust for this, the longest PIs and their associated RTs of five elderly subjects and the shortest PIs and their associated RTs of one nonathlete were eliminated. In this way, elderly and nonathletic young subjects had PIs which were not significantly different. When this equating was accomplished, the age comparisons of the RTs remained the same, i.e., elderly and nonathletic young subjects were not significantly different in RT.

Fact or Artifact: Discussion

We do not think that the present data refute the "fact of aging"—the often demonstrated decline in speed to respond with increasing adult age.[2] We do think the present data open up the need for more investigation and, perhaps, broader and modified views of the significance of speed to respond. Most important, the present data emphasize that just as individual differences must be controlled or evaluated in aging samples they must also be considered in the younger controls to which the elderly are compared. We know that matters such as health and sickness in old age determine the extent of age differences in the statistical comparisons (e.g., Botwinick & Birren, 1963). We now suggest that matters such as physical fitness in young age also determine the extent of age differences. It is not suggested here that these physical items are all that we need to monitor; on the contrary, we believe that they are but one class of items, perhaps not even the most important class.

Although the present data may alert us to the need for a much finer analysis of the age-RT literature, we do not believe that the present data showed that all of the slowness to respond in later life is an artifact of

---

[2] The distinction between speed to respond and speed of carrying out the response must be recognized. This distinction is frequently phrased in terms of reaction time and movement time. The present study has to do *only* with reaction time.

exercise. First, we really do not know how typical or atypical our subject samples may be. Second, since we did not start out doing this particular study, we categorized some of the subjects only after viewing the data and suspecting a relationship between RT and cardiac function (with athletes tending toward slower heart rates). This may have unduly influenced the results. We do not know at this time how repeatable the present study may be, but we do know that it is not easy to schedule athletes and nonathletes for testing. Thus the present data may best be regarded as suggestive, demonstrating a direction of analysis. Third, the present results may be less general than we would like to believe, and more unique to the specific procedures. Table 5–5 and Figure 5–4 show that as RTs go, those in this study are not especially fast. Our subjects were not seated in an alert position at a desk or table, but they were seated in a deep, soft, lounge chair. Furthermore, both the warning signal and the stimulus were tones. We have a hunch that it is more difficult to be quick with two tones (one alerting and one as stimulus) than with an alerting light and a tone stimulus. If this is correct, then perhaps only the most able of subjects, i.e., young athletes, were able to overcome this disadvantage. Perhaps a less demanding RT situation would more easily differentiate elderly subjects from young nonathletes. Fourth, and perhaps most important, it may be seen in Figure 5–4 that some age difference in RT is inherent even in the present data.

Figure 5–4 shows that the very fastest old person had a mean RT of 0.14 seconds. Seven of the 20 athletes (35 percent) and 6 of the 17 nonathletes (also approximately 35 percent) had faster RTs than this. In addition, as already indicated, the lack of significant difference between the elderly and nonathletic subjects was due principally to five slow nonathletes. Figure 5–4 shows that these 5 nonathletes (29 percent of sample) plus 1 or 2 athletes (5–10 percent) may belong to a special yet-to-be-described category, one that is much more specific and indicative of the underlying mechanisms than the crude categories of athlete and nonathlete.

The major point here is that rather than representing different age groups simply by means, medians, and the like, they may be more meaningfully represented by percentages in combination with these measures of central tendency. For example, Figure 5–4 shows that of the 37 subjects in the total young group, 11 (or 30 percent) were slower in RT than a third of the elderly subjects. We wager that if all age comparisons were made on the basis of such a combination of percentage and central tendency statistics much of the age difference which may seem impressive at first would lose its interest. An obvious disadvantage of such indices is that they do not lend themselves to parametric statistical tests of significance.

A Final Note and Summary

The contribution of the present report may lie less in the specific considerations of reaction time than in its broad methodological sampling implications. When we identified a college population subsample of 16–19 percent whose performances were no different, probably were worse, than the performances of an elderly sample, implicit questions were raised regarding the relation between a person's history and his aging patterns. To make more meaningful our conceptions of aging processes we need to control or to evaluate individual differences in a large variety of factors. This is as true for aging samples as for their younger controls.

In this study, we separated our young adult subjects into athlete and nonathlete categories because, as a portion of the data was being collected, we thought that heart rate may be related to RT, and that both these variables may differentiate the two categories of subjects. It is important to note that the categorization was made independent of either heart rate or RT, and in the final analysis, athletes and nonathletes were not very different in these measures. During the course of the experiment, mean heart rate of athletes was 70.14 beats per minute, and of nonathletes, 76.96. Although the difference was in the direction of expectation, it was not statistically significant ($p > .05$). The corresponding mean heart rate of the elderly subjects was 71.58, not significantly different from either young group.

Despite these nonsignificant relationships, categorizing young adult subjects into groups of athlete and nonathlete proved interesting. The often-demonstrated age difference in RT was seen again with athletic young subjects but not with nonathletic young subjects, which suggests that exercise or its lack may be a factor in the slowing with age: we can expect that young people overall exercise more than elderly people. Although this may pose difficulties for CNS theories explaining the age-related slowdown, it is well to recognize that the diminution with age in the amount of exercise may be more a co-function of CNS deficits than it is an antecedent or cause of the slowdown.

In any case, as was indicated, the data of the present study emphasized the need to control or to evaluate individual differences in a large variety of factors, not only habits of exercise. Furthermore, emphasis on individual differences ought to be complemented with a similar emphasis on individual differences with respect to the main measures of study, as for example, RT in the present study. This emphasis may best be made by referring to percentage in combination with measures of central tendency.

# References

Botwinick, J. Theories of antecedent conditions of speed of response. In Welford, A. T., and Birren, J. E. (Eds.), *Behavior, aging, and the nervous system.* Springfield, Ill.: Charles C Thomas, 1965.

Botwinick, J., and Birren, J. E. Cognitive processes: Mental abilities and psychomotor responses in aged men. In Birren, J. E., Butler, R. N., Greenhouse, S. W., Sokoloff, L., and Yarrow, M. R. (Eds.), *Human aging: A biological and behavioral study.* Washington: Government Printing Office, 1963.

Botwinick, J., and Thompson, L. W. Components of reaction time in relation to age and sex. *Journal of Genetic Psychology,* 108:175–183, 1966.

# Chapter 6. Intelligence

It has been widely assumed that declining intelligence is also typical or normal in aging. However, the data from the Duke Longitudinal Study of Aging throw considerable doubt on the generality of this assumption. The first report indicates that the intelligence score norms that are generally used for the aged (based on Kansas City subjects) may not be applicable to other regions such as the Southeast. The second report shows little or no overall decline in intelligence over a three-year period. The next study found that Rorschach performance was more closely related to intelligence level than to chronological age. Finally, a longitudinal study of intelligence and cardiovascular disease found no significant relationship between the two when socioeconomic status was controlled. This indicates that the aged may be able to maintain their intellectual abilities despite serious physiological deterioration. Thus the idea of a general and substantial decline of intelligence with aging may prove to be more of a myth than a normal pattern.

## The Generality of the WAIS Standardization for the Aged*    *Carl Eisdorfer and Louis D. Cohen*

In establishing age norms for the Wechsler Adult Intelligence Scale (WAIS), some "1,700 subjects, both sexes, aged 16–64 plus an additional 475 subjects of both sexes, ages 60–75 and over" were used. In selecting the 1,700 subjects, "occupation and education, as well as sex and age, . . . also geography, urban *vs.* rural, and color" were simultaneously considered, and it was concluded that "the norms as they stand . . . seem to be reasonably representative of the country as a whole . . ." (Wechsler, 1958, pp. 86–88, 91). The additional 475 subjects aged 60–75 and over referred to here formed the basis for an extension of the WAIS norms beyond age 64, but caution was expressed about using tables derived from these data because they were "not based on cases tested throughout the country according to census specifications but came from a special old age

* Reprinted by permission from the *Journal of Abnormal and Social Psychology,* 62:520–527, 1961.

study" (Wechsler, 1955, p. 25). However, there was an overlap of groups aged 60–64 in both the national standardization and in the special old age study, which was conducted in Kansas City. The overlapping groups showed high comparability of performance with only one subtest, Picture Completion, indicating a reliable difference between groups at the .05 level (Doppelt & Wallace, 1955).

The generality of the Kansas City results for the United States population over 65 has needed testing, and the opportunity to make comparisons with a population in another part of the country arose in the course of an investigation conducted at Duke University in Durham, North Carolina, in connection with a longitudinal study of the aged. In a previous paper (Eisdorfer, Busse, & Cohen, 1959) some question was raised as to the generality of the Kansas City results in view of strikingly consistent discrepancies between the Verbal and Performance IQs in the Duke Project population when the Kansas City data were used for comparison. Using these latter criteria, it would have been expected that the relationship between the Verbal and Performance IQs in the Duke data would be random, neither one nor the other being consistently superior; but successive comparisons based on age, sex, race, socioeconomic status, high or low IQ status, and community vs. hospitalized status in the Duke Project data showed consistent and reliable differences favoring the Verbal over the Performance IQs.

In consequence, it seemed advisable to compare systematically the data obtained from the final population of subjects available in the Duke study with those from Kansas City. The present report is based upon this comparison.

## Method

### Sample

The Kansas City study set out to test 500 individuals, although some 659 were listed to be approached on the basis of a "two stage, stratified, systematic sample" in which every block in the area of four counties embracing Kansas City was geographically numbered and weighted by size, and a systematic primary sample of every $n$th block selected. Every $n$th dwelling in each $n$th block was selected further, and each person over 60 in these dwellings was selected for the study. Actually, the WAIS was administered to 475 subjects, of whom 352 completed the study. Only data from completed tests were used for the IQ tables—a total of 352 subjects (Wechsler, 1955, p. 23).

The Duke sample of 239 subjects who completed the full scale WAIS was drawn from volunteers in the community, originally recruited through requests on radio and television as well as through Golden Age Club meetings. . . .

There were 18 subjects who did not complete the full scale WAIS and so were not included in this analysis.

Certain biases entered into the selection of the Duke Project sample. Since all subjects had to come to the Medical Center for a two-day examination, only ambulatory, reasonably well-functioning individuals participated in the study. Bedridden, immobile, and socially isolated individuals are probably not represented in relation to their incidence in the

Table 6-1. *Comparisons of numbers of subjects and age, race, and sex characteristics of the Duke Project and Kansas City Studies on the WAIS.*

| | Duke Project | | | | | | | Kansas City Study[a] total sample | | |
| | White | | Negro | | Total sample | | | | | |
| Age | Male | Female | Male | Female | Male | Female | Total | Male | Female | Total |
|---|---|---|---|---|---|---|---|---|---|---|
| 60–64 | 15 | 16 | 5 | 11 | 20 | 27 | 47 | 44 | 57 | 101 |
| 65–69 | 19 | 26 | 11 | 11 | 30 | 37 | 67 | 42 | 44 | 86 |
| 70–74 | 25 | 21 | 7 | 9 | 32 | 30 | 62 | 38 | 42 | 80 |
| 75+ | 23 | 20 | 9 | 11 | 32 | 31 | 63 | 36 | 49 | 85 |
| Subtotal | 82 | 83 | 32 | 42 | 114 | 125 | 239 | 160 | 192 | 352 |
| Total | 165 | | 74 | | 239 | | | | | |

[a] Wechsler (1955, Table 15, p. 23).

Durham population. Since the sample was built up over time, many volunteers were not included in the study because they did not fit into the "cells" of the design that needed to be filled. Thus, toward the latter part of the study, "upper" socioeconomic Negro male volunteers were sought for and accepted, while "lower" socioeconomic white female volunteers were not. It may well be that some systematic bias was incurred by the inclusion of subjects who volunteered early, since those individuals may have been more socially alert and more assertive than others of their age in the Durham population.

In Table 6-1 may be seen the distribution of the subjects included in the Duke Study according to age, sex, and race characteristics. This distribution is compared with the Kansas City population on the same criteria. The total number of subjects in the Duke sample for the three age intervals 65–69, 70–74, and 75+ is 67, 62, 63; for the Kansas City sample, N = 86, 80, and 85. The Duke and Kansas City samples for the three older groups seem close enough to each other in number to warrant comparison. Both studies report a slightly higher number of female subjects in the sample. Although the Durham population characteristics show 57 percent females over age 60, our Duke sample shows 52 percent female. The white/Negro proportions are not mentioned in the Kansas City study, but in the Duke sample, 31 percent are Negro, which conforms to 29 percent Negro in the Durham population. Some of the sample characteristics of the Duke Project are attributable to placing sufficient numbers of subjects in each cell so that individual variations would not distort the values of any cell.

No data on social class are reported for the Kansas City sample, but subjects were dichotomized on this variable in the Duke Project on the basis of a modification of Warner's Index of Status Characteristics (Warner, Meeker, & Eells, 1957) described in detail earlier (Eisdorfer et al., 1959). The "higher" status group included 103 subjects, whereas the "lower" socioeconomic group included 149 subjects.

*Procedure*

The WAIS examinations were administered by one of three experienced examiners according to the standard procedure outlined in the WAIS manual (Wechsler, 1955). The results for each subject were treated as prescribed in the test manual, Scaled scores, Verbal, Performance, and Full Scale IQs were computed.

In order to assess the relationship between the performance of the Duke and the Kansas City samples, comparisons were made by utilizing the data on Kansas City subjects reported by Doppelt and Wallace (1955).

Results

Table 6–2 presents the means and SDs of the Scaled scores for each of the WAIS subtests as well as for Verbal, Performance, and Full Scale scores and IQs. To assess the relationship between these scores and the data reported for Kansas City, *t* tests were performed to compare the Full Scale, Verbal, and Performance scores reported by Doppelt and Wallace (1955), and the data obtained in the present study. Table 6–3 gives the results of this comparison.

There is evidently a larger variance in the Duke sample, but no reliable difference between the Full Scale scores was obtained from the two groups. The import of the slight differences between the Full Scale scores of the two groups becomes clear on study of Sections B and C of Table 6–3. In Section B, subjects in age groups 70–74 and 75+ in the Duke sample show significantly higher Verbal scores than do the subjects in the Kansas City

Table 6–2. *Means and standard deviations of all WAIS subtest Scaled scores and Full Scale, Verbal, and Performance IQs for Duke Project samples.*

|  | Age group 60–64 (N = 47) | | Age group 65–69 (N = 67) | | Age group 70–74 (N = 62) | | Age group 75+ (N = 63) | |
|---|---|---|---|---|---|---|---|---|
|  | M | SD | M | SD | M | SD | M | SD |
| Information | 9.76 | 4.02 | 9.19 | 3.46 | 10.16 | 3.82 | 9.12 | 4.65 |
| Comprehension | 11.63 | 4.71 | 10.74 | 3.62 | 10.75 | 3.99 | 9.74 | 4.06 |
| Arithmetic | 9.76 | 4.31 | 8.67 | 3.33 | 9.08 | 3.45 | 8.28 | 3.49 |
| Similarities | 8.72 | 4.32 | 7.17 | 3.75 | 7.62 | 4.15 | 6.65 | 4.02 |
| Digit Span | 9.34 | 3.40 | 7.91 | 2.73 | 8.11 | 2.76 | 7.41 | 2.82 |
| Vocabulary | 10.65 | 4.24 | 9.85 | 3.89 | 10.56 | 4.38 | 9.90 | 4.70 |
| Digit Symbol | 5.14 | 3.54 | 4.43 | 2.92 | 4.37 | 3.22 | 2.73 | 2.66 |
| Picture Completion | 6.97 | 2.60 | 6.05 | 3.11 | 5.91 | 3.16 | 5.52 | 3.36 |
| Block Design | 6.42 | 3.20 | 5.71 | 2.61 | 6.04 | 2.89 | 5.14 | 3.23 |
| Picture Arrangement | 5.93 | 2.58 | 5.31 | 2.46 | 5.25 | 2.70 | 4.38 | 2.84 |
| Object Assembly | 6.97 | 3.18 | 6.05 | 2.56 | 6.16 | 2.75 | 5.20 | 2.73 |
| Verbal score | 59.89 | 22.78 | 53.70 | 18.12 | 56.14 | 20.00 | 50.96 | 21.27 |
| Performance score | 31.46 | 12.95 | 27.61 | 11.62 | 27.75 | 12.43 | 23.00 | 13.23 |
| Full Scale score | 91.23 | 34.68 | 81.31 | 28.89 | 83.90 | 31.24 | 73.74 | 33.36 |
| Verbal IQ | 104.00 | 22.56 | 100.01 | 17.95 | 108.20 | 19.99 | 106.77 | 21.01 |
| Performance IQ | 92.68 | 16.92 | 91.26 | 15.51 | 97.72 | 16.58 | 97.69 | 17.17 |
| Full Scale IQ | 99.08 | 20.68 | 96.04 | 17.35 | 104.00 | 18.86 | 102.88 | 19.79 |

Table 6–3. *Means, standard deviations, and* t *tests of Full Scale, Verbal, and Performance scores between Duke Project and Kansas City samples.*[a]

|  | Duke Project sample | | | Kansas City sample | | | | |
|---|---|---|---|---|---|---|---|---|
|  | N | M | SD | N | M | SD | t | p |
| A. Full Scale score | | | | | | | | |
| 60–64 | 47 | 91.23 | 34.66 | 101 | 90.21 | 24.15 | 0.18 | ns |
| 65–69 | 67 | 81.31 | 28.89 | 86 | 88.13 | 22.92 | 1.57 | ns |
| 70–74 | 62 | 83.90 | 31.27 | 80 | 77.19 | 21.42 | 1.43 | ns |
| 75+ | 63 | 73.74 | 33.36 | 85 | 68.71 | 21.56 | 1.03 | ns |
| B. Verbal score | | | | | | | | |
| 60–64 | 47 | 59.89 | 22.78 | 101 | 55.24 | 14.51 | 1.27 | ns |
| 65–69 | 67 | 53.70 | 18.12 | 86 | 53.73 | 14.51 | 0.01 | ns |
| 70–74 | 62 | 56.14 | 20.00 | 80 | 47.66 | 13.73 | 2.83 | .05 |
| 75+ | 63 | 50.96 | 21.27 | 85 | 42.02 | 14.16 | 2.23 | .05 |
| C. Performance score | | | | | | | | |
| 60–64 | 47 | 31.46 | 12.95 | 101 | 34.97 | 10.94 | 1.59 | ns |
| 65–69 | 67 | 27.61 | 11.62 | 86 | 34.40 | 10.05 | 3.77 | .01 |
| 70–74 | 62 | 27.75 | 12.43 | 80 | 29.53 | 9.45 | 0.92 | ns |
| 75+ | 63 | 23.00 | 13.23 | 85 | 24.68 | 9.54 | 0.84 | ns |

[a] As reported by Doppelt and Wallace (1955, Table 15, p. 328).

Table 6–4. *Means, standard deviations, and* t *tests of Duke Project and Kansas City samples on WAIS Verbal subtests.*[a]

| | Duke sample | | | Kansas City sample | | | |
|---|---|---|---|---|---|---|---|
| | N | M | SD | N | M | SD | *t* |
| Information | | | | | | | |
| 60–64 | 47 | 9.76 | 4.02 | 101 | 9.55 | 3.17 | 0.320 |
| 65–69 | 67 | 9.19 | 3.46 | 86 | 9.63 | 3.22 | 0.791 |
| 70–74 | 62 | 10.16 | 3.82 | 80 | 8.48 | 2.86 | 2.867** |
| 75+ | 63 | 9.12 | 4.65 | 85 | 7.92 | 2.81 | 1.811 |
| Comprehension | | | | | | | |
| 60–64 | 47 | 11.63 | 4.71 | 101 | 8.96 | 2.27 | 3.661** |
| 65–69 | 67 | 10.74 | 3.62 | 86 | 8.76 | 2.43 | 3.830** |
| 70–74 | 62 | 10.75 | 3.99 | 80 | 7.98 | 2.09 | 4.930** |
| 75+ | 63 | 9.74 | 4.06 | 85 | 7.52 | 2.46 | 3.823** |
| Arithmetic | | | | | | | |
| 60–64 | 47 | 9.76 | 4.31 | 101 | 9.51 | 3.58 | 0.350 |
| 65–69 | 67 | 8.67 | 3.33 | 86 | 9.30 | 3.69 | 1.096 |
| 70–74 | 62 | 9.08 | 3.45 | 80 | 7.86 | 3.28 | 2.118* |
| 75+ | 63 | 8.28 | 3.49 | 85 | 7.11 | 2.60 | 2.232* |
| Similarities | | | | | | | |
| 60–64 | 47 | 8.72 | 4.32 | 101 | 8.77 | 2.82 | 0.066 |
| 65–69 | 67 | 7.17 | 3.75 | 86 | 8.45 | 3.00 | 2.247 |
| 70–74 | 62 | 7.62 | 4.15 | 80 | 7.40 | 2.75 | 0.371 |
| 75+ | 63 | 6.65 | 4.02 | 85 | 6.19 | 3.33 | 0.735 |
| Digit Span | | | | | | | |
| 60–64 | 47 | 9.34 | 3.40 | 101 | 8.82 | 2.89 | 0.898 |
| 65–69 | 67 | 7.91 | 2.73 | 86 | 8.01 | 2.69 | 0.223 |
| 70–74 | 62 | 8.11 | 2.76 | 80 | 7.70 | 2.83 | 0.868 |
| 75+ | 63 | 7.41 | 2.82 | 85 | 6.94 | 3.24 | 0.939 |
| Vocabulary | | | | | | | |
| 60–64 | 47 | 10.65 | 4.24 | 101 | 9.61 | 3.25 | 1.487 |
| 65–69 | 67 | 9.85 | 3.89 | 86 | 9.58 | 2.83 | 0.475 |
| 70–74 | 62 | 10.56 | 4.38 | 80 | 8.25 | 2.93 | 3.554** |
| 75+ | 63 | 9.90 | 4.70 | 85 | 8.35 | 3.11 | 2.263* |

[a] Doppelt and Wallace (1955, Table 9, p. 321).
* $p < .05$.
** $p < .01$.

sample. In Section C, we note that the Performance score of the 65–69-year-old group of the Duke sample is significantly lower than the corresponding score in the Kansas City sample. It is interesting to observe also that in age group 60–64, the Duke sample has a somewhat higher Verbal score and a somewhat lower Performance score. All of these comparisons confirm the previous report of Eisdorfer et al. (1959) of the consistent superiority of Verbal over Performance scores in an earlier Duke sample as compared with the Kansas City sample.

A more intensive analysis of the Verbal scale subtest scores is possible since Doppelt and Wallace (1955) present the means and SDs of all their

Verbal scale subtests. A comparison of the Verbal subtest performance of the Duke sample with that of the Kansas City sample is found in Table 6–4, which presents these data as well as the *t* tests for differences between the two samples.

Of special note is the Comprehension score of the Duke sample, which is significantly higher (*t* < .01) at every age level. Arithmetic and Vocabulary subtest scales also appear higher in the Duke sample, but the differences are significant only for the two oldest groups—70–74 and 75+.

In 19 of the 24 comparisons of the Verbal subtest scores, the Duke sample is higher, 9 of the 19 being significant at the .05 level or better. The two older groups in the Duke sample are higher in every comparison. In only one case, the Similarities score of the 65–69-year-old group, does the comparison go in the opposite direction at a significant level.

Table 6–5. *Differences between mean scaled score of men in the Duke and Kansas City samples on each performance test.*[a]

| Test | Age | Duke sample | | | Kansas City sample | | | *t* tests of difference |
|------|-----|---|---|----|---|---|----|----|
| | | N | M | SD | N | M | SD | |
| Digit Symbol | 60–64 | 20 | 5.90 | 3.09 | 50 | 4.68 | 2.80 | 1.49 |
| | 65–69 | 30 | 3.56 | 2.66 | 44 | 5.07 | 1.83 | 2.56* |
| | 70–74 | 32 | 4.31 | 3.03 | 44 | 3.00 | 2.50 | 1.97 |
| | 75+ | 32 | 3.03 | 2.55 | 40 | 2.40 | 2.40 | 1.05 |
| Picture Completion | 60–64 | 20 | 8.05 | 2.45 | 50 | 7.34 | 2.48 | 1.06 |
| | 65–69 | 30 | 6.16 | 3.14 | 47 | 7.47 | 2.48 | 1.89 |
| | 70–74 | 32 | 6.31 | 2.91 | 47 | 6.87 | 2.65 | 0.85 |
| | 75+ | 32 | 6.18 | 3.59 | 50 | 5.32 | 2.81 | 1.14 |
| Block Design | 60–64 | 20 | 6.30 | 3.51 | 46 | 7.52 | 3.13 | 1.31 |
| | 65–69 | 30 | 4.80 | 2.59 | 43 | 7.42 | 2.39 | 4.32** |
| | 70–74 | 32 | 5.90 | 2.96 | 44 | 6.02 | 2.62 | 0.17 |
| | 75+ | 32 | 4.93 | 3.30 | 42 | 4.69 | 2.41 | 0.35 |
| Picture Arrangement | 60–64 | 20 | 6.00 | 2.95 | 45 | 7.29 | 2.46 | 1.67 |
| | 65–69 | 30 | 5.00 | 2.44 | 43 | 6.86 | 2.51 | 3.11** |
| | 70–74 | 32 | 5.34 | 2.78 | 41 | 6.37 | 2.51 | 1.60 |
| | 75+ | 32 | 4.59 | 3.09 | 40 | 5.05 | 2.37 | 0.67 |
| Object Assembly | 60–64 | 20 | 6.65 | 3.01 | 46 | 7.33 | 2.77 | 0.84 |
| | 65–69 | 30 | 5.73 | 2.30 | 43 | 7.98 | 2.76 | 3.72** |
| | 70–74 | 32 | 5.87 | 2.56 | 40 | 6.25 | 2.95 | 0.56 |
| | 75+ | 32 | 5.50 | 2.67 | 41 | 5.12 | 2.66 | 0.59 |

[a] Doppelt and Wallace (1955, Table 7, p. 319).
* Significant at .05.
** Significant at .01.

Table 6–6. *Differences between mean scaled scores of females in the Duke and Kansas City samples on each performance test.*[a]

| Test | Age | Duke sample | | | Kansas City sample | | | t tests of difference |
|------|-----|---|---|----|---|---|----|---|
| | | N | M | SD | N | M | SD | |
| Digit Symbol | 60–64 | 27 | 4.46 | 3.74 | 60 | 5.72 | 2.83 | 1.33 |
| | 65–69 | 37 | 5.13 | 2.98 | 49 | 4.53 | 2.59 | 0.97 |
| | 70–74 | 30 | 4.37 | 3.50 | 46 | 3.41 | 2.02 | 1.33 |
| | 75+ | 31 | 2.41 | 2.77 | 61 | 3.02 | 2.29 | 1.02 |
| Picture Completion | 60–64 | 27 | 6.17 | 2.40 | 60 | 6.93 | 2.17 | 1.38 |
| | 65–69 | 37 | 5.97 | 3.13 | 54 | 6.54 | 2.49 | 0.90 |
| | 70–74 | 30 | 5.48 | 3.47 | 51 | 5.35 | 2.48 | 0.17 |
| | 75+ | 31 | 4.83 | 3.01 | 63 | 5.25 | 2.07 | 0.67 |
| Block Design | 60–64 | 27 | 6.50 | 2.96 | 59 | 7.83 | 2.69 | 1.98 |
| | 65–69 | 37 | 6.45 | 2.42 | 49 | 7.61 | 2.69 | 2.05* |
| | 70–74 | 30 | 6.20 | 2.90 | 49 | 6.55 | 2.53 | 0.52 |
| | 75+ | 31 | 5.35 | 3.20 | 59 | 5.54 | 2.81 | 0.26 |
| Picture Arrangement | 60–64 | 27 | 5.89 | 2.28 | 59 | 6.64 | 2.54 | 1.35 |
| | 65–69 | 37 | 5.56 | 2.47 | 46 | 6.30 | 2.27 | 1.37 |
| | 70–74 | 30 | 5.13 | 2.69 | 48 | 5.48 | 2.09 | 0.57 |
| | 75+ | 31 | 4.16 | 2.59 | 50 | 4.98 | 2.32 | 1.41 |
| Object Assembly | 60–64 | 27 | 7.28 | 3.29 | 57 | 7.96 | 3.13 | 0.88 |
| | 65–69 | 37 | 6.32 | 2.76 | 46 | 8.00 | 2.91 | 2.64* |
| | 70–74 | 30 | 6.37 | 2.98 | 45 | 7.24 | 2.85 | 1.21 |
| | 75+ | 31 | 4.90 | 2.79 | 55 | 5.51 | 2.93 | 0.93 |

[a] Doppelt and Wallace (1955, Table 7, p. 319).
* Significant at .05.

While Doppelt and Wallace (1955) presented the means and SDs of all Verbal scale subtests for all subjects according to age, their presentation of the Performance scale subtests was not organized in the same manner. They list Performance scale data for the four age groups separately for men and women. Thus it was necessary to treat data from the present study similarly. Table 6–5 contains the Performance scale scores of the men in the Duke and Kansas City samples, and Table 6–6 shows the mean Performance scale scores of women from the two samples.

The most striking finding appears in Table 6–5 in the age group 65–69, where the males in the Kansas City sample have higher scores than the corresponding Duke sample in four of the five Performance subtests at a significance level of $p < .05$. The Kansas City females in the age group 65–69 are significantly higher on two of the subtests, Block Design and Object Assembly (in both cases $p < .01$). Tables 6–5 and 6–6 reveal a

Table 6–7. Intercorrelations of the tests: age 60–64, Duke sample.[a]

(N = 47)

| | 1 | 2 | 3 | 4 | 5 | 6 | 7 | 8 | 9 | 10 | 11 | 12 | 13 |
|---|---|---|---|---|---|---|---|---|---|---|---|---|---|
| 1. Information | | | | | | | | | | | | | |
| 2. Comprehension | .819 | | | | | | | | | | | | |
| 3. Arithmetic | .830 | .855 | | | | | | | | | | | |
| 4. Similarities | .814 | .800 | .803 | | | | | | | | | | |
| 5. Digit Span | .566 | .681 | .683 | .669 | | | | | | | | | |
| 6. Vocabulary | .875 | .877 | .850 | .884 | .723 | | | | | | | | |
| 7. Digit Symbol | .819 | .749 | .823 | .807 | .547 | .805 | | | | | | | |
| 8. Picture Completion | .717 | .769 | .739 | .682 | .457 | .717 | .746 | | | | | | |
| 9. Block Design | .685 | .721 | .655 | .750 | .508 | .698 | .655 | .620 | | | | | |
| 10. Picture Arrangement | .623 | .671 | .679 | .654 | .502 | .655 | .653 | .662 | .613 | | | | |
| 11. Object Assembly | .678 | .704 | .585 | .633 | .492 | .645 | .652 | .571 | .728 | .731 | | | |
| 12. Verbal score[b] | .906 | .932 | .927 | .917 | .782 | .961 | .842 | .758 | .744 | .699 | .692 | | |
| 13. Performance score[b] | .829 | .845 | .816 | .830 | .589 | .827 | .877 | .831 | .853 | .843 | .866 | .876 | |
| 14. Full Scale score[b] | .903 | .928 | .913 | .912 | .733 | .939 | .878 | .806 | .805 | .775 | .779 | .983 | .947 |
| 15. Verbal IQ | .906 | .926 | .923 | .917 | .783 | .964 | .840 | .757 | .742 | .700 | .695 | | |
| 16. Performance IQ | .821 | .836 | .809 | .830 | .588 | .830 | .875 | .822 | .847 | .838 | .871 | .872 | |
| 17. Full Scale IQ | .902 | .922 | .908 | .910 | .732 | .941 | .879 | .802 | .803 | .770 | .784 | .981 | .947 |

[a] Compare with Doppelt and Wallace (1955, Table 10, p. 324).
[b] Correlation of tests with Verbal, Performance, and Full Scale scores before correction for contamination.

Table 6–8. Intercorrelations of the tests: age 65–69, Duke sample.[a]

(N = 67)

| | 1 | 2 | 3 | 4 | 5 | 6 | 7 | 8 | 9 | 10 | 11 | 12 | 13 |
|---|---|---|---|---|---|---|---|---|---|---|---|---|---|
| 1. Information | | | | | | | | | | | | | |
| 2. Comprehension | .846 | | | | | | | | | | | | |
| 3. Arithmetic | .767 | .679 | | | | | | | | | | | |
| 4. Similarities | .769 | .818 | .686 | | | | | | | | | | |
| 5. Digit Span | .503 | .576 | .493 | .396 | | | | | | | | | |
| 6. Vocabulary | .860 | .837 | .700 | .725 | .551 | | | | | | | | |
| 7. Digit Symbol | .767 | .703 | .632 | .686 | .496 | .774 | | | | | | | |
| 8. Picture Completion | .787 | .769 | .719 | .706 | .511 | .729 | .719 | | | | | | |
| 9. Block Design | .625 | .632 | .569 | .603 | .423 | .639 | .656 | .589 | | | | | |
| 10. Picture Arrangement | .719 | .685 | .634 | .733 | .370 | .729 | .652 | .643 | .627 | | | | |
| 11. Object Assembly | .572 | .586 | .557 | .628 | .324 | .548 | .594 | .707 | .674 | .533 | | | |
| 12. Verbal score[b] | .929 | .927 | .839 | .860 | .649 | .914 | .791 | .827 | .685 | .765 | .636 | | |
| 13. Performance score[b] | .828 | .802 | .740 | .794 | .509 | .813 | .866 | .876 | .834 | .812 | .826 | .881 | |
| 14. Full Scale score[b] | .916 | .904 | .824 | .859 | .612 | .901 | .845 | .871 | .766 | .807 | .731 | | .955 |
| 15. Verbal IQ | .927 | .924 | .840 | .867 | .639 | .908 | .792 | .828 | .681 | .768 | .641 | .981 | |
| 16. Performance IQ | .818 | .792 | .737 | .799 | .491 | .803 | .862 | .868 | .825 | .813 | .822 | .873 | |
| 17. Full Scale IQ | .910 | .897 | .823 | .866 | .599 | .894 | .847 | .867 | .761 | .809 | .730 | .976 | .953 |

[a] Compare with Doppelt and Wallace (1955, Table 11, p. 325).
[b] Correlation of tests with Verbal, Performance, and Full Scale scores before correction for contamination.

Table 6–9. *Intercorrelations of the tests: age 70–74, Duke sample.*[a]

(N = 62)

| | 1 | 2 | 3 | 4 | 5 | 6 | 7 | 8 | 9 | 10 | 11 | 12 | 13 |
|---|---|---|---|---|---|---|---|---|---|---|---|---|---|
| 1. Information | .854 | | | | | | | | | | | | |
| 2. Comprehension | .793 | .738 | | | | | | | | | | | |
| 3. Arithmetic | .762 | .794 | .573 | | | | | | | | | | |
| 4. Similarities | .577 | .622 | .584 | .620 | | | | | | | | | |
| 5. Digit Span | .876 | .832 | .708 | .817 | .630 | | | | | | | | |
| 6. Vocabulary | .772 | .760 | .670 | .670 | .563 | .699 | | | | | | | |
| 7. Digit Symbol | .819 | .759 | .688 | .666 | .576 | .720 | .731 | | | | | | |
| 8. Picture Completion | .681 | .640 | .596 | .605 | .581 | .593 | .733 | .736 | | | | | |
| 9. Block Design | .631 | .642 | .605 | .499 | .519 | .706 | .630 | .604 | .501 | | | | |
| 10. Picture Arrangement | .569 | .549 | .403 | .530 | .475 | .482 | .577 | .686 | .699 | .431 | | | |
| 11. Object Assembly | | | | | | | | | | | .576 | | |
| 12. Verbal score[b] | .926 | .921 | .831 | .876 | .746 | .934 | .796 | .802 | .705 | .681 | .801 | .850 | |
| 13. Performance score[b] | .830 | .800 | .708 | .709 | .646 | .763 | .880 | .898 | .873 | .746 | .687 | | .941 |
| 14. Full Scale score[b] | .923 | .907 | .813 | .842 | .734 | .901 | .859 | .870 | .798 | .732 | .579 | | |
| 15. Verbal IQ | .926 | .914 | .826 | .875 | .741 | .939 | .788 | .809 | .708 | .683 | .796 | .977 | |
| 16. Performance IQ | .827 | .789 | .705 | .704 | .640 | .770 | .864 | .902 | .867 | .751 | .685 | .846 | |
| 17. Full Scale IQ | .921 | .897 | .809 | .839 | .730 | .906 | .846 | .877 | .798 | .736 | | .973 | .940 |

[a] Compare with Doppelt and Wallace (1955, Table 12, p. 326).

[b] Correlation of tests with Verbal, Performance, and Full Scale scores before correction for contamination.

Table 6–10. *Intercorrelations of the tests: age 75+, Duke sample.*[a]

(N = 63)

| | 1 | 2 | 3 | 4 | 5 | 6 | 7 | 8 | 9 | 10 | 11 | 12 | 13 |
|---|---|---|---|---|---|---|---|---|---|---|---|---|---|
| 1. Information | | | | | | | | | | | | | |
| 2. Comprehension | .874 | | | | | | | | | | | | |
| 3. Arithmetic | .775 | .754 | | | | | | | | | | | |
| 4. Similarities | .801 | .749 | .768 | | | | | | | | | | |
| 5. Digit Span | .572 | .559 | .568 | .541 | | | | | | | | | |
| 6. Vocabulary | .849 | .857 | .757 | .837 | .655 | | | | | | | | |
| 7. Digit Symbol | .743 | .712 | .782 | .745 | .637 | .780 | | | | | | | |
| 8. Picture Completion | .807 | .767 | .770 | .798 | .597 | .795 | .735 | | | | | | |
| 9. Block Design | .625 | .544 | .625 | .639 | .525 | .611 | .716 | .610 | | | | | |
| 10. Picture Arrangement | .773 | .685 | .690 | .772 | .552 | .764 | .768 | .796 | .734 | | | | |
| 11. Object Assembly | .662 | .555 | .629 | .727 | .529 | .662 | .654 | .683 | .806 | .723 | | | |
| 12. Verbal score[b] | .912 | .896 | .869 | .900 | .698 | .946 | .812 | .861 | .666 | .803 | .716 | | |
| 13. Performance score[b] | .823 | .748 | .796 | .838 | .663 | .824 | .873 | .875 | .874 | .904 | .870 | .883 | |
| 14. Full Scale score[b] | .904 | .860 | .865 | .905 | .696 | .924 | .855 | .891 | .770 | .869 | .803 | .981 | .953 |
| 15. Verbal IQ | .910 | .891 | .869 | .903 | .700 | .946 | .816 | .860 | .672 | .802 | .721 | | |
| 16. Performance IQ | .821 | .742 | .786 | .834 | .639 | .820 | .870 | .872 | .880 | .908 | .873 | .875 | .954 |
| 17. Full Scale IQ | .905 | .859 | .861 | .903 | .693 | .923 | .852 | .890 | .775 | .862 | .803 | .980 | |

[a] Compare with Doppelt and Wallace (1955, Table 13, p. 327).
[b] Correlation of tests with Verbal, Performance, and Full Scale scores before correction for contamination.

consistently poorer Performance score on the part of the Duke sample; of the 40 comparisons, 31 favor the Kansas City sample. The differences are not large except for the 65–69 year group.

In the treatment of their data, Doppelt and Wallace (1955, Table 7, p. 319) present different numbers on the different Performance subtests for each age group. No explanation of this variation in numbers is offered in the text, but one may assume that all the subjects completing the subtest were used, even though some did not complete the entire WAIS, but WAIS norms for these age groups are reported to have been computed from data obtained from subjects completing all the subtests (Wechsler, 1958). Thus, the Performance subtest data offered by Doppelt and Wallace (Table 7, p. 319) do not correspond to the data incorporated in the WAIS standardization, nor does the criterion information appear to be presently available in published form. It seems clear, therefore, that the Performance subtest comparisons between the Duke and Kansas City samples are based upon data closely approximating the criterion data (collected from Kansas City) and used as the WAIS norms for the aged.

Correlation matrices of the tests were prepared and are shown in Tables 6–7 through 6–10. These findings are in substantial agreement with those reported by Doppelt and Wallace (1955). As they reported, intercorrelations are generally higher among Verbal subtests and there appears to be similarity among the age groups as the correlation pattern emerges. Thus these findings tend to support the contention of Doppelt and Wallace concerning the factorial composition of the WAIS for these age groups.

Discussion

The differences which appear between the Duke Project sample and the standardization sample derived from Kansas City favor the Duke sample on the Verbal scale and, to a lesser extent, the Kansas City sample on Performance scale items.

The Duke 65–69 age group appears to differ most from the pattern of the Duke sample. As Table 6–3 shows, on the Full Scale, Verbal, and Performance comparisons, this group scored lower than the next older group in every case, when one might expect that it would perform at a midpoint between the 60–64 and 70–74 age groups. It can be seen from Table 6–3 that this expectation holds for the Kansas City sample. With the one exception of this Duke age group, all the age groups in both samples show decreasing levels of performance with increasing age. This 65–69 group has the largest number and the lowest SDs of the Duke sample.

In subtest comparisons, as noted on Tables 6–4, 6–5, and 6–6, the

65–69 group is the most atypical of the Duke sample. It is significantly lower in one Verbal subtest in comparison with the Kansas City sample—the only Duke subgroup that was significantly lower on a Verbal subtest—and in four of the six Verbal subtest comparisons, it was also lower. On the Performance subtests, it was not only lower than the comparable Kansas City group, but it was the only subgroup significantly lower than the comparison sample.

If we assume that the Duke 65–69 group is closer to the national standard and that the results for our other age groups are atypical, we are unable to explain the even lower Performance score of these subjects. At the very least, we must conclude that our subgroups are different from the Kansas City sample.

Since the criteria for the selection of groups were similar for all ages, we cannot account for the performance of this group in terms of any systematic sampling bias. Since it included recently retired subjects, it perhaps involved a number of individuals who were under special emotional stress as a function of adaptation to their new status. This does not appear to have influenced the Kansas City sample, however, unless there are differences in retirement age practices in the different regions.

It should be observed that this 65–69 group is not the principal contributor to the differences between the two samples. In fact, with regard to the Verbal differences noted, this group goes contrary to the Duke sample's higher achievement.

It is, of course, possible that the Duke Project sample is a biased one since all subjects were volunteers. On the other hand, it seems quite clear that this is also true of the Kansas City sample. Of the group originally contacted in Kansas City, approximately one-half (54.2 percent) completed the examination. Of the 649 subjects identified as the "Sample for testing," only 352 subjects completed the examination and were used for establishing the tentative national norms. In the Eisdorfer et al. (1959) study, using a portion of the Duke sample, various population variables were investigated in an attempt to find a source of sample bias. It appeared that the relationship between Verbal and Performance scores was not a function of sex, race, intelligence, social class, age, or mental illness variables. The authors can think of no reasonable explanation for the differences found, apart from unidentified regional differences.

If regional differences in patterns of intellectual performance exist, it would seem logical to suppose that they would derive from regional influences and would be intensified during the life span, thus appearing more prominently in the aged. This presumption could be tested readily. Probably in order to offset such (possible) regional influences, the collection of data from the WAIS norms for younger individuals (16–60) was based upon a national sample (Wechsler, 1958). In view of the present findings, it is suggested that subjects to be used as the standardization sample for the aged (60+) should also be selected on a nationwide basis.

## Summary

This study reports WAIS data on 239 elderly subjects above age 60 from the Durham, North Carolina, area. In view of the absence of national norms above age 65 for the WAIS and the suggested use of data from 352 subjects from a Kansas City study as tentative norms, it seemed especially appropriate to compare these latter with the Duke data. Stable differences were found between the samples, with the Duke groups showing superiority in the Verbal subtest scores and lower achievement in the Performance subtests. No satisfactory explanation of these differences is offered, other than the possibility of regional influences. The need for establishing national norms on a national sample of the aged is demonstrated.

## References

Doppelt, J. E., and Wallace, W. L. Standardization of the Wechsler Adult Intelligence Scale for older persons. *Journal of Abnormal and Social Psychology*, 51:312–330, 1955.
Eisdorfer, C., Busse, E. W., and Cohen, L. D. The WAIS performance of an aged sample: The relationship between verbal and performance IQs. *Journal of Gerontology*, 14:197–201, 1959.
Warner, W. L., Meeker, M., and Eells, K. *Social class in America*. Gloucester, Mass., Peter Smith, 1957.
Wechsler, D. *Manual for the Wechsler Adult Intelligence Scale*. New York: Psychological Corporation, 1955.
Wechsler, D. *The measurement and appraisal of adult intelligence*. (2nd ed.) Baltimore: Williams and Wilkins, 1958.

# The WAIS Performance of the Aged: A Retest Evaluation*    Carl Eisdorfer

In an excellent article discussing longitudinal IQ changes in twins, Jarvik, Kallman, and Falek (1962) presented data on a one- and eight-year follow-up examination of old subjects on the Wechsler Bellevue Scale. In

* Reprinted by permission from the *Journal of Gerontology*, 18:169–172, 1963. The help of Mrs. Frances L. Wilkie is gratefully acknowledged.

order to explain a rise in scores after one year, Jarvik et al. suggest the hypothesis that "test wiseness" may have acted to counterbalance any declining trend operating within the test-retest year. A similar explanation was suggested for the findings of Bell and Zubek (1960), who reported that a five-year retest of inmates of a Canadian institute for mental defectives yielded elevated IQs.

The conflicting findings of Kaplan (1956) and the importance of examining this phenomenon with the Wechsler Adult Intelligence Scale (WAIS) on a broader sample serve as the basis for the present report.

## Procedure

Upon the completion of the subject panel for the original investigation of the Duke Geriatrics Project (Eisdorfer & Cohen, 1961) an attempt was made to contact each subject with a request that he participate in the longitudinal phase of the project. Of the 225 subjects for whom there was complete information at the end of the first phase of study, 182 subjects agreed to participate in the longitudinal investigation. The 73 subjects who were lost included 49 (67 percent) who had died or were immobilized by serious illness, 10 (14 percent) who moved away, and 14 (19 percent) who refused to return for another examination. The reexamination was similar to the original evaluation (Busse, Dovenmuehle, & Brown, 1960) and included a repetition of the Full Scale WAIS as well as additional psychological studies. These new studies were introduced to the subject after the WAIS was repeated. One hundred and sixty-five (165) subjects received the second Full Scale WAIS and comprised a sample upon which the present report is based. Seventeen additional subjects who agreed to come in did not receive their full examinations as a result of a miscellany of factors, e.g., scheduling conflicts, interruptions in the examination sequence, illness of one of the examiners.

For the statistical analysis, subjects were assigned to two age groups (on the basis of their last birthday at the time of the first examination). This separation into groups 60–69 and 70+ years of age also represents the approximate equivalent of a median split to the sample according to age. Subjects were further subdivided according to the Full Scale IQ they obtained on the first examination to correspond with the high (116+), middle (85–115), and low (below 85) groups studied previously (Eisdorfer, 1962). Analysis was based on a six-cell design with two levels for age and three rows for IQ.

Sample

Table 6–11 shows the original age, IQ category, and time interval in months between the original and longitudinal examination for each of the six groups. Identifying data as to race and sex are also included in Table 6–11. Within each of the two age groups, i.e., I, II, and III or groups IV, V, and VI, the time between examinations was approximately the same. Statistical analysis showed no difference between the test-retest interval for any of the six groups. The most conspicuous feature of this table seems to be the large standard deviation (SD) for the test-retest interval of Group I,

Table 6–11. *Characteristics of subjects receiving WAIS retest.*

| Group | Mean age | SD of age | IQ category[a] | Months between tests | SD in months | Race and sex[b] | | | | Total number |
|-------|----------|-----------|----------------|----------------------|--------------|------|------|------|------|--------------|
| | | | | | | NF | WF | NM | WM | |
| I | 64.8 | 2.92 | −85 | 43.2 | 12.3 | 8 | 4 | 5 | 1 | 18 |
| II | 65.0 | 2.57 | 85–115 | 39.1 | 8.9 | 3 | 16 | 10 | 18 | 47 |
| III | 64.7 | 2.87 | 116+ | 41.0 | 5.1 | 3 | 11 | 0 | 6 | 20 |
| IV | 74.5 | 4.12 | −85 | 38.5 | 8.2 | 6 | 1 | 4 | 1 | 12 |
| V | 74.3 | 4.27 | 85–115 | 39.0 | 10.0 | 6 | 14 | 5 | 16 | 41 |
| VI | 75.1 | 5.41 | 116+ | 38.5 | 10.8 | 1 | 11 | 0 | 15 | 27 |

[a] WAIS Full Scale IQ on first exam.
[b] W = white   N = Negro   M = male   F = female.

especially in comparison with the corresponding high IQ group (Group III). The significance of this difference is not clear; every attempt was made to stabilize the time of the repeat investigation, but clearly there was some difficulty encountered with members of this group. This phenomenon is not simply a function of IQ as is suggested by a comparison of Groups IV and VI, which does not reflect such a difference.

Table 6–12 compares the performance of subjects who received both examinations with subjects who received the original evaluation only. A simple analysis of variance demonstrates no significant difference between the overall performance of the 60–69-year-old returnees and nonreturnees. For the 70+ groups (IV, V, and VI) the nonreturnees score below the returnees. These differences were statistically significant only in the case of Group V; however, for this group $F$ tests were significant (at $p < .05$) for all but the Performance IQ scores. This pattern is consistent for virtually all of the subtests.

Table 6–12. *Initial examination results of returnees as compared with nonreturnees.*

| Group | Scale | Returned | | Nonreturned | |
|---|---|---|---|---|---|
| | | Mean | SD | Mean | SD |
| | | N = 18 Mean age = 64.8 | | N = 13 Mean age = 64.9 | |
| I | Verbal weighted | 32.50 | 8.91 | 34.31 | 6.56 |
| | Performance weighted | 14.72 | 5.30 | 16.23 | 5.88 |
| | Full Scale weighted | 47.22 | 12.83 | 50.54 | 10.74 |
| | Verbal IQ | 78.22 | 8.49 | 79.92 | 5.62 |
| | Performance IQ | 72.83 | 6.74 | 74.62 | 6.68 |
| | Full Scale IQ | 74.44 | 7.49 | 76.38 | 5.45 |
| | | N = 47 Mean age = 65.0 | | N = 10 Mean age = 66.7 | |
| II | Verbal weighted | 59.45 | 11.46 | 53.80 | 9.47 |
| | Performance weighted | 30.98 | 6.91 | 29.00 | 7.79 |
| | Full Scale weighted | 90.43 | 16.16 | 82.20 | 15.87 |
| | Verbal IQ | 104.60 | 11.20 | 99.60 | 9.18 |
| | Performance IQ | 94.04 | 8.83 | 92.40 | 9.77 |
| | Full Scale IQ | 100.11 | 9.36 | 96.40 | 9.46 |
| | | N = 20 Mean age = 64.7 | | N = 4 Mean age = 63.8 | |
| III | Verbal weighted | 82.50 | 7.70 | 88.50 | 10.91 |
| | Performance weighted | 45.30 | 6.06 | 43.25 | 6.90 |
| | Full Scale weighted | 127.80 | 11.71 | 131.75 | 11.84 |
| | Verbal IQ | 128.00 | 7.05 | 133.00 | 10.16 |
| | Performance IQ | 113.35 | 7.90 | 109.00 | 9.42 |
| | Full Scale IQ | 122.90 | 6.27 | 124.00 | 6.38 |
| | | N = 12 Mean age = 74.5 | | N = 10 Mean age = 76.3 | |
| IV | Verbal weighted | 27.75 | 7.90 | 25.50 | 7.23 |
| | Performance weighted (N = 13) | 9.83 | 7.30 | 7.20 | 3.52 |
| | Full Scale weighted | 37.33 | 9.96 | 32.70 | 9.12 |
| | Verbal IQ | 81.42 | 7.84 | 79.90 | 7.31 |
| | Performance IQ (N = 13) | 76.33 | 9.87 | 73.90 | 3.11 |
| | Full Scale IQ | 78.00 | 6.27 | 76.10 | 5.30 |
| | | N = 41 Mean age = 74.3 | | N = 28 Mean age = 77.7 | |
| V | *Verbal weighted | 50.54 | 10.70 | 44.36 | 9.26 |
| | *Performance weighted | 24.15 | 7.18 | 19.28 | 8.16 |
| | **Full Scale weighted | 74.44 | 15.97 | 63.82 | 14.39 |
| | *Verbal IQ | 104.20 | 10.25 | 99.11 | 9.30 |
| | Performance IQ | 95.49 | 9.48 | 91.18 | 10.68 |
| | *Full Scale IQ | 100.34 | 9.01 | 95.54 | 8.50 |

Table 6–12. (*cont.*)

| Group | Scale | Returned | | Nonreturned | |
|---|---|---|---|---|---|
| | | Mean | SD | Mean | SD |
| | | N = 27 Mean age = 75.1 | | N = 8 Mean age = 77.8 | |
| VI | Verbal weighted | 81.67 | 6.76 | 76.88 | 7.18 |
| | Performance weighted | 41.48 | 6.55 | 38.88 | 6.71 |
| | Full Scale weighted | 122.93 | 11.25 | 115.75 | 12.15 |
| | Verbal IQ | 135.15 | 7.19 | 131.75 | 6.41 |
| | Performance IQ | 118.37 | 8.58 | 117.12 | 7.20 |
| | Full Scale IQ | 129.59 | 7.12 | 126.50 | 6.14 |

\* *F* significant at < .05.
\*\* *F* significant at  < .01.


Results

Table 6–13 summarizes the results of the comparison between the test and retest examinations for the 60–69-year-old groups. For Group III, the high IQ group, there is essentially no difference between the Full Scale, Performance, or Verbal weighted scores of the two examinations, although IQ does increase slightly. For Group II the changes on retest parallel those of Group III. Group I shows a somewhat more striking change; Full Scale and Performance scores increase with retest. Table 6–14 shows that among the subjects 70 years of age and older, the high IQ group (VI) shows a decline: the middle IQ group (V) a decrease of 1 weighted score point, but an increase in IQ of 1 point, while the low IQ group (IV) manifests an increase corresponding to 1.83 Full Scale IQ points. It is clear that none of these changes approaches significance.


Discussion

The finding of a difference in the IQ level of returnees and nonreturnees (70+ age group) is difficult to assess. The ratio of nonreturnees to returnees in the 60–69 year group is 27 to 85 as compared with 46 to 80 in the 70+ group. Of the nonreturnees of the younger group 13 (48 percent) did not return because of death (9) or ill health (4); for the 70+ group 36 or (78 percent) were not able to return for the same reasons (25 died; 11 were ill). The relationship between the subsequent physical condition of the subjects and their WAIS score on initial examination leads to the speculation of a relationship between the physical and intellectual

Table 6–13. *Test-retest differences for 60–69-year age groups.*[a]

| IQ group | Full Scale weighted | | Full Scale IQ | | Verbal weighted | | Verbal IQ | | Performance weighted | | Performance IQ | |
|---|---|---|---|---|---|---|---|---|---|---|---|---|
| | Mean | SD | Mean | SD | Mean | SD | Mean | SD | Mean | SD | Mean | SD |
| I<br>IQ < 85 | 3.00 | 6.74 | 5.39 | 4.41 | 1.17 | 4.42 | 4.33 | 5.19 | 1.83 | 5.29 | 6.22 | 6.49 |
| II<br>85–115 | 0.91 | 6.85 | 3.96 | 5.20 | −0.40 | 5.84 | 2.55 | 6.56 | 1.30 | 4.08 | 5.26 | 6.40 |
| III<br>116+ | 0.20 | 6.56 | 3.20 | 5.35 | 0.00 | 5.40 | 2.70 | 7.27 | 0.20 | 5.40 | 3.35 | 6.56 |

[a] − = retest < original score.

Table 6–14. *Test-retest differences for 70+ age groups.*[a]

| IQ group | Full Scale weighted | | Full Scale IQ | | Verbal weighted | | Verbal IQ | | Performance weighted | | Performance IQ | |
|---|---|---|---|---|---|---|---|---|---|---|---|---|
| | Mean | SD | Mean | SD | Mean | SD | Mean | SD | Mean | SD | Mean | SD |
| IV IQ < 85 | 0.33 | 7.56 | 1.83 | 6.53 | −1.33 | 5.26 | 0.00 | 6.85 | 1.42 | 3.80 | −1.08 | 20.88 |
| V 85–115 | −1.05 | 8.15 | 1.05 | 5.22 | −1.39 | 6.16 | −0.10 | 6.09 | 0.07 | 4.04 | 2.17 | 6.21 |
| VI 116+ | −4.59 | 10.84 | −1.30 | 7.08 | −2.37 | 7.53 | −1.30 | 7.25 | −2.48 | 6.07 | −1.37 | 8.63 |

[a] − = retest < original score.

status of these older subjects. This would be in support of the position of Kleemeier (1961), who reported a decline in intellectual functioning associated with physical decline preceding death. The data from the present study do not lend themselves to more than speculation along this point, however. The present three-year follow-up shows no clear progressive intellectual decline of our aged subjects. The findings are in substantial agreement with those of Jarvik et al. (1962), whose one-year retest showed no decline and even some evidence for improved performance on the part of their subjects. It is interesting too that Jarvik et al.'s (1962) eight-year follow-up showed clear evidence of decline on only a limited number of subtests. These results raise the suspicion that the normative data for intelligence, collected by cross-sectional sampling, may exaggerate the pattern of decline of old persons at least for relatively short periods.

It should be noted that the mean age of the subjects (in all of the groups) is extremely close to the marginal age levels for the IQ conversion tables (Wechsler, 1955). Thus one effect of the three-year test-retest interval would be that on their second examination many subjects were being compared with a sample, the mean age of which was five years greater. Although the effect of this particular variable is difficult to assess, it could in some small measure contribute to a slight increase in IQs (it would, of course, have no effect on weighted scores which are not age-corrected).

In a study involving repeated administration of a test of intelligence such as the WAIS, the factor of learning or "test wiseness" is not readily ruled out. All of the subjects in the present study were functioning in the community and had manifested a long-standing ability to adapt to novel and complex situations. While a priori conjecture would lead us to the expectation that repeat administration of a test such as the WAIS favors individuals with high IQ, who are more capable of profiting from short-term learning, clearly this is not the case.

The tendency for scores to converge toward the mean in the retest situation named by Galton as regression toward "mediocrity" is of some importance in the interpretation of the present results. Based upon this phenomenon McNemar (1940) has pointed out that with the repetition of an intellectual evaluation it should be expected that a below average group will show an improved performance. The results here are thus in accord with this concept of phenomenal regression to the mean and no distinguishable pattern of decline or improvement may be in evidence. It should be added this criticism seems conspicuously absent in the interpretation of Bell and Zubek's (1960) findings of an increase in the Wechsler Bellevue performance of mentally defective persons.

On the basis of a cross-sectional comparison Eisdorfer (1962) suggested that there was evidence to support a hypothesis of differential rates

of decline in cognitive ability with increasing age, as a function of intellectual level. If we may consider the present findings to have relevance for
long-term follow-up, they tend rather to support Owens's (1957) position
that age is not "any kinder" to the initially more able. Eisdorfer's (1962)
statement that "any cross-sectional study involves a built-in bias involving
differential environmental effects" (p. 894) seems well taken in view of the
present data. The results of extended longitudinal studies are clearly
needed to illuminate this area.

## Summary

One hundred and sixty-five aged volunteers from the Duke Geriatrics
Project sample received a second Full Scale WAIS as one aspect of a
three-year follow-up study. The results of the retest demonstrated little
overall decline in scores and a tendency for subjects to show minor changes
in test performance, in the general direction of a regression toward the
mean.

## References

Bell, A., and Zubek, J. P. The effect of age on the intellectual performance of mental
    defectives. *Journal of Gerontology*, 15:285–295, 1960.
Busse, E. W., Dovenmuehle, R. H., and Brown, R. G. Psychoneurotic reactions of the
    aged. *Geriatrics*, 15:97–105, 1960.
Eisdorfer, C. Changes in cognitive functioning in relation to intellectual level in
    senescence. In Tibbitts, C., and Donahue, W. (Eds.), *Social and psychological
    aspects of aging.* New York: Columbia University Press, 1962.
Eisdorfer, C., and Cohen, L. D. The generality of the WAIS standardization for the
    aged: A regional comparison. *Journal of Abnormal and Social Psychology*,
    62:520–527, 1961.
Jarvik, L. F., Kallman, F. J., and Falek, A. Intellectual changes in aged twins.
    *Journal of Gerontology*, 17:289–294, 1962.
Kaplan, O. J. *Mental disorders in later life.* Stanford, Calif.: Stanford University
    Press, 1956.
Kleemeier, R. W. Intellectual changes in the senium, or death and the IQ. Presidential
    address, Division on Maturity and Old Age, American Psychological Associa-
    tion, September 1, 1961.
McNemar, Q. A critical examination of the University of Iowa studies of environ-
    mental influences upon the IQ. *Psychological Bulletin*, 2:63–92, 1940.
Owens, W. A., Jr. Is age kinder to the initially more able? In *Proceedings of the
    Fourth Congress of the International Association of Gerontology.* Fidenza, Italy:
    Tipographia Tito Mattioli, 4:151–157, 1957.
Wechsler, D. *Manual for the Wechsler Adult Intelligence Scale.* New York: Psycho-
    logical Corporation, 1955.

# Rorschach Performance and Intellectual Functioning in the Aged*    *Carl Eisdorfer*

In a study of Rorschach performance of aged persons, Klopfer (1946) obtained profiles of 50 subjects 60 years and older (of whom 30 were institutionalized and 20 in the community). He agreed with Rorschach (1942) that in comparison with individuals "in the general population" aged subjects are slower, less productive, and less efficient. In addition he suggested that "thought content seems rather restricted" and aged individuals respond "with an instinctive regression to a more infantile level" (Klopfer, 1946, p. 152). In conclusion Klopfer suggested that Rorschach's predictions were confirmed insofar as aged individuals manifested "coarctated experience types," unclear forms, marked stereotype, loose ties with reality, etc. He based his conclusion on a "paucity of R" (means 14.1) and "over-emphasized" ($\Sigma$) W and an "under-emphasized" ($\Sigma$) D with "normal" Dd (negligible), c, C, and K, 1, or 0 M in 60 percent of the cases, and FM greater than M in 70 percent of the cases.

The statements of Klopfer have been substantially supported in the literature since 1946. Prados and Fried (1947) obtained Rorschach protocols on 35 normal aged adults from 50 to 80, categorized them by decades, and concluded that with increasing age there is a progressive impoverishment of creative intellectual facilities. Davidson and Kruglov (1952) examined 46 institutionalized subjects and found low productivity, "little drive, faulty perception of reality, narrow range of interest," etc., which confirms the previous work of Klopfer. Caldwell (1954) found that the protocols which she obtained from 47 institutionalized aged women (whose mean IQ was 85) showed "a rather high degree of similarity" to the findings of Klopfer. Thaler (1952) examined 50 individuals over 60 years of age who were in the community and 25 aged who were institutionalized. She found that her community group was less prone to overlook practical aspects of situations than was her hospital group, and both groups showed "a type of ego deficiency." Grossman, Worshawsky, and Hertz (1951) examined 50 institutionalized aged; Kuhlen and Keil (1951) obtained Rorschach protocols from 100 male residents of a county home (50 aged

* Reprinted by permission from the *Journal of Gerontology*, 18:358–363, 1963.

50–69 and 50 aged 70–80); and Chesrow, Wosika, and Reinitz (1949) reported on 20 institutionalized white males. These investigators all found degrees of perceptual distortion, delay in response times, reduced number of responses, and constriction in intellectual and emotional spheres in the aged.

Ames, Learned, Metraux, and Walker (1954) analyzed the Rorschach performance of 200 men and women between the ages of 70 and 100, one-third of whom were institutionalized. These investigators used the Rorschach performance itself as a criterion for adjustment, and their data were presented by classifying subjects into groups representing senility, presenility, and normalcy as defined by the similarity between the obtained Rorschach examinations and protocols found in children. Subjects in the three categories were then compared.

Light and Amick (1956) stated that the failure to control for intelligence or institutional status in Rorschach investigations resulted in "manifest shortcomings" which prevent utilization of the results of these studies as normative data. It seems necessary, in order to use Rorschach data from aged subjects as normative standards, that such data be obtained from noninstitutionalized subjects with an independent measure of intellectual performance available for such subjects. Light and Amick (1956) made an initial effort in this direction in their examination of 50 noninstitutionalized subjects who were residents of a West Virginia community. Their subjects had a mean IQ of 112.75 and ranged in age from 65 to 85. While this is a significant study, the number and IQ range of the subjects made it of somewhat limited value. In addition it seems clear from the contribution of Prados and Fried (1947) that one cannot characterize all individuals over 60 as members of a homogeneous population; thus, age past 60 is itself an important variable in the study of Rorschach performance.

Materials and Methods

. . . The present report is based on the Rorschach and WAIS examinations of 242 subjects aged 60–94. For the purpose of this investigation, subjects were subdivided into three groups based upon intellectual performance (i.e., Full Scale WAIS IQ scores). Subjects with IQs below 85 were assigned to Group I (low IQ), subjects with IQs in the range 85–115 to Group II (average IQ), and subjects with IQs of 116 or higher were placed in Group III (high IQ). In addition to the divisions according to IQ, the subject groups were further subdivided into five age categories, 60–64, 65–69, 70–74, 75–79, and 80+. All Rorschach tests were scored according to Piotrowski's (1950) method.

Results

In Table 6–15 subjects are listed by age, race, sex, and Full Scale IQ. Several characteristics of the overall population may be noted; a paucity of Negro men in the high IQ group as well as the apparently disproportionate

Table 6–15. *Subjects divided according to age, race, sex, and Full Scale IQ.*

| IQ group: | Below 85 | | | | 85–115 | | | | 116+ | | | | |
|---|---|---|---|---|---|---|---|---|---|---|---|---|---|
| Race: | White | | Negro | | White | | Negro | | White | | Negro | | Sub-totals |
| Sex: | M | F | M | F | M | F | M | F | M | F | M | F | |
| Age | | | | | | | | | | | | | |
| 60–64 | 2 | 2 | 2 | 8 | 7 | 8 | 3 | 1 | 5 | 6 | 0 | 1 | 45 |
| 65–69 | 4 | 4 | 4 | 6 | 13 | 15 | 8 | 2 | 2 | 8 | 0 | 2 | 68 |
| 70–74 | 1 | 2 | 5 | 4 | 16 | 10 | 3 | 5 | 8 | 9 | 1 | 1 | 65 |
| 75–79 | 0 | 1 | 2 | 4 | 5 | 8 | 4 | 3 | 6 | 3 | 0 | 0 | 36 |
| 80+ | 0 | 1 | 2 | 1 | 6 | 6 | 1 | 2 | 7 | 1 | 0 | 1 | 28 |
| Subtotals | 7 | 10 | 15 | 23 | 47 | 47 | 19 | 13 | 28 | 27 | 1 | 5 | 242 |

Table 6–16. *Means and standard deviations of Rorschach scoring determinants for subjects aged 60–64 distributed according to IQ.*

| IQ group: | Below 85 | | 85–115 | | 116+ | |
|---|---|---|---|---|---|---|
| Mean IQ: | 75.8 | | 101.2 | | 125.1 | |
| N: | 14 | | 19 | | 12 | |
| Determinant | Mean | SD | Mean | SD | Mean | SD |
| ΣR | 14.6 | 6.1 | 17.9 | 11.0 | 22.0 | 10.3 |
| W percentage | 43.7 | 29.2 | 47.3 | 23.2 | 55.6 | 16.0 |
| D percentage | 50.1 | 25.7 | 48.4 | 20.7 | 41.5 | 15.1 |
| Dd percentage | 6.0 | 6.8 | 4.2 | 5.6 | 2.0 | 7.2 |
| S | 0.7 | 1.3 | 1.1 | 1.4 | 1.5 | 1.9 |
| M | 1.1 | 1.3 | 1.2 | 1.7 | 2.0 | 1.8 |
| FM | 1.2 | 1.2 | 2.1 | 3.0 | 2.6 | 1.4 |
| m | 0.1 | 0.3 | 0.3 | 0.7 | | 0.2 |
| F percentage | 75.8 | 12.0 | 65.2 | 22.4 | 55.5 | 13.0 |
| F+ percentage | 64.6 | 23.3 | 76.9 | 17.8 | 79.0 | 16.0 |
| FC | 0.4 | 0.6 | 0.8 | 1.4 | 2.5 | 2.7 |
| CF | 0.1 | 0.5 | 0.6 | 0.8 | 1.1 | 1.1 |
| C | 0.3 | 0.4 | 0.2 | 0.5 | 0.6 | 1.7 |
| Σc | 0.6 | 1.4 | 0.6 | 1.1 | 1.5 | 1.4 |
| ΣC′ | | 0.4 | 0.2 | 0.7 | 0.6 | 1.7 |
| A percentage | 36.5 | 15.6 | 41.9 | 24.1 | 38.5 | 12.3 |
| A+ percentage | 17.8 | 23.5 | 11.6 | 14.1 | 11.7 | 12.4 |
| H percentage | 10.5 | 9.1 | 8.3 | 8.5 | 8.0 | 5.9 |
| Σ Popular | 3.2 | 1.9 | 4.2 | 2.1 | 4.8 | 2.9 |

Note.—Mean values of less than 0.1 not entered in table.

number of white in the low IQ group, especially at the older age levels. One other notable characteristic is the high ratio of men to women in the high IQ 80+ group. This last probably reflects a bias in the sampling community in that several retired college professors were among the earliest volunteers.

Tables 6–16 through 6–20 list the means and standard deviations of

Table 6–17. *Means and standard deviations of Rorschach scoring determinants for subjects aged 65–69 distributed according to IQ.*

| IQ group: | Below 85 | | 85–115 | | 116+ | |
| Mean IQ: | 74.2 | | 98.1 | | 121.0 | |
| N: | 18 | | 38 | | 12 | |
| Determinant | Mean | SD | Mean | SD | Mean | SD |
| --- | --- | --- | --- | --- | --- | --- |
| ΣR | 14.6 | 6.4 | 18.9 | 9.8 | 18.8 | 8.9 |
| W percentage | 37.0 | 20.0 | 43.0 | 20.9 | 46.7 | 19.4 |
| D percentage | 58.0 | 19.4 | 50.6 | 17.7 | 50.2 | 18.9 |
| Dd percentage | .4.9 | 8.1 | 6.1 | 7.3 | 2.6 | 3.0 |
| S | 0.2 | 0.5 | 0.4 | 0.8 | 0.5 | 0.6 |
| M | 0.7 | 0.9 | 1.2 | 1.4 | 1.7 | 1.7 |
| FM | 1.5 | 1.3 | 2.6 | 2.4 | 4.0 | 2.3 |
| m | | | 0.1 | 0.3 | 0.3 | 0.6 |
| F percentage | 78.8 | 18.4 | 71.3 | 21.1 | 51.7 | 17.2 |
| F+ percentage | 74.3 | 17.6 | 80.8 | 15.7 | 83.7 | 17.0 |
| FC | 0.3 | 0.6 | 0.5 | 0.9 | 1.5 | 1.8 |
| CF | 0.3 | 0.9 | 0.5 | 1.0 | 1.2 | 1.5 |
| C | 0.1 | 0.5 | 0.2 | 0.5 | 0.3 | 0.4 |
| Σc | 0.6 | 1.3 | 0.9 | 1.6 | 1.3 | 1.7 |
| ΣC′ | 0.2 | 0.8 | 0.1 | 0.6 | 0.5 | 0.9 |
| A percentage | 46.8 | 17.8 | 48.1 | 19.1 | 44.3 | 19.3 |
| A+ percentage | 7.5 | 17.5 | 10.9 | 15.2 | 12.5 | 20.9 |
| H percentage | 9.5 | 10.7 | 7.1 | 7.1 | 8.7 | 11.2 |
| Σ Popular | 3.2 | 1.7 | 4.6 | 2.2 | 5.8 | 3.0 |

Note.—Mean values of less than 0.1 not entered in table.

the Rorschach scoring determinants for the subjects divided according to age and IQ. For the purposes of comparison, Table 6–21 was developed from the works of Klopfer (1946), Prados and Fried (1947), Dörken and Kral (1951), Chesrow et al. (1949), Ames et al. (1954), and Light and Amick (1956).

The fraction of whole responses (W percentage) which Klopfer reported as overemphasized with age seemed rather to decrease with age in the Prados et al. study and was quite small in Dörken and Kral's analysis of senile dementia. While W percentage does increase from normal to senile groups in the Ames et al. study, we must bear in mind their criterion variables for the selection of the senile group and that their *normal* old subjects do not show a significant increment in W percentage. The work of Light and Amick indicates that for noninstitutionalized subjects W percentage accounts for only 50 percent of the responses; in the Duke study W percentage ranged from a low of 32.8 percent (subjects 75–79 with average IQ) to a high of 55.6 (subjects 60–64 with high IQ). From the relationship between W percentage and age within IQ groupings, it seems

Table 6–18. *Means and standard deviations of Rorschach scoring determinants for subjects aged 70–74 distributed according to IQ.*

| IQ group:<br>Mean IQ:<br>N:<br>Determinant | Below 85<br>76.0<br>12<br>Mean | <br><br><br>SD | 85–115<br>98.2<br>34<br>Mean | <br><br><br>SD | 116+<br>128.3<br>19<br>Mean | <br><br><br>SD |
|---|---|---|---|---|---|---|
| $\Sigma$R | 12.5 | 5.3 | 16.3 | 8.2 | 29.2 | 16.6 |
| W percentage | 40.5 | 15.0 | 41.8 | 23.4 | 40.4 | 24.5 |
| D percentage | 55.0 | 10.5 | 53.4 | 21.3 | 50.5 | 18.8 |
| Dd percentage | 4.5 | 11.2 | 4.4 | 5.0 | 8.8 | 13.1 |
| S | 0.2 | 0.6 | 0.1 | 0.4 | 1.0 | 1.2 |
| M | 0.4 | 0.6 | 1.0 | 1.4 | 2.6 | 2.1 |
| FM | 1.5 | 1.4 | 2.5 | 2.3 | 4.0 | 2.1 |
| m | | | | 0.3 | 0.4 | 0.6 |
| F percentage | 79.4 | 20.5 | 70.2 | 19.0 | 56.6 | 15.6 |
| F+ percentage | 73.3 | 25.0 | 79.7 | 16.2 | 86.5 | 7.2 |
| FC | 0.5 | 1.0 | 0.6 | 0.8 | 1.8 | 1.9 |
| CF | 0.2 | 0.4 | 0.5 | 0.9 | 1.2 | 1.3 |
| C | 0.0 | 0.2 | 0.1 | 0.7 | 0.3 | 0.5 |
| $\Sigma$c | 0.3 | 0.7 | 0.6 | 1.2 | 1.8 | 1.9 |
| $\Sigma$C' | | | 0.9 | 0.3 | 0.2 | 0.5 |
| A percentage | 59.5 | 21.3 | 47.6 | 23.0 | 49.1 | 13.8 |
| A+ percentage | 7.6 | 10.8 | 7.4 | 19.3 | 9.4 | 7.1 |
| H percentage | 6.2 | 5.5 | 7.1 | 6.2 | 8.5 | 5.3 |
| $\Sigma$ Popular | 3.6 | 1.8 | 3.9 | 1.5 | 6.3 | 3.1 |

Note.—Mean values of less than 0.1 not entered in table.

quite clear that it is not possible to describe the W percentage as increasing with age, within the range of this study, nor do other reports support such a hypothesis.

A "paucity" of responses ($\Sigma$R) was described by Klopfer (1946) on the basis of a mean $\Sigma$R of 14.1 for his subjects' performance. This finding was partially supported by the findings for average and below average IQ groups in the Duke sample. Thus for the below average IQ groups $\Sigma$Rs ranged from 14.6 to 9.7 with almost a linear decrement with age. For the average IQ group the range is somewhat higher. Here we found that subjects in their sixties had a mean slightly above 18 responses, but this declined to approximately 12.7 for age 80+. The high IQ group did not show any age-related decline in ΣR. The subjects studied by Prados et al. gave a larger number of Rs than did the normal subjects of Ames et al. In the Duke sample the largest discrepancies were found on the basis of IQ grouping, and it is especially interesting to note that the slight decline found in the average IQ groups was not supported for the high intelligence group;

Table 6–19. *Means and standard deviations of Rorschach scoring determinants for subjects aged 75–79 distributed according to IQ.*

| IQ group:<br>Mean IQ:<br>N: | Below 85<br>76.7<br>7 | | 85–115<br>98.5<br>20 | | 116+<br>103.4<br>9 | |
|---|---|---|---|---|---|---|
| Determinant | Mean | SD | Mean | SD | Mean | SD |
| ΣR | 9.7 | 2.2 | 15.8 | 7.0 | 22.2 | 6.7 |
| W percentage | 49.7 | 22.7 | 32.8 | 20.3 | 34.4 | 21.8 |
| D percentage | 48.7 | 21.7 | 61.9 | 17.5 | 62.0 | 18.9 |
| Dd percentage | 1.5 | 4.1 | 5.2 | 7.7 | 3.0 | 5.7 |
| S | | | 0.3 | 0.9 | 1.0 | 0.7 |
| M | 0.5 | 1.5 | 0.8 | 0.9 | 2.4 | 1.8 |
| FM | 1.8 | 1.0 | 2.1 | 2.1 | 3.7 | 2.4 |
| m | 0.1 | 0.3 | 0.1 | 0.3 | 0.1 | 0.3 |
| F percentage | 79.1 | 25.3 | 78.6 | 17.1 | 58.8 | 11.1 |
| F+ percentage | 78.1 | 18.3 | 75.1 | 16.3 | 88.1 | 10.7 |
| FC | | | 0.4 | 0.9 | 1.3 | 1.3 |
| CF | 0.5 | 0.9 | 0.3 | 0.6 | 0.2 | 0.4 |
| C | | | 0.1 | 0.3 | 0.2 | 0.4 |
| Σc | | | 0.6 | 1.1 | 2.3 | 2.5 |
| ΣC′ | 0.2 | 0.7 | 0.1 | 0.4 | 0.5 | 1.0 |
| A percentage | 67.8 | 13.8 | 54.4 | 25.9 | 39.1 | 8.7 |
| A+ percentage | 1.2 | 3.4 | 7.5 | 11.3 | 6.6 | 8.4 |
| H percentage | 10.4 | 15.1 | 5.5 | 6.5 | 13.4 | 8.2 |
| Σ Popular | 2.8 | 1.3 | 3.4 | 2.1 | 7.1 | 1.9 |

Note.—Mean values of less than 0.1 not entered in table.

thus mean ΣR for the subjects 60–69 with high IQs is 20.4, and the equivalent for the high IQ 75+ group is 21.1. The data reported on ΣR by Klopfer (1946) do seem in substantial agreement with those reported by Dörken and Kral, as well as those of the presenile and senile groups of Ames et al. which suggested that the "paucity" in ΣR with age is a complex function involving age and intellectual level.

The suggestion that a low ratio of large details (D percentage) is a characteristic of the aged seems somewhat difficult to substantiate in view of the findings of the Duke study that subjects in the normal range of intelligence showed a D percentage which hovered around 50 percent (range 44.2 to 61.9); certainly there seemed to be no consistent pattern of change with age and no consistent effect within age and intelligence.

As anticipated, perception of human movement ($\Sigma$M) on the Rorschach was very closely related to intelligence. Thus we see that in subjects with IQs below 85 the mean number of M responses is quite limited. The size of the standard deviation (SD) in relation to the mean is probably a reflection of the fact that M responses were not given by many people. When they

Table 6–20. *Means and standard deviations of Rorschach scoring determinants for subjects aged 80+ distributed according to IQ.*

| IQ group:<br>Mean IQ:<br>N: | Below 85<br>78.0<br>4 | | 85–115<br>97.6<br>15 | | 116+<br>127.7<br>9 | |
|---|---|---|---|---|---|---|
| Determinant | Mean | SD | Mean | SD | Mean | SD |
| $\Sigma$R | 10.0 | 4.9 | 12.7 | 4.8 | 20.0 | 7.3 |
| W percentage | 52.0 | 15.3 | 47.4 | 21.0 | 44.1 | 15.7 |
| D percentage | 48.0 | 15.3 | 44.2 | 21.8 | 53.5 | 14.9 |
| Dd percentage | | | 7.6 | 9.9 | 2.3 | 3.9 |
| S | | | 0.5 | 1.0 | 0.3 | 0.5 |
| M | 0.2 | 0.5 | 0.6 | 0.8 | 2.5 | 1.9 |
| FM | 0.7 | 0.9 | 2.1 | 1.5 | 3.6 | 2.5 |
| m | | | | | 0.3 | 0.5 |
| F percentage | 75.2 | 19.2 | 72.5 | 17.8 | 54.2 | 12.9 |
| F+ percentage | 57.5 | 31.2 | 75.2 | 18.0 | 86.6 | 13.8 |
| FC | 0.5 | 1.0 | 0.2 | 0.5 | 2.0 | 2.0 |
| CF | 0.2 | 0.5 | 0.1 | 0.3 | 0.5 | 1.6 |
| C | 0.7 | 0.9 | 0.5 | 0.6 | 0.4 | 1.0 |
| $\Sigma$c | 0.7 | 1.5 | 0.8 | 1.3 | 1.1 | 1.7 |
| $\Sigma$C' | | | 0.1 | 0.5 | 0.1 | 0.3 |
| A percentage | 60.2 | 9.8 | 59.6 | 16.9 | 48.6 | 21.8 |
| A+ percentage | | | 2.5 | 5.1 | 3.1 | 4.1 |
| H percentage | 3.7 | 4.5 | 5.8 | 4.7 | 12.1 | 9.8 |
| $\Sigma$ Popular | 1.7 | 1.5 | 4.0 | 1.4 | 5.5 | 2.6 |

Note.—Mean values of less than 0.1 not entered in table.

were given however, they probably occurred more than once in the same record. In the case of the low IQ group the mean $\Sigma$M seemed to show a fairly consistent monotonic drop with age from a mean of 1.1 to 0.2. Within the middle IQ group there was a similar drop. The mean of approximately 1.2 for the decade 60–69 dropped gradually to 0.6 for the 80+ group. The high IQ group's $\Sigma$M of about 2 per protocol showed a slight increase with age. The 60–64 year group showed a mean $\Sigma$M response of 2.0; the 80+ group a mean $\Sigma$M of 2.5.

The number of animal movements (FMs) varied only slightly except at the oldest level. Here, too, differences seemed to be more a function of intelligence within an age group than of age itself. In the oldest group as

Table 6-21. *Comparative findings of different investigators.*

| | Klopfer | Prados and Fried Normal old age | | | Dörken and Kral Senile dementia | Chesrow et al. | Ames et al. | | | Light and Amick |
|---|---|---|---|---|---|---|---|---|---|---|
| | | 50–60 | 61–70 | 71–80 | | | Normal | Presenile | Senile | |
| Age (mean or range): | 73.5 | 50–60 | 61–70 | 71–80 | 76.3 | 72 | | 70–100 | | 65–85 |
| Number of subjects: | 50 | 13 | 12 | 10 | 30 | 20 | 41 | 140 | 19 | 50 |
| R | 14.1 | 20 | 23 | 20 | 15.1 | 18 | 25.9 | 15.7 | 13.5 | 15.92 |
| W percentage | high | 61 | 52 | 43 | 31 | | 36 | 43 | 46 | 50.00 |
| D percentage | low | 37 | 46 | 55 | 50 | | 47 | 47 | 45 | 40.90 |
| Dd percentage | | 2 | 2 | 2 | 17 | | 15 | 9 | 8 | |
| M | 1.4 | 2.6 | 1.9 | 1.8 | 1.1 | | 3.3 | 1.6 | 0.2 | 2.02 |
| FM | 3.2 | 4.8 | 5.0 | 5.1 | 2.8 | 1.6 | 2.7 | 2.0 | 0.3 | 3.24 |
| m | 0.1 | | | | 0.1 | | 0.7 | 0.3 | 0.0 | 0.16 |
| F percentage | | | | | 55 | 70 | 50 | 64 | 92 | 39.00 |
| F+ percentage | | | | | | | 93 | 81 | 50 | |
| FC | 0.3 | 1.8 | 1.7 | 0.2 | 0.7 | | 1.0 | 0.3 | 0.0 | 0.74 |
| CF | 0.7 | 1.5 | 1.6 | 0.2 | 0.4 | | 1.3 | 0.5 | 0.2 | 0.94 |
| C | | 0.2 | 0.2 | 0.3 | 0.2 | | 0.2 | 0.1 | 0.1 | |
| A percentage | high | 43 | 45 | 49 | 47 | 49 | 46 | 55 | 40 | 48.00 |

Note.—Mean values of less than 0.1 not entered in table.

compared with the youngest group (when intelligence is matched), there seemed to be no clear pattern with age.

Form dominance (as reflected in F percentage) showed no age change, although it was quite clear that this was highly related to intelligence, and in every case the high IQ group showed the least reliance on form-dominated precepts. Form accuracy (F+ percentage) was consistently highest in the high IQ group, and again no clear age changes emerged. The F+ percentage of the older subjects was higher than that of the 60–64 year group, and the absence of monotonicity or of any substantial difference in F+ percentage between the youngest and oldest groups suggested that this component did not show a major age-related change.

More color (C) responses were found in the records of the brighter subjects than in those of low IQ. Ratio of FC to C dominated response changes from approximately 2 to 1 to approximately 4 to 1 in the oldest group. FC remained the predominant color response throughout.

Analysis of the content indicated that there was a relatively consistent level of popular (P) responses which was larger for the high IQ group than for the low IQ group. The number of popular responses (P) seems fairly constant with age. The percentage of animal responses (A) does show an increase for the low and middle IQ group. The highest IQ group showed a nonmonotonic but rising tendency for this class of response. The percentage of animal responses seen by subjects in the 70+ low IQ group, as well as the subjects 75+ with average IQ, seemed especially noteworthy, since in both cases these represented more than half of the total number of responses. Klopfer (1956) suggested that this was associated with either low intellectual capacity or disturbed adjustment. The number of human responses (H) was fairly restricted in the lowest age groups of low and middle IQ subjects. These seemed to represent a slight decline from a previous level, but this pattern was not found in the high IQ group.

## Discussion

These data lend themselves only to limited discussion and they are presented primarily as a baseline measure for the interpretation of the Rorschach of the aged. The subjects in this study were adapting to their community and volunteered after contact through mass media, e.g., radio and television, as well as social and fraternal organizations, or other persons. While their motivation may have included a desire for a free physical examination (which is given all subjects and made available to a physician should they so choose) no treatment of any sort is offered by the research group, and the subjects are so informed before they volunteer. Such motivations as the need to find out about old age and an interest in participating as a research subject along with others of their community were doubtless also involved. Several subjects verbalized these as well as the feeling that since they had enough spare time it was appropriate for them to contribute to the advancement of the project. It is important also to realize that the subjects of the present report did not represent an isolated sample but were chosen from a group of volunteers which was more than twice as large.

The most striking finding presented by the data was the significance of measured intelligence rather than of old age in Rorschach performance. While, in comparison with the younger population, some of the responses seemed more restricted, W percentage somewhat higher, etc., these did not seem to be too remarkable in the group of persons with IQ 116+ when compared with young adults; e.g., Klopfer (1956) pointed out that the average $\Sigma R$ fell in the range of 20–45. It may be noted that (apart from the 65–69 subgroup) all of the old subjects in the high IQ group fell within this range. It may be that Rorschach findings reportedly pathognomonic of aging are artifacts of institutionalized status or the IQ of the older person. The present report suggests that the use of data from aged subjects whose adaptation is such as to require institutionalization, or from subjects whose intellectual level is unknown, is unwarranted as a basis for generalizing to the larger population of the aged.

## Summary

The Rorschach test was administered to 242 subjects, aged 60–94, who had received the WAIS examination as one aspect of a study of older persons in the community. Subjects were categorized according to age and intellectual status, and their protocols compared with the literature on Rorschach performance in the aged. The results indicated that level of intellectual functioning, perhaps more than age, plays an important role in the Rorschach performance of this aged sample. In addition, it was noted that generalizations about "the aged" made on the basis of Rorschach findings from institutionalized subjects, or without regard to intellectual level, were not supported by data from the present sample of aged persons of adequate intelligence and adaptation to the community at large. The results are presented in an effort to offer some baseline values for normal Rorschach performance in aged persons.

## References

Ames, L. B., Learned, J., Metraux, R. W., and Walker, R. N. *Rorschach responses in old age.* New York: Harper, 1954.
Caldwell, B. McD. The use of the Rorschach in personality research with the aged. *Journal of Gerontology,* 9:316–323, 1954.
Chesrow, E. J., Wosika, P. H., and Reinitz, A. H. A psychometric evaluation of aged white males. *Geriatrics,* 4:169–177, 1949.
Davidson, H. H., and Kruglov, L. Personality characteristics of the institutionalized aged. *Journal of Consulting Psychology,* 16:5–12, 1952.
Dörken, H., and Kral, A. V. Psychological investigation of senile dementia. *Geriatrics,* 6:151–163, 1951.
Grossman, C., Worshawsky, F., and Hertz, M. Rorschach studies on personality characteristics of a group of institutionalized old people (abstract). *Journal of Gerontology,* 6: Supplement to No. 3, 97, 1951.
Klopfer, B. *Developments in the Rorschach technique.* Vol. II. *Fields of application.* New York: World Book, 1956.
Klopfer, W. G. Personality patterns of old age. *Rorschach Research Exchange,* 10:145–166, 1946.
Kuhlen, R. G., and Keil, C. The Rorschach performance of one hundred elderly males (abstract). *Journal of Gerontology,* 6: Supplement to No. 3, 115, 1951.
Light, B. H., and Amick, J. H. Rorschach responses of normal aged. *Journal of Projective Techniques,* 20:185–195, 1956.
Piotrowski, Z. A. A Rorschach compendium, revised and enlarged. *Psychiatric Quarterly,* 24:543–596, 1950.
Prados, M., and Fried, E. G. Personality structure in the older age groups. *Journal of Clinical Psychology,* 3:113–120, 1947.
Rorschach, H. *Psychodiagnostics.* New York: Grune and Stratton, 1942.
Thaler, M. B. The application of three theories of personality to the Rorschach records of seventy-five aged subjects. Doctoral dissertation, University of Denver, 1952.

# Cardiovascular Disease and Behavioral Changes in the Elderly* *Larry W. Thompson, Carl Eisdorfer, and E. Harvey Estes*

There is a growing body of evidence suggesting that cardiovascular disease (CVD) is associated with behavioral deficits in middle-aged and elderly subjects. Speith (1965) found that mild to moderate degrees of

* Reprinted by permission from the *Proceedings of the Seventh International Congress of Gerontology,* 387–390, 1966.

cardiovascular disease were related to slower response speed and poorer performance. A reliable association between critical flicker frequency and cardiovascular disease has also been reported (Enzer, Simonson, & Blankstein, 1942). Jalavisto (1965) reported a relationship between cardiovascular and behavioral variables even when the age effect had been partialed out. Patients with essential hypertension have also been found to evidence signs of organic brain impairment on psychological tests (Apter, Halstead, & Heimburger, 1951; Reitan, 1954). Such findings emphasize the possible importance of the antecedents of disease in the development of senile deterioration. Although numerous studies offer support for this position, the follow-up studies of a longitudinal nature are noticeably absent from the literature. The present investigation was focused on the relationship between changes in CVD status and changes in intellectual measures over a three-year period.

## Subjects and Procedures

The subject group was composed of elderly persons (60–93 years) selected from a panel of 250 community volunteers who were participating in a longitudinal multidisciplinary study of aging. . . .

As part of this research program, subjects were periodically evaluated by a physical examination and various laboratory procedures, including an EKG and chest x-ray. Each time the subjects were brought in for study an overall assessment of cardiovascular disease was obtained from physical findings, EKG interpretation, estimates of heart size, extent of aortic calcification, hypertension, and cardiac decompensation. The subjects were rated on a 10-point scale according to the number and severity of their symptoms and the limitations these posed on their activities. Psychological tests were also administered; these included the Wechsler Adult Intelligence Scale, the Wechsler Memory Scale, and measures of simple and choice reaction time. Of the original panelists, 182 subjects were seen for a second . . . evaluation after approximately three years. . . . Any subjects with diseases involving related systems including evidence of cerebral-vascular or pulmonary disease were not considered. Nine subjects, who had hypertension but no other indications of cardiac disease on both examinations, were also excluded from the study.

## Results and Discussion

The Performance IQ scores in Table 6–22 were significantly higher for subjects with no CVD than for the group with CVD. A similar trend was apparent for the Verbal IQ scores, but this was not significant at the .05 level. The means for all groups increased from the first to second testing. None of the statistical tests for trial by group interaction effects was significant. These data tend to support the notion of a relationship between CVD and behavioral decline seen in the elderly, but they would have been more convincing if the group by trial interaction effect were such that the CVD group performed more poorly than the no-CVD group at the time of the second exam. However, a closer look at the composition of our subject group revealed obvious biasing effects which could account for the group

Table 6–22. *Mean Verbal and Performance IQ scores at the first and second exam for subjects with and without CVD.*

| | | Verbal IQ | | | | Performance IQ | | | |
|---|---|---|---|---|---|---|---|---|---|
| | | Exam I | | Exam II | | Exam I | | Exam II | |
| | N | X | SD | X | SD | X | SD | X | SD |
| Exam I | | | | | | | | | |
| No CVD | 41 | 102 | 22 | 104 | 21 | 96 | 18 | 99 | 16 |
| CVD | 43 | 96 | 20 | 97 | 19 | 88 | 16 | 92 | 15** |
| Exam II | | | | | | | | | |
| No CVD | 35 | 103 | 22 | 106 | 22 | 97 | 18 | 99 | 16 |
| CVD[a] | 49 | 96 | 20 | 97* | 19 | 88 | 16 | 92 | 15** |

[a] 23 subjects with CVD had an increase in severity of symptoms.
* $p < .10$, F tests, CVD vs. No CVD.
** $p < .05$, F tests, CVD vs. No CVD.

differences. For example, only 38 percent of the white subjects were in the disease group, while 70 percent of the Negroes had CVD. Similarly, 61 percent of the subjects in the higher socioeconomic level were in the healthy group, whereas only 33 percent of the lower socioeconomic group were found to be free of CVD. When these variables were taken into account in subsequent analysis the relationship between CVD and IQ scores was not discernible. Tables 6–23 and 6–24 list the IQ scores for high and low socioeconomic groups as determined by the Hollingshead classification system. An analysis of these data yielded no significant differences or interaction effects. The CVD group was further divided into two groups: those who had no limiting symptoms and those with restrictions on their activities. No significant differences between subjects with increased symptomatology and healthy subjects of comparable age, race, and socioeconomic status were apparent. It is also of interest that the subjects with more severe symptoms showed no decline in IQ scores over the three-year interval.

Table 6–23. *Mean Verbal and Performance IQ scores for the higher socioeconomic subjects with and without CVD.*

| | | Verbal IQ | | | | Performance IQ | | | |
|---|---|---|---|---|---|---|---|---|---|
| | | Exam I | | Exam II | | Exam I | | Exam II | |
| | N | X | SD | X | SD | X | SD | X | SD |
| Exam I | | | | | | | | | |
| No CVD | 17 | 122 | 16 | 124 | 14 | 111 | 12 | 111 | 12 |
| CVD | 11 | 118 | 19 | 118 | 20 | 109 | 11 | 103 | 11 |
| Exam II | | | | | | | | | |
| No CVD | 15 | 122 | 17 | 125 | 15 | 111 | 12 | 110 | 11 |
| CVD 1 | 13 | 118 | 18 | 118 | 19 | 110 | 11 | 110 | 13 |
| CVD 2 | 7 | 123 | 18 | 122 | 20 | 111 | 10 | 112 | 10 |

Note.—CVD 1 = total CVD group; CVD 2 = mild to moderate limitation of activity.

An analysis of the individual WAIS subtests, the Memory Scale, and measures of simple reaction time data suggested that the decline in response speed may be slightly greater in subjects with CVD than in healthy persons. A test of this interaction effect, however, only approached statistical significance.

It appears that distinctions in health in the present sample are not reflected in cognitive differences. Even subjects with CVD sufficiently severe to result in mild to moderate limitations of their activities were not appreciably impaired on measures of psychological functioning. Further, there was no evidence of decline over a three-year follow-up period compared with controls roughly equivalent with respect to variables known to influence performance on psychological tests. Although these findings are surprising in view of other results in the literature, one is tempted to

Table 6–24. *Mean Verbal and Performance IQ scores for the lower socioeconomic subjects with and without CVD.*

| | | Verbal IQ | | | | Performance IQ | | | |
|---|---|---|---|---|---|---|---|---|---|
| | | Exam I | | Exam II | | Exam I | | Exam II | |
| | N | X | SD | X | SD | X | SD | X | SD |
| Exam I | | | | | | | | | |
| No CVD | 24 | 88 | 12 | 90 | 13 | 85 | 14 | 91 | 13 |
| CVD | 32 | 89 | 15 | 90 | 14 | 81 | 10 | 86 | 11 |
| Exam II | | | | | | | | | |
| No CVD | 20 | 89 | 12 | 91 | 14 | 86 | 14 | 91 | 14 |
| CVD 1 | 36 | 88 | 14 | 90 | 14 | 81 | 10 | 86 | 11 |
| CVD 2 | 22 | 90 | 16 | 91 | 16 | 82 | 10 | 88 | 11 |

Note.—CVD 1 = total CVD group; CVD 2 = mild to moderate limitation of activity.

question the hypothesis that behavioral deficits are reliably associated with the initial development of disease processes. Rather the data are in agreement with the notion that the two are largely independent, even in the face of a noticeable deterioration of physiological functioning.

Such a position, however, is weakened by numerous factors which must be considered in the interpretation of the data. It could readily be argued, for example, that the testing procedures utilized in this study were not sufficiently sensitive to detect the early manifestations of impairment. This is supported by the suggested differential decline of response speed in a choice reaction time experiment. One must also raise the question whether a limiting or critical level of disease had been reached. In spite of the evidence of CVD, many of these subjects were active in community affairs and were following comparatively normal daily routines for persons within their general age range. None of the subjects were severely restricted in their activities, and many were following prescribed therapeutic programs. A failure to see a differential change in behavior in the two groups may be accounted for in part by the selective dropout. It might be speculated that a considerable number of subjects whose pathology had reached a critical level with respect to cognitive processes had been eliminated from the study, particularly since 68 percent of those who failed to return had died or were immobilized by illness. Taken together, such points impose restrictions on the interpretations of the present results. It should nevertheless be emphasized that at least under certain conditions the onset of impaired cardiovascular functioning may have a minimal effect on psychological functioning. The nature of this relationship appears to be a complex interaction on various factors which remain to be specified.

## References

Apter, N. S., Halstead, W. C., and Heimburger, R. F. Impaired cerebral functions in essential hypertension. *American Journal of Psychiatry*, 107:808–813, 1951.
Birren, J. E., Butler, R. N., Greenhouse, S. W., Sokoloff, L., and Yarrow, M. R. In Birren, J. E., et al. (Eds.), *United States Public Health Service Publication No. 986*. Washington, 1963.
Enzer, N., Simonson, E., and Blankstein, S. S. Fatigue of patients with circulatory insufficiency investigated by means of the fusion frequency of flicker. *Annals of Internal Medicine*, 16:701–707, 1942.
Jalavisto, E. On the interdependence of circulatory, respiratory, and neural-mental variables. *Gerontologia*, 10:31–37, 1964–1965.
Reitan, R. M. Intellectual and affective changes in essential hypertension. *American Journal of Psychiatry*, 110:817–824, 1954.
Speith, W. Slowness of task performance and cardiovascular diseases. In Welford, A. T., and Birren, J. E. (Eds.), *Behavior, aging, and the nervous system*. Springfield, Ill.: Charles C Thomas, 1965.

# Chapter 7. Perception and Affect

A well-known pattern of normal aging is that of increasing difficulty with hearing and seeing. Less well known are the consequences of these perceptual difficulties for the aged's emotions and cognitive functioning. The first two reports show that hearing loss seemed to result in more rigid emotions and lower vocabulary and perceptual organization levels, but that impaired vision did not seem to have such an effect. The third report shows that the aged occupied a middle position between young subjects and ill subjects in terms of expressions of affect and activity; that is, the aged expressed less emotion and activity than young persons but more than ill persons. The last report shows that the aged subjects perceived auditory stimuli as often and as rapidly as the young subjects (as measured by galvanic skin response). It also shows that the aged could recall as well as the young those phrases that had strong meaning (high arousal). In fact, the aged seemed to use various psychological defenses such as repression and denial even less than the young.

## Rorschach Rigidity and Sensory Decrement in a Senescent Population*    *Carl Eisdorfer*

With advancing age the sensory apparatus of the human organism is subject to breakdown or decline in function which may result in serious impairment to the individual's functioning (Covell, 1952; Friedenwald, 1952). It has been contended (Barker, Wright, Myerson, & Gonick, 1953) that individuals with sensory decrement show regression, withdrawal, and rigidity in interpersonal relationships. In dealing with a senescent group it becomes important, therefore, to evaluate the relationship between visual and auditory changes and personal adjustment.

In attempts to study the personality organization of aged individuals, investigators such as Klopfer (1946), Davidson and Kruglov (1952),

* Reprinted by permission from the *Journal of Gerontology*, 15:188–190, 1960. The author wishes to express his gratitude to Mrs. Shirley Crooke, Dr. C. R. Nichols, and Dr. M. E. Tresselt for their assistance in various aspects of this study.

Caldwell (1954), and others have turned to the Rorschach as a technique suited for this purpose. Investigators using the Rorschach have attempted to study the personality configuration of aged subjects in homes or institutions for the aged. In these studies results have been frequently analyzed in terms of a mean protocol and discussed as though they represented the Rorschach pattern of aged individuals in general. Often samples are not controlled for intellectual ability, community status, or physical intactness.

Piotrowski (Piotrowski & Lewis, 1950; Piotrowski & Berg, 1955) has discussed the use of the alpha formula as an outgrowth of his theoretical assumptions that, in the typical adult, psychodynamic control is directly proportional to the potential energy which will be elicited in psychosocial situations. In other words, the amount of control over impulses which may be observed in an individual is proportional to the amount of affect which may be generated in that individual. This relationship may be examined through the use of the alpha formula which is limited to adult patients whose Rorschach protocols contain no more than six Whole responses and $\Sigma c \geq \Sigma C$. According to Piotrowski, persons with high scores tend to manifest little stimulation in interpersonal situations and at the same time show marked rigidity and overcontrol. This control is said to reflect a defense characteristic of patients who realize that their organism is greatly dibilitated by some serious disease. Such persons have developed habits of great restraint. Thus, those individuals with high alpha scores are persons who are overcontrolled, underactive, and who manifest a withdrawn, rigid approach to the world.

### Hypotheses

This study was proposed in an attempt to evaluate the relationship between visual and auditory loss and rigidity, as reflected in Rorschach performance, in a group of socially adjusted elderly individuals. It was hypothesized that:

1. When visual loss was present but corrected to approximate normal vision, there would be no evidence of overcontrol in Rorschach performance. Where visual loss was present but not corrected to approximate normal functioning, an increase in rigidity of Rorschach performance might be anticipated.

2. Subjects with uncorrected hearing decrement would exhibit marked rigidity on the Rorschach.

3. Subjects with both hearing and visual decrement would show a greater amount of Rorschach rigidity than subjects with a major deficit in only one sensory system.

## Method

### Subjects

Subjects were drawn from volunteers who participated in the Duke Geriatrics Research Projects and who had been contacted through religious, fraternal, and civic groups. None were institutionalized. These individuals, all of whom had passed their sixtieth birthdays, were given physical,

Table 7-1. *Visual acuity* $(V_1, V_2, V_3)$[a] *and auditory acuity* $(H_1, H_2)$[b] *for each of six subgroups* ($N$ *for each subgroup* = 8).

| | $V_1$ | $V_2$ | $V_3$ |
|---|---|---|---|
| $H_1$ | Normal vision 20/15–20/40 | Corrected vision to 20/15–20/40 | Poor vision $20/40^{-2}$–20/200 |
| | Normal hearing 0–19 db loss | Normal hearing 0–19 db loss | Normal hearing 0–19 db loss |
| $H_2$ | Normal vision 20/15–20/40 | Corrected vision to 20/15–20/40 | Poor vision $20/40^{-2}$–20/200 |
| | Hearing loss 21 db or greater | Hearing loss 21 db or greater | Hearing loss 21 db or greater |

[a] Vision in better eye.
[b] Hearing in better ear: 256–2,048 cps range.

psychiatric, and psychological examinations, including the Rorschach and the Wechsler Adult Intelligence scale. Visual examinations were conducted by a member of the Ophthalmology Department of the Duke University School of Medicine. In order to study auditory functioning an examination was conducted by an otologist, and a pure tone (MAICO) audiometric study was performed.

Subjects were selected for the six cells in the experimental design according to three categories of far distance vision and two levels of hearing, as shown in Table 7-1. The three vision groups included subjects with normal vision (20/15 to 20/40); those with vision corrected to approximate normal; and those with poor functioning vision which was uncorrected. The mean acuity level for the third group was 20/99. The hearing groups were defined according to the mean decibel loss of the better ear in the range 256 to 2,048 cps. This range was chosen since it is based upon the range of human conversation. The levels of function were:

first, from 0- to 19-decibel loss (mean, 11.1-decibel loss); and second, 21-decibel loss or greater (mean, 39.7-decibel loss).

All subjects received a Full Scale Intellectual evaluation. Based upon WAIS Verbal Scale IQ, only subjects in the Normal range (plus or minus 5 IQ points) were studied in this experiment. All subjects received a neurological examination, and those with a history or signs of obvious CNS damage were eliminated.

The number in each of the six cells was 8 (total $N = 48$).

## Statistical Analysis

In the scoring of the alpha technique a cutoff of three points or more has been established to differentiate high from low scores (Piotrowski & Lewis, 1950; Piotrowski & Berg, 1955). It is thus possible to utilize a chi-square analysis for studying the frequency distribution of subjects who surpassed this cutoff point. Those subjects whose Rorschach protocols did not meet the requirements for alpha scoring were assigned the score of zero.

When this procedure is adopted, it is necessary to assume only that the alpha scale represents an ordinal scale, but not necessarily an interval scale. Chi-square seemed the appropriate method of analysis for the mitigation of such distortions as might result from utilizing the actual scores.

## Results

Table 7–2 Part A shows that there was no significant difference between the distributions of the high alpha scores in subjects with corrected vision. Thus, the results suggest that the wearing of corrective lenses does not seem to result in any special rigidity or impairment of Rorschach performance in aged subjects.

Since there was no difference in performance between subjects with normal and subjects with corrected vision, it was possible to combine these two groups to obtain a group with normal functioning vision, and then to compare this latter group with the group showing visual decrement. Table 7–2 Part B shows the results of this comparison. The hypothesis that visual decrement would lead to greater rigidity and impaired Rorschach performance was not supported.

Table 7–2 Part C shows the comparison between subjects with hearing decrement and subjects without hearing decrement. Chi-square analysis demonstrates that the incidence of subjects with alpha score three or above (the sign of Rorschach rigidity) is greater in the hearing decrement group than in the group with normal hearing. The chi-square is significant at the 105 level.

The test of hypothesis 3 is not presented in tabular form, since it was clear from inspection that there was no difference in the incidence of high alpha scores in the group with both visual and auditory decrement as compared with the other two hearing deficit groups. There were five subjects with high alpha scores in the $H_2V_3$ cell, but four in each of the other two hearing decrement cells ($H_2V_1$ and $H_2V_2$). Thus, while it is true that the cell which included subjects with multiple deficit showed the

Table 7–2. *Chi-square analysis of alpha scores.*

| | Alpha scores | | | |
|---|---|---|---|---|
| | $\geq 3$ | $<3$ | $x^2$ | $p$ |
| A: By normal and corrected vision | | | | |
| Normal vision | 5 | 11 | 0 | |
| Corrected vision | 6 | 10 | | |
| B: By normal functioning vision and visual decrement | | | | |
| Normal functioning vision | 11 | 21 | .533 | > .3 |
| Visual decrement | 8 | 8 | | |
| C: By auditory level | | | | |
| Normal hearing | 6 | 18 | 4.260 | < .05 |
| Hearing decrement | 13 | 11 | | |

greatest incidence of subjects with high rigidity scores, this was not statistically different from the incidence of such scores found in the groups showing only hearing decrement.

## Discussion

Hearing was chosen as a variable for the present study not only because auditory deficit occurs so frequently with increasing age but also because of the insidious role defective hearing plays in the impairment of human communication. While the victim of visual loss is usually able to recognize his own condition, personal knowledge of hearing decrement, at least in its early phases, is often received from others. This information is usually associated with frustration and hostility generated by the failure of others to communicate with the "hard of hearing" individual. This study would appear to suggest that the aged individual reacts to hearing loss by withdrawal and by increasing rigidity of personality.

# Summary

This study was an investigation of the relationships between visual and hearing decrement and Rorschach indices of rigidity in an aged population. The Rorschach was administered to 48 community volunteers aged 60 and over, divided into six groups on the basis of three visual and two auditory levels of functioning. Subjects were screened to eliminate those with neurologically definable CNS damage and those with extreme Verbal IQ scores. Piotrowski's alpha formulation was adopted as an index of extreme overcontrol on the Rorschach. The results indicate:

1. There is no difference in the incidence of high alpha scores between subjects with normal vision and those with vision which is impaired but functioning normally (through the use of corrective lenses).

2. There are no differences in the incidence of high alpha scores between subjects with normally functioning vision and those with "impaired" vision.

3. There are significant differences in the alpha scores between subjects with normal and subjects with "impaired" hearing.

4. The Rorschach performance of subjects with both vision and hearing impairments is not significantly different from that in subjects showing hearing decrement alone.

# References

Barker, R. G., Wright, B. A., Meyerson, L., and Gonick, M. R. *Adjustment to physical handicap and illness: A survey of the social psychology of physique and disability.* New York: Social Science Research Council, 1953.

Caldwell, B. McD. The use of the Rorschach in personality research with the aged. *Journal of Gerontology*, 9:316–323, 1954.

Covell, W. P. The ear. In Lansing, A. I. (Ed.), *Cowdry's problems of aging.* (2nd ed.) Baltimore: Williams and Wilkins, 1952.

Davidson, H. H., and Kruglov, L. Personality characteristics of the institutionalized aged. *Journal of Consulting Psychology*, 16:5–12, 1952.

Friedenwald, J. S. The eye. In Lansing, A. I. (Ed.), *Cowdry's problems of aging.* (2nd ed.) Baltimore: Williams and Wilkins, 1952.

Klopfer, W. G. Personality patterns of old age. *Rorschach Research Exchange*, 10:145–166, 1946.

Piotrowski, Z. A., and Berg, D. A. Verification of the Rorschach alpha diagnostic formula for underactive schizophrenics. *American Journal of Psychiatry*, 112:443–450, 1955.

Piotrowski, A. A., and Lewis, N. D. C. An experimental Rorschach diagnostic aid for some forms of schizophrenia. *American Journal of Psychiatry*, 107:360–366, 1950.

# Developmental Level and Sensory Impairment in the Aged*   Carl Eisdorfer

The Rorschach performance of aged subjects is reported to show an impoverishment of creative intellectual facilities, a faulty perception of reality, and a narrowing of the range of interest (Davidson & Kruglov, 1952; Klopfer, 1946). These interpretations often are based upon generalized clinical findings derived from mixed groups of institutionalized and noninstitutionalized aged subjects in comparison with hypothetical normal (young) groups. Although there is much evidence suggesting that aging is accompanied by sensory deficits (Lansing, 1952), and that sensory deficits are associated with lower levels of perceptual organization (Barker et al., 1953), the relationship between such deficits and Rorschach functioning has been overlooked in studies with the aged.

Structural aspects of Rorschach response determinants have been employed to formulate scoring techniques (Friedman, 1953; Phillips & Smith, 1953) based upon the principles of developmental psychology (Werner, 1948). The utility of these scores for discerning levels of maturity in a wide variety of contexts has been demonstrated (Hemmendinger, 1953; Lane, 1955; Phillips & Framo, 1954). The language used in Rorschach responses has been investigated by Grace (1956), who has formulated and validated a procedure for assessing the developmental level of content vocabulary. These scoring techniques make it possible to investigate Rorschach performance of aged subjects in terms of developmental level.

The hypotheses tested were concerned with the developmental level of Rorschach performance on the part of aged subjects with visual or auditory deficit (or both). Investigators (Barker et al., 1953; Zucker, 1947) have shown a relationship between deafness and poor Rorschach performance in children; in consequence, it was hypothesized that hearing decrement would be associated with a lower developmental level of Rorschach performance among aged subjects. In view of the obvious relationship between vision and the Rorschach test performance, it was anticipated that uncorrected visual deficit would be associated with a decline in the developmental level of Rorschach. Where visual decrement was corrected, however, no

* Reprinted by permission from the *Journal of Projective Techniques and Personality Assessment*, 24:129–132, 1960.

such developmental decline would be expected. Subjects with both auditory and visual deficit may be expected to perform at a lower level of Rorschach functioning than subjects with deficit in either sense system alone.

## Method

[The subjects and methods of classifying by vision and hearing are the same as in the preceding report.—*Editor*]

. . . Three dependent variables were utilized in the investigation: the Functional Integration score, associated with the highest form of perceptual organization (Rochwarg, 1954); Grace's (1956) Content score, which provides a developmental positive estimate of the vocabulary level of Rorschach responses; and the Index of Primitive Thought, reflecting the lowest level of perceptual organization.

## Results

The hypothesis that hearing decrement would be associated with a developmental decline in Rorschach performance was examined, using nonparametric techniques. Mann-Whitney U tests show a significant difference ($p < .01$) between the normal hearing ($H_1$) and hearing decrement ($H_2$) groups in the direction predicted on the Content ($z = 3.25$) and Functional Integration ($z = 3.13$) variables.

Primitive Thought was analyzed with a chi-square test of the distribution of subjects who exhibited this score. This procedure was adopted since the presence of Primitive Thought in a record is suggestive of psychopathology, and subjects who exhibited any Primitive Thought might be expected to manifest an inordinate number of such responses.

The distribution of Primitive Thought scores does not support this hypothesis. Table 7–3 demonstrates that only 4 of 48 subjects produced responses which could be identified as indicative of Primitive Thought. While three of these are in the $H_2$ group, there are not enough cases present to allow for a meaningful test of the hypothesis based upon this criterion.

In order to test the assumption that visual impairment (even when corrected) would affect Rorschach performance, Content score differences we examined with a Mann-Whitney U test. The resultant $z$'s (.62 and .57, respectively) do not refute a hypothesis of no difference. In the examination of the Primitive Thought score the chi-square obtained was essentially zero ($x^2 = .004$), again indicating no difference between the two groups being examined. Thus none of the (three) measures of Rorschach developmental level shows a significant difference between the normal vision ($V_1$) and usually corrected ($V_2$) groups.

The same procedures were adopted to test the hypothesis that normal functioning ($V_1$ plus $V_2$) and visual decrement ($V_3$) groups would differ. The results of Mann-Whitney U tests for Functional Integration and Content score and chi-square analysis of the distribution of Primitive Thought scores fail to reveal any systematic difference between the Rorschach developmental level of normally functioning and visually impaired subjects.

The fourth hypothesis relates to the performance of subjects who show decrement in both sensory parameters. While the eight subjects with both

Table 7–3. *Chi-square analysis and distribution of subjects showing primitive thought according to auditory group.*

| Group | Distribution of primitive thought scores | | $x^2$ | $p$ |
|-------|:---:|:---:|:---:|:---:|
| | $\geq 1$ | 0 | | |
| Normal hearing | 1 | 23 | 1.09 | .30 |
| Hearing decrement | 3 | 21 | | |

vision and hearing impaired show lower Content and Functional Integration scores than all other subjects combined (Mann-Whitney U tests yield scores significant at the .05 level), this hypothesis is not confirmed. When the subjects in this group ($V_3H_2$) are compared with the subjects showing hearing decrement alone ($V_1H_2$ plus $V_2H_2$), the developmental scores are not significantly different.

Discussion

*Auditory Deficit*

Auditory deficit, as defined in this investigation, appears to be related to a decline in the developmental level of Rorschach performance. Vocabulary level of Rorschach responses as measured by Grace's Content score and cognitive ability as reflected in the Functional Integration score were significantly lower in the hearing decrement group (in both cases $p < .01$). Aged individuals with impaired audition, when compared to their normally hearing peers, show a less mature perceptual approach to their environment and developmentally lower level of communication. It may thus be inferred that these subjects are exhibiting a more poorly integrated personality.

Primitive Thought scores appeared in the protocols of only 4 of 48 aged subjects in the present study. This finding is at variance with that of Rochwarg (1954), who reports that more than half of a group of 40 normal aged subjects (32 of whom resided in institutions) showed this sign. It seems clear that generalization of Rorschach performance or personality variables, from institutional to noninstitutional aged, should be made only with extreme caution. The subjects in this investigation would appear to show considerably less evidence of developmentally early thought processes than is found in a mixed institutionalized and community group.

Aged subjects with visual and auditory difficulty combined did not perform at a significantly lower developmental level than did subjects with hearing decrement alone. In view of the extremely low performance level of the auditory decrement group, a baseline effect may be operating in this situation. Since all subjects were making an adjustment in the community, it may be anticipated that the Rorschach response patterns will be within a "normal" range. The functioning of the auditory decrement group may be approaching the lower limits of normal.

### Visual Deficit

The results of this study indicate that visual impairment, within the limits defined in this study, corrected or uncorrected, is not reflected in a decline in Functional Integration score, Content score, or Index of Primitive Thought derived from the Rorschach. It may be inferred that visual decrement in the aged is not associated with personality change, as re-'flected in a developmental analysis of the Rorschach. The present study suggests that the Rorschach blot can be made a good deal more ambiguous to the subjects, without major changes in the response properties.

### Summary

A study was performed to investigate the effects of visual and hearing decrement on Rorschach performance in an aged population. The Rorschach was administered to 48 senescent community-adjusted volunteers divided into six groups on the basis of three visual and two auditory levels of functioning. All subjects were screened to eliminate those with neurologically definable CNS damage and extremes of Verbal IQ. Three dependent variables—Functional Integration score, Grace's Content score (Vocabulary), and the Index of Primitive Thought—were utilized to reflect various levels on a developmental continuum of Rorschach performance.

The results indicate that:

1. Impaired hearing is associated with a significantly lowered developmental performance as defined by vocabulary level and Functional Integration scores.

2. No differences appear between subjects with normal vision and those with vision which is impaired but corrected, nor were differences found between subjects with normally functioning vision and those with "impaired" vision.

3. The performance of subjects with both visual and auditory decrement is not worse than that of subjects showing auditory decrement alone; although the level of performance of these subjects is consistently the poorest of the subject population.

## References

Barker, R. G., Wright, B. A., Meyerson, L., and Gonick, M. R. *Adjustment to physical handicap and illness: A survey of the social psychology of physique and disability.* New York: Social Science Research Council, 1953.

Davidson, H. H., and Kruglov, L. Personality characteristics of the institutionalized aged. *Journal of Consulting Psychology,* 16:5–12, 1952.

Friedman, H. Perceptual regression in schizophrenia: An hypothesis suggested by the use of the Rorschach test. *Journal of Genetic Psychology,* 8:63–98, 1953.

Grace, N. B. A developmental comparison of word usage with structural aspects of perception and social adjustment. Doctoral dissertation, Duke University, 1956.

Hemmendinger, L. Perceptual organization and development as reflected in the structure of the Rorschach test response. *Journal of Projective Techniques,* 17:162–170, 1953.

Klopfer, W. G. Personality patterns of old age. *Rorschach Research Exchange,* 10:145–166, 1946.

Lane, J. E. Social effectiveness and developmental level. *Journal of Personality,* 23:274–284, 1955.

Lansing, A. E. (Ed.). *Cowdry's problems of aging.* (3rd ed.) Baltimore: Williams and Wilkins, 1952.

Phillips, L., and Framo, J. L. Developmental theory applied to normal and psychopathological perception. *Journal of Personality,* 22:464–474, 1954.

Phillips, L., and Smith, J. S. *Rorschach interpretation: Advanced technique.* New York: Grune and Stratton, 1953.

Rochwarg, H. Changes in the structural aspects of perception in the aged. Doctoral dissertation, Michigan State College, 1954.

Werner, H. *Comparative psychology of mental development.* (Rev. ed.) New York: Follet, 1948.

Zucher, L. Rorschach patterns of a group of hard of hearing patients. *Rorschach Research Exchange* and *Journal of Projective Techniques,* 11:68–73, 1947.

# Affective Expression among the Aged* *Martin Lakin and Carl Eisdorfer*

Systematic research in personality factors among the aged has largely been centered in the area of cognition. The need to assess intellectual capacities in this group has been reflected in such efforts as Wechsler's standardization of the WAIS (Doppelt & Wallace, 1955). Other studies have focused upon learning, retention, and thinking and have evaluated differences between younger and aged populations with respect to these intellectual dimensions (Birren, 1959).

At the same time, even apart from the important conceptual issues raised, the press for planned rehabilitation and therapeutic programs for the aged makes necessary assessment of emotional as well as intellectual resources of the aged.

The attempt to investigate more complex personality dimensions among the aged has been marked by the employment of clinical methods including some of the projective techniques. These have included Rorschach studies (Ames, Learned, Metraux, & Walker, 1954), Figure Drawings (Lorge, Tuckman, & Dunn, 1954; Lakin, 1958), and Ambiguous Figures (Korchin & Basowitz, 1956). While none of these studies focuses exclusively or directly upon affective status, the concept is frequently utilized in a manner which suggests its pervasive significance for an understanding of personality among the aged.

The emphasis upon affects as an important variable in understanding the aged is even greater in the clinical studies by psychotherapists. Here, of course, the interactional effects with age become a real problem, especially insofar as diagnosis and treatment for the individual aged person is concerned. The problem is clearly seen in recent reviews of the literature on psychotherapy with the aged (Rechtschaffen, 1959; Ross, 1959), where two points of view are apparent. One point of view is that limitations of emotional expression among the aged are due to the ego-disorganizing and anxiety-arousing experiences of physical and social impairment and the proximity of death. The other point of view posits a concept of modification and diminution of affective expression as a function of expected developmental decline. The problem of primary factor thus poses a problem equally difficult to that suggested by presumed interactional effects with

* Reprinted by permission from the *Journal of Projective Techniques and Personality Assessment*, 24:403–408, 1960.

respect to emotionality changes in aging. However, especially in regard to clinical populations, either position may denote psychopathologic implications.

Current understanding of emotionality among the aged has derived largely from observation of psychiatric populations. These must be subject to certain limitations. For one thing, the samples are, of course, biased—especially with regard to emotionality. In addition, the service orientation implicit in the therapist-patient relationship and the attendant lack of observer objectivity make it difficult to arrive at valid conclusions regarding modes of affective expression in patient samples, much less normal aged groups.

The focus of the present investigation is on affective expression among normal aged. The methodology derives from the projective techniques tradition where an indirect measure of emotionality, i.e., the perception and response modality, is employed. This indirect measure is admittedly limited in terms of the assessment of such variables as emotionality potential and is clearly dependent upon adequacy of perception and verbalization. Nevertheless, it should be helpful in discovery of the expressive aspects of affect as they may be affected by the aging process.

## Subjects

Group I (N = 24) were young normals and consisted of secretaries and ward attendants. The mean age for the group was 23.7 years. Group II (N= 55) was composed of aged "normally adjusted" persons living in the local community who had volunteered to be subjects for the Duke University Geriatrics Project. . . . The mean age for Group II was 73.2 years. Group III (N = 27) was composed of new outpatients of the Duke University Medical Center's Outpatient Clinic. These persons, who had come for examinations on the basis of presumed physical illness, were selected on the basis of their availability at a certain time. Their mean age was 39.6 years. The identifying characteristics of these subject samples are shown in Table 7–4.

## Procedures

A set (12) of stick figures devised by Reitman (1947) was shown to all the subjects of this investigation. These stick figures, because of posture of head and attitudes, body and limbs, suggest emotional states. Description of these figures by subjects is typically in affective terms. The subjects were instructed as follows: "I am going to show you some stick figures. Tell me what sorts of feelings you get from looking at them. Give me as many as you can." Subjects were examined individually. Incidental comments were recorded.

Responses to the stick figures were scored for four parameters as follows: (*a*) number of discrete affects used in describing a figure; (*b*) intensity of affective expression as rated along a four-point scale; (*c*) comments relating explicitly to the somatic state of the figure as seen by the

Table 7–4. *Population characteristics.*

| Group | N | Mean age | Sex | | Race | | |
|---|---|---|---|---|---|---|---|
| | | | M | F | Negro | White | Other |
| Group I Young | 24 | 23.7* | 11 | 13 | 0 | 24 | 0 |
| Group II Aged | 55 | 73.2 | 25 | 30 | 13 | 42 | 0 |
| Group III MOPC | 28 | 39.6* | 9 | 19 | 7 | 18 | 1 |

* Incomplete: Age data for one subject unavailable.

subject; (*d*) the attribution of activity to the figure (active, passive, none). Groups of subjects were compared with each other with respect to each of the above-mentioned factors.

Results

Table 7–5 lists the mean score for each of the dependent variables obtained by the three groups.

For two of the dependent variables, number of affects and action, the performance of the three subject groups was analyzed with the use of a simple random analysis of variance design; in each case the $F$ was significant at beyond the .01 level. In order to investigate the relationship between the scores of the various groups for these numbers further, $t$ tests were performed. Since a Bartlett test of homogeneity of variance had indicated differences between groups with respect to the variables of Intensity and Somatic Comments, nonparametric techniques were used to test the significance of differences for these variables. These were the Kruskal-Wallis and Mann-Whitney tests. For the first dependent variable (i.e., the number of affects expressed) the three groups all differed from one another ($t$ was $p < .01$). The second variable, intensity of affect, appears to show a

Table 7–5. *Mean score obtained by subject groups for each dependent variable.*

| Variable group | Affect | Intensity | Total somatic comment | Total action |
|---|---|---|---|---|
| Group I Young | 13.2 | 2.0 | 0.6 | 9.0 |
| Group II Aged | 8.8 | 1.9 | 0.8 | 5.6 |
| Group III MOPC | 6.2 | 3.8 | 3.0 | 3.5 |

statistical difference only between Groups II and III (Mann-Whitney U test significant at the .05 level).

For the third variable, while Groups I and II do not differ statistically in terms of total somatic comment, both differ from Group III (Mann-Whitney U test significant at the .01). In their expression of action (variable *d*) all groups differ from one another (in every case *t* is significant at beyond the .01 level).

Table 7–6 shows a matrix listing the *t* test and Mann-Whitney results which will summarize this material.

It may be seen from these results that the following distinctions can be drawn between the performances by the aged group, the somatically ill subjects, and those of the younger normal controls.

Table 7–6. *Matrices indicating results of tests of significance.*

| Variable A: Affect *t* test | | | Variable B: Intensity Mann-Whitney test | | |
|---|---|---|---|---|---|
| Group | II | III | Group | II | III |
| I | ** | ** | I | ns | ns |
| II | | ** | II | | * |

| Variable C: Total somatic comment Mann-Whitney test | | | Variable D: Total action *t* test | | |
|---|---|---|---|---|---|
| Group | II | III | Group | II | III |
| I | ns | ** | I | ** | ** |
| II | | ** | II | | ** |

* Significant beyond .05.
** Significant beyond .01.

In the comparison between the elderly subjects and the medical outpatients, the older persons produced a greater number of affectively toned statements. They showed a higher level of activity (more active and more passive as contrasted with static quality) in their descriptions of figures than did the outpatients. They produced less somatic content in their descriptions than did the outpatients. However, the intensity level of affect in their descriptions of figures was judged to be less than that of the latter.

In the comparison between the aged and the normal groups the findings were as follows: aged subjects were exceeded by younger normals in number of affective descriptions and in the activity levels (active and passive as contrasted with static quality) depicted for the figures. No differences with regard to somatic content and intensity level were found for these two groups.

A qualitative analysis of the affective expressions suggests a descending order for the three groups—young normals, aged, and outpatients—in terms of such factors as variety, presence of conflicting or alternate responses, and what might be termed "degree of personal involvement" in the expressions.

## Discussion

The performance of the elderly subjects relative to the two other groups may illustrate the problem of the differential in affective expression among the aged. The finding of differences along several of the dimensions with respect to chronological age per se, in the two nonclinic groups, conforms to the anticipation that the aging process will be associated with a decline in affective "energy," at least insofar as this is reflected in verbal material. A theoretical formulation which would emphasize the normative developmental decline in emotionality among the aged is that of Banham (1951). She emphasized the saliency of consolidation, constriction, and disintegration as sequential processes in emotional organization in later life. A limited number of emotional responses and their relative unchangeability are cited as characteristic of normal aged. The point is made that the emotions of older people are characterized by paucity rather than by abundance of affective energy. It is also pointed out—relevant to the mental health versus psychopathology issue—that there is psychologic economy in this relative constriction. The reduced affective sensitivity and changeability may actually be helpful factors in adjustment.

The views of Cumming, Dean, Newell, and McCafferty (1959), as elaborated in their theory of disengagement, closely parallel this position, and the results of the present study would seem to lend support to the concept they express as the *appearance of deviance* in old age (Cumming et al., 1959, p. 8.0), i.e., the disengagement of the aged from life outside themselves. That diminished ability of older individuals to perceive action or affect on the part of others may contribute to the phenomenon of *mutual withdrawal* seems readily apparent. A qualitative approach to the material would appear consistent with this interpretation insofar as aged show noticeably less personal involvement with the task than do the younger nonclinic subjects. Preoccupation with bodily ailments and impairments has been widely assumed to affect the emotional responsiveness of the aged, and the psychopathologic implications of this preoccupation have been emphasized in the categorization of the emotional traits and charac- teristics of the aged (Pollack, 1948). Consistent with this assumption would have been a finding of difference between old and young on the dimension of somatic content and similarity of performance between old and sick with regard to this dimension. Our findings do not support this assumption. It would appear that although their physical status is clearly an important area for the aged· group (a powerful motivation for participation by normal elderly persons in the Duke University Geriatrics Research Program is the physical examination given each individual) somatic preoc- cupation has not grossly affected them in terms of their emotional expres- siveness. In the cases of the outpatients, their somatic concerns are explicit and are, of course, heightened at the time of their self-presentation for diagnosis and treatment. A similar psychological process may underlie the findings of judged greater intensity of affect expression for this group.

Decrement in reactivity potential in emotionality among the aged ap- pears to be an empirical fact (Ames et al., 1954; Banham, 1951). While comparison with a group of somatically ill individuals shows a higher level of reactivity for aged (productivity, variety, activity) and fewer "regres- sive" features (bodily preoccupation), comparison with young normals seems to reveal the decrement. The issue as to primary etiological factors is yet to be resolved. To oppose the genetic and sequential constriction hypothesis in a context of general decline there is the viewpoint of Ross (1959) and Gitelson (1955), who emphasize the psycho-social as well as physical assaults on the aged to which the constricted emotionality is but an understandable response. That sampling and professional bias may compli- cate the evaluation of either position has been indicated elsewhere in the paper.

The present investigation has not focused upon etiological issues as such but has aimed at exploration of the dimensions of affective expression among the normal aged. Their performances in terms of productivity, activity level, and somatic emphasis by contrast with younger, somatically ill patients and with younger, normal controls accentuate the unique pattern of affect expressions among the aged. The question of etiology with regard to this pattern is complex, and there is need for further study to examine the principal hypothesis and to evaluate ameliorative approaches to the problem. It may be that methods such as those used here combined with appropriate physiological and biochemical techniques (e.g., improvement of blood circulation and correction of endocrine imbalance) could be applied to the problem of assessment of changes in affect expression among the aged. Such an orientation appears to be supported by research which has shown desirable changes in affect expression on the basis of those therapies involving emotional expressiveness.

## Summary

Inference about emotionality among the aged is derived almost exclusively from clinical data. It would seem important, therefore, to study affective expressions in normal aged.

In order to examine the range, intensity, and content of affective expression among the aged, the Reitman stick figure projective test was administered to a group of 55 elderly volunteers (mean age 73.2) and two control groups, one composed of 24 young normal subjects (mean age 23.7), and the second comprised of 28 new outpatients in the Duke University Medical clinic (mean age 39.6). Responses to the 12 card series were examined according to (*a*) number of discrete affects expressed, (*b*) intensity of affect, (*c*) sum of the somatic responses, and (*d*) activity level noted (active, passive, static).

In the comparison between normal elderly subjects and medical outpatient controls, aged subjects obtained significantly better scores in terms of number of affects, activity level, and less somatic content. Aged subjects were exceeded by younger controls on the dimensions of number of affects and activity level. No difference was obtained between these groups with respect to somatic content. The revealed unique pattern of affective responsiveness for the aged group was reviewed in the light of the genetic hypothesis of general developmental decline and that which emphasized defects based upon negative (traumatic) emotional experiences associated with aging in our society. Theoretical and practical implications in terms of further research were indicated.

## References

Ames, L. B., Learned, J., Metraux, R. W., and Walker, R. N. *Rorschach responses in old age.* New York: Paul B. Hoeber, 1954.

Banham, K. M. Senescence and the emotions: A genetic theory. *Journal of Genetic Psychology*, 78:175–183, 1951.

Birren, J. E. (Ed.). *Handbook of aging and the individual.* Chicago: University of Chicago Press, 1959.

Botwinick, J. Drives, expectancies, and emotions. In Birren, J. E. (Ed.), *Handbook of aging and the individual.* Chicago: University of Chicago Press, 1959.

Cumming, E., Dean, L. R., Newell, D. S., and McCafferty, I. Disengagement: A tentative theory of aging. Paper delivered at symposium on Developmental Theories of Aging, American Psychological Association annual meeting, Cincinnati, Ohio, September, 1959.

Doppelt, J. E., and Wallace, W. L. Standardization of the Wechsler Adult Intelligence Scale for older persons. *Journal of Abnormal and Social Psychology,* 51:312–330, 1955.

Gitelson, M. The emotional problems of elderly people. *Geriatrics*, 3:135–150, 1948.

Korchin, S. J., and Basowitz, H. The judgment of ambiguous stimuli as an index of cognitive functioning in aging. *Journal of Personality*, 26:81–95, 1956.

Lakin, M. Affective tone in human figure drawings by aged and by children. *Journal of the American Geriatric Society*, 6:495–500, 1958.

Lakin, M. Certain formal characteristics of human figure drawings by institutionalized aged and by normal children. *Journal of Consulting Psychology*, 6:471–474, 1956.

Lorge, I., Tuckman, J., and Dunn, M. B. Human figure drawings by younger and older adults (abstract). *American Psychologist*, 9:420–421, 1954.

Pollack, O. Social adjustment in old age: A research planning report. *Social Service Research Council Bulletin*, 59, 1948.

Rechtschaffen, A. Psychotherapy with geriatric patients: A review of the literature. *Journal of Gerontology*, 14:73–84, 1959.

Reigle, K. F. Personality theory and aging. In Birren, J. E. (Ed.), *Handbook of aging and the individual.* Chicago: University of Chicago Press, 1959.

Reitman, F., and Robertson, J. P. Reitman's Pin-Man Test: A means of disclosing impaired conceptual thinking. *Journal of Nervous and Mental Diseases*, 112:498–510, 1950.

Ross, M. A review of some treatment methods for elderly psychiatric patients. *American Medical Association Archives of General Psychiatry*, 1:578–591, 1959.

# Influence of Psychodynamic Factors on Central Nervous System Functioning in Young and Aged Subjects* *Sanford I. Cohen, Albert J. Silverman, and Barry M. Shmavonian*

Numerous research studies representing various disciplines have suggested that aged persons show a decreased perceptual acuity; a decrease in the ability to perform tasks requiring sensorimotor integration; a decrease

* Reprinted by permission from *Psychosomatic Medicine*, 23:123–137, 1961. The authors are indebted to Miss Joan Ware for her participation and assistance in conducting this experiment and handling the data.

in the efficiency of their cognitive processes, including memory functions, discrimination, response capacity; and a decrease in the capacity to be conditioned (Barnes, Busse, & Friedman, 1965; Birren, 1955; Bortz, 1957; Botwinick, Brinley, & Robbin, 1958a, 1958b; Bromley, 1957; Busse, Barnes, & Silverman, 1954; Busse, Barnes, Friedman, & Kelty, 1956; Dennis, 1953; Fraser, 1950; Freeman, Pincus, Elmadjian, & Romanoff, 1955; Inglis, 1957; Korchin, 1956; Kirschner, 1958; Nelson & Gellhorn, 1957, 1958; Silverman, Busse, Barnes, Frost, & Thaler, 1957; Wilcox, 1956).

The difficulties encountered by the aged individual in performing complex intellectual and psychomotor tasks have been attributed in part to a decrease in perceptual acuity. This decrease in perceptive abilities has been suggested as an explanation of the increased reaction latency noted when older subjects are asked to make a discrimination between sensory cues and then to give a motor response to a stimulus. This perceptual difficulty has further been assumed to be a function of, or related to, some change in the central nervous system (CNS) associated with the aging process. However, it has never been clarified whether the changes responsible for the decreased functioning in aged persons affect primarily the sensory end organs, the afferent conducting pathways, the central integrating and transmission systems, or the efferent pathways.

The specific aim of the study reported in this article was to examine the relationship of psychodynamic and neurophysiological factors in the perception, recording, recall, recognition, and reporting of a series of nonverbal and verbal auditory stimuli during an experimental situation involving young and aged subjects.

## Materials and Methods

### Subjects

A group of 10 white male college students 20–24 years old and 10 white elderly men 60–79 years old were tested. The elderly subjects were obtained from the pool of subjects available to the gerontology research group—the Aging Center—at Duke University Medical Center. These were persons who had been previously examined for their general state of health. All the subjects were matched for IQ (above 110), physical health (no overt medical disease or sensory defects), and mental health.

### Experimental Design

The subjects were asked to lie quietly in a dimly lit room. They were given a short introductory talk in which the purpose of the experiment was described as an attempt to see what changes various sound stimuli would produce in certain aspects of skin functioning. The instrumentation in the room, e.g., the electrodes and loudspeakers, was explained. A general outline of the procedure was given as follows: "You will hear various sounds and phrases over the loudspeaker. You are not expected to do anything. Just lie back, relax, and listen." No specific details were given the subjects. Skin-resistance electrodes[1] attached to cloth slippers were placed on the subjects' feet. The subjects were then left alone, and a recording was begun that could be heard by the subjects over one of the loudspeakers. First, the introductory instructions (identical to those given to the subjects prior to the experimenters' leaving) were repeated. Following this, previously recorded stimuli were presented. Continuous skin-resistance (GSR) records were obtained during the experimental period.

The experimental session was divided into five periods, as outlined in Table 7–7.

Period 1: Four clearly distinguishable sounds (of 250, 500, 1,000, and 2,000 cps) were presented at 20-second intervals and were repeated five times in the same sequence.

Period 2: Two phrases intended to be "bland" were presented at 20-second intervals, three times in the same sequence (e.g., "the books on the table" and "the clouds in the sky"). The pattern of presentation was then reversed, and the expressions again were presented three times.

Period 3: Statements that the investigators considered "charged" for a young college group (Cy) and "charged" for an elderly group (Co) were then presented. These were systematically associated with the previously named tones and bland statements (Table 7–7). The four sounds were briefly presented immediately prior to each of the four types of phrases. The phrase, "the books on the table," always preceded the statement directed at the young group, and the expression, "the clouds in the sky," always preceded the phrases directed at the aged group. This series was presented in sequence eight times (that is, a series of four expressions with their accompanying tones was presented eight times). In the last four presentations, the order of presentation was altered, but the time between stimulus presentation was not changed. The young and old statements, which were paired in any one sequence, were constructed so that they were associated with similar areas for each of the groups (e.g., "too young for sex," "too old for sex").

Period 4: The four tones that had been presented in Period 1 were repeated three times.

---

[1] The characteristics of the highly sensitive skin-resistance meter used in the laboratory as well as reports of previous research utilizing this device are described in other publications (Burch & Greiner, 1958; Silverman, Cohen, & Shmavonian, 1959).

Table 7–7. *Experimental design.*

| Period | Verbal stimuli |
|---|---|
| | |

1 (Tones)[a]
   $S_1$—20 sec.—$S_2$—20 sec.—$S_3$—20 sec.—$S_4$—20 sec.
2 (Phrases)[bc]
   $NC_1$—20 sec.—$NC_2$
3 (Tones and phrases)
   $S_1NC_1$—20 sec.—$S_2Cy_1$—20 sec.—$S_3NC_2$—20 sec.—$S_4Co_1$
   $S_1NC_1$—20 sec.—$S_2Cy_2$—20 sec.—$S_3NC_2$—20 sec.—$S_4Co_2$
   $S_1NC_1$—20 sec.—$S_2Cy_3$—20 sec.—$S_3NC_2$—20 sec.—$S_4Co_3$
   $S_1NC_1$—20 sec.—$S_2Cy_4$—20 sec.—$S_3NC_2$—20 sec.—$S_4Co_4$
   Order reversed
   $S_3NC_2$—20 sec.—$S_4Co_5$—20 sec.—$S_1NC_1$—20 sec.—$S_2Cy_5$
   $S_3NC_2$—20 sec.—$S_4Co_6$—20 sec.—$S_1NC_1$—20 sec.—$S_2Cy_6$
   $S_3NC_2$—20 sec.—$S_4Co_7$—20 sec.—$S_1NC_1$—20 sec.—$S_2Cy_7$
   $S_3NC_2$—20 sec.—$S_4Co_8$—20 sec.—$S_1NC_1$—20 sec.—$S_2Cy_8$
4[d]
   $S_1$—20 sec.—$S_2$—20 sec.—$S_3$—20 sec.—$S_4$
5
   $NC_1$—20 sec.—$NC_2$—20 sec.—$NC_2$—20 sec.—$NC_1$
Postexperimental interview—aimed at ability to perceive and recall portions of experiment and associations to phrases for affect-evaluation.

[a] Entire sequence—$S_1$–$S_4$—repeated five times; $S_1 = 1,000$ cps; $S_2 = 250$ cps; $S_3 = 500$ cps; $S_4 = 2,000$ cps.
[b] Phrases repeated three times, then *reversed* and repeated three times.
[c] Explanation of verbal stimuli abbreviations:

| | |
|---|---|
| $NC_1 =$ "Books on the table" | $Cy_8 =$ "Study more and play less" |
| $NC_2 =$ "Clouds in the sky" | $Co_1 =$ "Too old and careless" |
| $Cy_1 =$ "Too young to know anything" | $Co_2 =$ "Too old for sex" |
| $Cy_2 =$ "Too young for sex" | $Co_3 =$ "An old failing body" |
| $Cy_3 =$ "You might flunk out" | $Co_4 =$ "Old and not wanted" |
| $Cy_4 =$ "Not really an adult" | $Co_5 =$ "Mind is getting weaker" |
| $Cy_5 =$ "Too smart for your own good" | $Co_6 =$ "No more respect" |
| $Cy_6 =$ "Respect your elders" | $Co_7 =$ "Old and afraid" |
| $Cy_7 =$ "Young and cocky" | $Co_8 =$ "No pleasures left" |

[d] Entire sequence repeated three times.

Period 5: The two bland phrases were presented twice without tones. (The tones were presented in Period 4 and the noncharged expressions in Period 5 to determine if any autonomic conditioning had occurred.)

Postexperimental Interview: After an introductory statement intended to reassure the subject and encourage him to verbalize any thoughts, ideas, or feelings that he might have had during the experiment, the interviewer asked the subject to describe the experiment in detail (Spontaneous Account 1). No attempts were made to explore the subject's associations at this point. Following this, the subject's memory of the experimental situation was further evaluated on the basis of responses to specific questions about the sequence of the experiment and the specific stimuli used. The interview was structured in such a way that the subject was given an opportunity to report spontaneously whatever he recalled about the experiment. When the subject indicated that he was unwilling or unable to go on, progressively more informative cues were offered in a systematic way. If the subject could not identify a portion of the experiment, it was described, and the investigator tried to determine whether the subject recognized it. Following this part of the interview, the subject was asked to list all the experimental expressions he could recall. The interviewer then handed the subject 48 index cards, each containing an expression typed on it. The 18 expressions actually used in the experiment were included among others with a similar or strikingly different meaning. The subject was then shown the 18 expressions actually used in the experiment. He was asked if he recognized them and to give his associations to the expressions.

The subject was then asked to express his ideas, feelings, and attitudes toward the stimuli and the experimenters, and his responses and associations were explored in detail. At the end, the subject was again asked to describe the whole experiment (Spontaneous Account 2). The interview was structured to evaluate the degree of "memory" for the events of the preceding experimental period. (The "degree of memory" refers to variation in the level of memory ranging from spontaneous recall to recall after presentation of progressively more informative hints and questions, to recognition of the test stimuli only after presentation on printed cards.) The personal meanings of the test situation and the individual test stimuli, as well as the subject's affective response to them, were also evaluated.

This postexperimental interview was recorded, and its content was analyzed. The associations elicited in the associative anamnestic portion of the interview were analyzed together with the specific associations to each phrase that were requested near the end of the interview procedure.

## Results

### Measures of Central Nervous System Activity

The utilization of changes in skin resistance as a source of information on the rate of CNS conduction, the intensity of peripheral sympathetic discharge in response to specific stimuli, and the level of CNS arousal or activation over time has been described in previous publications (Burch & Greiner, 1958; Shmavonian, Silverman, & Cohen, 1958; Silverman et al., 1959).

The findings relevant to CNS activity will not be reported in detail, as they have been described elsewhere by Silverman et al. (1959) and Shmavonian et al. (1958). However, the findings are briefly summarized in this section.

There was no difference in the number of stimuli perceived by the young and old subjects; i.e., the young and old subjects showed no difference in the total number of "specific" GSR given in response to the 84 auditory stimuli presented during the whole experiment. The neural conduction rates of the young and old subjects (latency time from stimulus to GSR) also revealed no significant differences. The total number of "nonspecific" GSR fluctuations was almost twice as much for the young subjects as compared to the old subjects; this result was interpreted as reflecting a significantly higher overall level of "arousal" in the young subjects.

The total number of specific responses to the auditory stimuli presented during the experimental session was considered to be a reflection of the number of responses that were received and perceived. The occurrence of a GSR change was considered to be evidence that the stimulus had actually been perceived, although the absence of a GSR change is not evidence that the subject has not perceived a stimulus (e.g., if the stimulus has no noxious, startling, or alerting value, and the subject has become "adapted"). Treating the data in this way may have decreased the number of stimuli tabulated as having been received and perceived, but it allows one to make more definitive statements about the mechanisms involved in the failure to recall or recognize the stimulus.

The stimulus that caused specific GSR of the greatest amplitude and the highest number of poststimulus nonspecific GSR fluctuations was the charged phrases, which were related to each individual group. Not only did the older subjects respond more to the "charged old" phrases than to the other phrases and tone stimuli, but in spite of the fact that their overall responsiveness (amplitude of specific responses and number of nonspecific responses) was significantly less than that of the younger subjects, they responded more in absolute terms to the "charged old" statements. Hence, on presentation of an appropriate stimulus, the apparently lowered CNS responsiveness disappeared.

### Cognitive and Perceptual Functions

*Recognition Score.* The number of cards with expressions typed on them that were accurately identified during the interview as having been presented during the experiment was used as a criterion of recognition. The aged subjects recognized fewer cards correctly and "recognized" more incorrect cards than the younger subjects. There was a significant rank-order correlation ($r_s = .38$, $p < .05$) between the number of items correctly recognized and the overall level of CNS arousal during the experiment (Table 7–8).

The correlations of high CNS arousal as assessed by GSR and the ability to recognize the expressions after the experiment were determined for each age group and showed the same trend as when the total subject population was considered; i.e., in general young subjects had higher levels of CNS arousal and higher recognition scores, and the old subjects who had high levels of CNS activity had better recognition scores than old subjects with low levels of CNS arousal. The $r_s$ for arousal and recognition for the old subjects was .45 and that for the young was .35. The number of subjects in each group was too small for the significance of correlation to reach the .05 level.

Table 7–8. *Age, GSR arousal, and recognition of phrases.*

| Subjects (rank-ordered from lowest to highest GSR arousal) | Aged group | | Young group | |
|---|---|---|---|---|
| | Number of correct-cards identified | Number of incorrect cards identified | Number of correct-cards identified | Number of incorrect cards identified |
| 1 | 6 | 0 | 10 | 0 |
| 2 | 7 | 0 | 11 | 1 |
| 3 | 8 | 1 | 12 | 0 |
| 4 | 10 | 0 | 14 | 2 |
| 5 | 11 | 0 | 14 | 0 |
| 6 | 11 | 1 | 15 | 0 |
| 7 | 11 | 6 | 16 | 0 |
| 8 | 13 | 4 | 16 | 0 |
| 9 | 15 | 5 | 16 | 0 |
| 10 | — | — | 16 | 0 |
| | $r_s = .45$, ns at .05 level.[a] | | $r_s = .35$, ns at .05 level.[a] | |

[a] Correlation of total number of subjects (19) and GSR arousal: $r_s = .38$, $p = .05$.

*Recall and recognition of expressions causing high and low arousal.* As was mentioned previously, a higher overall level of arousal during the experimental period was associated with a higher score for recognition of cards presented at the end of the experiment.

The level of accuracy or recognition of the two subject groups was also examined in terms of how well each group recognized those specific charged expressions that were associated with the highest and lowest levels of arousal in each individual.[2] Table 7–9 demonstrates these findings.

[2] The expressions considered to be associated with high and low levels of arousal were identified on the basis of the total number of nonspecific GSR during a 10-second period before and after the presentation of the expression.

The four expressions that were related to the largest number of nonspecific GSR after their presentation were grouped as highest-arousal expressions for a particular subject, and the four expressions that were related to the smallest number of nonspecific GSR after their presentation were grouped as lowest-arousal expressions

The four words that caused the highest level of arousal in the old group were recognized by the greatest number of individuals in that group. The four words associated with the least arousal when the group was considered as a whole were recognized by the lowest number of individuals in the old group. The level of arousal for each of the expressions was determined in terms of the total number of nonspecific fluctuations occurring before and after the presentation of the word, as well as the change from before the presentation to afterward. A chi-square test of the significance of difference of recognition of four words causing highest and lowest level of arousal was significant at the .05 level.

Table 7–9. *Recognition and spontaneous recall of expressions causing highest and lowest CNS arousal.*

| | Number of spontaneous recalls during interview and spontaneous account | Number of spontaneous recalls when asked to list | Number of recognitions |
|---|---|---|---|
| Old subjects | | | |
| Expressions causing highest arousal (4.5–5) | 20 ($p < .001$) | 24 ($p < .001$) | 25 ($p < .001$) |
| Expressions causing lowest arousal (3–1) | 1 | 4 | 15 |
| Young subjects | | | |
| Expressions causing highest arousal (5.2–9) | 16 ($p < .05$) | 17 ($p < .05$) | 28 ($p =$ ns) |
| Expressions causing lowest arousal (5.7–4) | 7 | 7 | 29 |

Comparison of the young group's recognition of the four expressions causing the highest level of arousal with that of the four causing the lowest level of arousal yields an interesting finding: The total number of recognition responses shows no significant difference for the high- and low-arousal for a particular subject. The expressions varied from subject to subject, but what we are concerned with is an examination of the ability to recognize expressions causing high and low arousal and not the ability to recognize expressions with specific content.

A group score for both the young and the old groups was based on the number of recognitions made by each group of the four highest- and the four lowest-arousal expressions. These are listed in Table 7–9 in the third column (number of recognitions). A score of 25 means that there were 25 recognitions by the aged group out of a possible 40. That is, there were 10 subjects who could have recognized all four high-arousal expressions (the score for the aged group would then be $10 \times 4$).

The figures charted parenthetically under the words "highest arousal" and "lowest arousal" represent the mean of the pre- and poststimulus level for nonspecific responses of the aged and young groups for the lowest- and highest-arousal expressions.

expressions. This somewhat paradoxical result is the consequence mainly of the fact that 9 young subjects failed to recognize the expression associated with the highest level of arousal (this was not necessarily the same expression for each subject). Furthermore, none of the 10 subjects spontaneously recalled the expression causing the highest arousal level.

The young and old groups showed no significant differences in their recognition scores for words associated with high arousal. However, the recognition score of the young group for words associated with low arousal was significantly greater than the recognition score of the old group for low-arousal words; the difference was significant at $p < .01$ chi-square test.

The other columns of Table 7–9 show the number of subjects in each group who spontaneously recalled the highest and lowest arousal expressions when they were specifically asked to list all the expressions they could remember (second column).

The older subjects had a recall and recognition score for the "highest-arousal" words higher than for the "lowest-arousal" words (difference was significant at $p < .001$ level using the chi-square test). The young subjects also had a higher recall for the high-arousal expressions than for the low-arousal ones ($p < .05$ using the chi-square test) but showed no difference in recognition score for the two types of expressions. The recall score was slightly less for the young group than for the aged group for the high-arousal words (difference not significant), in spite of the fact that the young subjects had showed superior recall and recognition when evaluated on the basis of their recall and recognition of all of the phrases.

These results suggest that higher levels of CNS activity were, in general, associated with more efficient cognitive functioning. However, the young subjects demonstrated difficulties in recalling and recognizing some specific phrases that had led to the most intense response physiologically.

### Psychodynamic Content Analysis of Interview

The interview was also evaluated as to (a) the specific psychological meaning to the subject of the experimental stimuli (the phrases); (b) the subject's concept of the purpose of the experiment; (c) the subject's concept of, and reaction to, the experimenter's expectations; (d) the major source of affect during the experiment; (e) the subject's method of handling, and reaction to, the stimuli and the situation; and (f) the subject's concept of the criteria used to evaluate his responses.

Table 7–10 summarizes the results of the content analysis of the postexperimental interviews. The information could be charted since there was no overlap in the data from the two groups. No subject of one group gave a response also given by a member of the other group.

Table 7-10. *Psychological implications of experiment to young and old subjects.*

| | Old subjects (N = 10) | Young subjects (N = 10) |
|---|---|---|
| Significance of experimental stimuli | Discriminated "young" and "old" phrases but believed all phrases were either descriptive or applicable to themselves | Divided phrases into two types: a "young" type was directed at them, and the other type was directed at older people; particularly concerned with phrases that appeared to be applicable to their own personal psychological characteristics |
| Concept of purpose of experiment | Test of what they know and how well they can think; a test of "sanity" | Test of emotional reactions in order to "uncover" facts about their personality; similar to (1) brain washing, or (2) a lie detector, or (3) a "third degree" |
| Concept of and reaction to experimenter's expectation | Experimenters wanted the subjects to actively perform some task in response to stimuli and subjects were concerned about inadequacy of their response | Experimenters wanted subjects to be passive in order to influence them, control them, or uncover something personal about them; subjects were concerned about responding or revealing too much |
| Major sources of affect during experiment | Uncertainty over what they were supposed to do; feelings of inadequacy for having performed poorly; fear of some painful or harmful action by experimenters | Uncertainty over what the experimenters were trying to find out; anxious over being watched and observed; fearful about what would be discovered about their personalities |
| Method of handling the experimental situation | Attempted to determine the logical intellectual meaning of the experiment; attempted to "perform" to stimuli | Tried to determine the emotional significance of stimuli; used defensive inattention and sleep to avoid revealing themselves |
| Concept of criteria used to evaluate subject's responses | Expected to be evaluated as "right" or "wrong" in terms of performance | Expected to be evaluated as "good" or "bad" in terms of their personalities |

The aged subjects expressed a need to perform well, believed that the experiment evaluated their mental adequacy, and thought that the investigators wanted them to perform some task that they were expected to identify. Much of the confusion described by this group was based on the fact that they were unable to determine the putative task.

The young subjects, on the other hand, had the impression that the experimenters' intent was to encourage them to relax as much as possible and to make them passive, since this would facilitate opportunities to observe, investigate, and control them. Furthermore, they felt that in a relaxed, passive state they would be unable to defend themselves. The younger subjects, in general, appeared more defensive about relating their feelings during the experiment and those that they experienced during the interview. However, in contrast to the aged subjects, they seemed less concerned about how well they "performed," i.e., whether they could recall the stimuli.

The affect of the older subjects was more obvious during the interview; at least, it was more readily verbalized. The younger subjects apparently tried to meet their "peer" group standards in regard to how young males should react in experimental situations; that is, they behaved as though the felt one should not become emotionally aroused or "thrown" by the situation.

There were certain events and situations preceding the experiment that may have been extremely important as determinants of the psychological meaning that the experiment had for both the young and the old subjects.

That the young subjects had been tested with a clinical-psychological battery in the room in which the experiment was conducted several weeks earlier may have influenced their strong preoccupation with being observed and watched through the two-way mirror. In the previous testing situation the light was on in the other room, and they were aware of the two-way mirror. Moreover, the fact that the young subjects had been examined with a clinical battery that they undoubtedly realized was aimed at some type of personality assessment may have led them to feel that the experiment was an extension of testing concerned with evaluating their emotional responses and uncovering various aspects of their personality.

None of the older subjects had been seen by the authors prior to the experiment. However, they had been given an extensive medical, psychological, and psychiatric work-up in their previous visits to the hospital, and they referred to their previous visits as consisting of mental and physical examinations of "how well they were functioning." Hence, the attitudes and expectations of these subjects regarding the present experiment could be, in part, accounted for on the basis of their previous experience.

Of course, general psychodynamic factors related to the problems of aged and of young persons may reasonably account for the difference in the responses of the two groups. However, the consistency with which the two groups differed suggests that more specific determinants were present as well. . . .

Theoretical Considerations

The results reported in this and previous papers (Shmavonian et al., 1958; Silverman et al., 1959) suggest that the aged subjects spontaneously recalled, reported, and recognized those expressions to which they had the largest GSR. Furthermore, their associations to these expressions were invariably personal. Tentatively, it appears that if a verbal stimulus is arousing and can be personalized, then in a sense it can effect an integration of sensory and perceptual data so that such data are registered and available for recall. The wish to retain, recall, and report was conceived to be "the task" by the aged subjects, and it appeared that their major concern was to perform this task well. As long as the aged subject was able to relate the stimulus to himself in a meaningful way, the stimulus seemed to become "a personal experience" that was registered, retained, and reported.

Kral suggests that one type of memory dysfunction that may be related to advancing age is characterized by the subject's inability to recall names or data on certain occasions. Evidently dysfunction of this type does not selectively affect names or data of the recent or remote past. He feels that this type of memory dysfunction involves only certain components of former experiences but not "personal experiences," that is, memories of the person as an individual or integrated whole. Hence, memories that are personally applicable or those that can be related to the self might not be subjected to this kind of memory dysfunction. Our data seemed to support part of this concept in that those stimuli and events that became personal experiences were remembered best by the elderly individuals.

The young subjects responded in a variety of ways to the expressions that were physiologically most arousing and that appeared to be psychologically most meaningful to them.

The disturbance in the recall and recognition of those phrases that had caused the most intense CNS arousal in the young subjects appeared to be in part related to the "set" created by the younger subjects' expectations about the experiment. (They felt the experiment was an attempt to evaluate their inner thoughts and feelings and expressed some concern over revealing "bad things" about themselves.)

Most of the young subjects' "cognitive" responses—e.g., (a) not recalling or recognizing it, (b) recognition without spontaneous recall and no associations to the expressions, (c) recognition and recall with impersonal associations, and (d) recognition, recall, and personal associations to an expression that was related but not identical to the phrase eliciting the most arousal—tended to reduce the personal significance of these arousing and meaningful expressions.

The experimental findings can be speculatively viewed as analogues of various clinical phenomena. Furthermore, the findings may support some of the speculations of Linn and others regarding the neurophysiological mechanisms associated with various psychological defenses.

Linn (1953) calls attention to the point that all sensory stimuli are not equally capable of arousing or activating the organism and that the meaning of the stimulus is ultimately a matter of great importance. He describes the process of perception as taking place in the form of feedback in the following manner. An experience, which is a complex of sensory impulses, is perceived as it enters upper CNS structures. Collateral fibers from the sensory tracts carry impulses into the reticular activating system, leading to cortical arousal. The aroused cortex scans the incoming impulses for meanings, and corticifugal impulses are fired back to the reticular structures. The nature of the corticifugal influence depends on the meaning of the percept.

Linn further speculates that if a source of anxiety involves only some circumscribed aspect of the entire environment, the corticifugal impulses might result in deactivation at a thalamic level (at which circumscribed deactivation could take place). The result would be an alteration in awareness or attentiveness that would be limited to specifically traumatic perceptions. Circumscribed "deactivation" could conceivably express itself on a psychological level as denial, repression, and isolation.

One could draw the following analogies between the experimental findings and Linn's ideas:

1. The failure spontaneously to recall, recognize, or associate to expressions that caused the greatest degree of arousal as measured by GSR changes and/or that appeared related to major psychological problem areas is analogous to "repression."

2. The failure to recognize a statement after it has been presented and used during the interview by the subject (although not identified as an experimental expression) is analogous to "denial."

3. The failure to report a statement, even though there is evidence that when later recognized it is spontaneously recalled, is analogous to "suppression."

4. The failure to present any meaningful personalized associations to, or to demonstrate any affect concerning, an expression causing high levels of arousal that is recognized and recalled and for which there is evidence that it is meaningful to the subject is analogous to "isolation."

Responses of the young group of subjects that could be placed in the above categories were those made to the expression causing the highest level of emotional arousal and CNS activation as determined by GSR measures. The findings reported in this paper can only be considered as lending some support to the hypothesis proposed by Linn. Intensive investigations are certainly necessary that have as their primary focus the clarification of the relationship of CNS activation produced by emotionally arousing stimuli and the psychological defense mechanisms that the individual uses to handle the stimulus.

The experimental findings suggested that verbal symbolic expressions meaningful to subjects can cause marked changes in the CNS arousal as measured by an instrument reflecting peripheral autonomic nervous system activity. Hence, the potential physiological effects of psychological events are highlighted. The events provoking the autonomic discharge were in some cases consciously recognized, in others not. This, of course, supports the frequently reported thesis that "unconscious" ideas and affects may be significant determinants of physiological changes.

The findings presented in this paper do not allow any definitive formulations. The major implications of the results are concerned with the selective influence on physiological responses of verbal statements that have specific psychological implications.

It is conceivable then that an experiment such as this can aid in helping to identify the manner in which various individuals will respond to experimental or life situations in which specific stimuli are imposed upon the subject or patient (particularly if the response is based upon his ability to discriminate cues). An individual must be studied, then, not only from the standpoint of certain general psychological and physiological responses to a stimulus or situation, but specific psychodynamic factors should be assessed as well, since they may affect, by their physiological and psychological effects, the quality and accuracy of his perceptive and cognitive functions and the nature of his CNS responses.

## Summary

A matched group of 10 young and 10 old subjects were presented pure tones, neutral phrases, and phrases designed to be "charged" for the young and for the old subjects while continuous GSR recordings were obtained as a measure of CNS activity. The subjects were then interviewed by a technique structured to evaluate the degree of "memory" for the preceding experimental period, as well as the meaning of and the affective response to the test situation and stimuli.

Arousing expressions appeared to facilitate the older subjects' memories by allowing them to form highly personalized associations. The expressions causing the highest level of arousal in the young subjects were associated with a high degree of "forgetting," which appeared to be analogous to various psychological defenses such as repression and denial, in spite of the fact that the young subjects' overall recognition was superior to that of the older subjects.

The data suggested that the "cognitive" results were influenced by the old subjects' perception of the experiment as a test of their intellectual capabilities and the young subjects' perception of the experiment as an attempt to uncover information about their feelings, impulses, and values.

The results indicated that studies assessing perceptual and cognitive functions should take into consideration the influence of: (a) reception and conduction of specific sensory inputs, (b) the level of nonspecific CNS activation, and (c) the psychological adaptive mechanisms activated by the psychodynamic implications of the experimental stimuli and the emotional arousal produced.

## References

Barnes, R. H., Busse, E. W., and Friedman, E. L. The psychological functioning of aged individuals with normal and abnormal electroencephalograms: II. A study of hospitalized individuals. *Journal of Nervous and Mental Disease*, 124:585, 1956.

Birren, J. E. Age changes in speed of simple responses and perception: Their significance for complex behavior. In *Old age in the modern world*. London: Williams and Wilkins, 1955.

Bortz, E. L. Growth and aging. *American Journal of Psychiatry*, 114:414, 1957.

Botwinick, J., Brinley, J. F., and Robbin, J. S. The interaction effects of perceptual difficulty and stimulus exposure time on age differences in speed and accuracy of response. *Gerontologia*, 2:1, 1958. (a)

Botwinick, J., Brinley, J. F., and Robbin, J. S. The effect of motivation by electrical shocks on reaction time in relation to age. *American Journal of Psychology*, 71:408, 1958. (b)

Bromley, D. B. Some effects of age on the quality of intellectual output. *Journal of Gerontology*, 12:315, 1957.

Burch, N. R., and Greiner, T. Drugs and human fatigue: GSR parameters. *Journal of Psychology*, 45:3, 1958.

Busse, E. W., Barnes, R. H., and Silverman, A. J. Studies in the processes of aging. *Diseases of the Nervous System*, 15:1, 1954.

Busse, E. W., Barnes, R. H., Friedman, E. L., and Kelty, E. J. Psychological functioning of aged individuals with normal and abnormal electroencephalograms. *Journal of Nervous and Mental Disease*, 124:135, 1956.

Dennis, W. *Age and behavior*. Randolph Field, Texas; USAF School of Aviation Medicine, 1953.

Fraser, D. C. Decay of immediate memory. *Nature*, 182–1163, 1950.

Freeman, H., Pincus, G., Elmadjian, F., and Romanoff, L. Adrenal responsivity in aged psychotic patients. *Geriatrics*, 10:72, 1955.

Inglis, I. J. An experimental study of learning and "memory" functions in elderly psychiatric patients. *Journal of Mental Science*, 103:796, 1957.

Korchin, S. J., and Basowitz, H. The judgment of ambiguous stimuli as an index of cognitive functioning in aging. *Journal of Personality*, 25:81, 1956.

Kral, V. A. Senescent memory decline and senile amnestic syndrome. *American Journal of Psychiatry*, 115:36, 1958.

Kirschner, W. Age differences in short term retention of rapidly changing information. *Journal of Experimental Psychology*, 55:352, 1958.

Linn, L. Psychological implications of the "activating" system. *American Journal of Psychiatry*, 110:61, 1953.

Nelson, R., and Gellhorn, E. The action of autonomic drugs on normal persons and neuropsychiatric patients. *Psychosomatic Medicine*, 19:486, 1957.

Nelson, R., and Gellhorn, E. The influence of age and functional neuropsychiatric disorders on sympathetic and parasympathetic functions. *Journal of Psychosomatic Research,* 3:12, 1958.

Shmavonian, B., Silverman, A. J., and Cohen, S. I. Assessment of central nervous system arousal in the elderly. *Journal of Gerontology,* 13:443, 1958.

Silverman, A. J., Busse, E. W., Barnes, R. H., Frost, L. L., and Thaler, M. B. Studies on the processes of aging: IV. Physiologic influences on psychic functioning in elderly people. *Geriatrics,* 8:7, 1957.

Silverman, A. J., Cohen, S. I., and Shmavonian, B. Investigation of psycho-physiologic relationships with skin resistance measures. *Journal of Psychosomatic Research,* 4:65, 1959.

Silverman, A. J., Cohen, S. I., and Shmavonian, B. Psychophysiological response specificity in the elderly. *Journal of Gerontology,* 12:443, 1958.

Wilcox, H. H. Changes in nervous system with age. *Public Health Reports,* 71:1179, 1956.

# Chapter 8. Marriage, Family, and Sexual Behavior

The reports in this chapter challenge some of the most common beliefs about marital and family relations in normal aging. The first report shows that equal ages between spouses and mentally superior wives were characteristic of *less* happy marriages among the aged. As might be expected, the less happy marriages also had more psychoneurotic symptoms and less frequent sexual relations. The second report shows that although most of the panelists lived in separate households from their children, most still maintained close ties with their children based on mutual affection and some dependence. This finding is contrary to the common belief that the aged in our modern society tend to experience isolation and neglect by their children. The last three reports show that the majority of married panelists continue to be sexually active until over age 75, even though there is a gradual decline in sexual activity and interest with advancing age. Also, 13 to 15 percent show a pattern of *increasing* sexual activity and interest. Such activity is contrary to the common belief that aged persons usually have no sexual activity or interest. Careful comparisons of the reports of husbands with those of their wives show a high degree of agreement, which supports the reliability and accuracy of these reports.

## Two Thousand Years of Married Life    *Ewald W. Busse and Carl Eisdorfer*

This paper is a survey of relations between the state of happiness in marriages of elderly persons and psychological, psychiatric, and other variables. It is based on information derived from a study of 30 married couples who are a part of an intensive, longitudinal, interdisciplinary investigation of 265 elderly so-called normal subjects. The individuals included in this survey have experienced a total of approximately 2,172 years of marriage. Their average age is 69.4 years.

To evaluate success or the degree of satisfaction in a marriage is an extremely complex undertaking (Eisenstein, 1956). Marital adjustment can be considered from a variety of viewpoints. Obviously, there are marriages which are considered by observers to be successful as these marriages meet or exceed social standards. Other marriages are seen as objectionable by society but may be quite satisfactory as interpreted by the marriage partners. This report approaches marital adjustment on the basis of evaluation of the relationship by the partners. The subjects were asked to rate the status of their marriage on a five-point scale ranging from very happy to very unhappy. When the partners gave different responses, the lowest rating determined the placement of the couple. This permitted us to separate out two groups of 15 couples—the more happy and the less happy. The split into groups of equal size was a chance phenomenon. None of these couples were very unhappy and cannot be considered marriages that verged on dissolution—rather both groups are surviving as couples and have survived many years. Hence by most social criteria these are "successful marriages." This study should not be confused with observations made on couples seeking marital counseling or moving toward separation or divorce.

In exploring the relationship between marital adjustment and other parameters, it is evident that we must pay attention to what factors are involved in a marriage. Obviously, it is a close interpersonal relationship in which compatibility is essential. Compatibility can exist on a healthy or a neurotic basis, and it is rare that marital partners have a thorough conscious understanding of the process. It is assumed that compatibility includes easy communication, i.e., the two partners convey to one another in some manner their needs, their feelings, and their interpretation of events. Certainly, it would appear that the partners must have a similar interpretation of reality if they are to function smoothly together.

In recent years, because of the increased life expectancy of women, it has been suggested that women should marry younger men. This would reduce the number of years that a woman is likely to be a surviving widow, but it does not *necessarily* mean marital happiness. Recognizing that we are dealing with a limited sample which has been exposed to social and cultural influences which are altering, it appears that the couples where the man is older are happier. The average age difference between the husband and the wife in the happy group is 5.9 years; while in the less happy, the male is at most a month or so older than the wife.

The length of marriage should also be considered. Here, the median of years married places the less happy ahead by two and a half years. This is of doubtful significance, and no interpretations are justified. The number of previous marriages was essentially the same in the two groups.

In the entire series of 265 subjects, 149 have available sexual partners, and 54 percent are continuing to have sexual intercourse. The presence or absence of sexual intercourse is not significantly different in the two groups when they are compared with one another or with the large series previously mentioned. However, there is a difference in the frequency of sexual activity. The happy group has a higher frequency in that 28 percent of the happy females report sexual activities occurring more than once a week. None of the less happy females report intercourse more than every two to three weeks.

Psychiatric evaluation which includes a rating scheme of the presence and severity of functional and organic mental signs and symptoms reveals that 93 percent of the less happy women and 64 percent of the less happy men have some evidence of a psychic disturbance (Busse, Dovenmuehle, & Brown, 1960). In the happy group this compares to 67 percent in the females and 60 percent in the males. If the signs and symptoms are restricted to those of psychoneurotic origin, there is an even more striking difference. In the less happy group, 50 percent have neurotic features (57 percent of females and 43 percent of males). In the happy subjects, 16.7 percent are classified as psychoneurotic (20 percent of the females and 13 percent of the males). This difference in the incidence of psychoneurosis between the two groups is significant at beyond the .05 level ($x^2 = 5.8$). This greater difference suggests that organic mental decline is not as important as are psychoneurotic disturbances in this particular study dealing with marital relations.

A comparison of the sum of responses given to the Rorschach indicates that women show a tendency to respond more frequently than do men (mean sum of R for women is 18.6; mean sum of R for men is 13.7). The difference between men and women in the mean number of responses for the happily married is 3.3, while for the less happy married couples the mean difference in number of responses for each couple is 7.5. An analysis was done to determine the presence or absence of mental superiority of one sex over the other. The results of the analysis revealed that in the happily married group there is no difference between men and women; for the less happy group there appears to be a significant difference ($x^2$ is 8.04 significant at .01 level). This may be cautiously interpreted to indicate that the women in the less happy marriages tend to be more responsive than their husbands to the environment, i.e., they talk more, appear to be somewhat more capable of adapting to new and complex situations, while their spouses are less able to do so. In any event it appears that there is greater incompatibility in the less happy group than there is in the happily married group.

The examination of W percentage (percentage whole responses) in these groups indicates that there is a significant difference between the spouses in the less happy marriage. The males showed a heightened W percentage ($x^2 = 4.17$, $p < .05$). This appears to be at the expense of D

(Detail) and F+ percentage (Form accuracy) and follows the pattern reported by Klopfer (1946) for aged persons. This suggests that less happy males exhibit a need to organize a situation. This failure is seen in the F+ percentage of 70 as compared with the mean F+ for their spouses of 80 (*T* is significant at .05).

The male in the less happy marital situation also tends to overly restrict himself by conforming to the form dominant aspect of the blot (F percentage = 76), while his spouse tends to be more imaginative and shows a considerably lower F percentage (58). This difference in the happy couples is negligible.

## Summary

This study indicates that in this series of supposedly well-adjusted elderly couples:

1. Happy women have husbands older than themselves by an average of 5.9 years as compared to the less happy wives whose husbands are but slightly older.

2. Mental disturbances, particularly psychoneurotic signs and symptoms, are maximum in the less happy women (57 percent), high in the less happy men (43 percent), and significantly lower among the happy couples (women 20 percent, men 13 percent).

3. The presence or absence of the capacity to perform the sexual act does not appear to be different in the two groups. However, the happy couples have more frequent sexual relations, suggesting that good interpersonal relations increase the frequency of this type of expression. . . .

The less happily married couples are apt to include a wife who is mentally superior to her spouse. This difference was significant for both performance and Full Scale WAIS IQ scores. The relative mental superiority of the female over the male in the less happily married couples is further suggested by the Rorschach performance. In the less happily married couple, the wife shows a greater number of responses to the Rorschach and is more accurate and imaginative than her spouse.

## References

Busse, E. W., Dovenmuehle, R. H., and Brown, R. G. Psychoneurotic reactions of the aged. *Geriatrics*, 15:97–105, 1960.

Eisenstein, V. W. *Neurotic interaction in marriage.* New York: Basic Books, 1956.

Klopfer, W. B. Personality patterns of old age. *Rorschach Research Exchange*, 10:145–166, 1946.

# Family Structure and Social Isolation of Older Persons*
## Robert G. Brown

The past three-quarters of a century or more in the United States has been portrayed as a period of rapid social change in which there have been significant modifications in family social organization and structure. Changes in the American family are thought to have had especially important implications for older persons.

Among the modifications in family relations which have been reported in the literature are increased cultural diversity between older and younger generations, increased mobility of children, and reduced parent-child interdependence (Burgess, 1957; Drake, 1958; Parsons, 1949a, 1949b). Such changes have been seen as important factors in the emergence of the nuclear family group as predominant and in the lessening of the degree of family solidarity. These changes in the family are presumed, furthermore, to be occurring at a greater rate, or to have proceeded further, in urban than in rural areas.

It has been suggested that among the consequences of these modifications in family social organization and structure have been the isolation of older persons from their children and the development of feelings of neglect and loneliness (Parsons, 1949b, p. 230). Other authors, however, have suggested that, as a result of such changes, the older person is now drawn closer to his children by bonds of affection (Burgess, 1957, p. 171).

From this apparent disagreement in interpretation were derived the problems for investigation in this exploratory study: To what extent are older persons in an urban area physically and socially isolated from their children? Does isolation, where it exists, lead to feelings of neglect or loneliness? Or do such feelings tend to vary independently of isolation and to depend, rather, upon the relationship between older persons' expectations of their children and their children's actual behavior?

## Method

As part of a multidisciplinary research project on aging, 260 elderly persons, age 60 and over, were intensively interviewed about social factors in their life situations and about their attitudes toward a variety of life experiences. . . .

* Reprinted by permission from the *Journal of Gerontology*, 15:170–174, 1960.

For statistical analysis, 161 residents of the city of Durham, who had living children, were selected from the total study sample. These subjects had the following characteristics: 53 percent were male and 47 percent female; 59 percent were white and 41 percent Negro; about half were under and half over 70 years of age; 62 percent were married, 32 percent widowed, and 6 percent separated or divorced. They varied widely in social class, a point that will be elaborated below.

Findings

A majority of the elderly subjects were found to be maintaining a nuclear family pattern, as defined by living arrangements, at the time of the interviews. Our data, for example, showed that 60 percent of the older persons in the sample did not live with their children or other relatives. The predominance of such a separate dwelling pattern, also generally reported for older persons in present-day American society as a whole, usually is attributed, in part, to grown children's high degree of geographical mobility. Data in this study indicated that the children of our subjects apparently did not differ from the general pattern in this regard: A pattern of geographical mobility of their adult children was found to obtain for a majority of elderly parents. The extent of adult children's geographical mobility was measured by the percentage of an elderly subject's living children who resided in Durham at the time of the interview. Nearly two-thirds (64 percent) of the 157 subjects for whom there were complete data reported that one-half or more of their children did not live in Durham. Of these, 50 percent had none of their children living in Durham, and the other 50 percent had some, but no more than half, of them residing there. On the other hand, only 36 percent of the subjects stated that one-half or more of their children lived in Durham; of these, however, 58 percent had all of their children living there. In spite of this pattern of children's mobility, it is important to note that in 78 percent of the cases elderly parents and at least some of their children lived in the same community.

The distribution of subjects on an Albrecht "Role Activities" scale (Havighurst & Albrecht, 1953), "Role as Parent," served as an indicator of the nature of the subjects' relationships with their children. This scale, which was used as a rough measure of parent-child dependency, is constructed as follows:

0   Never visited by children. No interest in them; rejects them.
1   No interest in children; too old or too ill to care.
2   Knows little about children, where they are, etc. Seldom hears from them.

3   Sees children occasionally, or depends upon them.
4   Shares children's home; somewhat burdensome.
5   Shares home of children; a help rather than a burden.
6   Slight dependence on part of children; some responsibility for them.
7   Responsible for children full or part time (children dependent).
8   Independent; occasional advice to children or needs their advice. Child may live with parent.
9   Mutual independence, but close social and affectional relationship (Havighurst & Albrecht, 1953, p. 376).
In a parent-child relationship, for example, "some form of dependency" was defined as including: (a) the older person dependent on his child(ren); (b) child(ren) dependent on their parent(s); and (c) mutual dependence of parent(s) and child(ren). These constitute items 3–7 on the scale.

In 41 percent of the 156 cases for whom we had adequate data there existed some form of dependency in the relationships of children and aged parents. An additional 17 percent of the subjects and their children, though mutually independent, were reported to have close social and affectional relationships (Item 9 on the scale). Thus, 58 percent of the subjects had relationships with their children characterized either by some type of dependency, by affectional ties, or by both.

These data suggest that in spite of the existence of separate dwelling and geographical mobility patterns our older subjects lived in close proximity to at least some of their children. In addition, the relationships of most of these older persons with their offspring were characterized by some form of dependency, by close social and affectional relationships, or by both.

Furthermore, a majority of the subjects did not appear to live in social isolation from their children. Degree of social isolation, defined in terms of frequency of contact with children, was dichotomized into "sees children less than weekly" and "sees children weekly or oftener." Sixty-eight percent of the 145 elderly parents from whom complete data had been collected tended to maintain relatively frequent contacts (i.e., weekly or oftener) with their children. In addition, it would seem that this high frequency of parent-child interaction was closely related to a low prevalence of reported feelings of neglect.

In the course of the interviews our subjects were asked: "Do you think your family or close relatives neglect you?" Eighty-one percent of all subjects responded "Not at all" to this question, while 19 percent said they thought they had been neglected "completely" or "a little." This variable, which has been called "expressed feelings of neglect," represents a statement of a person's perception of the state of the relationship between members of his family and himself. Implicit in this notion is an underlying set of expectations which pertain to the maintenance of the relationships in some form so that (*a*) if the members of the subject's family conform to his expectations he will report no feelings of neglect, or (*b*) if they deviate from his expectations he will report feelings of neglect. An attempt has been made in this study to determine the nature of elderly parents' expectations, conformity to and deviation from which would explain the observed variation in expressed feelings of neglect.

A part of the variation in expressed feelings of neglect may be explained by the frequency of contact between parents and their children. Table 8–1 reveals that subjects who saw their children weekly or more

Table 8–1. *Relationship between expressed feelings of neglect and frequency of contact with children.*

| | Frequency of contact with children | |
|---|---|---|
| Expressed feelings of neglect | Percentage seeing children less than weekly (N = 47) | Percentage seeing children weekly or oftener (N = 98) |
| Neglect | 30 | 13 |
| No neglect | 70 | 87 |
| Total | 100 | 100 |

Note.—Sixteen subjects excluded because of insufficient data.
$x^2 = 5.05, p < .05$.

were significantly less likely to express feelings of neglect than those who saw them less than weekly. Furthermore, as shown in Table 8–2, subjects who did not live with their children were no more likely than those who lived with them (and therefore were assured of frequent contact) to

Table 8–2. *Relationship between expressed feelings of neglect and living arrangements.*

| Expressed feelings of neglect | Percentage not living with children but seeing them weekly or oftener (N = 51) | Percentage living with children (N = 47) |
|---|---|---|
| Neglect | 8 | 19 |
| No neglect | 92 | 81 |
| Total | 100 | 100 |

$x^2 = 1.823, p > .1$.

express feelings of neglect. At the same time, however, it should be noted (see Table 8–1) that whereas only 13 percent of the subjects who saw their children weekly or more expressed feelings of neglect, as many as 70 percent who saw their children less than weekly reported no feelings of neglect. This relationship suggests that, while infrequent parent-child interaction appeared to constitute a sufficient condition for reports of neglect, infrequent interaction was not a necessary condition.

Further investigation of these two variables revealed that expressed feelings of neglect were related to frequency of contact with children only among the upper-status subjects. The subjects' social status positions were obtained by use of Warner's Index of Status Characteristics (Warner, Meeker, & Eells, 1957). Arbitrarily, "upper-status" individuals were designated as those falling below the median on this continuous variable for the group studied here, and "lower-status" individuals as those falling above the median. In Table 8–3 it can be seen that upper-status subjects who had

Table 8–3. *Relationship between expressed feelings of neglect and frequency of contact with children.*

|  | Upper status | | Lower status | |
|---|---|---|---|---|
| Expressed feelings of neglect | Percentage seeing children less than weekly (N = 27) | Percentage seeing children weekly or oftener (N = 48) | Percentage seeing children less than weekly (N = 17) | Percentage seeing children weekly or oftener (N = 49) |
| Neglect | 30 | 6 | 29 | 20 |
| No neglect | 70 | 94 | 71 | 80 |
| Total | 100 | 100 | 100 | 100 |

Note.—Twenty subjects excluded because of insufficient data.
Upper status: $x^2 = 5.794$; $p < .02$.
Lower status: $x^2 = 0.183$; $p > .5$.

infrequent contacts with their children were more likely to express feelings of neglect than upper-status subjects who saw their children more frequently. On the other hand, lower-status subjects who had infrequent contacts with their children were not significantly more likely to express feelings of neglect than lower-status subjects who saw them more frequently. Thus, within the upper-status group of subjects it would appear that there existed an obligation for children to maintain frequent contacts with their parents; and failure to meet this obligation, in large part, accounted for the expression of feelings of neglect by these elderly parents.

Within the group of lower-status subjects in our sample variation in expressed feelings of neglect was found to be related to race. Table 8–4 reveals that lower-status Negroes were significantly more likely than lower-status whites to express feelings of neglect, while upper-status Negroes were no more likely than upper-status whites to report such feelings. However, race, in and of itself, is an ambiguous explanatory variable. In accordance with the reasoning above—i.e., expressions of feelings of neglect are produced when expectations for the maintenance of relationships within families are not met—it would appear that the observed dependence of expressed feelings of neglect upon race among our lower-status subjects could be explained in one of the following ways:

1. Negro-white differences in children's attitudes toward (or expectations of themselves in relation to) their parents: e.g., lower-status Negro children are less likely than lower-status white children to conform to parental expectations about the maintenance of a relationship between them.

2. Differences in societal contingencies faced by Negro and white children: e.g., lower-status Negro children are less able than lower-status white children to conform to parental expectations about the maintenance of a relationship between them.

Table 8–4. *Relationship between expressed feelings of neglect and race.*

|  | Upper status | | Lower status | |
|---|---|---|---|---|
| Expressed feelings of neglect | Percentage white (N = 58) | Percentage Negro (N = 20) | Percentage white (N = 34) | Percentage Negro (N = 45) |
| Neglect | 14 | 15 | 9 | 31 |
| No neglect | 86 | 85 | 91 | 69 |
| Total | 100 | 100 | 100 | 100 |

Note.—Four subjects excluded because of insufficient data.
Upper status: $x^2 = 0.057$, $p > .8$.
Lower status: $x^2 = 4.453$, $p < .05$.

3. Negro-white differences in family structure: e.g., lower-status white parents are less likely than lower-status Negro parents to have expectations about the maintenance of a relationship between their children and themselves.

Our data indicate that unmet expectations in the lower-status group apparently do not relate to frequency of contact with children. Beyond this, however, no data were collected in the present study which bear directly upon either the content of expectations or the congruence between expectations and actual behavior of lower-status Negroes and whites.

Conclusions

The findings of this exploratory study would seem to cast some doubt upon the degree of generality of certain of the present formulations about the older person and his children—i.e., that a high degree of geographical mobility of children, social isolation of older parents, and the changed structure of the family tend to produce feelings of neglect among the elderly. While the presence of social isolation was found to be related to the expression of feelings of neglect, it appeared that this was true only in one segment of our sample—the upper-status group. Thus it would appear that social isolation produces feelings of neglect only when there exists an expectation for close parent-child contact.

These factors lead to a tentative reformulation of the position of elderly persons in the kinship system. Although a separate dwelling pattern appears to predominate in urban areas for the most part, we are unable to conclude that intergenerational interdependence has been replaced by independence, isolation, and neglect for the majority of aged persons. Though physically separated to a certain extent, elderly parents and their children tend to maintain close ties based upon mutual affection and some measure of dependence. Finally, not only have some elderly persons not experienced these general changes attributed to the American family, but also the consequences of such changes, where present, have not been uniform for them. Here again, then, we find that the aged population is not a homogeneous one, a factor which has important implications for action programs and legislation.

It is important to note that evidence is accumulating to lend support to the point of view expressed here. A number of sociologists in recent years have described findings which have challenged the validity of certain of the prevalent stereotypes about older people and their family relationships (Friedman, 1959; Streib, 1958; Thompson, 1959; Townsend, 1957). While these research beginnings are noteworthy, it is suggested that family relations of older people, with special emphasis upon possible variable manifestations, are in need of further careful investigation.

References

Burgess, E. W. The older generation and the family. In Donahue, W., and Tibbitts, C. (Eds.), *The New frontiers of aging.* Ann Arbor, Mich.: University of Michigan Press, 1957.

Cavan, R. S., Burgess, E. W., Havighurst, R. J., and Goldhamer, H. *Personal adjustment in old age.* Chicago: Science Research Associates, 1949.

Drake, J. T. *The aged in American society.* New York: Ronald Press, 1958.

Friedman, E. Changing family status of the aged. Paper read at the American Sociological Society, Chicago, September, 1959.

Havighurst, R. J., and Albrecht, R. *Older people.* New York: Longmans, 1953.

Parsons, T. Age and sex in the social structure of the United States. In *Essays in sociological theory pure and applied.* Glencoe, Ill.: Free Press, 1949. (a)

Parsons, T. The kinship system of the contemporary United States. In *Essays in sociological theory pure and applied.* Glencoe, Ill.: Free Press, 1949. (b)

Streib, G. F. Family patterns in retirement. *Journal of Sociological Issues,* 14(2):46–60, 1958.

Thompson, W. E. Retirement and family relationships. Paper read at the American Sociological Society, Chicago, September, 1959.

Townsend, P. *The family life of old people.* London: Routledge and Kegan Paul, 1957.

Warner, W. L., Meeker, M., and Eels, K. *Social class in America.* Gloucester, Mass.: Peter Smith, 1957.

# Sexual Activities and Attitudes in Older Persons*   *Gustave Newman and Claude R. Nichols*

Recent emphasis in medical education has stressed the need for greater understanding of human behavior. This broadening scope of knowledge is of practical use to the physician in making possible more comprehensive care of his patients. With a rapidly growing geriatric population to attend, the physician of today needs more knowledge of what is ordinary or usual in the life of the older person. Little has been reported concerning the sexual activity and attitudes of older people. There have been many misconceptions, certainly, about the role of sex in the lives of older people in our society. One commonly recognized belief among younger people in our society is that older persons, especially grandparents, have no sexual feelings. As we now recognize, the feelings and attitudes of people are directly related to the expectations of the society in which they live. Thus, it is common for the physician to see in his daily practice older persons who feel guilty about having sexual feelings; often these feelings are not acceptable to the older person, to the physician, or to other people in the environment in which the older person is living. Guilt or anxiety over sexual feelings may interfere with the adjustment of the older person and with his interpersonal relations, among which is the doctor-patient relationship.

* Reprinted by permission from the *Journal of the American Medical Association,* 173:33–35, 1960.

Guilt or anxiety on the part of the patient may thwart the therapeutic efforts of the physician.

While recognizing that the attitudes of society are slow in changing, we believe that more knowledge of this area of human behavior would serve both the physician and his patient, as well as strengthening their relationship to each other. Kinsey and co-workers (Kinsey, Pomeroy, & Martin, 1948) devoted only two pages in their study of male sexuality to the specific area of sexual activity in the aging man. Similarly, a single table summarizes their data on the aging woman (Kinsey, Pomeroy, Martin, & Gebhard, 1953). Much more information is needed in this area in order to determine the role that sexual activity plays in the life of the older person. It is our purpose, then, to present some normative data on sexual activity and attitudes in a geriatric population.

## Materials and Methods

. . . The data on sexual activity and attitudes are but one part of the medical and psychiatric history in this study and, as such, have always been obtained by a psychiatrist member of the research team. . . . Subjects ranged from 60 to 93 years of age, with an average of 70 years. The study included both Caucasoid and Negroid men and women. A total of 250 subjects were included in this study.

## Results

One hundred and one subjects of the original 250 were either single, divorced, or widowed, the greatest proportion of these being widowed. Of these 101 subjects, only 7 reported any sexual activity; thus about 7 percent of this group were sexually active. The remaining 149 subjects were still married and living with their spouses, and of these, 81 or 54 percent indicated that they were still sexually active to some degree. Subjects with any degree of regularity and periodicity of sexual intercourse were included in the group called "active." Frequency of sexual relations for the persons in this group ranged from once every other month to three times weekly. Figure 8–1 indicates correlation of sexual activity with age. Statistical tests of significant differences (chi-square test) indicate that only the fourth group, consisting of those persons 75 years of age or older, showed a significantly lower level of sexual activity.

In Figure 8–2 the sample of married subjects is divided by race, sex, and socioeconomic status. Inspection of these data shows that in this

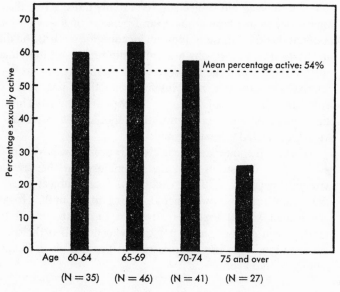

Figure 8–1. *Sexual activity related to advancing age in 149 married subjects.*

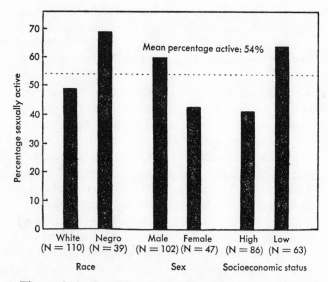

Figure 8–2. *Sexual activity related to race, sex, and socioeconomic status in 149 married subjects aged over 60 years.*

sample, the Negroid subjects were sexually more active than the Caucasoid, men more active than women, and persons of lower socioeconomic status more active than those of high socioeconomic status. The differences shown in these three bar graphs are valid differences by the chi-square test. We would like to point out, however, that there may be "cross-contamination," so that one variable may influence another; i.e., most of our Negroid subjects were also of lower socioeconomic status. Thus the graphs are descriptive of our total sample but should not be taken as independent variables related to sexual activity.

During the interview, each older person was asked to compare the subjectively felt strength of the sexual urge at the present time with its strength in youth. Without exception, every subject rated the strength of the sexual urge as lower in old age than in youth. However, those who rated their sexual urges as strongest in youth tended to rate them as moderate in old age; most persons who described their sexual feelings as weak to moderate in youth described themselves as being without sexual feelings in old age.

## Comment

The great difference between 7 percent of subjects sexually active in the group of single persons as compared to 54 percent of subjects sexually active in the married group confirms the great influence that marital status has on sexual activity, as pointed out by Finkle and co-workers (Finkle, Moyers, Tobenkin, & Karg, 1959). This difference is indicative of the gradual lessening of the sexual drive with increasing age; in the absence of a socially sanctioned or legally approved sexual partner, i.e., spouse, the sexual drive, although present, is not often strong enough to cause the elderly person to seek an extramarital sexual partner.

The abrupt lessening of sexual activity in the group of persons aged 75 years and older deserves comment. Many subjects in this segment of our sample had chronic illnesses such as arthritis, arteriosclerotic heart disease, and diabetes. Persons in this group also frequently reported such illness in their spouses. We have consistently found that chronic illness places limitations on all the activities of these persons, although there is an obvious variation in the degree of limitation which depends on the severity of the illness and the subject's attitude toward it. Thus it was not uncommon for a person of this age group to indicate the presence of sexual feelings in the absence of any sexual activity. These subjects usually stated that sexual activity was stopped because of poor health either of themselves or of their spouses.

The fact that the women in our sample reported less sexual activity than the men also deserves comment, since all persons in this group were still living with their spouses and therefore had adequate opportunity for sexual expression. The possibility exists that the women were somewhat more reluctant to give factual data about their sexual activity; however, we have generally felt that the data obtained in the face-to-face interviews have been reliable. We can point to one factor which may tend to explain this difference, which is that, while the average age of both men and women in this study was about 70 years, the men, by virtue of a trend to marry younger women, and conversely the women, marrying older men, were subjects who were individually reporting on sexual activity in marriages of significantly different age groups. For both males and females in our study, husbands were an average of four years older than wives. Another way of saying this is that our "average" male subject aged 70 had a 66-year-old wife, while our "average" female subject aged 70 had a 74-year-old husband.

## Conclusions

In a comprehensive, interdisciplinary study of geriatric subjects living in the Durham, North Carolina, community, data have been gathered and assessed regarding the sexual activity and attitudes of older people. Subjects averaged 70 years of age and ranged from 60 to 93 years. The study included both Caucasoid and Negroid men and women. Analysis of these data shows little correlation of sexual activity with age, but in this study, Negroid subjects were more active than Caucasoid, and men more active than women. The subjects also rated themselves on the relative strength of their sexual urge in youth and in old age, and a comparison of the two ratings shows a remarkable constancy of the experiencing of the sexual drive within individual persons throughout life. Although older people experienced a decline in sexual activity and strength of sexual drive, these data show that, given the conditions of reasonably good health and partners who are also physically healthy, elderly persons continue to be sexually active into their seventh, eighth, and ninth decades.

## References

Finkle, A. L. Moyers, T. G., Tobenkin, M. I., and Karg, S. J. Sexual potency in aging males, *Journal of the American Medical Association*, 170:1391–1393, 1959.

Kinsey, A. C., Pomeroy, W. B., and Martin, C. R.: *Sexual behavior in the human male.* Philadelphia: W. B. Saunders, 1948.

Kinsey, A. C., Pomeroy, W. B., Martin, C. R., and Gebhard, P. H. *Sexual behavior in the human female.* Philadelphia: W. B. Saunders, 1953.

# Sexual Behavior in Senescence*   *Adriaan Verwoerdt, Eric Pfeiffer, and Hsioh-Shan Wang*

. . . The first paper in this series (Verwoerdt, Pfeiffer, & Wang, 1969) reported on the frequency and the incidence of sexual intercourse and sexual interest. The approach followed was cross-sectional; that is, the subject groups were studied at three different points in time. Some of these data will be included in this report; in addition, data will be presented which are specifically longitudinal. The longitudinal approach focuses on changes in the course of time within the individual subject. The aim of this intrasubject method is to identify and study individual patterns of change in sexual behavior.

## Materials and Methods

. . . The number of subjects participating in the study declined over the course of the three studies. Data were collected on 254 subjects in Study I, 190 subjects in Study II, and 126 subjects in Study III. This decline was due principally to the death of some subjects and to serious illness in others. A smaller number of subjects dropped out after the first or the second study for a variety of personal reasons. In addition, not all of the subjects were always able to provide usable data in all areas of investigation. Thus one subject might give information on frequency of sexual intercourse but not on level of sexual interest, while the opposite might be true in another subject. Consequently, the number of responses available for analysis differs for each question, and it may be useful to note the number of responses (N) upon which each of the analyses is based.

The data on sexual behavior were gathered as part of each subject's medical history, and they were elicited during a structured interview. The interviewer was a psychiatrist who tried to obtain answers in the subject's own words but then scored the answers according to a prearranged system. The interview focused on the following areas of sexual behavior (the possible scores in each area are indicated in parentheses):

1. Enjoyment of intercourse in younger years (none, mild, very much)
2. Sexual feelings in younger years (none, weak, moderate, strong)
3. Enjoyment of intercourse at present time (none, mild, very much)

* Reprinted by permission from *Geriatrics*, 24:137–154, 1969.

4. Sexual feelings at present time (none, weak, moderate, strong)

5. Present frequency of intercourse (none, once per month, once every two weeks, once per week, more than once a week)

6. If intercourse has stopped, when stopped? (1 year ago or less, 2 to 5 years ago, 6 to 10 years ago, 11 to 20 years ago, 20 years ago or more).

7. Reason for stopping intercourse (death of spouse, illness of spouse, illness of self, loss of interest of spouse, loss of interest of self, loss of potency of spouse, loss of potency of self).

In order to gain information concerning individual patterns and changes in the course of time, the following approach was used: The subjects were classified in two groups according to the presence or absence of sexual activity at Study I; the former group was designated with a plus, the latter with a zero. A second classification was then made on the basis of the activity data in Study II. Compared with Study I, sexual activity in Study II could be either increased, decreased, or remain the same. Thus there were five possible patterns between Studies I and II as follows:

A: 0 → (not active in Study I; not active in Study II)
B: 0 ↑ (not active in Study I; active in Study II)
C: + → (active in Study I; equally active in Study II)
D: + ↓ (active in Study I; less active in Study II)
E: + ↑ (active in Study I; more active in Study II)

Likewise, the sexual interest data were studied by comparing intraindividual change between Studies I and II. The A to E patterns here have the same connotation as outlined for sexual activity.

For the purpose of simplification, patterns B and E were grouped together and called pattern R (rising activity). Thus we will be dealing with four patterns of change in a given subject: pattern A: continuously absent activity or interest; pattern C: sustained activity or interest; pattern D: decreasing activity or interest; pattern R: rising activity or interest.

## Findings

### Sexual Activity

*Degree of activity.* Frequency of intercourse was rated on a 5-point scale (0, no intercourse; 1, once a month or less; 2, once every two or three weeks; 3, once a week; 4, more than once a week).

There were 95 subjects who had data on the frequency of intercourse for all three studies. In this group, which included men and women (married and unmarried), there was a tendency toward a gradual decline

of sexual activity with advancing age. This tendency·reached statistical
significance only in the case of Study III ($p < .05$).

Figure 8–3 shows the linear regression curve representing the effect of
age on sexual activity (for Study III). The decline of activity in the group
was such that by the late eighties the frequency of intercourse approached
zero. Nevertheless, individual exceptions occurred. Among male subjects
surviving into the eighties and nineties, continued sexual activity was no
great rarity; about one-fifth of these men reported having sexual intercourse once a month or less.

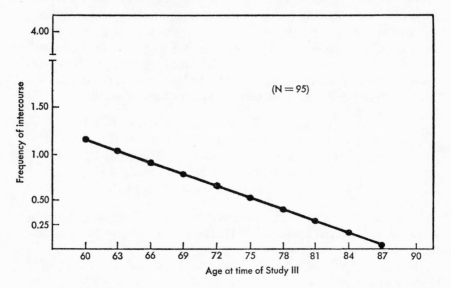

Figure 8–3. *Effect of age on sexual activity (Study III). Frequency scale:*
*0, no intercourse; 1, once a month or less; 2, once every two or three*
*weeks; 3, once a week; 4, more than once a week.*

Using the above scoring system, it was found that the mean sexual
activity scores for Studies I, II, and III, respectively, were 0.99, 0.71, and
0.52. In other words, at the time of Study I, the mean frequency of
intercourse was no more than once a month, and at the time of Study III
(about six years later), it had decreased by almost 50 percent.

*Incidence of sexual activity.* The subjects were grouped in two categories, depending on whether they had no sexual activity at all or some
activity, regardless of the degree. Thus the proportions of sexually active
subjects for various age groups could be determined, and this was done
separately for the three studies. In assessing the influence of age and other

factors, we decided to group the subjects by age intervals of three or six years. In comparing the data, it is useful to keep in mind that the mean age of the subjects at the time of Studies I, II, and III was 68.83, 73.04, and 76.01, respectively.

Figure 8–4 shows the proportions of sexually active subjects for Studies

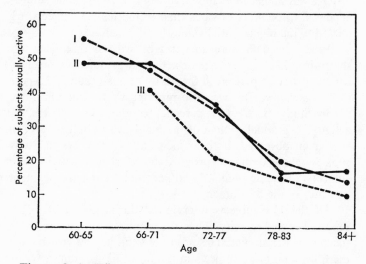

Figure 8–4. *Effect of age on incidence of sexual activity. Mean ages: Study I, 68.83 years; Study II, 73.04; Study III, 76.01.*

I, II, and III. In each study, N refers to all subjects who had data on activity for that particular study; in Studies I, II, and III, N was 215, 171, and 111, respectively. As can be seen, the incidence of sexual activity approached zero by the late eighties.

Table 8–5 shows the effects of age on the incidence of sexual activity

Table 8–5. *Effects of age and sex on the incidence of sexual activity.*

| Age group | Study I | | Study II | | Study III | |
|---|---|---|---|---|---|---|
| | M 116 Percent-age | F 99 Percent-age | M 86 Percent-age | F 85 Percent-age | M 67 Percent-age | F 64 Percent-age |
| 60–65 | 71 | 42 | 67 | 57 | none | none |
| 66–71 | 62 | 23 | 68 | 27 | 45 | 34 |
| 72–77 | 50 | 11 | 53 | 11 | 45 | 5 |
| 78+ | 21 | 7 | 39 | 0 | 29 | 5 |
| All ages | 53 | 20 | 56 | 18 | 39 | 13 |

for male and female subjects. In Study I, 38 percent of the 215 subjects were sexually active; of the 116 men, 62 (53 percent) reported sexual activity, while the incidence in the female group was 20 percent (20 of 99 subjects). With advancing age, there was a gradual decline in the proportion of sexually active subjects. For all age groups, the incidence of sexual activity was higher in men than in women. In the male subjects, the decline appeared to be more obvious than in the female subjects, which probably related to the higher initial values for the men.

When the data were analyzed by way of three-year age intervals, a sharp drop in the incidence of activity was noted for men in the mid-seventies—from 71 percent in the 72 to 74 age group to 20 percent in the 75 to 77 age range. This was also reported by Newman and Nichols (1960).

In Study II, 63 (37 percent) of the 171 subjects reported sexual activity. A gradual decline of the incidence of activity with increasing age was again observed, both in men and women. As in Study I, the male subjects showed higher proportions of sexual activity than the female subjects; of the 86 men, 48 (56 percent) were active, compared to 15 (18 percent) of the 85 women.

Of the 111 subjects interviewed during Study III, 29 (26 percent) reported sexual activity. Thus the incidence of activity was lower than in the two earlier studies. This group of subjects had grown older, so that now there were no more subjects in the 60 to 65 age range. Of the 57 men, 22 (39 percent) reported sexual activity compared with 7 (13 percent) of the 54 women. In comparison with Studies I and II, the age-related decline in the incidence of sexual activity among male subjects was not as clear.

Figure 8–5 shows the effect of marital status on the incidence of sexual activity for Studies I, II, and III (unmarried subjects include all those who were widowed, divorced, or single at the time of the study). The female group showed the most obvious differences; the sexual activity among unmarried women was almost negligible (4 to 5 percent). In contrast to this, the unmarried men reported a significant amount of sexual activity (35, 80, and 55 percent, respectively, in the three studies). In fact, in Studies II and III, the unmarried men had higher proportions than the married men. Of course, the number of unmarried male subjects was too small for definite conclusions. The incidence of activity among married men, for the three studies, was 57, 53, and 36 percent, respectively; for the married women these figures were 43, 41, and 42 percent. Thus, in the course of the three studies, male subjects showed greater change in the incidence of activity than did the women. Married men were more active than married women in Studies I and II, but, by the time of Study III, the activity of married women was slightly greater.

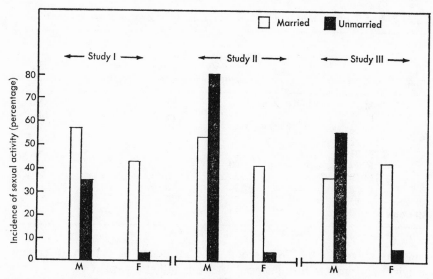

Figure 8–5. *Effect of marital status on incidence of sexual activity.*

*Patterns of sexual activity.* There were 160 subjects with data on sexual activity in both Studies I and II. Six of these, all women, were widowed between the time of Studies I and II and are therefore excluded from the data. In the remaining group of 154 subjects, 74 (48 percent) had pattern A, 26 (17 percent) had pattern C, 33 (21 percent) had pattern D, and 21 (14 percent) had pattern R.

In the overall group of 85 men, declining activity was the most frequent pattern (31 percent). Continuously absent activity occurred in 27 percent; in 22 percent of the men, sexual activity was sustained at the same level, and in 20 percent, activity showed an increase. In the overall group of 69 women, the pattern of continuously absent activity occurred in 74 percent of the subjects. The incidence of patterns C and D was 10 percent each. Only 6 percent of the women reported increased activity.

Table 8–6 shows the distribution of activity patterns by age for the 154 subjects. In men of the 60 to 65 age range, sustained and rising sexual activity were the most common patterns (each 33 percent). In the 66 to 71 age range, patterns A and D each occurred in 30 percent of the cases, while the incidence of patterns C and R was 25 and 15 percent, respectively. In men between 72 and 77, pattern D occurred most often (33 percent); and in the oldest group of men, pattern A was most frequent (50 percent). Thus, in men, the incidence of pattern A (continuously absent activity) increased with age; that of pattern C (sustained activity) declined with age

Table 8–6. *Effects of age and sex on incidence of sexual activity patterns.*

| Age group | Number | | A<br>Percentage<br>continuously<br>absent | C<br>Percentage<br>sustained | D<br>Percentage<br>decreasing | R<br>Percentage<br>rising |
|---|---|---|---|---|---|---|
| 60–65 | M | 18 | 6 | 33 | 28 | 33 |
|  | F | 22 | 50 | 18 | 18 | 14 |
| 66–71 | M | 36 | 30 | 25 | 30 | 15 |
|  | F | 22 | 77 | 14 | 4 | 14 |
| 72–77 | M | 21 | 29 | 19 | 33 | 19 |
|  | F | 17 | 90 | 0 | 10 | 0 |
| 78+ | M | 10 | 50 | 0 | 30 | 20 |
|  | F | 8 | 100 | 0 | 0 | 0 |
| All men | | 85 | 27 | 22 | 31 | 20 |
| All women | | 69 | 74 | 10 | 10 | 6 |

and was absent in the 78+ group. The incidence of pattern R (rising activity) appeared to be influenced relatively little by age.

In women, pattern A occurred most frequently in all age groups, and the incidence increased from 50 percent during the 60 to 65 age range to 77, 90, and 100 percent for the subsequent age groups. Patterns C and R occurred in a small number of younger subjects, but they were absent among the two older groups.

The effects of marital status on the incidence of activity patterns are shown in Table 8–7. There were 11 unmarried subjects among the 85 men

Table 8–7. *Effects of marital status on incidence of sexual activity patterns.*

| Group | Number | | A<br>Percentage<br>continuously<br>absent | C<br>Percentage<br>sustained | D<br>Percentage<br>decreasing | R<br>Percentage<br>rising |
|---|---|---|---|---|---|---|
| Married | M | 74 | 29 | 23 | 32 | 16 |
|  | F | 30 | 50 | 16 | 20 | 14 |
| Unmarried | M | 11 | 18 | 18 | 18 | 46 |
|  | F | 39 | 92 | 5 | 3 | 0 |

and 39 unmarried subjects among the 69 women. The unmarried men had a higher incidence of pattern R (increasing activity) than the married men. The unmarried women had a much higher incidence of pattern A than the married women (92 percent versus 50 percent).

When comparing married men and women, it became clear that the above described activity differences between men and women were now smaller. Married men, however, were still more active than married women, as evidenced by a lower incidence of pattern A and a higher incidence of pattern C. The higher incidence of pattern D among married men indicates that their sexual activity was more subject to change, generally a shift in the direction of pattern A. Interestingly, the incidence of pattern R (rising activity) was about the same for married men and married women.

## Sexual Interest

*Degree of interest.* Sexual interest was rated on a 4-point scale (0, no interest; 1, weak; 2, moderate; 3, strong). The inquiry was specifically restricted to interest in sexual intercourse. Thus we do not know if qualitative changes were associated with the quantitative changes, that is, a change from interest in heterosexual activity to interest in autoerotic or homoerotic activity.

There were 65 subjects who had data on sexual interest for all three studies. In this group, there was a significant (negative) correlation between age and interest (for Studies I, II, and III, $p = <.05$, $<.01$, and $<.01$, respectively). Sexual interest declined with age in such a manner that a strong degree of sexual interest became exceptional after the age of 70 and was practically nonexistent after 75. However, as will be shown below, there may have been a preservation of mild to moderate interest during the later years.

Using the above scoring system for degree of sexual interest, the mean interest scores for Studies I, II, and III, respectively, were 1.08, 0.83, and 0.91. In other words, the average degree of sexual interest in this group of subjects was weak in all three studies. The higher mean score for Study III reflected the preservation of mild to moderate degrees of sexual interest among subjects surviving to the time of Study III.

*Incidence of interest.* As in the case of sexual activity, the sexual interest data were also analyzed by classifying all subjects according to whether they reported having any interest, regardless of degree, or none at all. The percentages of subjects reporting sexual interest were determined separately for the three studies.

Figure 8–6 shows the proportions of subjects reporting sexual interest for Studies I, II, and III. In each case, the N is all subjects who had data on sexual interest for that particular study—150 in Study I, 171 in Study II, and 116 in Study III. In Studies I and II there was, with increasing age, a gradual decline of the number of subjects reporting sexual interest, with the exception of the 84+ age group. In Study III, the decline was less marked; in fact, the incidence appeared to change hardly at all. The incidence in the 84+ age range was close to 50 percent for all three studies.

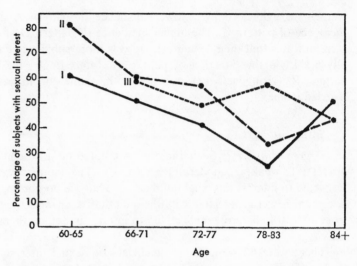

Figure 8–6. *Effect of age on incidence of sexual interest.*

Table 8–8 shows the effects of age on the incidence of sexual interest for male and female subjects. In Study I, the incidence of interest among the 150 subjects was 47 percent. Of the 71 male subjects, 48 (69 percent) reported sexual interest, while the incidence in the female group was 29 percent (23 of 79 subjects). With advancing age, the incidence of interest declined, in women more so than in men. For all age groups, women had a lower incidence than men.

In Study II, 95 (56 percent) of the 171 subjects reported sexual interest. The values were somewhat higher than in Study I. This was probably not due to differences in rating techniques but rather to the fact that the subjects in Study II were biologically advantaged in the sense of their greater longevity. Otherwise, the age-related decline in incidence was comparable to that in Study I.

Table 8–8. *Effects of age and sex on the incidence of sexual interest.*

| Age group | Study I | | Study II | | Study III | |
|---|---|---|---|---|---|---|
| | M 71 Percent-age | F 79 Percent-age | M 86 Percent-age | F 85 Percent-age | M 59 Percent-age | M 57 Percent-age |
| 60–65 | 77 | 50 | 88 | 71 | none | none |
| 66–71 | 74 | 23 | 88 | 35 | 77 | 43 |
| 72–77 | 65 | 26 | 78 | 33 | 76 | 23 |
| 78+ | 50 | 19 | 58 | 16 | 72 | 29 |
| All ages | 69 | 29 | 78 | 33 | 76 | 30 |

By the time of Study III, the group of subjects had aged so that there were no more subjects in the 60 to 65 age range. In the overall group of 116 subjects, 61 (53 percent) reported sexual interest. Compared with the previous two studies, the age-related decline of Study III was less obvious. The effects of marital status on interest are shown in Figure 8–7. In

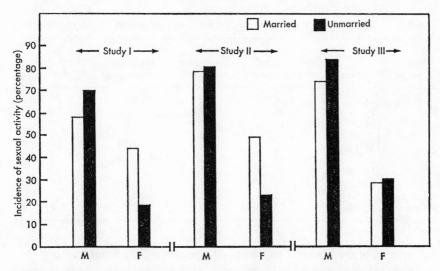

Figure 8–7. *Effect of marital status on incidence of sexual interest.*

unmarried men, the incidence of interest was somewhat higher than in married men (the greatest differences were found in the 60 to 71 age range). Compared with unmarried women, the married women had a higher incidence of interest in Studies I and II. The increasing incidence of sexual interest among unmarried women from Study I on to Studies II and III (a period of about nine years) was probably related to the increasing proportions of recently widowed women.

*Patterns of sexual interest.* There were 118 subjects (60 men and 58 women) with data on sexual interest in both Studies I and II. In this group, five women were widowed between the time of Study I and II; two had a pattern A, one a pattern C, and two a pattern R. These widowed female subjects are included in the sample in view of the fact that in women sexual interest is less influenced by marital status than is sexual activity.

In this group 42 (36 percent) reported pattern A, 27 (23 percent) reported pattern C, 31 (26 percent) reported pattern D, and 18 (15 percent) reported pattern R.

In the group of 60 men, patterns C and D each occurred in 31 percent of the cases, while the incidence of patterns R and A was 22 and 15 percent, respectively. In the group of 58 women, pattern A was most frequent (57 percent), pattern D occurred in 20 percent of the cases, while the incidence of patterns C and R was 14 and 9 percent, respectively.

Table 8–9 shows the distribution of sexual interest patterns by age and

Table 8–9. *Effects of age and sex on the incidence of sexual interest patterns.*

| Age group | Number | A Percentage continuously absent | C Percentage sustained | D Percentage decreasing | R Percentage rising |
|---|---|---|---|---|---|
| 60–65 M 12 | | 0 | 42 | 33 | 25 |
| 60–65 F 17 | | 35 | 18 | 35 | 12 |
| 66–71 M 26 | | 15 | 42 | 23 | 20 |
| 66–71 F 17 | | 76 | 12 | 12 | 0 |
| 72–77 M 14 | | 14 | 14 | 50 | 22 |
| 72–77 F 17 | | 65 | 6 | 17 | 12 |
| 78+ M 8 | | 37 | 13 | 25 | 25 |
| 78+ F 7 | | 43 | 29 | 14 | 14 |
| All men | 60 | 15 | 31 | 31 | 22 |
| All women | 58 | 57 | 14 | 20 | 9 |

sex. In men of the 60 to 65 and 66 to 71 age ranges, sustained interest was the most frequent pattern (42 percent). In men of 72 to 77, decreasing interest was the most frequent pattern (50 percent); and in the 78+ age range, pattern A had the highest incidence. Of interest is that even in the highest age group there were some men with a pattern of increasing interest.

In women, pattern A had, by and large, the highest incidence. However, there was no evidence of an age-related increase in the incidence of this pattern. It should be noted that the incidence was highest for the 66 to 71 age range. Likewise, there was no clear age-related decline of the incidence of pattern C; the incidence was lowest for the two middle age ranges, comprising the years 66 to 77. Nor was there any age-related decline in the case of pattern R. These findings suggest that it is during the age range of 66 to 77 that a woman is more likely to experience a decrease in sexual interest.

Table 8–10 shows the effect of marital status on sexual interest patterns of male and female subjects. Of the 60 men, 53 were married and 7 were unmarried; of the 58 women, 22 were married and 36 were unmarried.

In married men, sustained interest was the most frequent pattern (34 percent), but in unmarried men, rising interest had the highest incidence (43 percent). In both married and unmarried women, pattern A occurred

Table 8–10. *Effects of marital status on incidence of sexual interest patterns.*

| Group | Number | A<br>Percentage con-<br>tinuously absent | C<br>Percentage<br>sustained | D<br>Percentage<br>decreasing | R<br>Percentage<br>rising |
|---|---|---|---|---|---|
| Unmarried | M 53 | 15 | 34 | 30 | 21 |
|  | F 22 | 45 | 18 | 28 | 9 |
| Married | M 7 | 14 | 14 | 43 | 43 |
|  | F 36 | 64 | 11 | 16 | 9 |

most frequently (45 and 64 percent, respectively), while pattern R had the lowest incidence (9 percent for both groups).

Continued absence of interest was most common in unmarried women (64 percent) and least common in unmarried men (14 percent). Sustained interest was most common in married men (34 percent) and least common in unmarried women (11 percent). The incidence of decreasing interest was approximately the same for married men and women; it was highest in the married women (43 percent) and lowest in the unmarried women (16 percent). Increasing interest occurred more often in men than women, regardless of marital status; the highest incidence was among the unmarried men (43 percent).

Discussion

*The Effects of Aging*

Kinsey and associates (Kinsey, Pomeroy, & Martin, 1948) consider aging the most important single factor affecting the frequency of sexual outlets. In Kinsey's married male subjects, the mean frequency of total outlet at age 60 was 1.3 per week, declining to 0.9 per week at age 70. These frequencies were higher than those reported for our subjects. The reason for this must be that Kinsey's "total outlet" included activities other than heterosexual intercourse, while in our study, sexual activity refers specifically to heterosexual intercourse. Other types of sexual outlet may play an important role in aging individuals (Christenson & Gagnon, 1965).

Finkle and associates (Finkle, Moyers, Tobenkin, & Karg, 1959) reported that 65 percent of their male subjects below the age of 70 were potent in the sense of having had sexual intercourse at least once during the previous year. Freeman (1961) found that 55 percent of a group of men with a mean age of 71.1 years were sexually active and 75 percent showed a persistence of sexual desire. These findings appear to be in keeping with those presented here.

Sexual interest appears to be more intimately related to aging than is sexual activity. This is reflected in the fact that the degree of sexual interest showed a significant (negative) relationship to age in all of the three studies. The incidence of interest, however, does not show as clearly an age-related decline; this is due to the fact that, although strong degrees of sexual interest are absent after age 75, mild-to-moderate sexual desire may persist far beyond that age.

The data on activity and interest patterns provide information about change within the individual subject over a period of time. In men, there was, with increasing age, a gradual increase in the incidence of pattern A; this was true both for sexual activity and interest. In all age groups, the incidence of pattern A (activity) exceeded that of pattern A (interest); in other words, continuously absent interest occurred consistently less often than continuously absent activity. With the increasing incidence of pattern A, there was a concomitant decline of pattern C, more rapid for sexual activity than interest; thus, sustained interest appeared to hold up longer than sustained activity.

In women, pattern A was the most frequent pattern in all age groups; the incidence of this pattern was always higher than in men, regardless of marital status. Sustained and increasing activity occurred less frequently in women than in men. In the area of sexual interest, the differences between men and women were of similar nature, although less pronounced than in the case of activity. In women, the pattern of decreasing activity and interest occurred most frequently in the 60 to 65 age range, as compared to the 72 to 77 age group for men.

### The Effects of Marital Status

According to Masters and Johnson (1966), the aging human female is fully capable of sexual performance at orgasmic response levels, particularly if she is regularly exposed to effective sexual stimulation. There appears to be little evidence of aging in the sexual capacities of women until late in life (Kinsey et al., 1948; Kinsey, Pomeroy, Martin, & Gebhard 1953). To a large extent, the sexual activity of aging women is determined by the availability of a husband or sexual partner and his sexual capacity (Christenson & Gagnon, 1965). This is in keeping with our finding that in unmarried women the incidence of sexual activity was very low, but as far as sexual interest was concerned, the difference between married and unmarried women was much smaller. Christenson and Gagnon (1965) report that in postmarital women, the incidence of coitus decreases from 37 percent at age 50 to 0 percent at age 65. In this group, however, masturbatory activities were present in 25 percent at age 70. Thus, although unmarried women reported a negligible amount of heterosexual intercourse, this does not necessarily imply an absence of other types of sexual behavior.

In contrast to the unmarried women, unmarried men maintained sexual activity and interest at levels roughly similar to married men. In aging men, marital status appeared to play a negligible role in the frequency of sexual intercourse. Of course, it is probable that differences did exist between the married and unmarried men earlier in life. According to Kinsey and associates (1948) single men have slightly less frequent sexual outlets than married men, but by age 50, single and married men have the same frequency of outlets.

In our group of subjects, male subjects generally were sexually more active than female subjects. In the course of the three studies, however, the difference between married men and women became smaller to the point where, in Study III, the latter even had a higher incidence of sexual activity. In contrast to men, the group of married women showed no decline in the mean incidence of sexual activity in the course of the three studies.

Summarizing: In men, the factor of marital status has little or no effect on sexual activity and interest; in women, marital status has considerable effect on activity but relatively little effect on interest. Generally, the sexual activity and interest of men is greater than that of women, regardless of marital status, but with advancing age, marital status becomes less important in its effect on activity.

## Some Special Features of Sexual Behavior in the Aging

The final common path of human sexual behavior is under the influence of a great variety of factors, including genetic and biological endowment, developmental and age-related changes, psychodynamic forces, interpersonal relationships, and sociocultural factors. In addition, there are extremely complex interactional effects between these factors. It would be no surprise, therefore, to find a great deal of variability among aging individuals with regard to their sexual behavior. Some of these individual exceptions and variations in our group of subjects included the following:

1. Men were generally more sexually active than women, but in the married group, the differences became smaller in the course of the three studies, and by the time of Study III married women had higher incidence of sexual activity.

2. Among men surviving into the eighties and nineties, continued sexual activity was no great rarity; about one-fifth of these men reported they were still sexually active.

3. Although the degree of sexual interest declined with age, about

one-half of the subjects surviving into the eighties and nineties reported sexual interest of mild or moderate degree.

4. In women, sexual interest tended to be at a relatively low ebb during the late sixties and early seventies.

5. In both men and women, the incidence of interest usually exceeded that of activity. This interest-activity discrepancy was greater for men than for women. In men, the discrepancy tended to become greater with age, but in women it remained approximately the same.

6. Unmarried men had approximately the same level of activity and interest as married men. What is especially interesting is the finding that unmarried men more often reported a pattern of increasing activity and interest.

7. In women, the incidence of continuously absent activity patterns steadily increased with age, in contrast to the pattern of continuously absent interest. In men, on the other hand, the pattern of continuously absent interest became more frequent with age.

8. The difference between men and women with regard to sustained interest became less with increasing age to the point where, after the age of 78, women had a higher incidence of this pattern.

9. The configuration of decreasing activity and interest patterns occurred, in women, most frequently during the 60 to 65 age range, as compared to the 72 to 77 age range for men.

10. In men, the incidence of increasing activity or interest patterns changed relatively little with age. In other words, even though the overall picture in the subjects was one of decline, in roughly one-fourth of the male subjects an increase in the degree of activity or interest or both was observed, regardless of age.

### Men in the Mid-Seventies

According to Kinsey et al. (1948), the age-related decline in sexual activity is a gradual one—"after reaching a peak in adolescence, it gradually drops from then into old age and at no point does old age suddenly enter the picture—there are no calculations in all of the material on human sexuality which give straighter slopes than the data showing the age-related decline in outlets of single or married males." Although our data appear to confirm this generalization, there may be a possible exception: During the mid-seventies, a rather sudden drop in the frequency of sexual intercourse appears. This sudden decline might be due to the development (or exacerbation) of age-related infirmities or physical illness or both, which tend to interfere with the performance of sexual activity. That relatively major changes in sexual behavior may occur during the mid-seventies, especially in men, is suggested by the following findings:

1. A rather sudden drop in the incidence of sexual activity was noted among men of the 72 to 74 age range.

2. Absence of strong degrees of interest was evident beyond age 75 in all subjects.

3. In men, the configuration of decreasing activity and interest patterns had the highest incidence in the 72 to 77 age range. Prior to this age range, sustained activity and interest were prominent; and following this age range (i.e., 78+), continuously absent activity and interest patterns were most frequent. Thus the 72 to 77 age range appeared to be a period of transition.

4. The incidence of sustained interest was always higher than that of sustained activity, except in men of the 72 to 77 age range. At the same time, this is a rather marked reversal of the situation in the preceding age range, where we find that the incidence of sustained interest exceeded that of sustained activity by the widest margin. This reversal of the proportions of a pattern which refers to sustained behavior suggests a stressful disturbance of the status quo.

5. In the female subjects, we find that sexual interest was at its lowest ebb between the ages of 66 and 77, as manifested by high incidence of pattern A (interest), and low incidence of pattern C (interest) and R (interest). Possibly this is related to the above described changes in the men.

The importance of the aging husband as a factor may also be related to the finding (not shown) that in married women there was more age-related decline in interest than in the unmarried women. These differences between married and unmarried women suggest that the aging husband may be an important contributing factor to diminished sexual interest on the part of the married woman. Not only have men a greater activity-interest discrepancy than women, but this discrepancy tends to become greater with advancing age. This is obviously due to the fact that sexual activity after age 75 declines more rapidly than sexual interest. The existence of such a discrepancy, in combination with the other findings, implies the probability of psychological stress, arising from the need for a reorientation with regard to sexual aims. It may well be that, by the mid-seventies, many men are faced with the task of finding new outlets for their sexual desire and developing new ways of intimacy.

## Summary

The effects of age, sex, and marital status on degree, incidence, and patterns of sexual activity and interest were studied in a group of 254 men and women, ranging in age from 60 to 94. The data were obtained from three separate studies carried out at intervals of approximately three years. Degree of activity refers to frequency of sexual intercourse; degree of interest refers to interest in heterosexual activities. Incidence refers to the proportions of subjects with sexual activity or interest, regardless of degree. Intraindividual changes in activity and interest, in the course of time, were studied by way of four patterns: A (continuously absent), C (sustained), D (decreasing), and R (rising).

The data indicate that age and the degree of sexual activity are not related in a strictly linear fashion and that one or more intervening variables exist, probably age-related infirmities or physical illness or both. The incidence of sexual activity declined from a level of more than 50 percent during the early sixties to a level of 10 to 20 percent after age 80. The degree of sexual interest was more intimately related to aging than activity. Strong degrees of interest did not occur beyond age 75. However, the incidence of sexual interest did not show an age-related decline; mild-to-moderate degrees of interest tended to persist into the eighties. In general, the incidence of interest was higher than that of activity. This discrepancy was more prominent in male subjects, and it appeared to increase with age.

Marital status had little effect on the activity and interest of the aging men. Unmarried women had a negligible amount of sexual intercourse, but about 20 percent of the subjects did report sexual interest. The sexual activity and interest of men was greater than that of women, regardless of marital status, but with advancing age, marital status became less important in its effect on activity.

In men, generally, patterns of sustained activity and interest were relatively typical for the sixties, decreasing activity and interest for the mid-seventies, and continuously absent activity and interest beyond that age. On the other hand, the patterns of rising activity and interest occurred in 20 to 30 percent of the men, regardless of age. In women, sexual interest appeared to be at its lowest ebb during the early seventies. This may be related to the finding that men, during the mid-seventies, appeared to undergo a period of transition with regard to their sexual behavior.

## References

Christenson, C. V., and Gagnon, J. H. Sexual behavior in a group of older women. *Journal of Gerontology*, 20:351–356, 1965.

Finkle, A. L., Moyers, T. G., Tobenkin, M. E., and Kang, S. J. Sexual potency in aging males. *Journal of the American Medical Association*, 170:113–115, 1959.

Freeman, J. T. Sexual capacities in the aging male. *Geriatrics*, 16:37–43, 1961.

Kinsey, A. C., Pomeroy, W. B., and Martin, C. R. *Sexual behavior in the human male*. Philadelphia: W. B. Saunders, 1948.

Kinsey, A. C., Pomeroy, W. B., Martin, C. E., and Gebhard, P. H. *Sexual behavior in the human female*. Philadelphia: W. B. Saunders, 1953.

Masters, W. H., and Johnson, V. E. *Human sexual response*. Boston: Little, Brown, 1966.

Newman, G., and Nichols, C. R. Sexual activities and attitudes in older persons. *Journal of the American Medical Association*, 173:33–35, 1960.

Verwoerdt, A., Pfeiffer, E., and Wang, H. S. Sexual behavior in senescence: I. Changes in sexual activity and interest of aging men and women, *Journal of Geriatric Psychiatry*, 2(2), Spring, 1969.

# Sexual Behavior in Aged Men and Women* *Eric Pfeiffer, Adriaan Verwoerdt, and Hsioh-Shan Wang*

### . . . Reasons for Stopping Sexual Intercourse

In those subjects who have stopped sexual intercourse sometime before the completion of the entire study, we examined the reasons given for stopping. A total of 67 men and 73 women provided data in this regard. Death of the spouse was the most commonly given reason (30 percent). Apart from this, however, no particularly striking pattern emerged until we began to look at the stated reasons for men and women separately. When this was done, it became apparent that men on the whole tended to attribute stopping intercourse to themselves, while women overwhelmingly attributed stopping to their spouses. These findings are presented in Table 8–11. Thus, while there is seeming disagreement between the men and

Table 8–11. *Reasons for stopping intercourse.*

| Reason given | Men Number | Men Percentage | Women Number | Women Percentage | All subjects Number | All subjects Percentage |
|---|---|---|---|---|---|---|
| Spouse to blame | 28 | 42 | 63 | 86 | 91 | 65 |
| Death | 7 | 10 | 35 | 48 | 42 | 30 |
| Illness | 13 | 19 | 17 | 23 | 30 | 21 |
| Loss of interest | 7 | 10 | 1 | 1 | 8 | 6 |
| Loss of potency | 1 | 1 | 10 | 14 | 11 | 8 |
| Self to blame | 39 | 58 | 10 | 14 | 49 | 35 |
| Illness | 10 | 15 | 3 | 4 | 13 | 9 |
| Loss of interest | 10 | 15 | 7 | 10 | 17 | 12 |
| Loss of potency | 19 | 29 | 0 | 0 | 19 | 14 |
| Total (spouse + self) | 67 | 99 | 73 | 100 | 140 | 100 |

Note.—Entire sample, N = 140 subjects.

* Reprinted by permission from the *Archives of General Psychiatry*, 19:756–758, 1968. Parts of this article which repeat findings of the preceding article have been omitted.—*Editor.*

Table 8–12. *Reasons for stopping intercourse, death of spouse eliminated.*

| Reason given | Men | | Women | | All subjects | |
|---|---|---|---|---|---|---|
| | Number | Percentage | Number | Percentage | Number | Percentage |
| Spouse to blame | 21 | 35 | 28 | 74 | 49 | 50 |
| Self to blame | 39 | 65 | 10 | 26 | 49 | 50 |
| Total | 60 | 100 | 38 | 100 | 98 | 100 |

Note.—Entire sample, N = 98 subjects.

women as to whether oneself or one's spouse is to blame, there is actual agreement between the men and women that cessation of sexual intercourse is in general attributed to the man in the situation. Even when we subtract death of the spouse as a reason for stopping intercourse (see Table 8–12), the same agreement remains.

## Congruence in the Reporting of Sexual Data in Intact Couples

The presence of an intact couples group in the larger sample provided a unique opportunity to cross-check the reliability of reporting of sexual data within a marriage. The question of congruence was examined from two vantage points: (*a*) Did the two marriage partners agree or disagree on the then current frequency of sexual intercourse in their marriage? (*b*) Did the two marriage partners agree or disagree, in instances where intercourse has already stopped, on who was to blame for stopping intercourse?

### Congruence in Regard to Frequency of Intercourse

In the intact couples group there were 54 pairs of responses on frequency of intercourse available for analysis. A pair of responses was defined as a set of responses for both marriage partners obtained within one study, that is, within a matter of days of one another. Thus, any one couple might have provided from 0 to 3 responses, depending on whether one or both stayed alive and whether one or both answered all of the questions. Using these paired responses, the correlation between the frequency of intercourse reported by the husbands and that reported by their wives was calculated. The correlation was positive and highly significant ($r = .873$).

We also tabulated the 54 pairs of data on frequency of intercourse according to whether husband and wife agreed or disagreed. Again, the level of congruence is very high, as can be seen from Table 8–13. There was agreement in regard to presence or absence of sexual activity in 91 percent of the responses. Among the 18 responses in which husband and

Table 8–13. *Intact couples: congruence in regard to sexual activity.*

|  | Pairs of responses | |
|---|---|---|
|  | Number | Percentage |
| Agreement | 49 | 91 |
| No activity | 31 | 58 |
| Some activity | 18 | 33 |
| Disagreement | 5 | 9 |
| Total (agreement + disagreement) | 54 | 100 |

Note.—54 pairs of responses.

wife agreed that some activity was present, the breakdown was as follows: in 12 instances husband and wife indicated the same frequency; in 5 instances the husband indicated the greater frequency; and in 1 instance the wife reported the greater frequency. Among the 5 responses in which husband and wife disagreed on the presence of sexual activity, 3 of the husbands and 2 of the wives reported sexual activity while their partners reported that none was present.

## Congruence in Regard to Reasons for Stopping Intercourse

In the intact couples group there were eight couples in which both husband and wife were in agreement that sexual activity had ceased and in which both partners provided a reason for stopping. Congruence was taken to be present when husband and wife both agreed that cessation was attributed to the husband, or when husband and wife both agreed that cessation was attributable to the wife. These results obtained: both partners agree husband to blame, six couples (75 percent); both partners agree wife to blame, one couple (12.5 percent); and partners disagree, each blames self, one couple (12.5 percent).

Thus again in nearly 90 percent of this admittedly small number of couples there was congruence in the reporting of one aspect of sexual behavior. Incidentally, the data from these matched couples continued to bear out what was already demonstrated for the entire group: Men are most often responsible for cessation of sexual intercourse in a marriage in old age.

## Age at Which Intercourse Was Stopped

Finally, we tabulated the ages at which subjects reported they had stopped having sexual intercourse. Such data were available for 63 men

Table 8–14. *Age at which intercourse was stopped.*

| | Men | Women |
|---|---|---|
| 42–44 | — | 1 . |
| 45–47 | — | 4 .... |
| 48–50 | 1 . | 5 ..... |
| 51–53 | 2 .. | 4 .... |
| 54–56 | 4 ..... | 7 ...... .. |
| 57–59 | 5 ..... | 12 ..... ...... .. |
| 60–62 | 7 ..... .. | 13 ..... ...... ... |
| 63–65 | 6 ..... . | 8 ...... ... |
| 66–68 | 7 ...... .. | 3 ... |
| 69–71 | 5 ..... | 3 ... |
| 72–74 | 6 ..... . | 8 ...... ... |
| 75–77 | 9 ..... .... | 1 . |
| 78–80 | 3 ... | — |
| 81–83 | 6 ..... . | 1 . |
| 84–86 | 1 . | — |
| 87–89 | — | — |
| 90+ | 1 . | — |
| | 63 | 70 |

Note.—N = 133 subjects.

and for 70 women. These findings are presented in Table 8–14. The median age for stopping was age 68 for the men, age 60 for the women, thus indicating that the women ceased having sexual intercourse nearly a decade earlier than the men.

## Discussion

When Freud first attributed sexual thoughts and feelings to young children, he found that his ideas met with considerable resistance. When roughly half a century later data began to appear pointing to the existence of sexual thoughts and feelings in aged men and women, similar resistances were encountered. These resistances have not been massive, but they have nevertheless hampered investigation into this important area of human behavior. Researchers have sometimes limited their inquiries for fear of offending or embarrassing their experimental subjects or the subjects' families or both. Apart from the still extant notion that these matters ought not to be made the object of scientific inquiry, there also still exists the notion that there is no point in making such inquiries because the data which would result would be neither valid nor reliable, since people were either not truthful or not candid about such private matters, particularly in old age. It is true that many investigators can present anecdotal evidence of this old man or this old woman exaggerating beyond all belief their alleged sexual prowess. It is also true that certain details of sexual experience sometimes do not come to light even in intensive psychotherapy until many months have gone by. It is nevertheless the experience of long-term investigators in this field, W. H. Masters (oral communication, Spring, 1960) and W. B. Pomeroy (oral communication, June, 1967), that people are reasonably open about their sexual behavior when it is inquired into by an objective observer who is himself thoroughly comfortable with the subject of his inquiry. Our data revealed a high level of congruence in the reporting of sexual data between husbands and wives and thereby tended to strengthen the notion that useful data about sexual behavior can be obtained through interview techniques.

## Summary

. . . We found that among aged persons who had already ceased having sexual intercourse, men differed from women in that they tended to assign responsibility for stopping to themselves, while the women regularly attributed this blame to their spouses. Thus there was actual agreement that in general it was the husband who was the determining factor in the cessation of sexual intercourse in a marriage. The study also included a group of intact couples which provided an opportunity for studying congruence between marriage partners. There was a very high level of agreement between husbands and wives in regard to reported frequency of sexual intercourse and in regard to reasons for stopping sexual intercourse. Related data from the same research project will be presented in forthcoming publications.

## References

Kinsey, A. C., Pomeroy, W. B., and Martin, C. R. *Sexual behavior in the human male.* Philadelphia: W. B. Saunders, 1948.

Kinsey, A. C., Pomeroy, W. B., Martin, C. R., and Gebhard, P. H. *Sexual behavior in the human female.* Philadelphia: W. B. Saunders, 1953.

Newman, G., and Nicholas, C. R. Sexual activities and attitudes in older persons. *Journal of the American Medical Association,* 173:33–35, 1960.

Finkle, A. L., and Prian, D. V. Sexual potency in elderly men before and after prostatectomy. *Journal of the American Medical Association,* 196:139–143, 1966.

Maddox, G. L. A longitudinal multidisciplinary study of human aging: Selected methodological issues. *Proceedings of the American Statistical Association,* 280–285, 1962.

Masters, W. H. Personal communication.

Masters, W. H., and Johnson, V. E. *Human sexual response.* Boston: Little, Brown, 1966.

Pomeroy, W. B. Personal communication.

Verwoerdt, A., Pfeiffer, E., and Wang, H. S. Sexual behavior in senescence. *Geriatrics,* 24:137–154, 1969.

# Chapter 9. Activities and Satisfaction

Some of the most fascinating and controversial theories about normal aging deal with the relations of activities and satisfaction. These theories deal not only with the typical patterns of activities and satisfaction but with which pattern of activities produces the most satisfaction—and for which kinds of persons. To translate into practical terms: Does maximum satisfaction usually result from attempting to remain as active as possible, or does it result from quiet withdrawal from active roles (disengagement), or does it result from activity for some and from withdrawal for others?

The first report shows that poor health was clearly related to less activity in most areas but less clearly related to satisfaction in some areas. The second finds that socioeconomic status, rather than race, was more closely related to levels of activities and satisfaction. The last three reports present various longitudinal analyses that challenge the general applicability of disengagement theory, concluding that it has validity for only a small minority of the aged. They show that most of the panelists' activities and satisfactions tended to remain stable as they aged, indicating a "persistence of life style," and that those who maintained or increased activities tended to maintain or increase satisfactions, while those who reduced activities tended to have decreased satisfactions. These findings support the "activity theory" that the most normal and satisfying pattern of aging is to maintain as high a level of physical, mental, and social activity as is consistent with the person's life style.

## The Relationship of Activities and Attitudes to Physical Well-Being in Older People* _Frances C. Jeffers and Claude R. Nichols_

There has been very little research to date on the relationship of older peoples' physical capacities to their activities and attitudes. In Harold Meyer's North Carolina survey of recreation for the elderly, older people were asked, "Are there any reasons for your not taking up new hobbies or interests?" Fifty-five percent of those answering gave such reasons, and of

* Reprinted by permission from the *Journal of Gerontology*, 16:67–70, 1961.

these nearly half stated that health and/or afflictions were responsible (Institute for Research in Social Science, 1956). Cavan, Burgess, Havighurst, and Goldhamer (1949) and Havighurst and Albrecht (1953) have studied thoroughly the activities and attitudes of older people; but they did not obtain detailed medical examinations to measure objectively the physical functional capacities of these same older people.

The interdisciplinary research program at Duke University Medical Center . . . provides a unique opportunity to study the relationship between the older individual's physical functional capacity on the one hand, and his activities and attitudes on the other. . . .

## The Variables

*Physical Functional Rating* . . . [see Chapter 1].

*Activities and Attitudes*

This material was included as part of the social history obtained in personal interviews with the older subjects.

The Activity Inventory is that developed by Cavan et al. (1949) and consists of a series of 20 questions dealing with the older person's participation in the following areas: (*a*) intimate contacts (with family and friends); (*b*) leisure (ways of spending time, hobbies, reading, organizations); (*c*) security items (present work status, including housekeeping for women, and economic pressures); (*d*) health problems and difficulties; and (*e*) religious activities (attendance at religious services or listening to them on radio and TV, reading religious literature). A total activity score is obtained by adding the scores in these five categories.

The Attitude Inventory has a series of 56 agree-disagree items dealing with the older person's own satisfaction with his activities and status in regard to: friends, family, work, religion, health, economic status, general state of happiness, and feeling of usefulness. The total attitude score is obtained by adding the scores in eight areas. Since the items on the Attitude Inventory are composed of statements which all have references to self, they can be regarded also as indicators of self-image. Thus the scores might be interpreted as the degree of favorableness or unfavorableness with which the older person views himself in terms of the eight given areas of his experience.

A thorough discussion of these inventories, their purpose, use, reliability, and validity is to be found elsewhere (Cavan et al., 1949; Havighurst, 1951). The inventories have been used extensively throughout the United States.

Results

The variables in this study were analyzed by the chi-square technique, and coefficients of correlation were computed between the major variables. The following results were obtained:

1. Older people with no disability have higher total activity scores than do individuals with mild to severe disability. Of the individuals with low activity scores, there are about three times as many disabled as there are those with no disability. Conversely, of those individuals with high activity scores, nearly three times as many are not disabled compared with those having mild to severe disability. The biserial correlation coefficient between these two variables, although significant, is rather low, .39 (Table 9–1).

2. Older people with no disability have higher total attitude scores than do individuals with mild to severe disability. Total attitude score is not as strongly related to physical functional rating as is total activity score. However, among those having low attitude scores, there are twice as many disabled individuals as those who have no disability. The biserial correlation coefficient between physical functional rating and total attitude scores is .20 (Table 9–1).

Table 9–1. *Correlations between three major variables.*

|  | Correlation coeffecient | Level of significance |
| --- | --- | --- |
| Physical functional rating vs. total activity score | .39[a] | .001 |
| Physical functional rating vs. total attitude score | .20[a] | .01 |
| Total activity score vs. total attitude score | .54[b] | .001 |

Note.—Good physical functioning is associated with high activity and high attitude scores. High activity score is associated with high attitude score.

[a] Biserial coefficient of correlation (N = 245).

[b] Product-moment coefficient of correlation (N = 245).

3. High total activity scores are significantly associated with high total attitude scores. The product-moment coefficient of correlation between these two variables is .54 as shown in Table 9–1.

4. All categories of the activity scale are significantly related to physical functional rating except religious activity. High activity scores are associated with no disability. Table 9–2 lists the five categories of the activity scale and gives the significance level of chi-square for each.

5. In contrast to activities, none of the categories on the attitude scale is related to physical functional rating, except for attitude toward religion. In the latter case an inverse relationship was found, a high score being associated with disability. The majority of individuals with high religious

Table 9–2. *Relationships of activities and attitudes to physical well-being.*

| | Chi-square Level of confidence |
|---|---|
| Physical functional rating vs: | |
| Total activity scale | .001 |
| Total activity scale (minus health activity) | .001 |
| Health activity | .05 |
| Intimate contacts | .02 |
| Leisure activity | .01 |
| Security activity | .01 |
| Religious activity | .50 |
| Physical functional rating vs: | |
| Total attitude scale | .001 |
| Total attitude scale (minus health attitude) | .01 |
| Health attitude | .10 |
| Friends attitude | .30 |
| Work attitude | .10 |
| Economic security attitude | .20 |
| Religious attitude | .01 |
| Feeling of usefulness | .30 |
| Family attitude | .90 |
| Happiness | .10 |
| Total activity scale vs. total attitude scale | .001 |
| Health activity vs. health attitude | .01 |
| Intimate contacts vs. friends attitude | .001 |
| Intimate contacts vs. family attitude | .001 |
| Security activity vs. economic security attitude | .001 |
| Religious activity vs. religious attitude | .001 |

Note.—Good physical functioning is associated with high activity and high attitude scores with the exception of religious attitude, where an inverse relationship is found. High activity scores are associated with high attitude scores.

attitude scores are disabled. The eight separate categories on the attitude scale are given in Table 9–2 with the chi-square levels of significance.

6. High scores on the activity and attitude scales in the same categories are significantly related, i.e., health activity with health attitude, intimate contacts with attitude toward friends and toward family, security activity with economic security attitude, and religious activity with religious attitude. The relationships of these categories according to chi-square level of significance are shown in Table 9–2.

## Discussion

As shown above, when the sum of the scores of all the activity items was run against physical functional rating, a significant relationship was found. In order to avoid possible contamination of the results of plotting one health variable against another, the health item was deleted from the total activity score, which then was composed only of items in the areas of intimate contacts, leisure, security, and religion. Even with this deletion, the relationship remained statistically significant.

In a similar way, the health attitude item was deleted from the total attitude score. The relationship between total attitudes and physical functional rating was still significant.

So far as the separate items on the activity scale are concerned, it can be said that older people with no disability are more likely than those with mild to severe disability to have the following characteristics: (a) have few symptoms of illness and/or disability and days spent in bed (health item); (b) be married and have frequent contacts with family and friends (intimate contacts item); (c) engage in a variety of activities and hobbies, active in a number of organizations, and do much reading (leisure item); (d) be employed or occupied with housekeeping; (e) no change in standard of living because of lowered income (security item).

However, persons with no disability are no more likely than those with mild to severe disability to attend religious services, to listen to church services over the radio or television, or to read religious literature (religious item).

Concerning the findings on the attitude scale, on the other hand, the statistically significant relationship of the total attitude score to physical functional rating is presumably the result of a cumulation of nonsignificant relationships (all except for religion) reinforcing each other (Table 9–2). That is, for the seven other areas of an older person's attitudes, there are trends toward association but no statistically significant relationship shown to his physical well-being. It may be speculated that this is due to the persistence of attitudes which have developed slowly over a lifelong period.

In regard to the religious attitude item, there is evidence from most of the older subjects that religion means more to them as the years go by and the end of life approaches. For persons with disability this end is more imminent and they wish to become more closely associated with the solace and comfort of religion. This fact may account for the finding that disabled persons hold stronger religious convictions.

This finding may also explain why religious activity in turn is not significantly associated with physical functional rating. The disabled older person, although more handicapped and less able to take part in religious activity, is nevertheless much more highly motivated than the well person to do so.

Havighurst and Albrecht (1953) reported an overall study of older people in a small midwestern city. They devised a health handicap score based on subjective health evaluations, with half the number of these evaluations being reviewed by physicians. The product-moment correlations of the health handicap scores with two of the scores for which the Duke research team tested relationships with its objective physical functional ratings are as follows: health handicap score versus health activity, $-.56$. This indicates, as the authors point out, that the older person's "subjective feeling about his health was not completely determined by the extent and severity of his health handicaps." The defect in this calculation, which the authors would readily acknowledge, is that the health handicap score was largely a subjective rather than an objective health rating and not arrived at independently by a physician; thus the relationship tends to be predetermined. The Duke study accordingly offers a more objective evidence of the same relationship between physical disability and total activity and attitude scores.

In conclusion, a few interesting speculations occur as to how physical disability may operate on activities and attitudes. First, it tends to disqualify a person for certain activities, as in the case of a serious arthritic not being able to continue to play golf. However, disability does not act indiscriminately: locomotor activities, for instance, are cut off more quickly than the passive and more sedentary varieties. Second, if earning capacity is cut by disability, certain activities—such as travel, membership in expensive clubs, and the like—would need to be curtailed because of financial factors. Third, the discomfort of incapacity may be so depressing in itself as to limit the older person's activities, thus affecting both his motivation and his general attitudes quite severely. When an individual's physical functional capacity is handicapped, his family and friends may tend to be overprotective and fearful, again depressing his attitudes, motivation, and activities unless there is a strong compensating factor of resistance and determination. These speculations remain to be tested in future investigations.

## Summary

By means of a broad series of intensive interviews and examinations on a biracial group of 251 community volunteers over 60 years of age in North Carolina, it was found that older people with no disability have higher *total* attitude and activity scores than do individuals with mild to severe disability. But whereas all categories of the activity scale are significantly and positively related to physical functional rating except religious activity, the separate categories on the attitude scale are positively but unreliably related to physical functional rating except for attitude toward religion, where an inverse significant relationship was found.

References

Cavan, R. S., Burgess, E. W., Havighurst, R. J., and Goldhamer, H. *Personal adjustment in old age.* Chicago: Science Research Associates, 1949.
Havighurst, R. J. Validity of the Chicago Attitude Inventory as a measure of personal adjustment in old age. *Journal of Abnormal and Social Psychology,* 46:24–29, 1951.
Havighurst, R. J., and Albrecht, R. *Older people.* New York: Longmans, Green, 1953.
Institute for Research in Social Science, University of North Carolina. *Recreation for the aging in North Carolina.* Chapel Hill, N.C., 98–101, 1956.
Warner, W. L., Meeker, M., and Eells, K. *Social class in America.* New York: Harper Torchbooks, 1960.

# The Influence of Race and Socioeconomic Status upon the Activities and Attitudes of the Aged*   Dorothy K. Heyman and Frances C. Jeffers

The Negro segment of the aged population in contemporary society has hitherto been largely neglected in studies in social gerontology, i.e., either excluded (Cavan, Burgess, Havighurst, & Goldhamer, 1949) or included in a racially undifferentiated sample (Kutner, Fanshel, Togo, & Langner, 1956). The geriatrics research program at the Duke University Medical Center may have a unique contribution to make to this important area of investigation, since its panel of older subjects is both biracial and occupationally diversified.

The specific structure of the Negro community has for the most part not been differentiated in social stratification studies in the United States, which tend to be generalized to the population as a whole (Warner, Meeker, & Eells, 1949). However, several studies (Dollard, 1937; Davis, Gardner, & Gardner, 1941) have explored the concept of caste as well as of class. Frazier (1957b) questions whether the traditional concept of caste applies to the Negro in the United States but nevertheless states that "caste based upon race has been the most important feature of the occupational structure of the South."

Criteria for social status are evidently not the same for the two racial groups. Whereas occupation and income seem to be the chief distinctions for three-class structure (with subdivisions of these) in white society

* Reprinted by Permission from the *Journal of Gerontology,* 19:225–229, 1964.

(Warner et al., 1949), Frazier (1957a) points out that upper-class status in the Negro population in the South has been based upon (*a*) descent from Negroes freed before the Civil War, (*b*) mixed ancestry, and (*c*) conventional family and sex behavior. Moreover, restratification of the Negro population has occurred through the gradual emergence of a clearly defined dominant middle class, about which Warner (1962) notes ". . . this same group is drawing closer to the upper-middle class people of the white group . . . because of similar interests and political and economic forces." Frazier (1957a) labeled this middle class the "black bourgeoisie" and designated as its earlier capital the town of Durham, North Carolina, the same community in which this investigation was conducted.

The present study is in itself not an investigation into class differences between the races but more specifically into the relative influences of (*a*) race and (*b*) socioeconomic status on the activities and attitudes of older persons in a southern community. It was hypothesized that because of long-established cultural patterns, attitudes would remain consistent within a racial group and would transcend socioeconomic differences. Activities, on the other hand, would seem to be more modified by socioeconomic determinants and thus be less dependent upon the folkways.

## Materials and Methods

The relationships between (*a*) activities versus race and socioeconomic status, and (*b*) attitudes versus race and socioeconomic status were investigated by the use of the Activities and Attitudes Inventory developed by Burgess, Cavan, and Havighurst (1948). . . . A median split was used in the analysis of both activity and attitude ratings.

Socioeconomic status for the purpose of this investigation was assigned on the basis of whether the major lifetime occupation of the subject and/or spouse had been nonmanual or manual. Thus the biracial panel was divided into four groups: (*a*) white nonmanual, (*b*) white manual, (*c*) Negro nonmanual, and (*d*) Negro manual.

### Subjects

. . . The subject panel consisted of 125 men (48.0 percent) and 135 women (52.0 percent); 85 were Negro (32.7 percent) and 175 white (67.3 percent) (Table 9–3). . . .

The panel was drawn primarily from an urban population, but 21 percent of the subjects had spent most of their lives in rural areas. Only 5

Table 9–3. *Subject distribution on the basis of occupational status, sex, and race*
(*N = 260*).

|  | Nonmanual | | Manual | | Total | |
|  | Men | Women | Men | Women | Number | Percentage |
|---|---|---|---|---|---|---|
| White | 57 | 60 | 29 | 29 | 175 | 67.3 |
| Negro | 10 | 12 | 29 | 34 | 85 | 32.7 |
| Total | 67 | 72 | 58 | 63 | 260 | 100.0 |

percent were rural residents at the time of the study. However, the fathers
of 51 percent of the white and 68 percent of the Negro subjects had been
farmers.

The subjects' educational range varied from no formal schooling to
graduate work beyond the doctorate, with the median between the eighth
and ninth grades. . . .

Results

The relationships of the scores on the activity and attitude inventories
to socioeconomic status and race were analyzed by the chi-square technique. Analysis of variance was also computed on mean activity and
atttude scores for socioeconomic status and race.

*Activities*: *Socioeconomic Status versus Race Differences*

*Socioeconomic differences*. Significant socioeconomic differences on
total activities were found within both the white and the Negro populations.
i.e., there was a greater proportion of nonmanual subjects than of manual
with high total activity scores within both racial groups (*a* on Table 9–4).

No significant socioeconomic differences appeared for either race on
scores for health activities or intimate contacts.

More nonmanual than manual white subjects scored high on leisure-
time activities and on (economic) security. However, more of the white
manual than of the nonmanual scored high on religion.

Similarly, Negro nonmanual subjects outnumbered the manual in high
scores on security, but more Negro manual than nonmanual subjects had
high religious activity scores.

*Race differences*. No significant racial difference (*b* on Table 9–4) was
found for either the total or the subitems on the activity scale, with the

Table 9–4. *Relationship of activity scores (total and subitems) to socioeconomic status and race (N = 260).*

| | Total activities | | Health | | Intimate contacts | | Leisure | | Economic security | | Religion | |
|---|---|---|---|---|---|---|---|---|---|---|---|---|
| | $x^2$ | $p$ | $x^2$ | $p$ | $x^2$ | $p$ | $x^2$ | $p$ | $x^2$ | $p$ | $x^2$ | $p$ |
| a. Differences between nonmanual and manual | | | | | | | | | | | | |
| White | 3.84 | .05 | 0.25 | ns | 0.46 | ns | 10.54 | .01 | 8.39 | .01 | 4.06 | .05 |
| Negro | 7.99 | .01 | 0.42 | ns | 0.07 | ns | 2.90 | ns | 10.55 | .01 | 6.65 | .01 |
| b. Differences between white and Negro | | | | | | | | | | | | |
| Nonmanual | 0.36 | ns | 1.65 | ns | 0.50 | ns | 0.23 | ns | 1.70 | ns | 1.08 | ns |
| Manual | 1.84 | ns | 0.14 | ns | 3.35 | ns | 0.01 | ns | 0.91 | ns | 7.80 | .01 |

single exception that in the manual groups more Negro than white subjects had high religious activity scores.

Thus the differences found in activity patterns were socioeconomic rather than racial with the single exception of religion for manual subjects.

### *Attitudes: Socioeconomic Status versus Race Differences*

*Socioeconomic differences.* Total attitudes showed a socioeconomic difference only within the Negro population; more nonmanual than manual subjects scored high (*a* on Table 9–5).

For the subitems, in the white group the only attitude with a significant difference was that of economic security: more nonmanual than manual subjects had high scores.

In the Negro groups, more nonmanual than manual subjects rated high on attitudes toward work, toward economic security, and toward family. However, more manual than nonmanual subjects were in the high category in attitude toward religion.

*Race differences.* The only significant racial differences found in the nonmanual segment were on attitudes toward work and toward family, with proportionately more of the white than of the Negro in the high score categories (*b* on Table 9–5). The manual groups differed by race only as more Negro than white subjects had low scores on attitude toward economic security and contrariwise, more Negro than white subjects had high scores on attitude toward religion.

Accordingly, the overall findings as tested by chi-square technique were: (*a*) that activity scores tended to be associated with socioeconomic status; a racial relationship was apparent on only one item in the manual group (Table 9–4, *a* and *b*); (*b*) that socioeconomic relationships outnum-

Table 9–5. *Relationship of attitude scores (total and subitems) to socioeconomic status and race (N = 260).*

| | Total attitudes | | Health | | Friends | | Work | | Economic security | | Religion | | Usefulness | | Family | | Happiness | |
|---|---|---|---|---|---|---|---|---|---|---|---|---|---|---|---|---|---|---|
| | $x^2$ | $p$ | $x^2$ | $p$ | $x^2$ | $p$ | $x^2$ | $p$ | $x^2$ | $p$ | $x^2$ | $p$ | $x^2$ | $p$ | $x^2$ | $p$ | $x^2$ | $p$ |
| | a. Differences between nonmanual and manual | | | | | | | | | | | | | | | | | |
| White | 0.76 | ns | 0.18 | ns | 0.30 | ns | 0.00 | ns | 18.66 | .001 | 3.33 | ns | 0.28 | ns | 0.11 | ns | 1.87 | ns |
| Negro | 6.07 | .02 | 0.49 | ns | 0.00 | ns | 5.75 | .02 | 28.47 | .001 | 6.65 | .01 | 0.22 | ns | 5.14 | .05 | 1.50 | ns |
| | b. Differences between white and Negro | | | | | | | | | | | | | | | | | |
| Nonmanual | 1.87 | ns | 1.96 | ns | 0.25 | ns | 7.45 | .01 | 0.12 | ns | 0.59 | ns | 0.73 | ns | 5.50 | .02 | 0.00 | ns |
| Manual | 0.76 | ns | 0.24 | ns | 1.10 | ns | 0.10 | ns | 13.70 | .001 | 7.08 | .01 | 0.84 | ns | 0.09 | ns | 0.24 | ns |

Table 9–6. *Mean activity and attitude scores for racial and occupational groups.*

### Total activities

| | White | Negro | Combined racial groups |
|---|---|---|---|
| Nonmanual | 28.6 | 30.6 | 28.9 |
| Manual | 26.5 | 25.9 | 26.1 |
| Combined occupational groups | 27.9 | 27.1 | |

| White vs. Negro | p | Manual vs. nonmanual | p |
|---|---|---|---|
| Nonmanual | ns | White | .05 |
| Manual | ns | Negro | .005 |
| Combined occupational groups | ns | Combined racial groups | .005 |

### Total attitudes

| | White | Negro | Combined racial groups |
|---|---|---|---|
| Nonmanual | 34.6 | 36.4 | 34.9 |
| Manual | 33.4 | 33.1 | 33.2 |
| Combined occupational groups | 34.2 | 34.9 | |

| White vs. Negro | p | Manual vs. nonmanual | p |
|---|---|---|---|
| Nonmanual | ns* | White | ns |
| Manual | ns | Negro | .025 |
| Combined occupational groups | ns | Combined racial groups | .025 |

Note—p values indicate significance level of the differences obtained by analysis of variance.
* p < .10.

ber the racial on attitude scores and occur chiefly within the Negro group (Table 9–5, *a* and *b* ).

### Analysis of Variance

Analysis of variance was computed on the mean activity and attitude scores for the two racial and occupational groups with the following results (Table 9–6):

1. For total activities (mean scores) no significant racial difference was apparent in either occupational group separately or in the two combined. However, a socioeconomic difference was significant in both white ($p < .05$) and Negro ($p < .005$) groups, and when combined ($p < .005$).

2. For total attitudes (mean scores), no significant racial difference appeared. However, there was less overlap in total attitude scores of the two racial groups than in total activity, as evidenced by the trend ($p < .10$) toward racial difference in the nonmanual group.

3. Socioeconomic difference was not so pronounced for total attitudes as for total activities: for the white race, not significant, but for the Negro race significant at $p < .025$, and for the combined races at $p < .025$.

### Discussion

The present investigation reveals that socioeconomic differences were more important than those of race in regard to activities of the older population studied. This finding would tend to confirm the statement of Simpson and Yinger (1958) that "minority-group members almost always share with the other members of the society of which they are a part a great number of societal and cultural influences." Variations on the major finding may be accounted for in part, it is believed, by differences in education, in occupational level, and in the factor of urban or rural origin.

The only activity subitem which demonstrated consistent race and socioeconomic differences was that of religion. This is doubtless due in large part to the importance attached to religion in the South, particularly by the older generation (Jeffers, Nichols, & Eisdorfer, 1961). For the Negro especially, the church has long exerted a dominating influence in both personal and group life. The church serves as a social, educational, and recreational center as well as the source of great personal support and comfort to the individual. However, as Frazier observes (1957a), upward socioeconomic mobility has been reflected in religious behavior as the Negro middle class has "tended to leave the Baptist and Methodist churches, . . . the churches of the masses," to join the Episcopal, Congregational, or Catholic churches. This observation was confirmed by the present finding of no racial difference on religious activities and attitudes in the nonmanual groups, but only in the manual. Moreover, the socioeconomic difference found for religious activities in both racial groups did not obtain for religious attitudes in the white population, but only in the Negro.

The overall similarity of activities and attitudes of the white and Negro nonmanual subjects confirms another statement of Frazier's (1948) that "as the Negro acquires education and enjoys greater economic opportunities and participates in all phases of American life, he is taking over American patterns of behavior characteristic of different classes and regions." Thus, of the four groups studied here, the white nonmanual and manual, the Negro nonmanual and manual, the first three seem to be moving toward a common value system in regard to both activities and attitudes. The Negro manual group, on the other hand, tends to remain somewhat separate, so far as this investigation was able to determine, and perhaps continues to be more influenced by the folkways and values of a rural culture than the other groups.

## Summary

In a study of the activities and attitudes of a biracial older population (N = 260) in a southern community, it had been hypothesized (*a*) that activities would tend to be more closely associated with socioeconomic status than with race, but (*b*) that attitudes would tend to be more race-linked. Socioeconomic status (dichotomized by occupational classification into nonmanual and manual) and race were tested by chi-square technique for association with the total scores and subitems on the Activities and Attitudes Inventory (Burgess et al., 1948).

Analysis of the data indicated that: (*a*) differences in activity patterns were found to be socioeconomic rather than racial, (*b*) for attitudes, racial differences were again not dominant and socioeconomic differences were found only within the Negro group, (*c*) both activity and attitude subitems showed considerable variation in association with socioeconomic and race factors: religion and economic security revealed the most differentiation.

## References

Burgess, E. W., Cavan, R. S., and Havighurst, R. J. *Your attitudes and activities.* Chicago: Science Research Associates, 1948.

Cavan, R. S., Burgess, E. W., Havighurst, R. J., and Goldhamer, H. *Personal adjustment in old age.* Chicago: Science Research Associates, 1949.

Davis, A. W., Gardner, B. B., and Gradner, M. R. *Deep South.* Chicago: University of Chicago Press, 1941.

Dollard, J. *Caste and class in a southern town.* New Haven: Yale University Press, 1937.

Frazier, E. F. Ethnic family patterns: The Negro family in the United States. *American Journal of Sociology,* 53:435–438, 1948.

Frazier, E. F. *Black bourgeoisie.* Glencoe, Ill.: Free Press, 1957. (a)

Frazier, E. F. *Race and culture contacts in the modern world.* New York: Knopf, 1957. (b)

Jeffers, F. C., Nichols, C. R., and Eisdorfer, C. Attitudes of older persons toward death: A preliminary study. *Journal of Gerontology,* 16:53–56, 1961.

Kutner, B., Fanshel, D., Togo, A. M., and Langner, T. S. *Five hundred over sixty.* New York: Russell Sage Foundation, 1956.

Simpson, G. E., and Yinger, J. M. *Racial and cultural minorities.* (Rev. ed.) New York: Harper, 1958.

Warner, W. L. *American life.* (Rev. ed.) Chicago: University of Chicago Press, 1962.

Warner, W. L., Meeker, M., and Eells, D. *Social class in America.* Chicago: Science Research Associates, 1949.

# Fact and Artifact: Evidence Bearing on Disengagement Theory* *George L. Maddox*

The concept of disengagement has been introduced both to identify the modal process of mutual withdrawal of aging individuals and society and to describe the state of affairs most likely to produce optimal mutual satisfaction (Cumming & Henry, 1961). The adequacy of the theoretical formulations generated by these ideas is currently under critical review by the original proponents, Cumming (1963) and Henry (1963) and their colleagues (Havighurst, Neugarten, & Tobin, 1963) as well as by others (Rose, 1964; Maddox, 1964). There is every prospect that these critical discussions will contribute to more adequate theoretical formulations regarding the aging process and the conditions of successful aging, whatever the ultimate fate of the disengagement notion and its derivatives.

The logic of proof associated with testing various hypotheses generated by those who believe that disengagement is or is not a useful theoretical notion has been less adequately discussed. There have been occasional footnotes and incidental references in which unanswered questions have been raised about the adequacy of research that purports to describe a

* Reprinted by permission of S. Karger, Basel and New York, from *Human Development,* 8:117–130, 1965.

modal process. Moreover, there is demonstrated need to distinguish between aspects of the aging process which are attributable to aging per se, in contrast with aspects which more properly reflect continuities in personal life style or in situational constraints which are not attributable to aging. The implications for research strategy have not yet been adequately reflected in gerontological investigations (Williams, 1963; Anderson, 1963). To date, far too little attention has been given the adequacy of evidence purporting to support hypotheses bearing on the notion of disengagement. It will be argued in this paper that published research findings purporting to present evidence bearing on disengagement formulations have made it difficult, if not impossible, to distinguish artifacts produced by sampling bias and styles of data analysis from facts about the aging process and the process of successful aging. In the development of this argument, attention will be focused on selected problems of sampling, on panel maintenance in longitudinal research, and on styles of data analysis rather than on problems of reliability, validity, and comparability of research instruments. The latter problems continue to be substantial barriers to the accumulation of comparable evidence and, hence, to the resolution of some relevant theoretical issues, but they will not be discussed here.


Some Incidental Encounters

The methodological problems associated with the study of human aging were first encountered when the author became acquainted several years ago with the Duke Geriatrics Project, a multidisciplinary, longitudinal investigation of changes in the central nervous system and related phenomena among elderly individuals. A panel of some 250 volunteer subjects, 60 years of age and older, who continued to live in the local community, had been under observation for several years. At that time two questions were frequently being asked by project investigators: First, what are the characteristics of our elderly volunteer subjects which distinguish them from subjects who might have been accumulated in a random way? Second, what, if any, problems in data analysis are posed by any distinguishing characteristics of our subjects, and by the selective dropout among these panelists through time?

The attempt to answer the first question led to a comparison of the Duke panelists with other study populations of elderly subjects, particularly populations said to be randomly drawn. Since the details of these comparisons have been reported elsewhere (Maddox, 1962), it is sufficient to report simply a few conclusions from that analysis which are of particular relevance to the current discussion.

1. The Duke Geriatrics panelists, when compared with a similar population randomly drawn from the same locale, appeared to be quite advantaged physiologically, psychologically, and socially. These distinguishing characteristics became more pronounced among panelists through time as a result of selective dropout.

2. Comparisons of the Duke Geriatric panelists with nonlocal study populations described as randomly drawn, however, produced more similarities than differences. The inference was that refusal rates, which are pronounced in studies of older subjects, tend to produce study populations substantially similar to volunteers in spite of the randomizing procedures employed. Random sampling procedure does not necessarily produce representativeness.

3. In the absence of demonstrable representativeness of elderly subjects in a study population, the use of measures of central tendency to compare age-related differences among subjects becomes highly suspect. Gross cross-sectional analysis utilizing central tendencies as a basis for comparison maximizes the probability of spurious conclusions. Such gross comparisons make it difficult, if not impossible, to disentangle the artifacts produced by this style of analysis from the facts about the process under investigation. The problem is compounded if information on a panel of subjects is secured at various points in time and if gross comparisons are made without controlling for selective loss of subjects.

4. Randomly drawn but questionably representative populations of elderly subjects compared cross-sectionally provide an inadequate basis for generalizing about elderly populations and modal processes. The use of each subject as his own control minimizes but does not eliminate the difficulties described above.

An Illustration

The relevance of these conclusions was subsequently illustrated by an analysis of patterns of activity and satisfaction found among the elderly panelists participating in the Duke Geriatrics Project. At the time the data were first examined, 182 of the initial 256 subjects had completed a second series of medical and psychological examinations administered in a clinic setting. Both times a social history was taken which included activity and attitude inventories developed by Ruth Cavan and her associates (Cavan, Burgess, Havighurst, & Goldhamer, 1949). The activity and attitude inventories were originally proposed as a joint measure of personal adjustment. A brief description of each inventory and the rationale for its use have been presented elsewhere, along with the rationale for deriving subscores identifying *interpersonal* as distinct from *noninterpersonal* activity (Maddox, 1963). Investigation of the correlates of total activity scores using the Cavan inventories indicates that there is a positive relationship between total activity scores and both social class and health as determined by medical examination. This suggests reasonable validity. Moreover, various comparisons of the attitude scores with other purported measures of morale or life satisfaction indicate some justification for viewing the attitude inventory as an indicator or gross definition of satisfaction with self-in-relationship-to-environment. Evidence of the reliability of these measures is noted below.

The data in Table 9–7 present the relationship between reported activity and satisfaction among the 182 Duke Geriatric panelists who

Table 9–7. *Percentage distribution of satisfaction scores by activity score (initial interview and three years later).*

Initial interview[a]

| Satisfaction score (quartile) | | Activity score (quartile) | | | |
| --- | --- | --- | --- | --- | --- |
| | | Low | | High | |
| | | 1 | 2 | 3 | 4 |
| Low | 1 | 55 | 29 | 9 | 2 |
| | 2 | 23 | 39 | 29 | 6 |
| | 3 | 3 | 17 | 41 | 43 |
| High | 4 | 19 | 15 | 21 | 49 |
| | | 100 | 100 | 100 | 100 |
| | | N = 33 | N = 42 | N = 59 | N = 43 |
| | | | $x^2 = 70.1, p < .001$ | | |

Three years later

| Satisfaction score (quartile) | | Activity score (quartile) | | | |
| --- | --- | --- | --- | --- | --- |
| | | Low | | High | |
| | | 1 | 2 | 3 | 4 |
| Low | 1 | 59 | 23 | 12 | 5 |
| | 2 | 23 | 30 | 24 | 16 |
| | 3 | 18 | 28 | 27 | 37 |
| High | 4 | 0 | 19 | 37 | 42 |
| | | 100 | 100 | 100 | 100 |
| | | N = 44 | N = 43 | N = 51 | N = 41 |
| | | | $x^2 = 56.5, p < .001$ | | |

[a] Based on the Cavan activity and attitude inventories.

participated in a second series of interviews approximately three years after they were first seen. The substantial majority of subjects obtained activity and satisfaction scores which were either both high or both low; and 7 out of 10 subjects with such congruent scores presented the same pattern of response in the first and second examinations. The data in Table 9–7, however, also show that approximately 1 in 3 subjects in the first examination and/or the second presented incongruent scores; that is, high satisfaction but low activity, or low activity but high satisfaction scores. These incongruent patterns of activity and satisfaction were unstable through time. Only about one-third of the subjects with such incongruent responses presented the same response from one interview to the next. This is in contrast to subjects who presented congruent patterns. Over 2 out of 3 congruent patterns were stable over the three years between the first and second interview. The data in Table 9–7 lead to the conclusion that, among these elderly subjects, activity is a positive correlate of satisfaction. Because the concept of *disengagement* is not reducible to *inactivity*, however, these data do not provide a crucial test of the disengagement hypothesis regarding the independence of engagement and satisfaction (morale) with increasing age. In any case, satisfaction is not independent of activity in the evidence cited.

The data in Table 9–8 introduce the format and style characteristic of

Table 9–8. *Mean activity and satisfaction by age* (*Initial interview and three years later*).

| Age category[a] | Mean activity scores | | Mean satisfaction scores | |
|---|---|---|---|---|
| | Initial | Later | Initial | Later |
| 60–64 (N = 38) | 30.7 | 31.0 | 34.4 | 34.4 |
| 65–69 (N = 54) | 29.9 | 29.6 | 34.3 | 34.4 |
| 70–74 (N = 51) | 28.6 | 28.6 | 33.9 | 34.0 |
| 75–79 (N = 25) | 28.1 | 28.1 | 34.3 | 34.3 |
| 80 and over (N = 14) | 25.7 | 25.9 | 34.7 | 34.1 |
| N = 82 | | | | |

[a] Age at time of initial interview.

most research currently available on the topic under discussion: measures of central tendency controlled by age categories. Here the suggestion is that, the positive relationship between activity and satisfaction reported in Table 9–8 notwithstanding, as age increases, activity may decrease without affecting satisfaction. This finding may be complementary to the first since the observed minority with incongruous patterns of activity and satisfaction might be the oldest subjects. In fact, the number of older panelists (those above the mean age) who maintained high satisfaction scores in association with low *interpersonal* activity subscores (the principal source of decrease in activity) was twice as high as among the younger ones initially (38 percent versus 19 percent) and was as great as among the younger ones three years later (40 percent for each).

These data certainly argue that, for a minority of the panelists, satisfaction scores can be and are maintained in spite of lowering activity scores, particularly interpersonal activity. Since at this point, however, no other important characteristics of these individuals are known except that they are older, it is appropriate to give more attention to other characteristics which might help explain the relationship.

Three types of test factors were introduced into the analysis of the relationship between activity and satisfaction: (*a*) physical and psychological (e.g., clinical estimate of degrees of physical disability, self-health estimate, absence of clinical depression, subjective feelings of usefulness); (*b*) social structural (e.g., occupational classification, work-role maintenance); and (*c*) type of activity (interpersonal, noninterpersonal). With one exception, all of these factors were found to be significantly related, at least at the 5 percent level of confidence, to both activity and satisfaction; and in important ways they elaborated the relationship between activity and satisfaction. In both phases of the investigation, the effect of each type of factor on the activity/satisfaction relationship can be summarized as follows:

1. All of the physical and psychological test factors modified the activities/satisfaction relationship, regardless of reported high or low activity. Satisfaction was more likely to be high when both physical and mental health status were good than when either was poor.

2. The social structural test variables, only two of which were significantly related to both activity and satisfaction among these panelists, did not appreciably elaborate the relationship between activity and satisfaction. Measures of lifetime occupation of the subject (or of the spouse in the case of women who had not had regular gainful employment after marriage) and work-role maintenance indicate that subjects at the upper end of the socioeconomic continuum (as indicated by a nonmanual occupational background) and those who had experienced a minimum work-role change were more likely than others to report both high activity and high satisfaction. Neither of these characteristics, however, improves significantly the probability that high satisfaction would appear in the presence of low activity.

3. Introduction of subtypes of activity as test variables modified the activity/satisfaction relationship, but in a very complex way. In an analysis not shown, a subject's total activity score was a somewhat better predictor

of his satisfaction score than of either the interpersonal or noninterpersonal activity subscore alone and much better than when one subscore was high and the other low. Yet, also in an analysis not shown, the mean satisfaction score was higher among subjects who reported high noninterpersonal but low interpersonal activity than among those for whom the relationship between the subscores was reversed. This relationship was more pronounced among older subjects than younger ones. It is suggested, then, that the combination of subscores more likely to be associated with high satisfaction cannot be specified without reference to the age of the subject.

A review of the test variables which modify the activity/satisfaction relationship would lead one to ask about the distribution of the characteristics known to modify the relationship among those subjects who present high satisfaction scores along with low activity scores. A comment on the distribution of the physical and psychological characteristics of panelists will illustrate the relevance of this inquiry. It was noted above that relatively good health, as indicated by a medical evaluation and by the subject's self-assessment, increased the probability that high satisfaction would be found even when activity was low. A sense of personal adequacy as indicated by psychiatric evaluation (absence of depression) and by expressed feelings of usefulness also contributed to the achievement of maintenance of high satisfaction in spite of reported low activity. Moreover, although both interpersonal and noninterpersonal activities contributed to the maintenance of satisfaction, high satisfaction was more likely to be maintained in the absence of high activity only among the very oldest subjects.

The relationship between activity and satisfaction originally demonstrated by cross-sectional analysis is clearly a complex one, modified not only by age but also by particular combinations of physical, psychological, and social characteristics which are not necessarily age related. The combinations of characteristics known to modify the activity/satisfaction relationship were peculiarly concentrated among the oldest subjects, who, incidentally, were the subjects most likely to maintain high satisfaction in the face of low activity. The probability that the observed distribution of relevant characteristics reflects sampling bias is high. Consequently, conclusions about aging process and the process of successful aging based on the cross-sectional analysis of these data are suspect.

A more powerful as well as cautious test of the relationship between activity and satisfaction among the panelists is the analysis of stability and change of both variables and of their relation through time with each subject providing his own baseline; i.e., the use of each subject as his own control. By way of illustration, 59 subjects whose change in reported activity over a period of three years exceeded plus or minus one standard

Table 9-9. *Changes in satisfaction among subjects with extreme changes in activity.*

| Subjects with extreme change in activity scores[a] | Change in satisfaction score | | | | |
|---|---|---|---|---|---|
| | −4 or more | −3 to −1 | 0 | +1 to +3 | +4 or more |
| Upward (N = 28) | 3 | 2 | 2 | 8 | 13 |
| Downward (N = 31) | 7 | 10 | 3 | 4 | 7 |

[a] Plus or minus at least one standard deviation from the mean change found in the panel (N = 182) during the years between the first and second interviews.

The observed distribution is significant, $p < .001$, Goodman's chi-square adaptation of the Kolmogorov-Smirnov two-sample test (Siegel, 1956, p. 131).

deviation of the mean change were selected (Table 9-9). In these cases, an increase in reported activity scores predicts an increase in satisfaction scores, and a decrease in activity scores predicts the opposite. The number of subjects involved here was too small to introduce the test variables mentioned above, although the analysis discussed in the previous paragraphs suggests the direction in which such an analysis should proceed. It is relevant that age was not a distinguishing factor in the distribution of the 59 panelists between the activity-change categories. . . .

A Note on the Cumming-Henry Morale Measure

As noted at the outset of this paper, the disengagement concept has been introduced to describe not only processes of aging but also processes of optimum aging. Perhaps the most novel aspect of this formulation has been the suggestion that mutual withdrawal is necessarily a typical condition in successful aging (that is, in achieving and maintaining high morale).

The disengagement concept cannot be reduced to a measure of activity. Yet contact with the social environment is one dimension of disengagement, and the inference has been invited in various discussions of disengagement that activity can decrease in the long run without loss of morale. It has been argued, moreover, that this is the typical case.

The Duke data do not support this conclusion unambiguously; moreover, the data suggest that typical styles of cross-sectional analysis really do not provide a crucial test of relevant hypotheses. Case analyses suggest that maintenance of activity is typically a positive correlate of satisfaction. This is also the conclusion of Havighurst, Neugarten, and Tobin (1963, 1964).

Since the measure of satisfaction used in the Duke project is not the same as the measure of morale used by Cumming and Henry, the latter measure was introduced in the third round of observations. This was done in the interest of comparability; but more than this, in the initial reports of Cumming and Henry, the morale scale scores, which include items on satisfaction with activity, are not analyzed in relationship to the amount of activity reported. Hence, it was quite possible that those who were most satisfied were also most active. Table 9–10 reports an analysis of Duke

Table 9–10. *Activity scores for selected panelists by morale.*

| Morale scores | Male | | | | Female | | | |
| | Total activity | Inter-personal activity | Non-inter-personal activity | Number | Total activity | Inter-personal activity | Non-inter-personal activity | Number |
| --- | --- | --- | --- | --- | --- | --- | --- | --- |
| 4 | 32.0 | 15.0 | 17.0 | 2 | 33.0 | 17.2 | 15.8 | 4 |
| 3 | 25.8 | 11.2 | 14.6 | 12 | 25.6 | 12.7 | 12.9 | 12 |
| 2 | 24.2 | 10.4 | 13.8 | 17 | 26.3 | 12.4 | 13.9 | 24 |
| 1 | 24.0 | 9.8 | 14.2 | 5 | 27.9 | 14.3 | 13.6 | 13 |
| 0 | | | | 0 | 25.0 | 11.0 | 14.0 | 3 |

[a] See Cumming and Henry (1961, Appendix 3).
[b] Cavan activity inventory.
[c] Derivation explained in Maddox (1963).

activity scores (total, interpersonal, and noninterpersonal) in relation to the Cumming-Henry morale score for 92 Duke panelists who have thus far appeared for their third series of clinical observations and interviews. Among males there is a positive relationship between activity and morale scores. Among females the pattern is less clear, a higher mean total activity score is found among women with morale scores of 1 and 2 than.among those with a morale score of 3. In a review of the array of activity scores for females it was found that among females who had a morale score of 3, there was a single, extraordinarily low score; and among subjects with a morale score of 1 there were three extraordinarily high activity scores. If these four scores are removed, the mean activity score of females with a morale score of 3 becomes 26.7; and the mean activity score of subjects with a morale score of 3 becomes 24.2. The pattern observed among males is thus repeated for females. These data suggest that the Cumming-Henry measure of morale is not independent of activity.

Conclusions

In much of the research purporting to deal with processes of aging and optimum aging, cross-sectional analyses have been used in which central tendencies of various questionably representative age groups are compared. Such studies run a very high risk of producing as many artifacts as facts. Even when a longitudinal format is introduced, the situation is not greatly improved so long as the style of analysis involves the central tendencies on one or another characteristic, and when the effect of selective dropout is not controlled.

The use of individual case analysis seems recommended for several reasons. First, since each subject provides his own control, it is possible to keep reasonable control in data analysis over particular combinations of characteristics known to modify the relationship between the principal variables, such as, in the instance illustrated above, the relationship between activity and satisfactions. Second, analysis of the individual case makes possible the identification of the persistence of life style of the individual.

The use of each individual as his own control minimizes the chance of producing artifacts which are, in fact, spurious information about social and psychological processes. Such a precaution does not, however, obviate the problem of limited generalizability of findings based on samples or panels which are not demonstrably representative. Thus, while precautions such as described above would permit one to identify with confidence the existence of various patterns of activity in relation to patterns of satisfaction, one could not generalize with equal confidence about the relative distribution of such patterns among elderly persons. The fact that, for example, a pattern of low activity and high satisfaction is found to exist and to persist among a minority of Duke subjects does not allow one to generalize with confidence about how frequently this state of affairs would be found among elderly persons in general.

The disengagement concept has stimulated a useful discussion in social gerontology. Its proponents and opponents have been ingenuous in their development of research instruments and candid in describing the limitations of the study populations used in the testing of hypotheses. But a complaint must be lodged against the continued use of styles of analysis that are methodologically unsuited to the adequate study of the aging process. The emerging demonstration of continuity of life style as an important variable in the process of optimum aging adds a theoretical objection to the methodological objection which has been the focus of this paper.

## Summary

The concept of disengagement has been introduced both to identify the modal process of mutual withdrawal of elderly individuals and of society and to describe the state of affairs most likely to produce optimum mutual satisfaction. It is argued that in most published research purporting to evaluate hypotheses derived from disengagement theory it is difficult, if not impossible, to distinguish the *artifacts* produced by sampling bias and styles of data analysis from the *facts* about social and psychological aspects of aging processes, on the one hand, and about the process of successful aging, on the other. Data from the Duke University Geriatrics Project—a longitudinal, multidisciplinary investigation of a panel of elderly subjects (original N = 256) over a period of seven years—are used to illustrate research strategies which have a high probability of producing artifacts, and to outline procedures which minimize this problem.

## References

Anderson, J. Environment and meaningful activity. In Williams, R., Tibbitts, C., and Donahue, W. (Eds.), *Processes of aging.* Vol. I. New York: Atherton, 1963.

Cavan, R., Burgess, E., Havighurst, R., and Goldhamer, H. *Personal adjustment in old age.* Chicago: Science Research Associates, 1949.

Cumming, E. Further thoughts on the theory of disengagement. *International Social Science Journal,* 15:377–393, 1963.

Cumming, E., and Henry, W. *Growing old: The process of disengagement.* New York: Basic Books, 1961.

Havighurst, R., Neugarten, B., and Tobin, S. Disengagement and patterns of aging. International Social Science Seminar on Social Gerontology, Markaryd, Sweden, 1963 (unpublished paper).

Havighurst, R., Neugarten, B., and Tobin, S. Disengagement, personality and life satisfaction in the later years. In Hansen, P. F. (Ed.), *Age with a future.* Philadelphia: Davis, 1964.

Henry, W. The theory of intrinsic disengagement. International Social Science Seminar on Social Gerontology, Markaryd, Sweden, 1963.

Henry, W. The theory of intrinsic disengagement. In Hansen, P. F. (Ed.), *Age with a future,* Philadelphia: Davis, 1964.

Maddox, G. A longitudinal, multidisciplinary study of human aging: Selected methodological issues. *Proceedings of the Social Statistics Section of the American Statistical Association,* 280–285, 1962.

Maddox, G. Activity and morale: A longitudinal study of selected elderly subjects. *Social Forces,* 42:195–204, 1963.

Maddox, G. Disengagement theory: A critical evaluation. *Gerontologist,* 4:80–83, 1963.

Rose, A. A current theoretical issue in social gerontology. *Gerontologist,* 4:46–50, 1964.

Siegel, S. *Non-parametric statistics for the behavioral sciences.* New York: McGraw-Hill, 1956.

Williams, R. Styles of life and successful aging. In Williams, R., Tibbitts, C., and Donahue, W. *Processes of aging.* Vol. I. New York: Atherton, 1963.

# Persistence of Life Style among the Elderly*   *George L. Maddox*

In the analysis of behavioral or attitudinal phenomena among the elderly, change rather than persistence is more often the focus. Concentration on change, usually decremental, within some aggregate of elderly individuals in the typical case results in attention being given neither to distinguishing *changers* from *nonchangers* nor to establishing baselines against which individual change may be measured in a meaningful way. This state of affairs is part the result of the use of cross-sectional, in contrast to longitudinal, design. Both theoretical and methodological considerations suggest, however, the relevance of studying persistence as well as change in the patterns of behavior and attitudes among elderly longitudinally. Data from the Duke Geriatrics Project support this contention. . . .

With few exceptions, research in the United States has consistently supported the hypothesis that, among the elderly, maintenance of contact with the social environment is a condition of maintaining a sense of life satisfaction. The principal exception is, of course, the work of Cumming and Henry on disengagement (1961), which draws exactly the opposite conclusion; that is, reduction of interaction with the environment among the elderly is eventually a condition of the maintenance of life satisfaction or morale. Although the evidence against disengagement theory as a general explanation of aging process cannot be reviewed here (see preceding report), one issue raised by the critics of Cumming and Henry is especially relevant to the concern of this paper. This is the suggestion that the disengaged state is most likely to be observed primarily among the very old, whose declining health reduces their capacity to play any social roles successfully, and among those for whom disengagement is a life style antedating old age. The evidence presented below reinforces these probable explanations.

Elsewhere it has been shown that among the Duke panelists activity, on the average, does tend to decrease somewhat with age (Maddox, 1963). Decrease in contact with the environment, however, must be interpreted in relation to an individual's own baseline. Gradual decrease in activity through time for an elderly person with a history of active contact with his environment when, even with the experienced decrease, he is relatively more active than his peers must be distinguished from more consequential

* Reprinted by permission from *Proceedings of the Seventh International Congress of Gerontology*, 309–311, 1966.

modifications in activity. The persistence of a life style involving a relatively high level of involvement with the environment is as much a possibility as its opposite, as indicated by the report of the panelists under consideration. For example, individuals who ranked high or low in activity initially tended to maintain their ranking in the panel through time (see Table 9–11). This was also true of reported life satisfaction. In fact, such

Table 9–11. *Patterns of activity and life satisfaction*[a] *among selected panelists, three reports available.*

| Pattern | Male | | Female | | Total | |
|---|---|---|---|---|---|---|
| | Number | Percentage | Number | Percentage | Number | Percentage |
| Activity and satisfaction | | | | | | |
| Consistently above mean[b] | 14 | 21.9 | 24 | 28.5 | 38 | 25.7 |
| Predominantly above mean[c] | 13 | 20.3 | 13 | 15.4 | 26 | 17.6 |
| Consistently below mean | 12 | 18.7 | 9 | 11.0 | 21 | 14.2 |
| Predominantly below mean | 6 | 9.5 | 5 | 5.9 | 11 | 7.4 |
| Activity below, satisfaction above mean | | | | | | |
| Consistently | 4 | 6.2 | 3 | 3.6 | 7 | 4.7 |
| Predominantly | 7 | 10.9 | 7 | 8.3 | 14 | 9.4 |
| Other patterns | 8 | 12.5 | 23 | 27.3 | 31 | 21.0 |
| Total | 64 | 100.0 | 84 | 100.0 | 148 | 100.0 |

[a] Based on the Cavan activity and attitude inventories (Maddox, 1963).
[b] *Consistent* refers to all three reports.
[c] *Predominant* refers to two of the three reports.

persistence was characteristic of a large majority of the panelists (79 percent). Fourteen percent of the panelists did display persistently what might be called the disengaged pattern, in which life satisfaction is maintained in spite of a low level of activity. But these data suggest that a pattern of disengagement is more adequately viewed as the continuing life style of particular individuals than as a likely culmination of a process characteristic of all aging individuals. This conclusion is reinforced by other data about panelists variously categorized in Table 9–11.

Consider, for example, the categories "predominantly above," "predominantly below," and "other." Is there a tendency for the last observation in these nonuniform series to indicate a disengaged state? Of the 68 subjects in the three relevant categories, only 4 displayed a pattern of low activity and high life satisfaction at the time of the third observation. Clearly there is not a tendency for this pattern to emerge among individuals who at the initial observation did not display it.

Four characteristics did differentiate somewhat the panelists who displayed one or another pattern of activity in relation to life satisfaction. The pattern of high activity–high life satisfaction was associated with being younger, with better health, with higher socioeconomic status, and with above average intelligence (WAIS); the pattern of low activity–low life satisfaction was associated with the absence of these characteristics. The differences are not, however, particularly remarkable. The difference in age, for example, is only about two years. This means that at the third round of observations the average age of the former category would be approximately 74, and the latter, 76. Relatively more importance is attached to factors of social status, health, and intelligence. The individuals displaying the disengaged patterns are in fact the oldest in the panel (average age 80) at the third observation, but there is a considerable range of ages in each category. This would argue again for the conclusion that the disengaged pattern is not simply a function of age. Moreover, individuals at an advanced age who eventually display the disengaged pattern may have arrived there by very different routes, some as a result of a persistent life style and others as a result of the gradual modification in advanced age of a lifetime pattern of high activity and high life satisfaction.

This research reinforces the hypothesized importance of assessing persistence in individual life styles which reflect differences in the degree of contact with the environment and the relevance of this contact for the maintenance of life satisfaction. If life style is, as it appears to be, such an important variable; the longitudinal study of individual careers is crucial in the understanding of social processes of aging.

Contact with the panelists in the Duke study continues. Whether, through time, the disengaged pattern appears with increased frequency is of special interest. Of particular relevance will be the experience of those individuals who, at the third observation, presented both high activity and high life satisfaction. It is hypothesized that, excluding those with a disengaged life style, these individuals are more likely than others to present a disengaged pattern in subsequent observations.

## References

Cumming, E., and Henry, W. E. *Growing old.* New York: Basic Books, 1961.
Maddox, G. Activity and morale: A longitudinal study of selected elderly subjects. *Social Forces*, 42:195–204, 1963.
Maddox, G. Fact and artifact: Evidence bearing on disengagement theory from the Duke geriatrics project. *Human Development*, 8:117–130, 1965.

# The Effects of Aging on Activities and Attitudes* *Erdman B. Palmore*

Does aging reduce activities and attitudes? Most cross-sectional surveys agree that it does, but recent longitudinal evidence tends to question the extent of this reduction. Are decreases in activities related to decreases in satisfacton? Disengagement theory maintains that high satisfaction in aging usually results from acceptance of the "inevitable" reduction in interaction, while "activity theory" maintains that reduction in activity usually results in reduction of satisfaction. Is there a persistence of life style among the aged? There is evidence that regardless of the average effects of aging, individual persons tend to maintain relatively high or relatively low levels of activity and satisfaction during their later years. Does aging increase homogeneity or differentiation? Again, theories have been advanced supporting both positions.

Such questions and theories have fascinated social gerontologists for at least the two decades since the Chicago group developed their Activity and Attitude Inventory (Cavan, Burgess, Havighurst, & Goldhamer, 1949). A major reason for the uncertain answers and conflicting theories is that usually cross-sectional data were used even though these questions deal with change over time. It was not until 1963 that longitudinal data were first presented in an attempt to clarify these uncertainties (Maddox, 1963). The present paper discusses new longitudinal findings relevant to these questions from data that now cover a 10-year period of tests and retests.

## Methods

One hundred and twenty-seven (out of 256) volunteer participants in a longitudinal, interdisciplinary study of aging were examined and interviewed the first time during 1955–1959 and were reinterviewed at approximately three-year intervals so that they had completed four waves of interviews by 1966–1967.[1] When interviewed the fourth time, they ranged in age from 70 to 93 with a mean age of 78. Fifty-one were men and 76 were women. There was less than one year's difference between the mean age for men and the mean age for women. . . . Analysis of selection and

* Reprinted by permission from the *Gerontologist*, 8:259–263, 1968.
[1] A few subjects missed the second or third wave of interviews, but all 127 returned for the fourth wave.

attrition factors indicates that the panelists were a social, psychological, and physical elite among the aged and became more so through time (Maddox, 1962a). However, since longitudinal analysis uses each subject as his own control and examines changes over time rather than comparing younger with older subjects, the degree to which the sample of an age category represents the universe of an age category is a less critical issue than in cross-sectional studies.

We need not discuss here the various advantages of longitudinal analysis for studying aging, such as its greater sensitivity and its ability to measure change directly rather than inferentially (Goldfarb, 1960; Maddox, 1965), but we might point out one advantage of repeated measurements that has not been widely recognized. This is the ability to use *consistency* as a test of reliable and significant change when one has three or more repeated measurements on the same sample. When a change is observed between two points in time, there is always the possibility that this change might be due to temporary or chance fluctuations. But when the same change is observed between the second and third points in time, our confidence in the reliability and significance of this change can be greatly increased because the probability of two such changes occurring by chance is much smaller. Thus, in the present discussion we shall focus on consistent changes (or lack of consistency) as well as on the statistically significant changes.

The Inventory of Activity and Attitudes questions were read to the subjects by a social worker as part of a longer social history. The Activity Inventory consists of 20 questions dealing with five areas of activities (about 4 questions for each area): health (physical capacity to act); family and friends (frequency of contacts); leisure (ways of spending time, hobbies, reading, organizations); economic (amount of work or housework and lack of economic restrictions on activity); and religious activity (attendance at religious services, listening to them on radio or television, reading religious literature).[2] Each subscore could range from 0 to 10 with the higher scores indicating more activity. The total activity score is the sum of the subscores in these five areas (total range: 0–50).

The Attitude Inventory consists of 56 agree-disagree items about the subject's satisfaction with eight areas of his life (7 items in each area): health, friends, work, economic security, religion, usefulness, family, and general happiness.[3] The score in each area could range from 0 to 6 (1 item

[2] Typical questions: How many days did you spend in bed last year? How often do you see some of your family or close relatives? How many club meetings do you usually attend each month? Are you working now? (Full-time, part-time, or not working) How often do you attend religious services?

[3] Typical items: I feel just miserable most of the time. I have all the good friends anyone could wish. I am satisfied with the work I now do. I am just able to make

of the 7 is neutral in the scoring) with the higher scores indicating more satisfaction. The total attitude score is the sum of the scores in these eight areas (total range: 0–48). Further discussion of the development, purpose, scoring, reliability, and validity of these inventories may be found in Cavan et al. (1949) and Havighurst (1951). These inventories have been used in more than 20 different studies, and the results show a relatively high degree of reliability and validity.

As a check on the Inventory of Activity and Attitudes, the social worker interviewing the subjects used the Cavan Adjustment Rating Scale to give her estimation of the subjects' activities and attitudes (Havighurst & Albrecht, 1953). In general, the results from these scales were similar to those from the Activity and Attitude Inventory.

Some may question the appropriateness of comparing mean scores and correlations on the grounds that such analysis assumes equal intervals in the scales even though we are not sure this assumption is justified. However, several statisticians have recently pointed out that treating ordinal scales as equal-interval scales (a) involves assumptions that may be no more misleading than the use of arbitrary cutpoints that obscure differences in amount of variation (Blalock, 1964, p. 94); (b) has been useful in developing more accurate measurements and theory in most sciences (Burke, 1963, p. 149); (c) usually involves relatively little error (Labovitz, 1967); and in general allows much more powerful and sensitive analysis. Since we are interested primarily in direction of change and relative changes rather than absolute amounts of change, this type of analysis seems worth the risk of assuming equal intervals.

## Results

### Small Reductions

The men had almost no overall reduction over the ten years in either activities or attitudes (Tables 9–12 and 9–13). The women had significant but quite small (less than 7 percent) reductions in both activities and attitudes. This lack of substantial reduction in activities is contrary to disengagement theory, which asserts that marked withdrawal from activities is the modal pattern in aging (Cumming & Henry, 1961). It is also contrary to the findings of most cross-sectional surveys (for example, Havighurst & Albrecht, 1953) and contrary to the commonly held assumption that most people become less active as they age. On the other hand, it is consistent with previous longitudinal findings from this panel (Maddox,

ends meet. Religion is a great comfort to me. My life is meaningless now. I am perfectly satisfied with the way my family treats me. My life is full of worry.

Table 9–12. *Mean activity scores at four points in time.*

| Activity | Time 1 | Time 2 | Time 3 | Time 5 |
|---|---|---|---|---|
| **Men** | | | | |
| Health | 2.4 | 3.9* | 3.1 | 2.6 |
| Family and friends | 6.8 | 7.5 | 6.8 | 6.9 |
| Leisure | 6.9 | 5.8* | 5.7* | 5.6* |
| Economic | 4.8 | 4.9 | 5.3 | 6.0 |
| Religious | 6.3 | 6.1 | 5.5 | 6.0 |
| Total | 27.2 | 28.4 | 26.1 | 27.3 |
| **Women** | | | | |
| Health | 2.5 | 3.2 | 2.6 | 2.5 |
| Family and friends | 5.9 | 6.1 | 5.5 | 5.3* |
| Leisure | 7.7 | 7.2 | 6.6 | 6.3* |
| Economic | 7.4 | 7.5 | 8.1 | 8.4* |
| Religious | 6.7 | 7.1 | 6.4 | 6.7 |
| Total | 30.1 | 31.1 | 29.4* | 28.8* |

\* Difference between this score and score at Time 1 is significant at .01 level according to the *t* test for paired observations.

Table 9–13. *Mean attitude scores at four points in time.*

| Attitudes | Time 1 | Time 2 | Time 3 | Time 4 |
|---|---|---|---|---|
| **Men** | | | | |
| Health | 3.8 | 3.7 | 4.1 | 3.5 |
| Friends | 4.6 | 4.4 | 4.3 | 4.2 |
| Work | 3.7 | 3.6 | 3.8 | 3.4 |
| Economic security | 3.3 | 3.6 | 4.0* | 3.7 |
| Religion | 5.2 | 5.3 | 5.3 | 5.5* |
| Usefulness | 4.3 | 4.3 | 4.3 | 4.0 |
| Family | 4.9 | 4.6 | 4.9 | 5.0 |
| Happiness | 4.3 | 4.4 | 3.6* | 4.1 |
| Total | 34.0 | 33.8 | 34.2 | 33.3 |
| **Women** | | | | |
| Health | 4.0 | 3.8 | 3.7 | 3.6* |
| Friends | 4.5 | 4.4 | 4.5 | 4.3 |
| Work | 3.9 | 3.8 | 3.7 | 3.5* |
| Economic security | 3.8 | 3.9 | 4.0* | 4.0* |
| Religion | 5.5 | 5.6 | 5.7* | 5.6 |
| Usefulness | 4.6 | 4.3 | 4.4 | 4.1* |
| Family | 4.7 | 4.8 | 4.9 | 4.8 |
| Happiness | 4.2 | 4.1 | 3.6* | 3.6* |
| Total | 35.3 | 34.6 | 34.2* | 33.3* |

\* Difference between this score and score at Time 1 is significant at .01 level according to the *t* test for paired observations.

1963, Table 3). There are two plausible explanations for this apparent contradiction. While the aged may disengage or reduce activities in *some* areas, such as belonging to organizations and attending meetings (as shown by the declining leisure activities scores) or retiring from work (most of our panel was already retired), they may compensate by increasing activities in other areas, such as contacts with family and friends or reading religious literature. Or a temporary decrease may be compensated for by a subsequent increase. Or some may reduce while others increase. The net effect would then be little or no change in the average total activities score. Second, this panel represents those relatively healthy aged who were community residents and who survived for over 10 years from the first wave to their fourth wave "ripe old age" of 70 to 93. It may be that the relatively healthy aged do maintain a fairly stable plateau of activity up until just before death and that it is only the ill or disabled aged who pull the average activity level down in cross-sectional studies. The cross-sectional association of poor health and low activity is well established (Jeffers & Nichols, 1961; Havighurst & Albrecht, 1953). The same explanations would apply to the mixed changes in attitudes which show some increases, some decreases, and no significant net decrease in total attitudes among men.

It is unlikely that this pattern of small or insignificant decreases could be attributed to unreliability in the tests, because the reliability of these tests has been demonstrated elsewhere and is confirmed in this study by the moderately high correlations of earlier scores with later scores (Table 9–15).

The fact that women had larger and more consistent decreases in both activities and attitudes seems to indicate that aging produces greater net changes for women than men, at least in this age range. This may be related to the fact that most of the men had already retired before the beginning of this study and thus did not have to adjust to that change in status during the course of the study. Indeed, their increasing economic activity scores indicate that many men went back to work or increased their work during the study.

The small but significant increases of interest in religion, despite no increase in religious activities, confirm the findings of the cross-sectional studies (Moberg, 1965). This has been related to approaching death and increasing concern with afterlife. However, Havighurst (1951) found that religious attitudes had practically no correlations with the total scores nor with the other subscores. He suggested that since the religious items seemed to be measuring a different kind of dimension from the rest of the attitude scale, they should not be included in the total score. We also found that the religious attitude scores had almost no correlation with the total attitude score at any point in time (most of the correlations were less than .15) and that many of the correlations with the other subscores were even negative. We agree with Havighurst that the religion items should be dropped or considered separately from the rest of the attitude scale.

### Activity Correlates with Attitudes

Changes in total activities were significantly and positively correlated with changes in total attitudes (Table 9–14). This means that those who

Table 9–14. *Correlations* (r) *of changes in activities with changes in total attitudes* (*Time 1 to Time 4*).

| Activity | Men | Women |
|---|---|---|
| Health | .07 | .09 |
| Family and friends | .12 | .27* |
| Leisure | .22 | .10 |
| Economic | .36* | .30* |
| Religious | .26 | .13 |
| Total activity | .42* | .40* |

\* The probability of this correlation occurring by chance is less than .01.

reduced their activities as they aged tended to suffer a reduction in overall satisfaction; and conversely, those who increased activities tended to enjoy an increase in satisfaction. This finding is contrary to what might be predicted from disengagement theory, which asserts that disengagement is usually associated with the maintenance of high morale (Cumming & Henry, 1961). Even though disengagement is more than reducing activity, and morale is not exactly equivalent to our measure of satisfaction, it is fair to say that disengagement theory would probably predict no association or a negative association between changes in activity and changes in attitudes. That is, when activities decrease, attitudes should remain high or even increase, rather than declining as in our study.

This positive correlation of activity with attitudes supports rather the activity theory of aging, which has been stated as the "American formula for happiness in old age . . . keep active" (Havighurst & Albrecht, 1953, p. 55). This theory is favored by most of the practical workers in the field of gerontology:

They believe that people should maintain the activities and attitudes of middle age as long as possible and then find substitutes for the activities which they must give up—substitutes for work when they are forced to retire; substitutes for clubs and associations which they must give up; substitutes for friends and loved ones whom they lose by death. (Havighurst, 1961)

It may well be that disengagement theory is applicable to some and the activity theory is applicable to others; that some find most satisfaction in disengaging and others find most satisfaction in remaining active. But apparently in our panel the activity theory was most applicable to most of the participants.

Among the specific activities related to attitudes, change in economic activities were the most closely related to changes in total attitudes. This is congruent with Kutner's (1956) finding that having a job is more closely associated with high morale than is keeping busy with recreational activities. However, because the economic activities subscale contains an item on the restrictions on activities resulting from lower income we cannot be sure at this point whether it is the change in job status or change in income or both that account for the association with attitudes.

Changes in health had almost no association with changes in total attitudes. This is surprising in view of the substantial associations between health and activity on the one hand and between activity and attitudes on the other. Perhaps this indicates that unless health changes activity, there is little effect on attitudes.

### Persistence of Life Style

There is a clear tendency for aged people to persist with the same relative levels of activities and attitudes as they grow older. Most of the correlations of earlier scores with scores three years later were .57 or higher; half were over .70 (Table 9–15). This means that over half of the

Table 9–15. *Correlations* (r) *of earlier score with later score for total activities and total attitudes.*

| Variable | Time 1 with Time 2 | Time 2 with Time 3 | Time 3 with Time 4 | Time 1 with Time 4 |
|---|---|---|---|---|
| Men | | | | |
| Total activities | .57 | .57 | .46 | .27 |
| Total attitudes | .74 | .73 | .71 | .65 |
| Women | | | | |
| Total activities | .75 | .65 | .74 | .60 |
| Total attitudes | .67 | .66 | .79 | .56 |

variance in later scores can be accounted for by the earlier scores in the majority of comparisons. Correlations between scores at Time 1 with scores at Time 4 (10 years later) were much lower because of the greater time lapse which made possible a greater number of events that could change the relative levels of activity and attitudes.

This persistence in scores over three-year periods and even over the entire 10 years indicates both that the inventories are fairly reliable and that patterns of behavior and attitudes among the aged tend to be fairly stable over long periods of time. This also supports the results of a different type of persistence analysis (Maddox, 1966).

However, the correlations do not show consistent trends toward increasing persistence in the later intervals. The men's correlations actually decline somewhat in the third interval. Thus the idea that the aged become increasingly rigid and "set in their ways" is not supported by these data.

### Increasing Homogeneity

The standard deviations show no consistent trend toward either increasing homogeneity or differentiation (Table 9–16). The women's standard deviations remained about the same while the men's decreased in

Table 9–16. *Standard deviations for activity and attitude scores at four points in time.*

| Variable | Time 1 | Time 2 | Time 3 | Time 4 |
|---|---|---|---|---|
| Men | | | | |
| Total activities SD | 6.2 | 6.5 | 6.1 | 5.4 |
| Total attitudes SD | 4.9 | 5.3 | 5.3 | 5.7 |
| Women | | | | |
| Total activities SD | 5.8 | 6.3 | 6.6 | 5.7 |
| Total attitudes SD | 5.5 | 5.5 | 5.5 | 5.8 |

activities but increased in attitudes. However, there was a generally consistent decrease in differences between the mean scores for men and women (Tables 9–12 and 9–13). There is practically no difference left between men and women in their total attitude scores by Time 3 and 4.

Thus these data do not support the ideas that the aged become more differentiated in their behavior or attitudes (Havighurst, 1957) or that the "sexes become increasingly divergent with age" (Neugarten, 1964). On the contrary, the decrease in differences between men and women is consistent with Cameron's (1968) recent finding of converging interests between aged men and women.

## Summary

Changes in activities and attitudes over a 10-year period among 127 panelists in a longitudinal study of aging were assessed by use of the Chicago Inventory of Activity and Attitudes. There was no significant overall decrease in activities or attitudes among men and only small overall decreases among women. This was interpreted as evidence contrary to the findings of most cross-sectional surveys and the commonly held assumption that most people become less active as they age. It was suggested that normal aging persons tend to compensate for reductions in some activities or attitudes by increases in others or to compensate reductions at one point in time with increases at other times. The greater decreases among women seem to indicate that at this stage in life aging causes more overall changes among women than men.

Changes in activities were positively correlated with changes in attitudes so that reductions in activity were associated with decreases in satisfaction. This was interpreted as contrary to disengagement theory but supportive of activity theory: the "American formula for happiness in old age . . . keep active."

There was a strong tendency for the panelists to persist with the same overall level of activities and attitudes over time, but there was no evidence that patterns of behavior or attitudes became increasingly rigid or differentiated. In fact, mean differences between men and women tended to disappear.

## References

Blalock, H. M. *Causal inferences in nonexperimental research.* Chapel Hill, N.C.: University of North Carolina Press, 1961.

Burke, C. J. Measurement scales and statistical models. In Marx, M. H. (Ed.), *Theories in contemporary psychology.* New York: Macmillan, 1963.

Cavan, R. S., Burgess, E. W., Havighurst, R. J., and Goldhamer, H. *Personal adjustment in old age.* Chicago: Science Research Associates, 1949.

Cameron, P. Masculinity-femininity in the aged. *Journal of Gerontology,* 10:63–65, 1968.

Cumming, E., and Henry, W. E. *Growing old.* New York: Basic Books, 1961.

Goldfarb, N. *Longitudinal statistical analysis.* Glencoe, Ill.: Free Press, 1960.

Havighurst, R. J. Validity of the Chicago Attitude Inventory as a measure of personal adjustment in old age. *Journal of Abnormal and Social Psychology,* 46:24–29, 1951.

Havighurst, R. J. The social competence of middle-aged people. *Genetic Psychology Monographs,* 56:297–375, 1957.

Havighurst, R. J. Successful aging. *Gerontologist,* 1:3–7, 1961.

Havighurst, R. J., and Albrecht, R. *Older people.* New York: Longmans, 1953.

Jeffers, F. C., and Nichols, C. R. The relationship of activities and attitudes to physical well-being in older people. *Journal of Gerontology,* 16:67–70, 1961.

Kleemeier, R. W. Leisure and disengagement in retirement. *Gerontologist,* 4:180–184, 1964.

Labovitz, S. Some observations on measurement and statistics. *Social Forces,* 46:151–160, 1967.

Maddox, G. A longitudinal, multidisciplinary study of human aging. *Proceedings of the Social Statistics Section of the American Statistical Association,* 280–285, 1962. (a)

Maddox, G., and Eisdorfer, C. Some correlates of activity and morale among the elderly. *Social Forces,* 40:254–260, 1962. (b)

Maddox, G. Activity and morale: A longitudinal study of selected elderly subjects. *Social Forces,* 42:195–204, 1963.

Maddox, G. Disengagement theory: A critical evaluation. *Gerontologist,* 4:80–83, 1964.

Maddox, G. Fact and artifact: Evidence bearing on disengagement theory from the Duke Geriatrics Project. *Human Development,* 8:117–130, 1965.

Maddox, G. Persistence of life style among the elderly. *Proceedings of the Seventh International Congress of Gerontology,* 309–311, 1966.

Moberg, D. O. Religiosity in old age. *Gerontologist,* 5:78–87, 1965.

Neugarten, B. L. A developmental view of adult personality. In Birren, J. E. (Ed.), *Relations of development and aging.* Springfield, Ill.: Charles C Thomas, 1964

# Chapter 10. Attitudes toward Health and Cautiousness

Changes in health are assumed to be a normal concern to the aging. Some exaggerate these changes and exhibit hypochondriasis. Others tend to deny any deterioration in their health. But about two-thirds of the panel members were fairly realistic in evaluating their health. Further, the majority tended to be consistent over time in their health evaluations, whether realistic or unrealistic. Persons with unrealistic self-evaluations had typical characteristics: those unrealistically considering themselves healthy tended to be older, active, retired, male, and nonmanual when compared with the hypochondriasis type. Despite the assumed concern for health among the aged, few of the panelists admitted much concern or planning for chronic illness. It is difficult to determine how much of this is due to denial and how much to feelings of security in areas related to health.

A related study found that although the aged tend to avoid choosing among risky alternatives when possible, their cautiousness is no greater than that of young persons when they are forced to decide which odds of success they would accept in choosing a risky alternative.

## Effect of Time Lapse on Consistency of Self-Health and Medical Evaluations of Elderly Persons*    *Dorothy K. Heyman and Frances C. Jeffers*

The validity of the self-health rating of elderly people in a selected sample was tested by Maddox (1962), who found that "for two out of three subjects (65 percent) self-assessment and medical evaluation of health are congruous." The results of an opportunity to test this cross-sectional finding on a longitudinal basis are reported in this study. How is health evaluated as aging progresses? Is a change in health faced realistically, or do those in poor health assess themselves less realistically than do those in good health?

Age, sex, and occupational classification are commonly assumed to

* Reprinted by permission from the *Journal of Gerontology*, 18:160–164, 1963.

have some bearing on health inasmuch as with age: (*a*) disability in general seems to increase, (*b*) women tend to outlive men, and (*c*) "there is a tendency toward increasing disability in the poorer occupational groups," as Hobson and Pemberton (1955), among others, point out. In spite of this, according to a National Opinion Research Center survey, "most older persons interviewed considered themselves as being well. Only one of every five people thought his health was poor" (Shanas, 1961). There remains, however, the problem of consistency of self-health and medical evaluations.

The questions to be explored in the present investigation are: (*a*) whether people tend to remain realistic in their own health estimates, without substantial change, over a period of time, (*b*) whether changes with time in both subjective and objective evaluations of health are affected by the factors of age, sex, and occupational classification.

## Methodology

### Subjects

. . . The 256 subjects composing the original panel represent a wide spectrum within the occupational groups in the Piedmont region of North Carolina, with 54.7 percent of the subjects or their spouses in the upper socioeconomic level and 45.3 percent in the lower when dichotomized into nonmanual and manual occupational groups according to the United States Census Bureau classification. . . .

The present study is based on information obtained from the 182 subjects (71.0 percent of the original panel) who returned on an average of three years later, for a second series of two-day examinations. Of the 256 on the original panel, 32 (12.5 percent) had died in the interim, 8 (3.0 percent) had moved from the community, 19 (7.4 percent) could not return because of serious illness of self or in the home, and employment (full or part-time) prevented 3 (1.1 percent) from returning. The remaining 12 (5.0 percent) were reluctant to continue the series for a variety of reasons. . . .

### Variables

The three principal variables in this study were: physical functional rating, self-health rating, and health attitude score. The instruments for the measurement of these variables were identical on the two series of exami-

*Physical functional rating.* The physical functional rating (PFR), mod-ified and adapted in the Duke University geriatrics research program from that in use by the United States Army and Veterans' Administration, was the physician's estimate of the subject's capacity to function effectively in daily living and was determined after comprehensive examinations, which included a medical history, physical and neurological examinations, as well as ophthalmological and dermatological examinations. The tests also in-cluded an audiogram, chest x-ray, electroencephalogram, electrocar-diogram, ballistocardiogram, and routine blood and urine studies. The physician indicated the existence of physical impairment in the subject and assessed on a rating scale the degree of limitation of function in everyday life situations.

The frequency distribution of PFR for the subjects in this study is presented in Table 10–1. For the statistical purposes of this particular

Table 10–1. *Physical functional rating: distribution score in Duke group of elderly subjects on two series of examinations by per-centage (N = 182).*

| Condition | First examination | Second examination |
|---|---|---|
| No diseases or limitation | 23.0 | 2.8 |
| Disease present. No limitation of social or industrial function | 32.6 | 31.7 |
| Limitation, 20 percent or less | 25.3 | 31.7 |
| Limitation, 21–50 percent | 14.1 | 23.3 |
| Limitation, 51–80 percent | 3.9 | 8.9 |
| Limitation, over 80 percent | 1.1 | 1.6 |

study, subjects have been divided into those with 20 percent or less degree of physical disability (high PFR) and those with more than 20 percent disability (low PFR). This table indicates that on the initial series of examinations, 80.9 percent of the total subjects fell into high PFR, while only 66.2 percent were in this high category on the second series, a decline with time on this health rating.

*Self-health rating.* The second variable was the subject's own rating of his health. In the course of securing a detailed social history, the subject was asked, "How would you rate your health at the present time?" (Table 10–2).

The dividing point for the total group of subjects in this study was between the combined categories of *Poor* and *Fair* responses on the one hand (in the initial series, 29.7 percent; in the second, 30.3 percent) and

Table 10–2. *Self-health rating: distribution on two series of examinations by percentage (N = 182).*

| Subject's reply | First examination | Second examination |
|---|---|---|
| Very poor | 3.3 | 2.2 |
| Poor | 6.0 | 6.6 |
| Fair "for my age" | 2.8 | 5.0 |
| Fair | 17.6 | 16.5 |
| Good | 9.3 | 36.8 |
| Good "for my age" | 30.8 | 13.2 |
| Excellent | 10.4 | 12.6 |
| Excellent "for my age" | 19.8 | 7.1 |

those of *Good* and *Excellent* on the other (initial series, 70.3 percent; second, 69.7 percent).

*Health attitude score.* The third variable was the Health Attitude score (based on eight agree-disagree items) taken from the Activities and Attitudes Inventory developed by Cavan, Burgess, Havighurst, and Goldhamer (1949). This inventory and tests of its validity and reliability are described in detail in *Personal Adjustment in Old Age* (Cavan et al., 1949) and *Older People* (Havighurst & Albrecht, 1953).

The health attitude score, as seen in Table 10–3, also remained essen-

Table 10–3. *Health attitude score: distribution on two series of examinations by percentage (N = 182).*

| Scoring | First examination | Second examination |
|---|---|---|
| 0 | 1.1 | — |
| 1 | 1.1 | 3.3 |
| 2 | 4.9 | 7.7 |
| 3 | 31.9 | 30.8 |
| 4 | 31.3 | 30.8 |
| 5 | 18.2 | 17.0 |
| 6 | 11.5 | 10.4 |

tially unchanged for the present subjects from the first examination to the second. As indicated in this table, 61.0 percent of the subjects scored high (4 or higher) on the initial series and 58.2 percent on the second. That is, statements such as, "I feel just miserable most of the time," "I am perfectly satisfied with my health," or "My health is just beginning to be a burden to me" and others of similar import were answered on the second examination much as they had been answered on the first.


## Results and Conclusions

Three problems were investigated, with findings as follows:

1. Consistency of the first and second series of examinations on (*a*) medical evaluations, (*b*) self-health estimates, and (*c*) health attitude scores.

In order to measure change with time, ratings on each of the principal variables were compared for the two series of examinations.

(*a*) Of the total subjects reevaluated by the examining physician on the physical functional rating scale, 75.4 percent tended to remain unchanged, that is, in the same category of either high or low PFR on both examinations. Analysis for consistency in this distribution proved statistically significant ($x^2 = 33.68$, $df = 1$, $p < .001$) with 61.3 percent of those rating high on the first series of examinations remaining so on the second, and 14.1 percent who rated low initially remaining in the low category on the second examination. Thus the generally held assumption that striking changes in physical health occur with time alone in the elderly is not supported in this investigation.

Subjectively, however, the geriatrics research staff noted that many of these older persons evidenced a relative decline in both appearance and motor activity. Confirming this impression, for the 24.6 percent who changed categories on the PFR from the first to the second series, 19.8 percent were found to have moved from good to poor, and 4.8 percent from poor to good ($x^2 = 16.09$, $df = 1$, $p < .001$).

(*b*) A similar consistency on the two series of examinations was apparent for the self-health estimate. Of the subjects who returned, 76.3 percent remained unchanged, while 58.2 percent rated their health as good and 18.1 percent as poor on both series of examinations ($x^2 = 34.74$, $df = 1$, $p < .001$). For those who changed (23.7 percent), there was no statistically significant difference in the movement from good to poor or from poor to good.

(*c*) The health attitude score maintained consistency ($x^2 = 22.37$, $df = 1$, $p < .001$) on the two examinations, with 43.9 percent of the total subject group on the second examination remaining in the high score category and 24.7 percent continuing in the low. Although the other 31.4 percent changed from good to poor or vice versa, there were not significantly more subjects moving in one direction than in the other.

While the findings on consistency over time of the three principal variables are similar and statistically significant, it should be noted that only on the PFR rating was there a marked downward trend between the two series of examinations.

2. The interrelationships of the three principal variables on the two series of examinations.

When the three principal variables were compared with each other on the two series of examinations, a significant relationship was found between the PFR and the self-health rating on both series (initial series $x^2 = 2.23$, $df = 1$, $p < .05$; second series $x^2 = 17.85$, $df = 1$, $p < .001$). This indicates clearly that older persons seem to be reliable in self-health assessment, since self-evaluation tended to remain consistent to a significant degree with the evaluation by the physician.

The comparison of scores on PFR versus health attitude did not yield a significant relationship on the initial series ($x^2 = 2.23$, $df = 1$, ns). However, on the second examination these variables showed a statistically significant relationship ($x^2 = 16.15$, $df = 1$, $p < .001$), revealing consistency between objective health rating and subjective health attitude.

Self-health rating was found to be significantly associated with health attitude score on the two series of examinations ($x^2 = 13.23$, $df = 1$, $p < .001$ on the initial series; $x^2 = 27.53$, $df = 1$, $p < .001$ on the second series). Thus these two measures of the subject's own health appraisal were found to be significantly associated to each other on both sets of examinations.

An additional measure of consistency between subjective and objective health appraisals was provided by study of the ratings on the first series for the 32 subjects who died before the second series of examinations took place. (As stated above, an additional 42 subjects, 16.5 percent, of the original 256 did not return for the second examination for reasons other than death.) Those subjects who lived to the time of the second series of examinations and those who had died in the interim were found to be statistically significantly different on each of the three principal variables (Table 10–4).

Of the total subject group originally classified as in good health (that is, 20 percent or less degree of physical disability) by the physician, only 7.6 percent died between the examinations, while of those classified as in poor health (more than 20 percent disability), 39.4 percent had died ($x^2 = 36.89$, $df = 1$, $p < .01$).

The finding on self-health estimate approximated this closely, with 8.8 percent deaths among the subjects who had described themselves as in good or excellent health and 28.9 percent deaths for those described in fair or poor health ($x^2 = 18.03$, $df = 1$, $p < .001$).

The health attitude scores for the same two groups of subjects indicate

Table 10–4. *Comparison of two subject groups—living and deceased[a]—on three principal variables.*

| | | PFR (N = 251) | | Self-health estimate (N = 256) | | Health attitude score (N = 255) | |
|---|---|---|---|---|---|---|---|
| | | Good | Poor | Good | Poor | Good | Poor |
| Living | Number | 171 | 40 | 145 | 69 | 126 | 87 |
| | Percentage | 92.4 | 60.6 | 91.2 | 71.1 | 88.7 | 77.0 |
| Deceased | Number | 14 | 26 | 14 | 28 | 16 | 26 |
| | Percentage | 7.6 | 39.4 | 8.8 | 28.9 | 11.3 | 23.0 |
| Total | Number | 175 | 66 | 159 | 97 | 142 | 113 |
| | Percentage | 100.0 | 100.0 | 100.0 | 100.0 | 100.0 | 100.0 |
| | | $x^2 = 36.89, df = 1,$ $p < .001$ | | $x^2 = 18.03, df = 1,$ $p < .001$ | | $x^2 = 6.32, df = 1,$ $p < .02$ | |

[a] I.e., those subjects who later returned for the second series compared with those who had died in the interim period.

that those who died also had lower health attitude scores than those who returned for the examinations; that is, of those with high health attitude scores only 11.3 percent were deceased ($x^2 = 6.32$, $df = 1$, $p < .02$). This reinforces the assumption that older persons are realistic about their own health

3. The relationship between changes with time in the principal variables and the factors of age, sex, and occupational classification.

Upon analysis of the present data, no significant association with age-difference was found on changes with time in the (*a*) PFR ($x^2 = 1.83$, $df = 2$, ns), (*b*) self-health rating ($x^2 = .3736$, $df = 2$, ns), nor (*c*) health attitude score ($x^2 = 1.25$, $df = 2$, ns). The finding is in agreement with observations by Kutner, Fanshel, Togo, and Langner (1956), who stated that "with respect to age differences, although there is a decline with advancing age in the number of people without a major health problem, the Physical Health Index indicates relatively little difference in health status as age increases."

Interesting differences have been reported in self-health assessments examined in relation to sex. Women have been found by some investigators to be less realistic in self-health estimates than men, tending to complain more and to underrate their health, although over a period of time greater changes occurred in the health of men than in women. In *Personal Adjustment in Old Age* (Cavan et al., 1949), it was reported that for every *subjective* measure of health, the women in the early sixties indicate poorer health than do men. "Fewer women believe their health is good; fewer feel satisfied with their health; fewer report lack of illness. . . . The preponderance of poor health reported by women continues into the later age periods." In the study of old people in Sheffield (England), Hobson and Pemberton (1955) found that "age for age, a smaller proportion of women than men assessed themselves as fit. There was a falling off in the percentage assessing themselves as fit with advancing age which was more marked in women." In the present longitudinal investigation, however, changes with time on the three principal variables studied, PFR ($x^2 = .03$, $df = 1$, ns), self-health rating ($x^2 = .62$, $df = 1$, ns), and health attitude score ($x^2 = 1.79$, $df = 1$, ns), were not significantly related to sex.

Unlike the factors of age and sex, occupational classification, however, was found to be significantly related both to PFR and to self-health rating; that is, a greater percentage of the manual workers than of nonmanual manifested changes both in the PFR ($x^2 = 4.77$, $df = 1$, $p < .05$) and in the self-health rating ($x^2 = 5.80$, $df = 1$, $p < .02$), although no such difference was found in regard to health attitude score ($x^2 = .01$, $df = 1$, ns). Change for the manual workers was in the direction of poorer health, while the nonmanual workers by comparison remained stationary on both PFR and self-health evaluation. This supports a finding by Kutner et al. (1965), who stated that socioeconomic position bears a positive relationship to good health, with the upper economic group tending to deny health deterioration.

## Summary

In a longitudinal study of 256 elderly community volunteers, changes with time were investigated on three measures: physical functional rating (PFR), self-health rating, and health attitude score. Inquiry was also made into the extent of agreement of these two measures of self-health with objective health evaluations by a physician (PFR).

The greater proportion of subjects remained, to a statistically significant degree, unchanged during the time interval studied: (*a*) PFR (75.4 percent), (*b*) self-health rating (76.3 percent), and (*c*) health attitude score (68.4 percent).

The PFR on the initial examination tended to be related to self-health rating but not to health attitude score, although the health attitude score itself related significantly to the self-health rating. On the second series, all three variables were found to be significantly related to each other.

Realistic self-health appraisals in older persons are further substantiated by the findings on the initial examinations for those subjects who died prior to the second test series. These subjects had relatively lower ratings on all three variables to a statistically significant degree.

The incidence of change between the two examinations on the three principal variables was further examined in relation to age, sex, and occupational classification. Occupational classification alone showed a significant relationship both to PFR and self-health rating, in the direction of a downward trend for manual workers as compared to those in the non-manual classification.

## References

Cavan, R. S., Burgess, E. W., Havighurst, R. J., and Goldhamer, H. *Personal adjustment in old age.* Chicago: Science Resesarch Associates, 1949.

Havighurst, R. J., and Albrecht, R. *Older people.* New York: Longmans, 1953.

Hobson, W., and Pemberton, J. *The health of the elderly at home.* London: Butterworth, 1955.

Kutner, B., Fanshel, D., Togo, A. M., and Langner, T. S. *Five hundred over sixty.* New York: Russell Sage Foundation, 1956.

Maddox, G. L. Some correlates of differences in self-assessment of health status among the elderly. *Journal of Gerontology,* 17:180–185, 1962.

Shanas, E. *Family relationships of older people.* Health Information Foundation Research Series, No. 20. Chicago: Health Information Foundation, 1961.

# Self-Assessment of Health Status*    *George L. Maddox*

This paper explores some medical, social, and attitudinal factors associated with differences in subjective responses of individuals to illness and the threat of illness. The data reported here form part of a comprehensive study of (*a*) hypochondriasis and denial of illness and (*b*) the implications for medical management of incongruity between medical and subjective assessments of health status.

The theoretical perspective underlying this continuing study of differences in self-assessment of health status has been outlined in an earlier paper (Maddox, 1962a). There it was argued that what an individual believes his health status to be is logically an intervening variable between the objective state of his health, as it is or might be determined by clinical evaluation, and his occupancy or rejection of the sick role. Medical evaluation and self-assessment of health status are expected to be and in most cases are in agreement, and the sick role tends to be accepted or rejected

* Reprinted by permission from the *Journal of Chronic Diseases,* 17:449–460, 1964.

accordingly. An individual's assessment of his health, however, may be faulty. He may believe that he is ill, when in fact this evaluation of his health status is not or would not be confirmed by a medical examination. Or he may exaggerate the state of his good health to a degree which, from the medical standpoint, would seem unwarranted. Such faulty assessments of health status, whether conscious or not, logically precede the inappropriate occupancy or rejection of the sick role implied in cases of hypochondriasis or denial of illness.

Although differences in self-assessment of health status can be observed and might be studied in any age category of a population, an elderly population offers certain advantages in such investigation. In any elderly population a wide range in health status and fairly rapid changes in health status for at least some members of such a population are assured. In addition to the experience or threat of illness, elderly persons become increasingly vulnerable socially as they experience changes in important social roles and increasingly lose control of the environment. Cumulatively, these experiences might be expected to increase the probability of unrealistic perceptions of health among the elderly.

In this characterization of elderly persons it is not meant to imply that they necessarily are limited to choosing between denial of illness and hypochondriacal manipulation of the environment through the inappropriate assumption of the sick role. Whether persons 60 years of age and over are in fact more likely than others to assess their own health status inappropriately is a matter for subsequent research and is not under consideration here. In this paper it is argued only that in an elderly population there is a maximum opportunity to observe variety in response to the experience and threat of illness. Also, while specification of whether, how, and under what conditions faulty self-assessments of health status lead to inappropriate acceptance or rejection of the sick role are important questions needing further investigation, they are not the concern of this paper. The focus here is rather on the related but logically prior question: What factors are associated with a person's predisposition to be optimistic or pessimistic in self-assessment of health status and with the stability or change of that assessment? For purposes of exploring the answer to this question, elderly subjects provide a useful source of information.

Methodology

This report is based on data concerning a panel of volunteer subjects participating in a comprehensive longitudinal study of human aging made available by the Department of Psychiatry, Duke Medical Center. . . .

For 176 of the 182 subjects remaining in the panel at the second study there were data sufficiently complete for our purposes. These 176 subjects provide the data for this report.

The phenomenon to be explored is self-assessment of health status. Classification of subjects both initially and later was based on answers to the question, "How do you rate your health at the present time?" Subjects were permitted to indicate, without prompting, their preference for one of four basic answers. The health status of subjects who answered "excellent" or "good" was designated *subjectively good* and, of those who answered "fair" or "poor," *subjectively poor*.

Three types of factors were both initially and later considered as possible correlates of subjective estimates of health status. These were: (*a*) objective health status, (*b*) placement in the social structure, and (*c*) indicators of preoccupation with health and of morale. The *objective health status* of a subject was rated in terms of a five-point scale of physical functioning following extensive clinical evaluation (Dovenmuehle, Busse, & Newman, 1961). A subject's health was assumed to be *medically good* if no symptoms of disease were present or, if symptoms of disease were present, he suffered no more than 20 percent limitation of his normal functioning. On the other hand, a subject's health was considered to be *medically poor* if, as a result of disease processes, he suffered more than a 20 percent limitation of his normal functioning.

*Social placement factors* were considered in relationship to differences in self-assessments of health status among these elderly subjects. These factors included age, sex, the major lifetime occupation of subject or spouse (as a crude indicator of socioeconomic status), the type and level of activity maintained and the extent of change in work role. The work role was considered to be *maintained* for a male or a female with a history of employment outside the home who was working at least part time and for females with no history of regular employment outside the home who continued to assume major responsibility for household management.

*Attitudinal factors* of two kinds were considered: (*a*) preoccupation with health and (*b*) morale. Specifically, preoccupation with health was assumed to be indicated by "high body concern," a psychiatric evaluation of subjects who exhibit overconcern with health. Morale was measured in terms of the Havighurst attitude scale (Maddox & Eisdorfer, 1962). This attitude inventory includes items which, cumulatively, assess what might be called an individual's master definition of satisfaction with self in relation to others and to the environment; items such as feelings about health, friends, work, economic security, religion, personal usefulness, and family relationships. The mean scale score initially for the subjects described here was 34.7.

In the initial phase of the study objective health status appeared to be the single most important correlate of a subject's self-estimate of health. Two out of three subjects evaluated their health status in agreement with the medical evaluation. Among the one in three subjects whose self-evaluation was not in agreement with the medical evaluation, on the other hand, there was an approximately even distribution among those who were optimistic (i.e., whose health status was subjectively good/medically poor) and those who were pessimistic (i.e., subjectively poor/medically good). When the medical evaluation of health was controlled, it was found that optimism and pessimism were related both to social placement and to attitudinal factors. For example, optimism about health was found to be positively associated with subjects who were: (*a*) older, (*b*) had experience in nonmanual (higher status) occupations, (*c*) were relatively active (the mean activity score for all panelists was 28.8) with a major component of this score derived from activity not involving contact with other persons,[1] (*d*) were male, and (*e*) had maintained their major lifetime work roles. Pessimism about health status was associated with the absence of these characteristics. Optimism, in contrast to pessimism, about health was also found initially to be associated with the absence of preoccupation with health and with above average morale.

These initial findings suggested that in the longitudinal analysis of data:

1. Self-assessments of health status would continue to be positively associated with medical evaluations of health. This proposition has as its corollary that a change in objective health status would tend to be accompanied by a corresponding change in subjective assessment.

2. In cases of incongruity between objective and subjective assessments, optimism in contrast to pessimism about health would continue to be associated positively with the previously identified pattern of social placement and attitudinal factors. This proposition has as its corollary that the presence of these characteristics in the initial phase of the analysis would identify a predisposition to optimism about health; their absence would identify a predisposition to pessimism.

This research also bears on two methodological issues raised in the initial phase of the investigation which required longitudinal observations for resolution. First, reliability of subjective assessment of health for a given subject cannot be assumed. It is possible for an individual's response to a question about his current assessment of health status to be idiosyncratic, to express momentary feeling states or his assessment of the situa-

[1] The author has argued elsewhere (Maddox, 1963) that it may be useful in the analysis of activity patterns of elderly subjects to distinguish between *interpersonal* activity, in which evaluation by others is maximized, and *noninterpersonal* activity, which is relatively free from evaluation by others.

tionally appropriate answer quite apart from his actual or his usual feelings. This issue is addressed indirectly in the test of the principal hypotheses noted above. These hypotheses suggest that self-assessment of health is not random but is predictably related to objective health status as well as to a syndrome of social and attitudinal characteristics. To the extent that these hypotheses are supported, the reliability of the self-assessments under consideration is implied.

Second, in any assessment of the meaning of disagreement between subjective and objective evaluations of health status, it is necessary to know whether or not the individual is aware of his objective health status. A distinction needs to be made, for example, between a subject with an incongruous self-evaluation of health who is unaware of his medical status and one who maintains the incongruous evaluation in spite of contrary medical information. Only in the latter instance would an incongruous self-assessment be crucial in our analysis.

The subjects considered here had a high probability of being informed about their objective health status. Between the first and second phases of this study, subjects were exposed to the findings of clinic physicians to some extent directly; that is, conditions serious enough to warrant immediate medical attention were indicated to the subject. Moreover, a letter evaluating the subject's health status was sent to a local physician designated by each subject. In brief, each subject probably had a greater chance than the average person to be informed about his objective health status. In this context, then, incongruous assessments of health status cannot easily be dismissed as idiosyncratic, especially not those incongruous assessments which persisted between the two sets of observations. The possibility of continuing ignorance about objective health status, while not ruled out, was minimized.


Analysis of Data

Over the 38 months between the initial and second phases of the study, both medical and subjective assessments of health, considered separately, tended to remain stable for these subjects. In analyses not shown but derivable from Table 10–5, three out of four (76 percent) of them had the same medical evaluation of health status both initially and later. Exactly the same proportion of these panelists displayed the same self-assessments of health status on both occasions. The stability of both objective and subjective assessments is greater in both instances than one would expect by chance alone ($p < .001$).

The relationship between medical and self-assessments of health status initially and later is more complex (Table 10–5). The difference in the proportion of subjects with congruent assessments initially (68 percent) and later (70 percent) is slight. In both instances self-assessments are not simply a reflection of objective medical status. Some incongruities observed initially persist. Others emerge or are resolved over the three-year period.

Of the four categories of medical/subjective assessments (Table 10–5), only the first is highly stable. Of the subjects who initially were assessed objectively and subjectively to be in *good health,* 74 percent are found to be in the same category three years later. In the other categories (II–IV) there is a slight but consistent tendency for a subject to remain in his initial category in contrast to movement to any other single category. However, the subjects who remained in the same category over the three years constitute minorities in initial categories II, III, and IV.

From Table 10–5 it can be determined that 68 percent of the subjects

Table 10–5. *Persistence and change in the relationship between medical and subjective assessments of health status, initially and later.*

|  | Type[a] | Initial assessment (percentage to nearest whole) | | | | |
|---|---|---|---|---|---|---|
|  |  | I | II | III | IV | |
| Later assessment | I | 74 | 30 | 21 | 9 | N = 94 |
|  | II | 6 | 35 | 10 | 9 | N = 22 |
|  | III | 14 | 5 | 37 | 40 | N = 30 |
|  | IV | 6 | 30 | 32 | 42 | N = 30 |
|  |  | 100 | 100 | 100 | 100 | |
|  |  | N = 105 | N = 37 | N = 19 | N = 15 | Total = 176 |

[a]  I. Health medically "good"; subjectively "good."
II. Health medically "good"; subjectively "poor."
III. Health medically "poor"; subjectively "good."
IV. Health medically "poor"; subjectively "poor."

initially expressed subjective evaluations congruent with medical evaluation; 70 percent did so later. Of the subjects who experienced a change in objective health status, 52 percent displayed a congruent self-assessment.

These data give modest support to the hypothesis that medical health status is an important factor in the determination of subjective health assessment. A number of subjects, nevertheless, continued to be deviant cases from the standpoint of the first hypothesis. Of the 134 subjects who experienced no change in medical health status, 24 percent displayed incongruent subjective evaluations in the later observations. Of the 42 subjects who experienced a change in medical assessment of health, 48 percent failed to change their subjective assessments congruently. The existence of both these deviant types leads to a consideration of the second hypothesis, which suggests that the deviant cases are not random but can be explained, at least in part, by a pattern of social placement and attitudinal factors.

Specifically, the hypothesis indicates that a pattern of certain social placement and attitudinal factors would predict a subject's tendency to become or remain optimistic about his health status between initial and later observations. The absence of these factors, on the other hand, would predict a tendency to remain or become pessimistic about health.

The data summarized in Table 10–6 permit limited testing of the second hypothesis. A major limitation in this testing is a consequence of the large number of possible health status types in relation to the panel size. Some health status types include only one or two subjects, and only one type (I/I) includes a large number. Characterization of all types in terms of the selected social placement and attitudinal factors, regardless of the number of subjects involved, is presented only in the interest of complete reporting. Moreover, when comparisons between health status types are made, attention is focused on the direction of differences as hypothesized rather than on the magnitude of the differences and on the pattern of differences rather than on any single characteristic.

Consider as a case in point the 13 subjects found both initially and later to be pessimistic (Type II/II) and the 7 subjects who were found to be optimistic (Type III/III). The persistently optimistic subjects are distinguished from the pessimistic ones as predicted for all factors considered except in the case of maintenance of work roles. The differences, though sometimes small, are predominantly in the expected direction. Unexpectedly, subjects optimistic about their health are more likely than those who are pessimistic to be out of the work force if male and to have given up major responsibilities as a homemaker if female. This discrepancy will be noted in subsequent comparisons often enough to warrant comment later. With regard to activity, optimistic subjects, in comparison with pessimistic ones, tend to have a relatively greater proportion of their activity scores derived from noninterpersonal activity.

As expected, the persistently optimistic subjects also tend to be male, to have relatively higher status, and to be older. Moreover, they are less likely to display high body concern and are more likely to indicate high morale.

Additional confirmation that optimism and pessimism about health are not idiosyncratic individual responses is provided by a characterization of subjects who changed from one health assessment category to another between the initial and later phases of the study. For example, among subjects initially in Type I (medically good/subjectively good), 6 of them three years later are found in Type II and 15 in Type III (Table 10–6).

Table 10–6. *Selected characteristics of subjects by type of health status assessment, initially and later.*

| Type[a] | | | | | | | | | | | | | | | | |
|---|---|---|---|---|---|---|---|---|---|---|---|---|---|---|---|---|
| Initially: | I | I | I | I | II | II | II | II | III | III | III | III | IV | IV | IV | IV |
| Later: | I | II | III | IV | I | II | III | IV | I | II | III | IV | I | II | III | IV |
| N | 78 | 6 | 15 | 6 | 11 | 13 | 2 | 11 | 4 | 2 | 7 | 6 | 1 | 1 | 6 | 7 |
| **Characteristic** | | | | | | | | | | | | | | | | |
| **Social placement factors** | | | | | | | | | | | | | | | | |
| 1. Male | 49%[b] | 50% | 80% | 0% | 55% | 15% | 50% | 36% | 50% | 100% | 71% | 83% | 100% | 0% | 83% | 57% |
| 2. Nonmanual occupation | 71% | 67% | 53% | 33% | 73% | 62% | 50% | 82% | 75% | 0% | 71% | 33% | 100% | 100% | 33% | 14% |
| 3. Work role maintained | 63% | 67% | 40% | 100% | 55% | 100% | 50% | 36% | 100% | 50% | 43% | 50% | 100% | 0% | 50% | 43% |
| 4. Mean age, initially | 70.0 | 71.0 | 72.7 | 75.7 | 65.0 | 67.0 | 65.5 | 69.3 | 67.5 | 73.0 | 79.0 | 74.6 | 70.0 | 66.0 | 69.4 | 69.5 |
| 5. Mean total activity score initially | 30.2 | 29.2 | 27.0 | 27.0 | | 27.8 | 31.5 | 26.4 | 27.5 | 25.5 | 28.6 | 25.7 | 22.0 | 31.0 | 24.2 | 25.2 |
| 6. Percentage of total activity score from noninterpersonal sub-score | 53% | 45% | 53% | 48% | 49% | 54% | 52% | 50% | 52% | 55% | 65% | 52% | 55% | 48% | 54% | 56% |
| **Attitudinal factors** | | | | | | | | | | | | | | | | |
| 7. High body concern, initially | 29% | 33% | 20% | 17% | 45% | 85% | 0% | 45% | 25% | 0% | 29% | 83% | 100% | 100% | 29% | 100% |
| 8. Mean morale score, initially | 36.0 | 34.0 | 35.5 | 34.3 | 36.0 | 32.8 | 36.0 | 29.0 | 37.0 | 35.5 | 37.6 | 35.2 | 36.0 | 35.0 | 35.0 | 28.0 |

a   I. Objectively good/subjectively good.
  II. Objectively good/subjectively poor.
 III. Objectively poor/subjectively good.
 IV. Objectively poor/subjectively poor.
b All percentages to nearest whole.

Comparison in terms of the selected social placement and attitudinal factors reveals the hypothesized pattern with three exceptions. Type I subjects who experienced a change in objective health but nevertheless remained optimistic (Type I/III) show a tendency to be of lower status and a lower mean total activity score than those whose objective health status remained good but who became pessimistic (Type I/II). The third exception is that the subjects who remained optimistic are less likely than others to have maintained work roles, an exception already observed in the comparison of persistently optimistic and pessimistic subjects.

Another illustration of the pattern of characteristics predicting optimism or pessimism is found among subjects who were initially Type I, 21 of whom (20 percent) experienced a change in medical health evaluation over the three years. Six of these subjects modified their subjective evaluations to be consistent with the change in medical evaluation (Type I/IV); but 15 subjects who also experienced an objective change in health remained optimistic (Type I/III), as noted above. A comparison of these two types of responses (Table 10–6) again illustrates the expected pattern of attitudinal and social factors with three exceptions. The exceptions are that the emergent optimists (Type I/III) in this instance are (a) younger, (b) do not display the expected distribution of "high body concern," and (c) are less likely to have maintained their work roles. The last exception is now "expected."

Attention now shifts to a comparison of subjects objectively in poor health initially. Among subjects initially in Type IV (medically poor/subjectively poor), 7 of them remained in this category later and 6 had moved to Type III (medically poor/subjectively good). Again the hypothesized pattern of attitudinal and social placement characteristics in association with differences in subjective evaluation is observed with few exceptions (Table 10–6). Subjects who in this instance became optimistic (Type III) are, unexpectedly, about the same age as those who remained Type IV and do not show the expected distribution of noninterpersonal activities in relation to the total activity score.

Similarly, among the 19 subjects initially optimistic (Type III), 7 of them later remained in this type, and 6 had become a congruous Type IV (Table 10–6). Only the sex distribution presents an exception to the expected characteristics of optimistic subjects.

Overall, then, the second hypothesis tends to be supported by these data. Other relevant comparisons of health status types not introduced as illustrations here lead to the same conclusion. Subjects who remained or became optimistic about their health status displayed a definite pattern of social and attitudinal characteristics, a pattern distinguishing them from those who remained or became pessimistic. The predisposition toward optimism is positively associated with being male, higher status, and older. While optimistic subjects do not display consistently greater activity, their activity does tend to be predominantly noninterpersonal. The subject who tends to be optimistic about his health, moreover, is inclined to be less preoccupied than others with his health and to indicate higher morale. The only unexpected characteristic frequently found in association with a predisposition to be optimistic about health is the tendency to have experienced a change in the major lifetime work role.

## Discussion

These findings indicate that subjects in this study displayed a predominantly realistic orientation toward health status. Between the initial and later observations, panelists had sufficient access to information about objective health status to make it unlikely that misperceptions reflect simple ignorance about the actual state of affairs. However, ignorance of health status cannot be ruled out categorically as a source of misperceptions.

In order to minimize the possibility that the observed optimism or pessimism about health does not simply reflect differences in the ability of the person to attach meanings to the various symptoms of disease processes experienced or brought to their attention, variation in intellectual functioning of individuals in different health status types was explored. Little difference was found, for example, in the full-scale WAIS scores of various types of health status assessment. When subjects who were persistently pessimistic (Type II/II) both initially and later are compared with those subjects who were persistently optimistic (Type III/III), the average WAIS score of the optimistic subjects was higher (97.8 versus 92.2). Moreover, the subjects initially in good health objectively and subjectively (Type I) who, over the three years, became either pessimistic (Type II) or optimistic (Type III) were compared. The optimistic subjects in this comparison, in spite of poorer health, were found to have essentially the same WAIS scores (113.5 versus 112.3). Both optimistic and pessimistic subjects in the study not only had a high probability of being informed about objective medical status but also had comparable levels of intellectual functioning.

It has been noted that, for those subjects who displayed incongruous self-evaluations of health status, the predisposition to optimism or pessimism was predictably related to a pattern of social-placement and attitudinal factors. The importance of these nonmedical factors is emphasized when it is recalled that subjects typed as optimistic are by definition objectively in poorer health than those typed as pessimistic. To illustrate, subjects who were persistently optimistic (Type III/III) between observations exhibited, as expected, more pathology than their counterparts who were pessimistic (Type II/II) when compared in terms of the presence or absence of seven chronic processes.[2] These persistently optimistic subjects were found to present on the average 4.1 of these pathological conditions, as compared with 2.8 for their pessimistic counterparts. Moreover, among the Type I (medically good/subjectively good) subjects initially who subsequently became either pessimistic (Type II) or optimistic (Type III), the latter displayed on the average 3.1 of the 7 pathological conditions, as compared with 2.2 by the former. In an analysis not shown, no pattern was observed in the distribution of the selected chronic disease processes among the health status types.

The predisposition to optimism or pessimism about health, then, is explained, at least in part, by a pattern of social placement and attitudinal factors. Optimistic subjects as compared with pessimistic ones tend to be: (a) older; (b) relatively active (particularly activity which does not involve contact with other persons); (c) to have modified their work role; (d) to be male; and (e) for the male or head of household, to have had experience in a nonmanual occupation.

The association between being older and displaying optimism about health status probably reflects such factors as the concentration of the trauma associated with major role changes for the individual in the decade 60 to 70. Increasingly, after age 70, the individual might be expected to have made some kind of working adjustment to these changes. Moreover, for the very old individual, relative to his age peers with whom he has continuing contact, there is a decreasing likelihood that their situation will be very different from his own (see Blau, 1961). There is also some evidence that, with increasing age, the very old person increasingly disengages from the social structure (Maddox & Eisdorfer, 1962; Maddox, 1963; Cumming & Henry, 1961). This structural disengagement is reflected in a gradually decreasing level of activity, with such activity as remains focused largely in the noninterpersonal sphere (for example, reading or hobbies).

Disengagement from the social structure possibly is reflected also in the observed relationship between optimism about health and having experienced a change in work role. That is, it is the individual who has experienced no change in work role who is more likely than others to be pessimistic about his health. This finding is anticipated by the work of Thompson and Streib (1958); they report that self-assessments of health

[2] The indices of chronic processes included evidence of impaired heart functioning, arthritis, neurological deficit, psychiatric abnormality, EEG abnormality, pulmonary disease, and greater than 25 percent hearing loss.

tend to improve after retirement for many individuals. Such a conclusion is consistent with the observation that a predominance of interpersonal activity, which implies evaluations of personal competence by others, is related among the subjects studied to pessimism about health.

The observed association between nonmanual occupational experience for self or spouse and a predisposition to optimism about health probably follows from the above argument. The higher the status of the individual, the greater the probability that he has control over his work situation and the greater the possibility of staging an orderly withdrawal from the work force. In an analysis not shown, there is a positive relationship between socioeconomic status and the probability of having developed reading skills, hobbies, and other activities which permit the individual to keep in touch with his environment without having to do so through direct contact with other individuals.

The relationship between being male and being optimistic about health status has been noted by other investigators. But ordinarily it has not been possible to determine whether the explanation lies in different sex-related expectations about appropriate responses to illness or whether older females are as a matter of fact physically more impaired than males of comparable age. In an analysis not shown, when objective health status was held constant, among those assessed to be in "poor" health, 64 percent of the male panelists, in contrast to 28 percent of the comparable females, evaluated their health subjectively as "good." In this particular case, then, objective differences in health seem less likely than sociocultural factors to explain the association between maleness and optimism about health. Males are *expected* to be stronger than females, and this expectation may be reflected in the tendency to deny poor health rather than to attempt to manipulate the environment by means of using illness as a defensive maneuver.

Optimism and pessimism about health are also associated with predispositions to be oriented respectively away from and toward preoccupation with the body. The pessimistic (Type II) subjects, who were objectively in good health, rather consistently showed a tendency to have "high body concern" when compared with their optimistic counterparts. Moreover, the pessimistic subjects who displayed a tendency to be preoccupied with the body and its ills also were inclined to be dissatisfied with their relationship to the environment as indicated by their lower morale scores.

At the beginning of this paper it was noted that no attention would be given explicitly to the problem of hypochondriasis and denial. That is, in the context of one paper, whether or not the pessimistic subject in contrast to the optimistic one is more likely to assume the sick role inappropriately, to make greater utilization of health facilities, and so on, cannot be explored. The particular pattern of characteristics displayed would lead one to hypothesize, however, that the pessimistic subject, in contrast to the optimistic one, would in fact tend to display the characteristic behavior of the hypochondriac. This is a subject for subsequent consideration. Also the generalization of these findings to individuals in other age categories is recognized as problematic. Clarification of this issue will require additional research.

## Summary

Two of three elderly subjects (N = 176) displayed a reality orientation in their subjective evaluations of health status. Among the one subject in three who disagreed with the physician's assessment of his health, a pattern of social and attitudinal factors was found to distinguish between subjects with incongruous subjective assessments who were predisposed to be optimistic and those predisposed to be pessimistic. The relationship between these predispositions and the inappropriate rejection of the sick role remains to be investigated. A related issue for investigation is the implications of incongruity between medical and subjective assessment of health status for medical management.

## References

Blau, Z. Structural constraints on friendship in old age. *American Sociological Review*, 26:429, 1961.

Cumming, E., and Henry, W. *Old age*. New York: Basic Books, 1961.

Dovenmuehle, R., Busse, E. W., and Newman, E. G. Physical problems of older people. *Journal of the American Geriatric Society*, 9:209, 1961.

Maddox, G. L. Some correlates of differences in self-assessment of health status among the elderly. *Journal of Gerontology*, 17:180, 1962. (a)

Maddox, G. L. A longitudinal multidisciplinary study of human aging: Selected methodological issues. *Proceedings of the Social Statistics Section of the American Statistical Association*, 280, 1962. (b)

Maddox, G. L. Activity and morale: A longitudinal study of selected elderly subjects. *Social Forces*, 42:195–204, 1963.

Maddox, G. L., and Eisdorfer, C. Some correlates of activity and morale among the elderly. *Social Forces*, 40:254, 1962.

Thompson, W. E., and Streib, G. Situational determinants: Health and economic deprivation in retirement. *Journal of Social Issues*, 14(2):18, 1958.

# Observations on the Extent of Concern and Planning by the Aged for Possible Chronic Illness*  *Dorothy K. Heyman and Frances C. Jeffers*

According to a recent study (United States Department of Health, Education, and Welfare, 1962) of the aging population in this country, persons 65 years of age and over are increasing in absolute numbers as well as in proportion to the total population. The highest proportionate increases are occurring in the oldest age bracket, and additional significant increases are likely to occur should the three most common causes of death among middle-aged and older people (heart disease, cancer, and stroke) be affected by advances in medical research.

Aging and illness should not be thought of as synonymous terms. The most common affliction in the older age groups is the presence of one or more chronic illnesses (Von Mering & Weniger, 1959); this occurs in 77 percent of persons over 65 years of age as compared with 38 percent of those under age 65 (United States Senate, 1961a). For the purposes of the present paper, chronic disease has been defined as "a disabling or non-disabling chronic pathological condition known to the informant," the symptoms of which have been recognized for at least three months (Parrott, 1945). Relatively few categories of these illnesses (arthritis, rheumatism, heart disease, and high blood pressure) account for much of the disability in later life. However, blindness or progressive visual or auditory impairment often add distress to the aging process. Although comprising only a small segment of the total population (about 9 percent), the aged account for more than 55 percent of all persons who have limitations resulting from chronic illness (United States Senate, 1961a). This striking age-related incidence of chronic disease is also supported by the following findings of the National Health Survey (1961): (a) three-fourths of all aged persons not in institutions have one or more chronic disorders; (b) of these, two out of every five have a chronic disorder which prevents or limits their usual activity; and (c) among those 75 or older, almost every third person is confined to the house or needs help to get around outside (United States Senate, 1961b).

Does this extension of life span with the accompanying greater likelihood for the occurrence of various types of chronic illnesses arouse in-

* Reprinted by permission from the *Journal of the American Geriatrics Society*, 13:152–159, 1965.

creased concern in the elderly themselves? Burgess (1960) believes that "one of the two major anxieties of retired people is the possibility of prolonged illness against which there is no complete protection. . . ." Bortz (1958) states that chronic illness, though present in all age groups, is likely to be more devastating for older persons in our society, adding that Rusk has emphasized "the fear of chronic disease and disability as the most haunting specter of increasing age." A recent study (Lipman, 1962) of an older population group in Dade County, Florida, showed that insecurity regarding future health rather than present disability accounts for anxiety.

In view of the widespread interest manifested in the problem of chronic illness in the elderly, a brief study was made within the framework of a comprehensive investigation of aging now being conducted at Duke University to determine: (a) the extent of the anxiety of elderly persons regarding a prolonged illness in the future, and (b) the extent of their planning for such a possible illness.

The two variables—degrees of concern and planning—were explored for relationship to age, race, sex, occupational classification, self-health assessment, and physical functional ratings.

Methods and Results

The study included a biracial group of 180 community volunteers 60–94 years old (median age, 72). . . . The variables to be studied were obtained in the course of the second longitudinal series in the interdisciplinary geriatrics research program at the Duke University Medical Center.

*Questions and Responses*

During the social history interview, exploration was made of the extent of the subject's concern about and planning for a possible prolonged illness in the future (defined as one "that would keep you in bed for a long time or prevent you from getting around much"). Table 10–7 gives the frequency

Table 10–7. "*How concerned (or worried) do you feel about a long illness which you might have?*" (*N = 180*).

| Reply | Number | Percentage |
| --- | --- | --- |
| No concern | 91 | 50 |
| Moderately concerned | 61 | 34 |
| Very concerned | 28 | 16 |

distribution of the replies to the question, "How concerned (or worried) do you feel about a long illness which you might have?"

The responses usually indicated that a long disabling illness would not come as a surprise since friends or relatives had had such experiences. Many incidental comments were made concerning the dread of a long illness or of complete physical dependency upon others. There was also the common feeling that an early death was preferable by far to a lingering incapacitating illness. However, only 16 percent of the subjects stated directly that they were *very* concerned that they might have a long illness; of these 28 subjects, 18 were women and 10 were men. This bears out the observation that women in general tend to express more concern about their health than do men (Von Mering & Weniger, 1959; Peterson & Peterson, 1960). It is noteworthy that 50 percent of all the subjects declared that they had *no* concern over the possibility of such a long illness.

To the next question—"In the event of a long-term illness, have you made plans of any kind (i.e., financial, or for housing or nursing care)?" —25 percent said that they had no plans of any kind, and 64 percent indicated that some financial plans had been undertaken (Table 10–8).

Table 10–8. *"In the event of a long-term illness, have you made plans of any kind?"* (*N = 180*).

| Reply | Number | Percentage |
|---|---|---|
| None | 45 | 25 |
| Financial planning only | 115 | 64 |
| Specific plans (housing, nursing care, etc.) | 15 | 8 |
| Other | 5 | 3 |

However, this did not mean that the latter 115 persons had made specific provision in case of chronic illness. Actual planning was vague in many instances, the subjects saying they believed (or sometimes simply hoped) they would be able to cope financially with such a contingency by means of current income, usually from multiple sources such as pensions, social security benefits, savings, insurance, and/or assistance from relatives. Although worry was often expressed about the adequacy of income to meet the great expense of illness over and above ordinary living costs, the regularity and dependability of pension payments or of social security payments, although limited, seemed to furnish to most of the subjects some "peace of mind." Acute anxiety over the financial aspects of chronic illness was expressed by relatively few of the total group. Forty percent of those who had hospital expenses in the previous two years had had some form of health insurance to defray at least part of these expenses.

More specific planning was explored with the question, "How would you manage at home in the event of a long illness?" (Table 10–9). Only 26

Table 10–9. *"How would you manage at home in the event of a long illness?" (N = 180).*

| Reply | Number | Percentage |
|---|---|---|
| Not applicable; would need to move | 46 | 26 |
| Spouse would take over | 59 | 33 |
| Other relative would take over in subject's home | 26 | 14 |
| Hire help to come in | 49 | 27 |

percent of the group anticipated having to make other housing arrangements (e.g., county home, nursing home). The remaining 74 percent thought that, with the assistance of the spouse, other relatives, or hired help, they would not have to move. The strong desire to remain at home was often expressed, although frequently qualified by the recognition that the family might not be able to cope physically, emotionally, or financially with a bedridden patient for an extended period of time. Subjects at present living alone or with a spouse in poor health were usually certain that in case of long illness a change in living arrangements would have to be made.

On the assumption that the subject's present state of health, both subjective and objective, might affect the degree of anxiety regarding the prospect of a future illness, a self-health rating was obtained in addition to the findings of the physical examination by a physician. To the question, "How would you rate your health at the present time?" (Table 10–10), 30

Table 10–10. *"How would you rate your health at the present time?" (N = 180).*

| Reply | Number | Percentage |
|---|---|---|
| Very poor | 4 | 2 |
| Poor | 12 | 7 |
| Fair or "Fair for my age" | 38 | 21 |
| Good or "Good for my age" | 90 | 50 |
| Excellent or "Excellent for my age" | 36 | 20 |

percent of the panel subjects responded "poor" or "fair" and 70 percent responded "good" or "excellent." These self-health evaluations were found to be: (*a*) objectively realistic according to the rating of the examining physician, and (*b*) stable over a period of time as compared with the responses to the same question some three years earlier (Heyman & Jeffers, 1963).

## Objective Ratings

The examining physician's objective rating was obtained by converting the results of a series of medical examinations to a score on a physical functional rating scale (PFR). This scale, modified and adapted by the Duke University geriatrics research program (Dovenmuehle, Busse, & Newman, 1961) from that in use by the United States Army and Veterans Administration, rated the capacity of the subject to function effectively in *daily living*. The comprehensive series of clinical examinations and laboratory studies included: a medical history; physical, neurologic, ophthalmologic, and dermatologic examinations; an audiogram, an electroencephalogram, an electrocardiogram, and a ballistocardiogram; a chest roentgenogram; and laboratory determinations on blood (including cholesterol levels) and urine.

It will be noted in Table 10–11 that for about two-thirds (66.2

Table 10–11. *Physical functional rating* ($N = 180$).

| Physical status | Number | Percentage |
|---|---|---|
| No diseases or limitation | 5 | 2.8 |
| Diseases present; no limitation of social or industrial function | 57 | 31.7 |
| Limitation, 20 percent or less | 57 | 31.7 |
| Limitation, 21–50 percent | 42 | 23.3 |
| Limitation, 51–80 percent | 16 | 8.9 |
| Limitation, over 80 percent | 3 | 1.6 |

percent) of the total group there was no limitation of social or industrial function as measured by the PFR. Eighty-six percent of all subjects reported that they had had to spend few or no days in bed during the previous year.

## Analysis

The association of subjective and objective health evaluations with the variables of the extent of concern and the extent of planning for chronic illness was analyzed by the chi-square technique (Table 10–12). With regard to the self-health rating item, those subjects who evaluated their present health as poor exhibited only a tendency ($p < .10$) toward greater concern than did those who assessed their health as good. Otherwise there

Table 10–12. *Factors analyzed for association with concern and planning for long-term illness (N = 180).*

| | Level of significance (chi-square) | |
| --- | --- | --- |
| Factor | Concern | Planning |
| Self-health rating | ns | ns |
| Physical functional rating | ns | ns |
| Occupational classification | ns | ns |
| Age | ns | ns |
| Race | ns | ns |
| Sex | ns | .05 |

was no significant relationship between concern and planning for chronic illness on the one hand and subjective or objective health evaluations on the other.

Furthermore, there were no statistically significant differences regarding the degree of concern or of planning for long-term illness between: (*a*) manual and nonmanual occupational groups, (*b*) younger and older age groups, (*c*) Negroes and whites, or (*d*) males and females, *except* that in the last category there was a tendency ($p < .05$) for more men than women to indicate some financial planning.

In an analysis not described here, the relationship of concern to planning was examined, since the degree of concern over a long illness might reasonably be expected to be reflected in planning *for* such illness. However, it was found that there were no statistically significant differences in the extent of planning (financially or otherwise) between persons who expressed little or no concern over a long illness and those who expressed some or even great concern.

Discussion

How is this lack of expressed concern and planning for possible chronic illness to be interpreted on the part of those persons belonging to the age group in which such illness is most prevalent? Questions on the inventory (Table 10–13) yielded additional material: 44 percent of the subjects said they were not concerned about their present health; half of the total group stated that health troubles did not interfere with the activities in which they currently were most interested; a substantial number (77 percent) believed themselves to be in better health than their contemporaries; 86 percent had had to spend few or no days in bed within the previous two years; and 47

Table 10–13. *Selected health-related items* ($N = 180$).

| Item | Number | Percentage |
|---|---|---|
| PFR—"20 percent or less disability" | 119 | 66 |
| Self-health concern ("not concerned") | 79 | 44 |
| Health did not interfere with activities | 91 | 50 |
| Self-health better compared to health of others in same age group | 139 | 77 |
| Days in bed within previous two years ("none or few") | 155 | 86 |
| Age-group feeling ("young" or "middle-aged") | 85 | 47 |

percent classified themselves as "young" or "middle-aged" (instead of "elderly," "old," or "aged").

In spite of these rather optimistic attitudes toward their own present health, many of the subjects, according to the impression of the two interviewers, reacted quite emotionally when faced with a direct question about the possibility of a future illness. Often they became tearful and hesitant. Yet 50 percent of the subjects, when questioned, denied that they had any concern over a possible future illness, and only 15 percent admitted that they were extremely concerned. When these replies were explored for a relationship to objective health status (PFR), it was noted that, with two exceptions, the persons with the most deteriorated health were not the most anxious. The 28 persons expressing the greatest degree of concern were in relatively good health as measured by PFR, whereas the 3 in poorest health (again by PFR rating) were among those "not very concerned." Is it that the persons in good health felt more free to admit concern, whereas for those in poor health the question exposed a possibility too uncomfortable to face? Further studies of denial, the "sick role," hypochondriasis, and depression are currently under investigation by other members of the Duke geriatrics research staff. It is recognized that wide generalizations cannot be drawn from the findings on this group of subjects because of the necessary exclusion of those who were bedridden or too ill to participate.

Another possible explanation for the lack of expressed concern might be the presence of certain environmental factors which may have served to minimize anxiety. These subjects had, in fact, considerable security in three important areas—social, financial, and domestic—and it is quite possible that this might have had at least some bearing on the degree of concern about the future (Table 10–14).

As to living arrangements, 62 percent of the subjects were married and living with a spouse, and 88 percent were living in their own homes, two-thirds having resided in the same location for a decade or longer. Close

Table 10–14. *Socioeconomic factors* ($N = 180$).

| Factor | Number | Percentage |
| --- | --- | --- |
| Married and living with spouse | 111 | 62 |
| Living in own home | 158 | 88 |
| Living in same location for previous 10 years or longer | 121 | 67 |
| Did not feel neglected by others | 167 | 93 |
| Sources of income—"multiple" | 135 | 75 |

family ties were indicated by the finding that only 7 percent of the total group said they felt "neglected by family or close relatives." The income of three-fourths of the subjects came from two or more sources, such as social security or public assistance benefits, pensions from former employment, help from relatives, rentals, or other investments.

Other studies at Duke have shown the important role of religion in the lives of older persons in this southern community (Jeffers, Nichols, & Eisdorfer, 1961; Jeffers & Nichols, 1961). Frequent expressions of confidence in the "will of the Lord" indicate strong religious feeling and an acceptance of whatever the future may hold. Furthermore, in the Piedmont region of North Carolina, which is predominantly rural–small town in nature, there appears to be a lifetime pattern of stability which reflects less tension and fewer changes than are usually found in great urban areas. The more extensive social mobility in large cities doubtless infuses the thought of illness with an uncertainty which is less prevalent in the slower, quieter small towns.

We might speculate further that anxiety regarding illness may be much more acute in middle age, since health maintenance and health management are vital for either the breadwinner or the homemaker in a family. Most of the group of elderly persons in this study believed they were quite well in comparison with some of their contemporaries. They looked upon their state of health as a distinct achievement in itself, viewing it with pride and pleasure not unlike that which might be displayed toward a valuable material possession. This increased the impression they gave of postponing as long as possible any consideration of future illness. A frequent comment was, "I'm grateful just to be alive at my age."

Thus we may conclude that in this group of elderly subjects, concern about illness was not significantly related to either objective or subjective health evaluations or to certain demographic items but probably was more influenced by a constellation of various socioeconomic and attitudinal factors. Further investigation will be needed to identify such factors with more certainty.

# Summary

A study of 180 elderly ambulatory subjects (median age, 72) in a southern small-town area was made to ascertain the extent of their concern and planning for chronic illness in the future. Although they were aware of the possibility of their incurring such an illness, only 15 percent stated that they were very much concerned about it, and 50 percent expressed no concern at all. Any planning undertaken for future illness was chiefly in the area of adequate financial provision (64 percent), with dependence on more than one source of income.

Although the mechanism of denial may have been present, the lack of expressed concern over long-term illness appeared to be based chiefly on the security these elderly persons found in family life, religion, a stable environment, financial resources, and their relative good health at the time of the study.

# References

Bortz, E. L. The challenge of chronic illness. In Committee on Medical Care and Teaching (Ed.). *Readings in medical care.* Chapel Hill, N.C.: University of North Carolina Press, 1958.

Burgess, E. W. (Ed.). *Aging in Western societies.* Chicago: University of Chicago Press, 1960.

Dovenmuehle, R. H., Busse, E. W., and Newman, E. G. Physical problems of older people. *Journal of American Geriatrics Society,* 9:208–217, March, 1961.

Heyman, D., and Jeffers, F. Effect of time lapse on consistency of self and medical evaluations of health of elderly persons. *Journal of Gerontology,* 18:160–164, April, 1963.

Jeffers, F., and Nichols, C. The relationship of activities and attitudes to physical well-being in older people. *Journal of Gerontology,* 16:67–70, January, 1961.

Jeffers, F., Nichols, C., and Eisdorfer, C. Attitudes of older persons toward death: A preliminary study. *Journal of Gerontology,* 16:53–56, January, 1961. Also in Tibbits, C., and Donahue, W. (Eds.), *Social and psychological aspects of aging.* New York: Columbia University Press, 1962.

Lipman, A. Health insecurity of the aged. *Gerontologist,* 2:99–101, 1962.

Parrott, G. St. J. The problem of chronic disease. *Psychosomatic Medicine,* 7:22–27, January, 1945.

Peterson, J. S., and Peterson, V. J. The health of the aging. In Burgess, E. W. (Ed.), *Aging in Western societies.* Chicago: University of Chicago Press, 1960.

United States Department of Health, Education, and Welfare. The aging population: National and state trends, 1950–60–70. *Aging,* 91:12–17, May, 1962.

United States Senate. Basic facts on the health and economic status of older Americans. A Staff Report to the Special Committee on Aging, United States Senate. Washington: Government Printing Office, 1961. (a)

United States Senate. Health and economic conditions of the American aged. Prepared for the use of the Special Committee on Aging, United States Senate. Washington: United States Government Printing Office, 1961. (b)

Von Mering, O., and Weniger, F. L. Social-cultural background of the aging individual. In Birren, J. (Ed.), *Handbook of aging and the individual.* Chicago: University of Chicago Press, 1959.

# Disinclination to Venture Response versus Cautiousness in Responding: Age Differences*  *Jack Botwinick*

## Introduction

A distinction may be made between a pattern of cautiousness which takes the form of a reluctance to make decisions or to take action and a pattern of cautiousness which takes the form of doing these things, but in a manner which minimizes risk even if it means minimizing potential gain. Although future research may demonstrate that these two patterns are correlated and stem from a common base, for the present at least, it may be useful to differentiate between a person who avoids problems and a person who is cautious in his solutions of them.

This differentiation was implicit in the conclusions of a recent study (Botwinick, 1966) in which young and elderly adults were compared in their decisions involving risk. That study replicated with subjects from central North Carolina that which Wallach and Kogan (1961) reported with subjects from eastern Massachusetts, viz., elderly adults were more cautious in their decisions than were young adults. The proposition under test in the present study is that this cautiousness of the elderly is more a matter of a reluctance to be involved with problems of risk than of cautiousness in the decision process. The test of this proposition was made by repeating the previous study (Botwinick, 1966), as much as it was practical to do so, except for eliminating from the arena of choice an option to eschew a risky course altogether. Each subject was obliged to make a decision in which some risk was unavoidable.

## Method

### Subjects

The subjects were 126 white men and women volunteers, selected on the basis of education and general health criteria. All subjects had at least one year of college training, or its equivalent, and none had apparent incapacitating illnesses; all were well enough to come to the laboratory and to carry out the instructions of the procedure. Subjects were men and women of two age and two education subgroups (13–15 years of formal

* Reprinted by permission from the *Journal of Genetic Psychology*, 115:55–62, 1969.

schooling, and 16 years and over). The elderly subjects were aged 65 to 88 years (the mean was middle seventies in each of the sex-education sub-groups). The younger subjects were aged 18 to 27 (the mean was 19–20 for men and women of 13–15 years education and 23–24 years for the graduates). In the elderly group there were 7 men and 13 women of 13–15 years of schooling and 10 men and 8 women with 16 or more years of education. The comparable numbers of the younger group were 27 and 35, 13 and 13. Of the 17 aged male and 21 aged female subjects, 7 and 9, respectively, served in the earlier study (Botwinick, 1966).

All except 4 elderly subjects were community residents. These 4 were in an old peoples' home, but they were not regarded as comprising a different sample because they traveled or walked to the laboratory and did not require custodial care. The younger subjects were comprised of under-graduate and graduate students and employees of Duke University.

### Procedure

A questionnaire of 24 "life situations" was presented to each subject: 12 of these situations were developed by Wallach and Kogan (1961), and each involves a central character who is a young adult facing problems typical of young people. Twelve situations were developed by Botwinick (1966), each involving an aged central character facing problems more unique to the aged. Each of the 24 central characters considered two alternatives—a rewarding but risky course of action and a less rewarding but safer one. The subject had to make a choice for the central character by indicating the probability or likelihood of success that was judged sufficient to decide upon the risky course. To each of the 24 "life situations," five alternative probabilities were presented from which the subject had to choose one. The five alternatives were 1 chance in 10 that the risky course would succeed, 3 chances in 10, 5 in 10, 7 and 9 in 10. Thus each subject was obliged to decide upon a risky course even if he insisted that the risk be small. The option available in the earlier study (Botwinick, 1966), not to risk a new course of action regardless of the probabilities (scored as 10 chances in 10), was not available here.

### Assumptions and Analyses

Using the same "measuring instrument" twice, elderly subjects were found more cautious than younger subjects (Wallach & Kogan, 1961; Botwinick, 1966). Since many elderly subjects in at least the more recent of these two studies exercised an option to not choose risky alternatives regardless of the probabilities (scored 10 in 10), it is assumed that when in the present study this option is not provided, a failure to demonstrate statistically significant age differences in scores of cautiousness would reflect, not negative results demanding equivalent conclusions, but rather, a basis for drawing positive conclusions. The results of the present study in comparison with the two previous studies would provide information regarding the role of the option scored as 10; i.e., the option not to choose the risky course regardless of the probabilities. A failure to demonstrate age differences without this option, when twice before age differences were demonstrated with it, would be taken as evidence of an interest in avoiding risky situations rather than a cautiousness as such.

The methods of analysis in this study were similar to those used in the previous study (Botwinick, 1966). In addition to analyzing for the overall difference between age groups in their relative levels of cautiousness, an analysis was made of the interaction between age of the subjects and the age of the central characters portrayed in the "life situations." This analysis should indicate whether needs, values, and attitudes as reflected by the age and circumstance of the central characters would differentially affect the decision processes of the old and young. In addition, this interaction was studied in relation to the sex of the subject and in relation to level of education (13–15 versus 16 and over years of schooling).

The data were examined with two types of variance analyses. In one, each subject was represented by 24 scores, one for each of the 24 situations. Also, separate analyses were carried out for the 12 situations of the young central characters and the 12 situations of the old central characters. In the second type of variance analysis, each subject was represented by 2 scores, each the mean of one set of 12 situations. The variations of "life situations" are presented as "Treatments" in Table 10–15. The unweighted means approach for unequal cell frequencies was used (Winer, 1962, pp. 222–224).

Results

The results were unequivocal: in the present study, elderly subjects were not more cautious than younger adults. Table 10–15 shows that the two age groups were not significantly different ($p > .05$). It is always tenuous to draw positive conclusions from such negative results, even when the necessary assumptions and hypotheses were established beforehand. It is therefore of special interest that when an analysis of variance of the type reported in Table 10–15 was carried out with the 12 "life situations" of young central characters, a statistically significant age difference was found ($p < .05$), but in the opposite direction! That is, the young adult subjects were more, not less, cautious than the elderly subjects. The actual mean

Table 10–15. *Analyses of variances of scores of cautiousness.*

| Source | 24 situations | | | 2 sets of 12 situations | | |
|---|---|---|---|---|---|---|
| | *df* | Mean square | *F* | *df* | Mean square | *F* |
| Between subjects | 125 | 44.39 | | 125 | 1.43 | |
| Age (A) | 1 | 27.23 | 0.59 | 1 | 3.38 | 2.42 |
| Sex (S) | 1 | 50.20 | 1.10 | 1 | 3.71 | 2.66 |
| Education (E) | 1 | 24.86 | 0.54 | 1 | 1.56 | 1.12 |
| A × S | 1 | 29.08 | 0.64 | 1 | 3.43 | 2.46 |
| A × E | 1 | 4.86 | 0.11 | 1 | 0.38 | 0.28 |
| S × E | 1 | 0.00 | 0.00 | 1 | 0.00 | 0.00 |
| A × S × E | 1 | 9.94 | 0.22 | 1 | 1.08 | 0.77 |
| Error | 118 | 45.79 | | 118 | 1.40 | |
| Within subjects | 2898 | 0.61 | 0.11 | 126 | 0.66 | 1.04 |
| Treatments (T) | 23 | 35.37 | 6.24[b] | 1 | 0.26 | 0.42 |
| A × T | 23 | 32.06 | 5.64[b] | 1 | 2.52 | 3.96[a] |
| S × T | 23 | 6.35 | 1.12 | 1 | 0.89 | 1.40 |
| E × T | 23 | 5.68 | 1.00 | 1 | 0.24 | 0.38 |
| A × S × T | 23 | 6.78 | 1.20 | 1 | 2.08 | 3.27 |
| A × E × T | 23 | 4.64 | 0.82 | 1 | 0.00 | 0.00 |
| S × E × T | 23 | 5.74 | 1.01 | 1 | 0.83 | 1.30 |
| A × S × E × T | 23 | 5.87 | 1.03 | 1 | 1.66 | 2.61 |
| Error | 2714 | 5.67 | | 118 | 0.64 | |
| Total | 3023 | 4.40 | | 251 | 1.04 | |

Note.—The *F* ratio may not equal exactly the ratio of the respective mean square to the error term due to rounding off to two decimal places. Differences are only in the decimals.
[a] Significant at .05 level.
[b] Significant at .01 level.

difference, however, was small (5.31 versus 4.85). A comparable analysis of variance of the 12 situations in which the central characters were aged showed no significant age difference ($p > .05$).

It may be seen in Table 10–15 that there was a statistically significant interaction between age and the "life situations" (Treatments) in both the 24 situations analysis ($p < .01$) and the 2 sets of 12 situations analysis ($p < .05$). The conclusion from these analyses is the same as that in the previous study (Botwinick, 1966), i.e., the interaction between age of the subject and the 24 different "life situations" is accounted for, at least in part, by the significant interaction between the ages of the subjects and the ages of central characters facing the problems of the aged. Again, the mean differences were very small. The mean of young subjects for the situations of young and aged central characters, respectively, were 5.30 and 5.00; for elderly subjects, 4.80 and 4.96, respectively.

For each of the 24 "life situations," *t* tests of age differences were made by grouping all elderly subjects together and grouping all younger subjects together (disregarding disproportionate subgroup numbers). Of the 12 situations with young central characters, the younger subjects were more cautious in their response in 4 of them ($p < .01$); the older subjects were more cautious in 1 ($p < .01$). Of the 12 situations with aged central characters, the elderly subjects were more cautious in 4 ($p < .05–.01$), and the younger subjects were more cautious in 3 ($p = .05–.01$). These results explain further the statistically significant interaction between age of subject and Treatments in Table 10–15.

Still another analysis was carried out to test the proposition that when a decision of risk is unavoidable, older people are not more cautious than

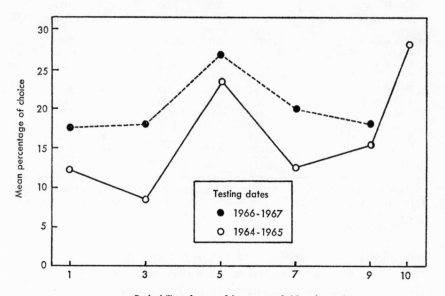

Probability of successful outcome of risky alternative

Figure 10–1. *A comparison of responses in two questionnaire contexts. The same questionnaire of 24 "life situations," with one difference, was presented to 21 elderly subjects on two occasions, 23–40 months apart. The one difference involved the number of alternatives presented for each situation. In the present study five alternatives were presented, among which it was necessary to choose one; in the earlier study six were presented. The alternatives were ordered on the abscissa from lesser to greater cautiousness. Alternative 1 represents a decision to follow a course of action which has a low likelihood of success. There are rewards if it does succeed, but there are negative consequences if it does not. Alternative 9 is to follow this course only if there is a high likelihood of its success. Alternative 10, presented only in the earlier study, was not to follow the risky course regardless of the probabilities.*

younger people. This analysis involved a longitudinal comparison. It was indicated that 7 elderly men and 9 elderly women were subjects in both the previous (Botwinick, 1966) and present studies. In addition, five subjects with 7–12 years of education were tested in both studies.[1] The time between testings was 23 to 40 months, with a mean of 33.8 and a median of 35. Figure 10–1 shows that in the earlier testing of these 21 subjects, the alternative scored as 10 (not to choose the risky course regardless of the probabilities) was decided upon in about 28 percent of the situations. When this option was unavailable to the subjects in the present study, they did not decide upon number 9 (the next most cautious alternative) but, instead, distributed their decisions more or less normally around the central values. This was the mode of response of the younger subjects both in the present study and in the previous study when the number 10 alternative was available to them.

## Discussion

If the results of the present study are examined in relation to the results of two previous studies (Wallach & Kogan, 1961; Botwinick, 1966) a most clear concept emerges. To the extent that the present data permit generalizations, the results show that when obliged to make decisions involving risk, elderly people are not more cautious than younger adults. They may appear more cautious in that, when given the opportunity, they often avoid the risky possibilities altogether.

Accepting this idea, it may be of interest to speculate as to the underlying mechanisms. Perhaps there is a hint in the conclusion of a study carried out in an entirely different context. Basovitz and Korchin (1957, p. 96) concluded that for the elderly there seems to be "a defensive reluctance to venture response for fear of recognizing their inadequacy." In related fashion, Botwinick, Brinley, and Robbin (1958) suggested that older people may require a higher "confidence level . . . before responding." In still a different context, Eisdorfer (1965) found that elderly subjects scored poorly in a learning task not so much because of incorrect responses but because they often tended not to respond. These errors of

[1] Figure 10–1, which includes the data of these 5 subjects, is very similar to a figure based upon only those 16 subjects with 13 or more years of formal education. These 5 subjects were part of a total of 22 elderly subjects with 7–12 years of education who were given the questionnaire. Age comparisons involving these 22 subjects were not made since young adults of comparable education were not available for testing at the time data were collected. When the 3 education groups of elderly subjects (7–12, 13–15, and 16 and over) were compared in a variance analysis, statistically significant group differences were not found ($p > .05$).

omission, he thought, could be attributed to a high level of anxiety, resulting in a withdrawal from the problem.

Each of these studies is distinguished from the present study in that special abilities or capacities such as learning and perception were measured. In the present study, not abilities, but choice or preference in making decisions was measured. If the general pattern of the aged is to withhold response because of an overriding lack of self-confidence, and fear of failure, even when the situation does not involve a threat to presumed deteriorating abilities, how uncomfortable must life be. . . .

There is some relationship between the present discussion and the theory of "disengagement" as elucidated by Cumming and Henry (1961): with increasing age there is increasing tendency to dissociate oneself from people and activities. The similarity involves withdrawal and inhibition of responses. There is a major difference, however. The notion of "disengagement" suggests that with age there is a loss of interest in life—there is a psychological withdrawal as a counterpart to impending physical death. The notions growing out of the present data, on the other hand, suggest not a loss of interest but a great engagement with the social forces of life. There is confrontation and pain involving self-acceptance and social approval. There is fear and perhaps expectation of failure.

Admittedly, these speculations are several orders of inferences removed from the data of the present study. The data show no special cautiousness on the part of the elderly when decisions involving risk are unavoidable.


## Summary

An examination was made of the proposition that cautious behavior on the part of old people is more a reluctance to be involved with problems of risk than an inclination to seek relatively safe, even if unrewarding, alternatives. This examination was made by comparing decisions within two questionnaire contexts. One context required subjects to commit themselves to risky courses of action in order to improve upon poor situations. Their decisions were simply of the extent of the risks to be taken. The other questionnaire context involved this same requirement but, in addition, included the option to not choose the risky course of action regardless of its likelihood of succeeding.

Elderly subjects tended to choose this option, and younger subjects did not. When, however, this option was unavailable, the elderly subjects did not select the safest, most cautious alternatives; instead, they selected alternatives very similar to those of young adults. This was interpreted as a tendency to avoid decisions of risk rather than a cautiousness in solving problems. The possibility that a lack of self-confidence and a fear or expectancy of failure may underlie this tendency was discussed.


## References

Basovitz, H., and Korchin, S. J. Age differences in the perception of closure. *Journal of Abnormal and Social Psychology*, 54:93–97, 1957.

Botwinick, J. Cautiousness in advanced age. *Journal of Gerontology*, 21:347–353, 1966.

Botwinick, J., Brinley, J. F., and Robbin, J. S. The interaction effects of perceptual difficulty and stimulus exposure time on age differences in speed and accuracy of response. *Gerontologia*, 2:1–10, 1958.

Cumming, E., and Henry, W. *Growing old*. New York: Basic Books, 1961.

Eisdorfer, C. Verbal learning and response time in the aged. *Journal of Genetic Psychology*, 107:15–22, 1965.

Wallach, M. A., and Kogan, N. Aspects of judgment and decision making: Interrelationships and changes with age. *Behavioral Science*, 6:23–36, 1961.

Winer, B. J. *Statistical principles in experimental design*. New York: McGraw-Hill, 1962.

# Chapter 11. Age and Death

This final chapter of reports deals, appropriately, with attitudes toward age and death and includes a report on longevity. Studies of the panelists' concepts of their own age cast doubt on the general applicability of the old saying, "A man is as old as he feels he is." If that saying means that a person's own age concept is independent of his chronological age, then it clearly does not apply to most of these panelists. Although there are a few exceptions, the age concepts were usually related to the actual chronological age. If the saying is interpreted to mean that the age concept is important in determining other attitudes and actions, again the evidence is to the contrary. Most of the variables one might expect to be influenced by the age concept were not significantly related to age concepts. Furthermore, half of the panelists shifted their own age concepts toward older categories, which were presumably more realistic, after having assigned chronological ages to the various age categories.

Similarly, the evidence on attitudes toward death contradicts the ideas that most aged persons are fearful about death or that death attitudes strongly influence the rest of an aged person's life and attitudes. The last two reports indicate that only a small percentage say they are afraid to die and the majority say they think about death rarely or only occasionally and that death thoughts do not affect enjoyment of life. Furthermore, only 6 out of 52 variables tested were found to be significantly related to fear of death. Thus these studies indicate that most aged persons do not have strong fears about death and those few with fears are not strongly affected by such fears.

The final report shows that actuarial predictions about how long a person will live can be improved by about one-third when physical functioning, intelligence, and work satisfaction are taken into account. It also found that while physical functioning was generally the most important of these three variables, intelligence and work satisfaction were more important in some subgroups. The report concludes that among normal aged, maintaining health, mental activities, and satisfying social roles are the most important factors related to longevity.

# Factors in Age Awareness* *Ewald W. Busse, Frances C. Jeffers, and Walter D. Obrist*

In an examination of the aging process and its meaning to the individual, it has been stated that "the importance of the self-concept in aging cannot be overestimated" (Greenleigh, 1953). We believe that *age-concept*, as a fundamental component of the self-concept, should also be emphasized in a study of the process of aging. This is another way of stating that "a man is as old as he feels he is." Accordingly, we have explored some of the factors which might be associated with the subjective feeling of age awareness. The factors studied fell in the categories of chronological age, health, environment, intelligence, race, and attitudes. Investigation has shown us that some of these variables are significantly related to awareness of age, and it is hoped that further study of these, as well as of other factors, will contribute to a better understanding of self-concept as an important variable in the aging process.

## Methodology

The subjects in the present study were 134 white and 28 Negro persons, all 60 years of age or older, who volunteered to come in for a two-day series of physical, psychological, psychiatric, and social evaluation on the Geriatrics Research Project at Duke University School of Medicine. . . .

Statistical treatment of the data was confined to the larger white group. Because of the small size of the Negro sample, it was used only for cross-cultural comparisons.

## Age Awareness

The principal variable investigated was age awareness, that is, how old the individual feels himself to be. This was determined by the subject's placing himself in an age category in response to the question, "Do you feel that you are now—

* Reprinted by permission from the *Proceedings of the Fourth Congress of the International Association of Gerontology*, 349–357, 1957.

Table 11–1. *Subjects included in study on age awareness.*

Characteristics: 60 years of age or older
                Nonhospitalized community volunteers
                Functioning at various levels in family and/or community life.

| | |
|---|---:|
| I. White group | |
|   a. Socioeconomic status: | |
|     1. Mostly lower middle class and below, rural and urban | 67 |
|     2. Professional and upper-level business group, usually urban | 67 |
|                         Total | 134 |
|   b. Age range = 60–94. Median age = 70. | |
| II. Negro group | |
|   a. Socioeconomic status: All subjects in 1 as above | 28 |
|   b. Age range = 60–89. Median age = 73. | |
|                         Total | 162 |

Table 11–2. *Factors influencing age awareness.*

| | Confidence level of chi-square | |
|---|---|---|
| | Not matched | Matched for age |
| I. Factors which were found to influence age awareness | | |
| Chronological age | .01 | |
| Race | | .01 |
| Feeling of health | | .01 |
| II. Factors which were found not to influence age awareness | | |
| Sex | | ns |
| Health | | |
|   Physical status (based on functional capacity) | .10 | |
|   Depression | ns | |
|   Sexual adjustment | ns | |
|   Personal adjustment | ns | |
| IQ (WAIS adjusted for age) | ns | |
| Environment | | |
|   Socioeconomic level | | ns |
|   Marital status and living arrangements | .01 | ns |
|   Change in location since age 55 | ns | |
| Present activities | | |
|   Vocational and avocational status | .02 | ns |
|   Religious activity | .02 | ns |
| Attitudes | | |
|   Feeling of permanent financial security | ns | |
|   Change in religious interests | ns | |
|   Fear of death | ns | |
|   Feeling toward family | ns | |
|   Feeling of happiness | .10 | |
| Advantages-disadvantages of aging | ns | |
| Chronological age at which he feels aging began | ns | |

A young adult person . . . . . . . . . . . . . ?
A middle-aged person . . . . . . . . . . . . . ?
An elderly person   . . . . . . . . . . . . ?
An old person   . . . . . . . . . . . . ?
An aged person   . . . . . . . . . . . . ?"

The question was asked in the course of securing a detailed social history from the older person and occurred during the latter third of the history, after one or two hours of interviewing. By this time it was felt that sufficient rapport had been secured so that the older person was answering questions freely.

A statistical study was made of some of the factors that might be related to age awareness. Twenty-one variables were analyzed, using the chi-square technique to test the probability of relationship. Three of these factors were found to be significantly related, while 18 appeared not to be significantly related to age awareness. Some of the latter showed trends toward significance, and it is felt that future exploration of these should be made by refining the methodology and increasing the size of the sample (Table 11–2).

Chronological Age and Sex

Chronological age was found to be significantly related to age feeling. The older a person actually is, the more likely he is to think of himself as belonging to an older age group (Table 11–3).

Table 11–3. *Test for chronological age differences in age feeling.*

| Chronological age | Age feeling | | | |
| --- | --- | --- | --- | --- |
| | Young and middle-aged | Elderly | Old or aged | Total |
| I. White group[a] | | | | |
| 60–64 | 18 | 7 | 1 | 26 |
| 65–69 | 22 | 15 | 3 | 40 |
| 70–74 | 11 | 18 | 10 | 39 |
| 75+ | 7 | 12 | 10 | 29 |
| Total | 58 | 52 | 24 | 134 |
| II. Negro group[b] | | | | |
| 60–64 | 1 | 1 | 0 | 2 |
| 65–69 | 1 | 1 | 6 | 8 |
| 70–74 | 0 | 4 | 5 | 9 |
| 75+ | 3 | 3 | 3 | 9 |
| Total | 5 | 9 | 14 | 28 |

[a] Significant at .01 level of confidence.
[b] Too small a group for statistical tests.

Burgess has noted that people in their sixties and seventies tend to regard themselves as middle-aged or elderly and not to think of themselves as old or aged. (*Old Age in the Modern World,* 1954). Our findings for the white group are in agreement with his, as shown in Table 11–3.

One of the stereotypes in our culture is that women tend to understate their age, since a high premium is placed upon the younger female. However, in this study, when the sexes were matched for chronological age, there was no appreciable difference in age feeling—that is, the women in our study did not take this opportunity to place themselves in a younger age group.

Socioeconomic Level

As has been shown in Table 11–1, the 134 white subjects had been divided equally between two socioeconomic levels: (*a*) those belonging mostly to the lower-middle and lower classes, and (*b*) those subjects who were in the upper business and professional classes. These two levels were matched for chronological age and tested for differences in age feeling. No significant trends were obtained.

Race

Table 11–4 shows that Negroes tend to think of themselves as older for their chronological age than do members of the white race. A chi-square

Table 11–4. *Test for differences between races in age feeling (matched for age).*

|  | Young or middle-aged | Elderly | Old or aged | Total |
|---|---|---|---|---|
| Total white group | 42 | 42 | 20 | 104 |
| Negro group | 4 | 9 | 13 | 26 |
|  |  |  | Total | 130 |

Note.—Significant at .01 level of confidence.

test of this trend was performed, matching the races for chronological age. There was a statistically reliable difference in the direction of the Negroes tending to consider themselves older.

We are perhaps not justified in concluding that there is a racial difference per se with respect to age feeling, since in the sampling, the white group includes many professional and upper-level business people, which was not the case for the Negro group. However, when the white group was confined to a socioeconomic level comparable to the Negro subjects, there was still a significant difference at the .05 level of confidence. In addition, a test for differences in age feeling between socioeconomic levels in the white group was negative, making it unlikely that this variable can account for the racial difference.

In exploring factors which might be associated with age feeling, four of them were tested for racial differences without reference to age feeling. These all gave significant chi-squares.

A glance at the factors listed in Table 11–5 may explain in part why the

Table 11–5. *Factors showing racial differences in old people— without references to age feeling (not matched for age).*

|  | Confidence level of chi-square |
|---|---|
| 1. Physical status (based on functional capacity) | .02 |
| 2. Feeling of financial security | .01 |
| 3. Listing of advantages-disadvantages of aging | .05 |
| 4. Change in religious interest | .02 |

Negro tends to think of himself as older than his white counterpart. An additional factor may be that of life expectancy. A comparison in life expectancy of the white and Negro populations in North Carolina is shown in Table 11–6.

When physical status was evaluated directly . . . it was found that the older Negro subjects were actually in poorer health than the white subjects (Table 11–7). Considering the factors of lower longevity, poorer physical

Table 11–6. *Longevity in North Carolina (based on three-year study 1949–1951).*

| At beginning of year of age | Number living of 100,000 born alive | | | |
|---|---|---|---|---|
|  | White males | White females | Nonwhite males | Nonwhite females |
| 60 | 73,293 | 84,883 | 53,557 | 61,024 |
| 65 | 63,802 | 78,843 | 43,169 | 51,270 |
| 70 | 52,829 | 70,202 | 33,651 | 41,663 |
| 75 | 39,472 | 56,646 | 25,252 | 37,844 |
| 80 | 25,295 | 40,127 | 17,625 | 25,076 |
| 85 | 13,143 | 23,480 | 11,208 | 18,064 |
| 90 | 4,519 | 10,141 | 5,462 | 10,726 |

Table 11-7. *Test for racial differences in regard to physical status (not matched for age).*

|  | 0 | 1 | 2 | 3, 4, 5 | Total |
|---|---|---|---|---|---|
| White group | 33 | 45 | 31 | 25 | 134 |
| Negro group | 0 | 9 | 0 | 10 | 28 |
|  |  |  |  | Total | 162 |

Note.—Significant at .02 level of confidence.

status, and greater feeling of financial insecurity (Table 11–5), it is apparent that the Negro is faced with three basic threats. This may account for his regarding himself as older than does his white contemporary.

However, the paradox occurs that having attained this older age and in spite of the threats mentioned, the Negro probably feels grateful for the added years and thus lists more advantages to aging than does the older white person (significant at the .05 level). Further study is indicated with respect to the prestige and privileges attached to aging in the Negro culture.

Another interesting racial difference between the older subjects is in regard to the change in religious interest. Compared with 65 percent of the white group who showed increased religious interest with aging, 93 percent of the Negroes indicated increased interest. This difference was significant at the .02 level. . . .

Physical Evaluation and Feeling toward Health

It is often conjectured, both by older people and the rest of the population, that a person's health usually determines how old he feels. If this is true, physical status in terms of present functional capacity might well be one of the important factors in awareness of age.

Our older subjects were given an extensive battery of examinations, including many in the physical and physiological areas. Based on these results, an overall rating scale for physical status in terms of functional capacity was constructed. . . .

When the ratings for physical evaluation based on functional capacity were tested in relation to age feeling, a trend only was obtained (Table 11–8).

However, the picture was quite different when the older individual's attitude toward health was plotted against age feeling. The subject's attitude toward health had been determined by his answers on the inventory, Your Activities and Attitudes (Havighurst & Albrecht, 1953), which is part of our social history. The findings on this test (when matched for age)

Table 11–8. *Test for relation of physical status to age feeling (not matched for age).*

| | Young and middle-aged | Elderly | Old or aged | Total |
|---|---|---|---|---|
| I. White group[a] | | | | |
| 0. No pathology | 19 | 11 | 3 | 33 |
| 1. Pathology, no disability | 18 | 17 | 10 | 45 |
| 2. Pathology, 20 percent disability (mild) | 14 | 16 | 1 | 31 |
| 3. 4. 5. } Pathology, 20 percent or more disability | 7 | 8 | 10 | 25 |
| | | | Total | 134 |
| II. Negro group[b] | | | | |
| 0. No pathology | 0 | 0 | 0 | 0 |
| 1. Pathology, no disability | 3 | 4 | 2 | 9 |
| 2. Pathology, 20 percent disability (mild) | 1 | 2 | 6 | 9 |
| 3. 4. 5. } Pathology, 20 percent or more disability | 1 | 3 | 6 | 10 |
| | | | Total | 28 |

[a] A trend only—not statistically significant—.10 level of confidence.
[b] Too small a group for statistical tests.

revealed that the older person's feeling toward his health was significantly related to age awareness—that is, the poorer he feels his health to be the older he tends to consider himself (Table 11–9).

The above results seem to indicate that a person's awareness of age depends more upon psychological than upon physiological factors. These two factors are probably independent, as suggested by the finding that health feelings show only a chance relation to actual physical status. The latter is consistent with the observations of our research staff in a separate study on hypochondriasis (Busse, Barnes, & Dovenmuehle, 1956).

Other factors were explored in the area of health, intelligence, environ-

Table 11–9. *Test for relation of feeling of health to feelings of age (matched for age).*

| White group | Young and middle-aged | Elderly | Old or aged | Total |
|---|---|---|---|---|
| 4–6 | 32 | 21 | 5 | 58 |
| 0–3 | 16 | 27 | 15 | 58 |

Note.—6 = feeling of excellent health, 0 = very poor health. Significant at the .01 level of confidence.

ment, present activities, and attitudes (see Table 11–2). As stated earlier, none of these variables showed a significant relationship to feeling of age. . . .

## Summary

1. A study was made to discover factors which influence awareness of age in a group of white and Negro nonhospitalized subjects over 60 years old, presently functioning at various levels in family and/or community life.

2. The following variables were found to be significantly related to age awareness: chronological age, race, and feeling of health.

3. Since there was a statistically reliable tendency for the Negroes to consider themselves older than do white persons, further investigation was made of racial differences. The following four factors varied significantly with race: physical status (based on functional capacity), feeling of financial security, listing of advantages-disadvantages of aging, and change in religious interest.

4. Eighteen other variables in the areas of health, intelligence, environment, present activities, and attitudes were studied, but none of these gave statistically significant results, when related to age awareness.

## References

Barnes, R. H., Busse, E. W., and Silverman, A. J. The interrelationship between psychic and physical factors in the production of mental illness in the aged. *North Carolina Medical Journal*, 16:No. 1, January, 1955.

Burgess, E. W. Status and prospects of research in aging: Sociological aspects. Paper presented at the Gerontological Society, September, 1952.

Busse, E. W., Barnes, R. H., and Dovenmuehle, R. H. The incidence and origins of hypochondriacal patterns and psychophysiological reactions in elderly persons. Paper presented at the First Pan-American Congress on Gerontology, Mexico City, September, 1956.

Cavan, R. S., Burgess, E. W., Havighurst, R. J., and Goldhamer, H. *Personal adjustment in old age*. Chicago: Science Research Associated, 1949.

Dovenmuehle, R. H., and Busse, E. W. Studies of the processes of aging: A review of the findings of a multi-disciplinary approach. *British Journal of Physical Medicine*, 19:100–103, 1956.

Friedman, E. L., Busse, E. W., and Cohen, L. D. Level of aspiration and some criteria of adjustment in an aged population (abstract). *American Psychologist*, 11:368, 1956.

Greenleigh, L. F. *Psychological problems of our aging population*. Washington: National Institute of Mental Health, United States Department of Health, Education, and Welfare, 1952.

Greenleigh, L. F. *Changing psychological concepts of aging*. Washington: National Institute of Mental Health, United States Department of Health, Education, and Welfare, 1953.

Havighurst, R. J. The validity of the Chicago Attitude Inventory as a measure of personal adjustment in old age. *Journal of Abnormal and Social Psychology*, 7:24–29, 1951.

Havighurst, R. J., and Albrecht, R. *Older people.* New York: Longmans, 1953.

Jeffers, F. C. A method of evaluation of social attitudes and activities in psychiatric research. Paper presented at the Regional Research Conference, American Psychiatric Association, Chapel Hill, N.C., November, 1955.

Kafta, G. Uber das erlebnis des lebensalters (The experience of age). *Acta Psychologica*, 6:178–189, 1949. Abstracted in *Psychological Abstracts*, 25:1664, 1951.

Mason, E. P. Some correlates of self-judgments of the aged. *Journal of Gerontology*, 9:324–337, 1954.

*Old age in the modern world.* Report of the Third Congress of the International Association of Gerontology, 1954. Edinburgh and London: E. and S. Livingstone, 1955.

Perlin, S. Psychiatric aspects of aging. Paper presented at the American Psychiatric Association, May 16, 1957.

Rethlingshafer, D., Bliss, W. D., and Maag, C. H. (U. E.). The degree to which a person's age acts as an anchor in his judgment of others' ages (abstract). *Florida Psychiatric Association Newsletter*, 2:7, 1957.

Tuckman, J., and Lorge, Z.: Classification of the self as young, middle-aged, or old. *Geriatrics*, 9:534–536, 1954.

Tuckman, J., and Lorge, I. When aging begins and stereotype about aging. *Journal of Gerontology*, 8:489–492, 1933.

Vaughan, C. L., and Reynolds, W. A. Reliability of personal interview data. *Journal of Applied Psychology*, 35:61–63, 1951.

# Measurement of Age Identification*    *Frances C. Jeffers, Carl Eisdorfer, and Ewald W. Busse*

It has been hypothesized (Greenleigh, 1953) that age identification is an important aspect of the self concept particularly relevant in older persons. In a study of an elderly community population in conjunction with the Duke geriatrics research program, Busse, Jeffers, and Obrist (1957) found that age identification was significantly related to chronological age, race, and subjective evaluation of health. They employed the technique of self-age category placement as defined in the Activities and Attitudes Inventory developed by Burgess, Cavan, and Havighurst in 1948. A thorough discussion of this inventory, its purpose, use, reliability, and validity is to be found elsewhere (Cavan, Burgess, Havighurst, & Goldhamer, 1949; Havighurst, 1951; Havighurst & Albrecht, 1953). Continued investigation, including retest evaluation of earlier subjects, has led the investigators at

* Reprinted by permission from the *Journal of Gerontology*, 17:437–439, 1962.

Duke to suspect that for their (older) subjects there might be idiosyncratic differences in the use of terminology relating to advanced age. Accordingly, an exploration of these differences and their possible significance was undertaken.

The purposes of the present investigation are: (*a*) To compare the age order sequence defined by the Duke elderly subjects by means of individual card sorts, with the age order sequence assigned by the Activities and Attitudes Inventory (in which the age category question is included). (*b*) To compare the subjects' responses to the inventory question with those to a similar inquiry an hour later, immediately after the card sort.

## Procedure

### Subjects

The subjects were 168 community volunteers who came to the Duke University Medical Center for a two-day series of comprehensive physical, psychological, and social evaluations. . . .

### Method

On the series of follow-up examinations in the Duke geriatrics research program, the age identification question appearing in the Activities and Attitudes Inventory (Burgess, Cavan, & Havighurst, 1948) was asked of all subjects, i.e., "Do you feel that you are now: Young, Middle-Aged, Elderly, Old, or Aged?"

Approximately an hour later, a card sort and inquiry were employed with each subject. As indicated in Table 11–10, each subject was asked (*a*) to do a card sort of five life periods, (*b*) to assign chronological ages to each of these life periods, and (*c*) to respond to a variation of the inventory self-age identification question.

Data from the card sort were ordered to form a five-point rating system so that each subject's response appears as a number from one to five (with one indicating the earliest period of life and five the last). This is dependent upon his own concept of the sequence of life periods and independent of the word he used in the earlier inventory question or in the inquiry (Table 11–10*c*) after the card sort.

The responses on section *a* of the card sort were studied to determine whether the order of life periods as defined by the Duke elderly subjects was the same as the order assigned in the inventory. To the inventory items were assigned the numbers: young, 1; middle-aged, 2; elderly, 3; old, 4; and aged, 5.

**Table 11–10.** *Card sort and inquiry.*

Examiner: "We have sometimes used certain names for the periods of life we all go through and we don't know exactly which ages correspond to these." (Present 5 cards shuffled randomly with one of the following categories printed on each card: Young, Middle-aged, Elderly, Old, Aged.)

a. "Please arrange these as they should come in order of age of a person." (After subject has made arrangement, interviewer will at once place numbers according to order made in the brackets below. Number 1 is assigned to the earliest period of life, 5 to the most advanced stage.)

b. "What are the years of life for each one of these?" (Point to cards in order the subject has given them.)

Age interval

( ) Young.....................
( ) Middle-aged.................
( ) Elderly......................
( ) Old.........................
( ) Aged.......................

c. "In which of these life periods would you place yourself at the present time?" (Again pointing to cards in order in which the subject has given them.)

( ) Young.....................
( ) Middle-aged.................
( ) Elderly......................
( ) Old.........................
( ) Aged.......................

## Results

Table 11–11 shows that for only 26 percent of the subjects is there agreement between their card sort of the sequence of life periods and the inventory items. Even if the reversal of the last two items were to be admitted as partial agreement, a total of 40 percent of the subjects still show disagreement involving three or more items.

Table 11–12 presents the relationship between the semantic ordering of the three words associated with the later years of life as defined by the

**Table 11–11.** *Consistency of activities and attitudes inventory items[a] with responses on card sort (Table 11–10a) (N = 168).*

|  | Percentage |
|---|---|
| Complete agreement of card sort with inventory items | 26 |
| Reversal of last two items (old and aged) | 34 |
| Changes in order of last three items (elderly, old, and aged) | 34 |
| Other rearrangements of life periods | 6 |

[a] To the inventory items are assigned the numbers: young, 1; middle-aged, 2; elderly, 3; old, 4; and aged, 5.

Table 11–12. *Frequency distribution of word placement order in card sort* (*N = 168*).

|  | Elderly | Old | Aged | Other[a] | Total |
|---|---|---|---|---|---|
| Last word | 33 | 71 | 59 (35%)+ | 5 | 168 |
| Next to last word | 21 | 53 (32%)[b] | 94 | 0 | 168 |
| Third (or middle) word | 101 (60%)[b] | 43 | 15 | 9 | 168 |
| First or second word | 13 | 1 | 0 | — | — |

[a] Inappropriate answer: Young or middle-aged.

[b] Percentage of agreement between subject's card sorts and order assigned by inventory scale.

inventory and the order in which the subjects placed them in the card sort. The inventory defined *elderly*, *old*, and *aged* to indicate increasingly advanced age. Consequently, for agreement with the Activities and Attitudes Inventory order, 168 subjects should have chosen *elderly* as the third or middle term in the aging sequence, *old* as the next to last, and *aged* as the last term. As Table 11–12 indicates, 60 percent of the subjects in this study placed *elderly* as the third term in the sequence, 32 percent agreed with the inventory placement of *old*, and 35 percent used *aged* as the term representative of the most advanced age.

In order to determine the relationship between the subjects' responses to the inventory question and their responses to their own placement of the age categories (*c* on Table 11–10) administered approximately one hour later, these two sets of ratings were compared. To make this comparison, the age placement term used by a subject in the inventory question was given the value assigned this particular term by the subject's (subsequent) card sort. Thus a subject who had labeled himself as *old* would have received a placement rating of four on the inventory order (as determined by Burgess et al., 1948). If, however, he had given *old* as the last (i.e., fifth) position on his own card sort, his rating would be changed to five. If, on the other hand, *old* had been in the third position on his card sort, his rating would be three. In this way the inventory and inquiry (i.e., Table 11–10*c*) responses were compared. Since the inquiry question had been scored directly from the subject's card sort results, it was possible to make direct comparisons between the ratings.

Table 11–13 presents the frequency distribution of the two self-age placement questions. It should be noted that *A* lists the responses to the inventory question on self-age placement according to the Burgess et al. (1948) order; *B* gives the same responses (to the inventory question) redefined according to the age order resulting from the subject's card sort (Table 11–10*a*); and *C* shows the responses to the inquiry in self-age

Table 11–13. *Frequency distribution of self-age placement (N = 168).*

|  | 1 | 2 | 3 | 4 | 5 | Total |
|---|---|---|---|---|---|---|
| A. Inventory question: | | | | | | |
|    Inventory age order[a] | 4 | 76 | 53 | 26 | 10 | 168 |
| B. Inventory question: | | | | | | |
|    Subject's card sort order[b] | 5 | 79 | 49 | 15 | 21 | 168 |
| C. Inquiry question: | | | | | | |
|    Subject's card sort order[c] | 0 | 22 | 73 | 38 | 36 | 168 |

[a] Burgess et al. (1948).   [b] Table 11–10a.   [c] Table 11–10c.

placement (Table 11–10c) which came after the card sort and was defined in terms of that card sort.

It is clear from this frequency that the chief rearrangement in age order sequence between the inventory placement and the card sort was in the sequence of the last two age groups—*old* and *aged*. It is also clear that subjects faced with a situation requiring self-age identification after having assigned ages to the placement categories show a marked shift from younger to older self-age category placement.

Table 11–14 shows the changes of individual subjects from the first

Table 11–14. *Comparison of self-age placements one hour apart (N = 168).*

|  | No change | Total change group | Unit of deviation of self-age placements: | | | | | |
|---|---|---|---|---|---|---|---|---|
|  | | | To older groups | | | | To younger group | |
|  | | | +1 | +2 | +3 | Total | −1 | Total |
| Percentage | 41 | 59 | 35 | 15 | 5 | 55 | 4 | 4 |
| Number | 68 | 100 | 58 | 26 | 9 | 93 | 7 | 7 |

Note.—Inventory question was asked one hour before card sort, and inquiry question immediately after card sort. In this table, age order sequence is defined in terms of the card sort (Table 11–10a).

(inventory) to the second (inquiry) request for self-age categorization. Of the total of 168 subjects, 41 percent retained the same age placement as when questioned an hour earlier, but 59 percent rated themselves in a different category (as defined by their own card sort) and only 4 percent to a younger one. That is, 93 percent of those who shifted did so in the direction of older age placement.

It seems probable that the necessity for the subjects to consider specific chronological periods in relation to age categories (Table 11–10b) had served to remind them of their own aging and hence to adopt a more realistic attitude in regard to the relationship between their chronological age and the age categories. This factor would seem to account for the shift to older age placements in the inquiry than those assigned by the same persons to the inventory question an hour earlier.

## Summary

The relationship of the semantic units of the self-age categorization index in the Activities and Attitudes Inventory developed by Burgess et al. in 1948, now in common usage in gerontological research, was investigated. With the use of a card sort technique, 168 elderly subjects who had earlier answered the Activities and Attitudes Inventory, ordered the sequence of life stages represented by the terms *young, middle-aged, elderly, old,* and *aged.* Differences were found between the card sort ordering of individual subjects and the order defined by Burgess et al. The context of the question also seemed to have a significant effect upon the subjects' responses to their own self-age placement.

It seems to the present authors that it might be more appropriate to attempt a rating of age placement with a scaling device lacking in specific reference to such terms as *elderly, old, aged.* Thus a card sort might be arranged in terms of major life events on a birth-death continuum with present placement of the subject in the sequence of such events; in addition, his attitudes toward the different phases of life could be examined concomitantly.

Finally, this study seems to have demonstrated a lack of consistency in the use of common words such as *young, middle-aged, elderly, old,* and *aged.* Individual and perhaps regional differences in usage seem to make it important to examine subjects' definitions of terms in specific contexts. Since the terms in this study are shown to have idiosyncratic meanings, their use as a scaling device is not yet justified except as validated for each subject in a given population.

## References

Burgess, E. W., Cavan, R. S., and Havighurst, R. J. *Your activities and attitudes.* Chicago: Science Research Associates, 1948.
Busse, E. W., Jeffers, F. C., and Obrist, W. D. Factors in age awareness. *Proceedings of the Fourth Congress of the International Association of Gerontologists,* Merano, Italy, 349–357, 1947.
Cavan, R. S., Burgess, E. W., Havighurst, R. J., and Goldhamer, H. *Personal adjustment in old age.* Chicago: Science Research Associates, 1949.
Greenleigh, L. F. *Changing psychological concepts of aging.* Washington: Public Health Service, National Institute of Mental Health, 1953.

Havighurst, R. J. Validity of the Chicago Attitude Inventory as a measure of personal adjustment in old age. *Journal of Abnormal and Social Psychology*, 46:24–29, 1951.

Havighurst, R. J., and Albrecht, R. *Older people.* New York: Longmans, 1953.

# Attitudes of Older Persons toward Death*   *Frances C. Jeffers, Claude R. Nichols, and Carl Eisdorfer*

Scheler (1953) has said that death is viewed by mankind merely as the end point of aging. It may be hypothesized, however, that attitudes toward death may have a direct effect upon adjustment and upon attitudes toward life. The first step in research undertaken to test this hypothesis will necessarily be an exploration of methods to determine attitudes toward death; the second, an attempt to see what these attitudes may be; and the third, an investigation of the other factors to which these attitudes may be related.

A few earlier studies bear upon these points. Feifel (1956, 1959), for instance, studied white male veterans living at a Veterans Administration Domiciliary. When asked, "What does death mean to you?" 40 percent thought it meant the end of everything; 40 percent expressed religious belief, with a new life expected after death; 10 percent thought death would mean relief and a peaceful sleep; 10 percent did not know. When asked, "What do you think happens to us after we die?" 25 percent said, "When you're dead, you're dead"; 60 percent had some religious orientation, with hope of a hereafter (15 percent of those who thought death was the end now asserted a belief in some kind of hereafter); 10 percent still did not know; and 5 percent thought it would mean a long sound sleep.

In another study (1956) on what age groups least and most fear death, 45 percent of Feifel's same older subjects thought that people most feared death in the seventies and beyond, "Because you're close to it then; you're at the end of your rope"; 15 percent thought the period at which death was most feared was in the forties, and 15 percent saw it as in the twenties. On the other hand, old age was singled out by 35 percent of the older subjects as the time most people least fear death because, "You accept and are resigned to it; you've lived your life." The inference was that certain people fear idleness and uselessness in old age more than they do death.

* Reprinted by permission from the *Journal of Gerontology*, 16:53–56, 1961.

Feifel found that there was a religious outlook evident in those 48 percent who "occasionally" and those 20 percent who "frequently" thought about death as distinguished from the 32 percent who "rarely" thought about it. He also reported that older persons who are religiously inclined give more thought to concepts about death than do those to whom death represents the inexorable end. Do the former master their anxiety about death by thinking of it as a precursor of a new life? It was interesting that 77 percent of this older age group viewed old age as "the end of the line," with only 15 percent seeing it as a time of leisure and contentment. In conclusion, Feifel pointed out that his data pertain to conscious and public attitudes of his respondees more than to the deeper layers of the personality.

Shrutt (1958) compared attitudes toward death of a group of 30 ambulatory aged white female residents in the apartment section of the Home for Aged and Infirm Hebrews in New York with those of 30 similar persons who lived in the larger and more institutionalized Central House of the same home. He used clinical impressions based on a sentence completion test and 10 TAT cards, plus three questionnaires on health, adjustment, and participation in activities. He found that the subjects living in the apartments, which were more like their previous living arrangements, showed less fear of or preoccupation with death; which might mean, he said, that they enjoyed better mental health. He reported that both groups of subjects revealed at least mild anxiety with regard to thoughts of death.

Schilder and Bromberg (1933, 1942) studied responses to a series of questions on death given by 70 normal adults of various ages and by mental patients in whom death thoughts were prominent. They concluded that "there seemed to be no essential difference as far as age of the subject was concerned. . . . It is possible to correlate closely the attitudes toward one's own death with attitudes toward death of other people."

Faunce and Fulton (1958) have reported that "emotional responses suggesting either fear of death or of the dead were more frequent among spiritually oriented than among temporally oriented individuals."

## The Data

As part of a two-day series of examinations involving a variety of disciplines, the biracial group of 260 community volunteers, 60 years of age and older, were asked, during the course of a two-hour social history interview, "Are you afraid to die?" and "Do you believe in a life after death?"

## Fear of Death

Answers to the first question were distributed as shown in Table 11–15.

Fear of death was explored in relation to 52 other variables: demographic (race, age, sex, marital status, education); physical (functional rating, cardiac status, symptom count); psychological (taken from three WAIS and four Rorschach ratings); psychiatric (classification, subjective emotional reaction, hypochondriasis); and social (activities, attitudes, self-health rating and concern, religious items, adjustment ratings). Analysis by

Table 11–15. *Percentage of answers to "Are you afraid to die?"* (*N = 254*).

| | | |
|---|---:|---:|
| Yes | | 10 |
| No | | 35 |
|   No, but want to live as long as possible | 13 | |
|   No, but dread pain of dying | 2 | |
|   Mixed feelings (balanced ambivalence) | 16 | |
| | | 31 |
|   No, but don't want to be sick or dependent a long time | 4 | |
|   No, but it's inevitable | 17 | |
|   No, other elaboration | 3 | |
| | | 24 |
|       Total | | 100 |

chi-square yielded the statistically significant associations shown in Table 11–16.

Since many of the older subjects answered the question, "Are you afraid to die?" in religious terminology, an analysis of these answers yielded associations as follows ($x^2$ significant at the .001 level):

1. The *unqualified no* answers were associated with religious terminology.

2. The answers suggesting *ambivalence* were associated with an absence of religious connotations.

3. The answers *admitting fear of death* tended to have no religious connotation.

It therefore appears that the factors associated with *no* fear of death include a tendency to read the Bible oftener, more belief in a future life, reference to death with more religious connotations, fewer feelings of rejection and depression, higher scores on Full Scale and Performance IQ, and more responses on the Rorschach (with the suggestion also of more leisure activities).

*Belief in Afterlife*

The inquiry on belief in life after death revealed that very few of the subjects denied such a belief outright. Only 2 percent said "no"; 21 percent said "not sure"; and 77 percent said, "yes, sure of it."

Belief in life after death was examined in relation to 37 demographic, physical, psychological, psychiatric, and social variables. Statistically significant association was obtained for 10 of these variables (Table 11–17).

Religious activities and attitudes appear to be the most important variables associated with belief in life after death, but depression, intelligence, and socioeconomic status are also probably associated.

Clinical Impressions

The clinical impressions and experience of the present investigators, who have had extensive study and contact with not only the 260 community volunteer subjects in the present group but also with other groups of older persons during the past six years or more, may be useful in interpreting the empirical data.

1. As Schilder (1942) has suggested, there may be no common human idea of death, but it may be an extremely individualized concept. He hypothesized that individual experiences become the determining factors for the picture which one develops of death. Gardner Murphy, in his discussion of the contributions to Feifel's book (1959), concludes that "it is apparent that fear of death is not psychologically homogeneous at all, even in a narrowly defined cultural group."

2. The technique of direct questioning may be inappropriate for reaching the real feelings of the subject, even though in the present study the

Table 11–16. *Fear of death in relation to other variables.*

| Fear of death is associated with | Chi-square level of confidence |
| --- | --- |
| Less belief in life after death | .01 |
| Less frequent Bible reading | .01 |
| Feelings of rejection and depression | .05 |
| Lower Full Scale IQ | .05 |
| Lower Performance IQ | .001 |
| Fewer number of Rorschach responses | .02 |
| Fewer leisure activities | .10 |

questions were asked near the end of a social history taken in an informal setting, and even though the interviewer was previously known to the subject and good rapport had been established. In addition, in all such inquiries, a semantic factor which needs clarification is that of differentiation between the words *death* and *dying*.

3. Bearing in mind that the subjects were community volunteers living in their own homes and neighborhoods, and following Shrutt's finding (1958) that those older persons having less institutionalized living arrangements show less fear of or preoccupation with death, it is perhaps to be anticipated that only a small proportion of the present sample should express fear of death.

4. Religion is a very great part of community life in the North Carolina region in which the study was carried out. Only 6 percent of these older subjects had no church membership. It is accordingly to be expected that most of them would think of death in religious terminology.

5. The distribution of responses to the question, "Are you afraid to die?" (Table 11–15) confirms the clinical impressions of the Duke geriatrics research group that denial is a very important mechanism for dealing with anxiety in old age. The mental mechanism of denial may be among the most common adaptive techniques employed in personality adjustment by persons beyond the fifth decade of life. Its use may be promoted chiefly by three factors: (*a*) perceptual distortions, as suggested by Linn (1953), during the later period of life due to concomitant changes in cortical and receptor processes; (*b*) changes in body image with age and chronic disease (this parallels the frequent utilization of this same regressive maneuver by younger persons who have devastating chronic diseases); (*c*) gradual deterioration of the central nervous system, which causes reversal

Table 11–17. *Belief in life after death in relation to other variables.*

| Belief in life after death is associated with | Chi-square level of confidence |
|---|---|
| Less fear of death | .01 |
| More frequent church attendance | .01 |
| More frequent Bible reading | .001 |
| Greater number of religious activities | .001 |
| Stronger religious attitudes | .001 |
| Feeling that religion is the most important thing in life | .001 |
| Less depression (psychiatric rating) | .001 |
| Lower scores on Full Scale IQ | .02 |
| Lower socioeconomic status | .05 |
| More women than men | .05 |
| Less high level of education | .10 |

of the mental processes toward those of early childhood, when the denial mechanism of unacceptable reality situations is quite universally utilized.

## Suggested Techniques for Studying Attitudes toward Death

It is the feeling of the investigators that fear of death and illness plays an important part in the unconscious psychological life of the individual, but it is clearly evident that much further research is needed in this area. Several avenues are suggested for the further study of attitudes of older persons toward death:

Direct questioning has certain advantages even though, as Feifel (1956) has noted, the answers to direct questions tap the conscious and public attitudes of the subjects rather than the deeper layers of the personality. Direct questioning on the topic of death may prove too threatening to aged or ill persons, and such affects need to be given careful consideration. We have, however, found a willingness on the part of older subjects to speak freely on the topic of death. This confirms the finding of Beard in her study of centenarians (1956) who, she said, have "no morbid fears about death or any special reticence in discussing it."

Clinical depth interviews, preferably repeated through time, would doubtless be the most valuable single method for determining an individual's attitude toward death. Considerations of staff time and of the psychotherapy which might be involved necessarily limit the widespread utilization of this method.

Projective methods such as focused thematic pictures, sentence completions, and word association tests specifically designed to elicit responses to death and illness are fruitful methods. The sorting of TAT responses, as has been done by Neugarten and Gutmann (1958), and the utilization of sentence completion data for assessing attitudes as by Golde and Kogan (1959) and their colleagues provide possible models for dealing with such data.

The work of Osgood et al. (1958), Nunnally and Kittross (1958), and more recently that of Altrocchi and Eisdorfer (1960) suggests that semantic differential procedures are useful for assessing attitudes toward such concepts as illness, death, and dependency.

It would also be useful to obtain psychophysiological correlates of the aged person's discussion of concepts involving death. Psychophysiological measurements could be studied either as a measure of the response to focused projective material or in conjunction with a series of interviews designed to elicit the aged individual's affects and his defensive techniques in dealing with feelings in this area.

## References

Altrocchi, J., and Eisdorfer, G. A comparison of attitudes toward old age, mental illness and other concepts. In Donahue, W., Tibbitts, C., and Williams, R. H. (Eds.), *Social and psychological aspects of aging*, New York: Columbia University Press, 1962.

Beard, B. B. Social adjustment in extreme old age. Paper presented at the First Pan-American Congress on Gerontology, Mexico City, 1956.

Bromberg, W., and Schilder, P. Death and dying: a comparative study of attitudes and mental reactions toward death and dying. *Psychoanalysis Review*, 20:133–185, 1933.

Faunce, W. A., and Fulton, R. L. The sociology of death: A neglected area of research. *Social Forces*, 3:205–209, 1958.

Feifel, H. Older persons look at death. *Geriatrics*, 11:127–130, 1956.

Feifel, H. (Ed.). *The meaning of death*. New York: McGraw-Hill, 1959.

Golde, P., and Kogan, N. A sentence completion procedure for assessing attitudes toward old people. *Journal of Gerontology*, 14:355–363, 1959.

Linn, L. The role of perception in the mechanism of denial. *Journal of the American Psychoanalytical Association*, 1:690–705, 1953.

Neugarten, B. L., and Gutmann, D. L. Age-sex roles and personality in middle age: A thematic apperception study. *Psychological Monographs*, 72:(470), No. 17, 1–33.

Nunnally, J., and Kittross, J. M. Public attitudes toward mental health professions. *American Psychologist*, 13:589–594, 1958.

Osgood, C. E., Suci, G. J., and Tannenbaum, P. H.. The measurement of meaning. Urbana, Ill.: University of Illinois Press, 1957.

Scheler, M. Tod und Fortleben. Berlin: Schriften aus dem Nachlass, 1953.

Schilder, P. Goals and desires of man. New York: Columbia University Press, 1942.

Shrutt, S. D. Attitudes toward old age and death. *Mental Hygiene*, 42:259–266, 1958.

# Factors Associated with Frequency of Death Thoughts in Elderly Community Volunteers* *Frances C. Jeffers and Adriaan Verwoerdt*

The present investigation continues an earlier study, "Attitudes of Older Persons toward Death" (Jeffers, Nichols, & Eisdorfer, 1961), which analyzed factors associated with verbalized fear of death and belief in life after death. As Fulton (1964) has since pointed out in a review of the literature on attitudes toward death, research to date in this area has often

* Reprinted by permission from *Proceedings of the Seventh International Congress of Gerontology*, 149–152, 1966.

led to seemingly contradictory conclusions, largely due to differences both in methodology and in sampling procedures. The topic itself is doubtless heavily loaded emotionally for our current society, with evidence suggesting great efforts toward death denial. Parsons (1962) believes that there may be ambivalence as well, manifesting itself in "apathy . . . a withdrawing from the situation in order to avoid facing an insoluable dilemma" (which of course may be another aspect of denial). The present study revealed not only individual ambivalence but also a high degree of variation in response. Welford (1959) discusses the increased variability which occurs in old age so far as psychological performance is concerned and suggests it may be partially due to the highly individual character of (lifetime) experience. Butler (1964) states in a different context, "It is likely that the fact of approaching death varies as a function of individual personality in the degree to which it is a crisis."

The present investigation is concerned with frequency of death thoughts as reported by subjects on the Duke University geriatrics research panel and with the factors which appear to differentiate those persons who say they never think about death from those who say it is always in mind. Is the variation due to experiential and personality factors, as suggested by Welford and Butler, or is it as well a matter of degree of physical and psychological intactness and hence better prognosis for longer survival? Is the sheer fact of propinquity to death a more critical variable?

## Methodology

1. Elderly community volunteers (N = 140) were asked four questions during the course of a social history by an interviewer known from earlier research periods. The resulting frequencies are given on Table 11–18. The two extreme groups of those who said they never think about death and those who said death is always in their minds (Table 11–18, b, 1 and 5) were selected for further analysis.

2. The subjects were then given orally the first 2–8 words of 10 incomplete sentences and asked to complete them (repetitions were given as often as requested). The results were rated (blind, at a later date, by one of the interviewers) for degree of positive, negative, or neutral reaction, with frequency findings as indicated on Table 11–18.

3. The clinical impression of the subject's (a) willingness to speak about death and (b) his feeling tone toward the topic of death were then rated on a seven-point scale, with resulting frequencies as given on Table 11–20. (Rating done by interviewer on basis of subject's total reaction to the four questions and to the incomplete sentences).

4. The two extreme groups were then analyzed for cluster of other factors based on data drawn from the Duke longitudinal study of these same subjects. . . .

## Results

Of the 140 elderly community volunteers, 5 percent reported (in a section of a social history) that they *never think about death* (Table

Table 11–18. *Frequency on inventory questions, total subject group* (*N = 140*).

|  | Percentage |
|---|---|
| a. How frequently do you believe people your age think about death (as compared with before 55 years old)? | |
| 1. More often now | 80 |
| 2. Less often now | 1 |
| 3. Undecided | 15 |
| 4. Same as ever | 4 |
| b. How often do you think about death? | |
| 1. Never | 5 |
| 2. Rarely (less than once a week) | 25 |
| 3. Occasionally (once a week) | 20 |
| 4. Frequently (daily) | 42 |
| 5. Always in mind | 7 |
| 6. Undecided | 1 |
| c. Do death thoughts affect enjoyment of life? | |
| 1. Yes | 40 |
| 2. No | 47 |
| 3. Undecided | 13 |

11–18, *b*, 1), and 7 percent reported that *death is always in mind* (Table 11–18, *b*, 5). These two groups were differentiated in the present investigation in that *those who never think about death* (1): (*a*) did not believe that thoughts about death come more frequently with age, whereas those in 5 tended to disagree; (*b*) said that death thoughts affect enjoyment of life —those in 5 were in disagreement; (*c*) were more willing to talk about death and had a more pleasant and accepting feeling tone toward the topic of death than those in 5. However, there was no difference found between the two groups insofar as positive or negative reactions to the sentence completions.

Factors drawn from the Duke longitudinal study further differentiated the two groups on general characteristics (with reference noted to earlier studies on death attitudes). Those in 1: (*d*) were more active, less "disengaged" (Klopfer 1947), with higher ratings on the Activity Inventory; (e) had higher self-health evaluation (confirming Rhudick and Dibner, 1961) but with no difference on health evaluation by physicians; (f) had higher IQ scores (confirming Jeffers et al., 1961); (g) were in the nonmanual rather than manual occupational group (Jeffers et al., 1961); (h) were younger chronologically; and (i) had higher morale as scored by the Attitude Inventory.

Discussion

The subjects who reported that they *never think about death* (Table 11–18, b, 1), as differentiated from those who say *it is always in mind* (Table 11–18, b, 5) believed that older people do *not* think more about

Table 11–19. *Frequency of reactions indicated by sentence completions.*

|  | Percentage | | | |
|---|---|---|---|---|
|  | Positive | Neutral | Negative | |
| Total subject group | 57 | 13 | 30 | = 100 |
| Extremes (Table 11–18): | | | | |
| 1. Never think about death | 51 | 20 | 29 | = 100 |
| 2. Death always in mind | 50 | 17 | 33 | = 100 |

death than they used to do before age 55 and that death thoughts *do* affect enjoyment of life. It would appear that a subject in this group was saying in effect that he does not think about death but that if he did so it would affect his enjoyment of life. On the sentence completion test, however, the subject was confronted with the topic of death, i.e., "When a man dies, he——," "Death is——," "I feel that when I die——," etc. He was accordingly more or less forced to consider the prospect of death, which placed him in the same position temporarily as those who said they always think about death. The resulting data on reactions to sentence completions indicated that thoughts about death affected the total subject group in the same direction (Table 11–19).

The difference noted between groups 1 and 5 was that those subjects in 1 somehow managed to keep thoughts of death at a distance. It may be that this "distance" made it easier for them to talk about it (Table 11–20, 1). Since it was less of an immediate personal reality to them, with accordingly a less immediate painful impact of the idea of personal death, the feeling tone may have thus been more accepting and pleasant (Table 11–20).

The further data on general characteristics indicated confirmation that those in group 1 were in better shape—in regard to activity, morale, self-health evaluation, IQ, occupational level, and younger age—and hence actually were and felt more distant from death than those in group 5. Accordingly, those who were more active, more engaged, with higher morale, were the ones with fewer thoughts about death; they perceived themselves as more "distant" from death and hence were more willing to talk about it (Table 11–20, 1), as well as being more accepting and pleasant

Table 11–20. *Frequency of (1) willingness to speak about death and (2) feeling tone toward the topic of death (rated by interviewers).*

|  | Percentage | | |
| --- | --- | --- | --- |
|  |  | Extremes (Table 11–18): | |
|  | Total subject group | 1. Never think about death | 5. Death always in mind |
| **1.** | | | |
| a. Willingness to speak or no affect perceived | 70 | 85 | 55 |
| b. Reluctance or blocking | 30 | 15 | 45 |
|  | 100 | 100 | 100 |
| **2.** | | | |
| a. Feeling tone pleasant or accepting | 57 | 71 | 33 |
| b. Sad, ambivalent, depressed or disturbed | 43 | 29 | 67 |
|  | 100 | 100 | 100 |

about the prospect (Table 11–20, 2) since it was far enough in the future to be no immediate threat. However, when they were actually confronted with the topic of death and became involved with it at least temporarily, they appeared to react basically in the same way as did the total subject panel (Table 11–19).

## References

Butler, R. N. The life review: An interpretation of reminiscence in the aged. In Kastenbaum, R., *New thoughts on old age.* New York: Springer, 1964.

Fulton, R. Death and the self. *Journal of Religion and Health,* 3:359–368, 1964.

Jeffers, F. C., Nichols, C. R., and Eisdorfer, C. Attitudes of older persons toward death: A preliminary study. *Journal of Gerontology,* 16:53–56, 1961.

Klopfer, W. G. Attitudes toward death in the aged. Doctoral dissertation, City College, New York, 1947.

Parsons, T. The aging in American society. *Law and Contemporary Problems,* 27:22–35, 1962.

Rhudick, J., and Dibner, A. S. Age, personality, and health correlates of death concerns in normal aged individuals. *Journal of Gerontology*, 16:44–49, 1961.

Swenson, W. M. Attitudes toward death in an aged population. *Journal of Gerontology*, 16:49–52, 1961.

Welford, A. T. Psychometer performance. In Birren, J. E. (Ed.), *Handbook of aging and the individual*. Chicago: University of Chicago Press, 1959, pp. 562–613.

# Physical, Mental, and Social Factors in Predicting Longevity*    Erdman Palmore

Actuaries predict how many years a person will live simply on the basis of his age, sex, and race. The predictions are summarized in standard life expectancy tables and are widely used by life insurance companies, government agencies, and others to establish premium rates, annuity payments, benefit levels, etc.

Jarvik and Falek (1963) and Riegel, Riegel, and Meyer (1967) have shown that intellectual functioning is associated with longevity. Theoretically, physical and social factors should also be related to longevity. If we were able to give a person a complete series of physical, mental, and social examinations and if we knew how these examinations correlated with longevity, we should be able to improve the accuracy of longevity predictions by adjusting for individual differences in these variables. Data from a 13-year longitudinal study of aging now allow us to test this hypothesis. We can also examine the relative importance of physical, mental, and social factors in predicting longevity and how their importance varies by age, sex, and race. We can even construct prediction equations based on these factors, which can be used to predict, with a specified standard error, the number of years remaining for persons similar to those in the longitudinal study.

## Methods

. . . The measure of longevity used in this analysis is simply the number of years a panelist lived after initial testing or, for a living person, an estimate of the number of years he will have lived after initial testing. This estimate of years remaining for those living (N = 147) is made by

* Reprinted by permission from the *Gerontologist*, 9:103–108, 1969.

adding the present number of years since initial testing (about 13) to the estimated number of years now remaining according to actuarial life expectancy tables. In order to know exactly how many years each person will live after initial testing we would have to wait another 20 or more years until all participants have died. In the meantime this estimate can be used for purposes of analysis because it will probably not be off by more than a few years for most persons, and in a sample of this size many of the errors tend to cancel each other out. If one were to analyze only those who have already died, he would have a one-sided picture because his sample would include only those on the lower end of the longevity distribution, the sicker and less able persons. The pattern of correlations for the dead panelists is similar to that of the total but is generally lower because of reduced variance.

The multiple regression in this analysis uses four variables to predict longevity:

1. *Actuarial expectancy at initial testing.* This is derived from the standard life expectancy table by age, sex, and race for North Carolina (Public Health Service, 1959–1961). These life expectancies ranged from 2.5 to 20.0 years, with a mean of 11.5 years and a standard deviation of 3.6 years.

2. *Physical functioning rating.* This is a score given by the examining physician for the level of physical functioning in everyday activities on the basis of the medical history, the physical and neurological examinations, audiogram, chest x-ray, electroencephalogram, electrocardiogram, and laboratory studies of the blood and urine. For the present analysis the scores were reversed so that they range from 1 (total disability) to 6 (no pathology), with a mean of 4.4 and standard deviation of 1.2.

3. *Work satisfaction.* This is part of an attitude questionnaire designed to measure a person's satisfaction with various areas of life (Burgess, 1949). The work satisfaction scale awards one point for agreement with each of three positive statements (I am happy only when I have definite work to do; I am satisfied with the work I now do; I do better work now than ever before) and one point for disagreement with each of three negative statements (I can no longer do any kind of useful work; I have no work to look forward to; I get badly flustered when I have to hurry with my work). Thus the score could range from 0 to 6 with a mean of 3.7 and a standard deviation of 1.2. If a subject asked what was meant by "work," it was defined to include any useful activity such as housework, gardening, etc.

4. *Intelligence.* This is the weighted performance score of the Wechsler Adult Intelligence Scale (Wechsler, 1955). It is made up of tests on digit symbols, picture completions, block designs, picture arrangement, and

object assembly. The mean score for our panelists was 27.1, with a standard deviation of 13.1.

Results

*Zero-Order Correlations*

From among the hundreds of measures taken during the two-day examinations, we selected 38 items to test for correlations with longevity (Table 11–21). This shows that actuarial life expectancy is usually the best single predictor of longevity ($r = .56$). However, we shall see that this is not true among the younger age-sex groups.

Table 11–21. *Correlations of 38 items with longevity.*

| Independent variable | Number | r with longevity | Independent variable | Number | r with longevity |
|---|---|---|---|---|---|
| Actuarial life expectancy at time 1 | 268 | .56 | Attitudes | | |
| | | | Total attitudes | 263 | .15 |
| | | | Work satisfaction | 266 | .19 |
| Health | | | Health evaluation | 266 | .19 |
| Physical functioning rating | 261 | .43 | Usefulness | 266 | .16 |
| Cardiovascular disease | 187 | .29 | Religious attitude | 266 | .11 |
| | | | Happiness | 265 | .10 |
| Cholesterol | 139 | .19 | Economic security | 266 | .07 |
| Self-health rating | 268 | .13 | Attitudes toward family | 264 | .04 |
| Tobacco use | 263 | .09 | | | |
| Hypochondria | 265 | .02 | Attitudes toward friends | 266 | .00 |
| Obesity and emaciation | 262 | .01 | Adjustment ratings | | |
| | | | Secondary group contacts | 252 | .24 |
| Intelligence (WAIS) | | | Primary group contacts | 251 | .14 |
| Performance weighted score | 259 | .31 | Nongroup activities | 252 | .12 |
| Full Scale weighted | 259 | .26 | Emotional security | 252 | .05 |
| Verbal weighted score | 268 | .22 | Prestige feelings | 252 | .04 |
| | | | Master rating | 253 | .03 |
| Performance IQ | 258 | .14 | Happiness rating | 252 | .01 |
| Full Scale IQ | 258 | .13 | Socioeconomic status | | |
| Verbal IQ | 268 | .11 | Education | 268 | .13 |
| Activities | | | Occupation | 267 | .09 |
| Total activity | 263 | .23 | | | |
| Leisure activities | 263 | .23 | | | |
| Economic activities | 255 | .18 | | | |
| Health activities | 262 | .11 | | | |
| Family and friends contact | 259 | .07 | | | |
| Religious activities | 263 | .02 | | | |

The second best predictor was the physical functioning rating (r = .43). This means that next to a person's age-sex-race, the most important factor related to his longevity is usually his general health and functioning. The absence of cardiovascular disease was also related to longevity at a fairly strong level (r = .29). Most of the other health measures have a weak or nonexistent relationship to longevity, such as the self-health rating, the hypochondriasis rating, obesity or emaciation, and the amount of tobacco used. The presence of higher levels of cholesterol was positively related to longevity (r = .19). This is contrary to the widely held belief that higher levels of cholesterol contribute to cardiovascular disease and thus tend to shorten a person's life. In these correlations, cholesterol shows no association with cardiovascular diseases and is moderately related to longer life. However, this factor was not used in the multiple regression analysis because only about one-half of the subjects had cholesterol tests at the initial examinations.

The third highest factor related to longevity was the weighted performance score of the Wechsler Adult Intelligence Test (r = .31). The performance intelligence scores were more closely related to longevity than the verbal intelligence scores, probably because the former involve physical functioning abilities such as coordination and speed of reaction and thus are more closely related to a person's general health. The intelligence quotient measures have only one-half the correlation with longevity as do the weighted scores because the IQ measures attempt to control for age while the longevity measure does not.

Among the activity measures, total activity (the sum of the five types of activity scores) has the same correlation with longevity as does leisure-time activities (r = .23). Both of these measures were included in a preliminary multiple regression. However, they were dropped from the final analysis because they did not contribute a significant improvement in the prediction equation. Apparently they are so closely related to the other factors that they had little independent association with longevity.

Among the attitude scores, work satisfaction and self-health evaluations had the two highest correlations with longevity (r = .19). Work satisfaction was included in the multiple regression, but self-health evaluation was not because it is largely a reflection of general health which is better measured by the physical functioning rating (for purposes of predicting longevity). Feelings of usefulness also had a moderate correlation with longevity (r = .16) presumably because it measures a similar dimension to that of work satisfaction. The rest of the attitude scores had only low or even negative correlations with longevity.

The adjustment rating of secondary group contact had a substantial correlation with longevity (r = .24). This is a rating given by the social worker of the extent to which a person participates in formal groups such as churches and clubs or spends time reading or watching television. It was included in the preliminary regression, but did not contribute any significant improvement and so was dropped from the final equation.

Contrary to other evidence, neither of the measures of socioeconomic status had a substantial correlation with longevity. This seems to suggest that the usually assumed association between higher socioeconomic status and longevity may be more related to their better health, higher intelligence, and greater work satisfaction than to their higher education and occupation as such. Part of the explanation may also be that despite the inclusion of persons from lower occupations and educational groups, these persons may have been among the most favored in those groups. There is evidence that the sample is generally biased toward an "elite" group (Maddox, 1962). This would tend to reduce the variance attributable to socioeconomic status.

### Multiple Regressions

When life expectancy, physical functioning, work satisfaction, and performance intelligence were combined in a step-wise multiple regression with longevity, the addition of the last three factors improved by about one-third on the amount of variance explained by actuarial life expectancy alone (Table 11–22). Physical functioning was second in importance for the total group and explained substantially more of the variance than the latter two factors. Although work satisfaction had a lower zero-order correlation than intelligence with longevity, work satisfaction entered the equation before intelligence, presumably because performance intelligence was more closely associated with the first two variables. When the last three factors are put in a multiple regression without the life expectancy factor, the multiple correlation is .45 compared to .64 when life expectancy is included.

There are interesting variations on this basic pattern among specific sex, age, and race groups. For men in general, physical functioning no longer contributes any significant improvement to the prediction equation, and performance intelligence is second most important. Among the women in general, both work satisfaction and performance intelligence drop out as significant predictors. Among the men aged 60–69 work satisfaction is the best predictor of longevity, even better than life expectancy. This suggests that among these younger men the maintenance of a satisfactory and useful work role is more important for longevity than is their chronological age. Similarly, physical functioning is the most important factor among women aged 60–69, which suggests that their general health and functionings are

Table 11–22. *Step-wise regression of four predictors with longevity* ($N = 234$).

| Predictors | Zero-order correlation | Cumulative variance | Additional variance | Percentage final cumulative variance |
|---|---|---|---|---|
| Life expectancy at $T_1$ | .56** | .315 | .315** | 78 |
| Physical functioning | .39** | .374 | .059** | 92 |
| Work satisfaction | .19** | .393 | .019* | 97 |
| Intelligence (Performance) | .32** | .404 | .011* | 100 |
| Total *r* with four predictors | .64** | | | |
| All men N = 107 | | | | |
| Life expectancy at $T_1$ | .47** | .224 | .224** | 64 |
| Intelligence (Performance) | .35** | .306 | .082** | 88 |
| Work satisfaction | .27** | .348 | .042* | 100 |
| Total *r* with three predictors | .59** | | | |
| All women N = 127 | | | | |
| Life expectancy at $t_1$ | .55** | .305 | .305** | 86 |
| Physical functioning | .35** | .356 | .051** | 100 |
| Total *r* with two predictors | .60** | | | |
| Men aged 60–69 N = 47 | | | | |
| Work satisfaction | .36* | .130 | .130* | 61 |
| Life expectancy at $T_1$ | .34* | .212 | .082* | 100 |
| Total *r* with two predictors | .46** | | | |
| Men aged 70+ N = 60 | | | | |
| Life expectancy at $T_1$ | .46** | .213 | .213** | 51 |
| Intelligence (Performance) | .44** | .416 | .203** | 100 |
| Total *r* with two predictors | .65 | | | |
| Women aged 60–69 N = 66 | | | | |
| Physical functioning | .38** | .140 | .140** | 56 |
| Life expectancy at $T_1$ | .37** | .249 | .109** | 100 |
| Total *r* with two predictors | .50** | | | |
| Women aged 70+ N = 61 | | | | |
| Life expectancy at $T_1$ | .48** | .235 | .235** | 80 |
| Intelligence (Performance) | .36** | .292 | .057* | 100 |
| Total *r* with two predictors | .54** | | | |
| Whites N = 153 | | | | |
| Life expectancy at $T_1$ | .59** | .346 | .346** | 86 |
| Work satisfaction | .20** | .384 | .038** | 95 |
| Intelligence (Performance) | .29** | .404 | .020** | 100 |
| Total *r* with three predictors | .64** | | | |
| Negroes N = 81 | | | | |
| Physical functioning | .56** | .316 | .316** | 77 |
| Life expectancy at $T_1$ | .53** | .413 | .097** | 100 |
| Total *r* with two predictors | .64** | | | |

Note.—Multiple regressions shown only through the last variable, which yields an increment in variance significant at the .05 level.

\* $p < .05$.
\*\* $p < .01$.

more important for their longevity than their chronological age. Among both the men and women over 70, life expectancy is most important and intelligence is the only other factor significantly improving the equation. Among Negroes, physical functioning had a slightly higher correlation than life expectancy, and their physical functioning alone explained over three-fourths of the cumulative variance. In contrast, physical functioning drops out of the equation for whites.

### Prediction Equation

As one would expect from the differences in the step-wise regressions, the longevity prediction equations vary for different age, sex, and race

Table 11–23. *Prediction equations for longevity.*

| Group | Equation | Standard error |
|---|---|---|
| Total | $Y = 12.7 + 0.87x_E + 1.07x_P + .71x_W + .06x_I$ | 5.2 |
| Men 60–69 | $Y = 13.0 + 1.30x_E + 1.71x_W$ | 6.1 |
| Men 70+ | $Y = 9.0 + 1.33x_E + 0.20x_I$ | 4.6 |
| Women 60–69 | $Y = 16.8 + 1.24x_E + 2.02x_P$ | 5.6 |
| Women 70+ | $Y = 11.7 + 0.86x_E + 0.09x_I$ | 4.3 |
| Whites | $Y = 13.0 + 0.95x_E + 1.03x_W + .08x_I$ | 5.2 |
| Negroes | $Y = 12.2 + 0.75x_E + 2.32x_P$ | 5.3 |

Note.—Y = Predicted longevity: years remaining after initial testing; $x = x - \bar{X}$; E = Life expectancy at time 1; P = Physical functioning; W = Work satisfaction; I = Intelligence (Performance).

groups in terms of the relative effects of the various factors as measured by their beta weights (Table 11–23). The first or constant term in the equation, which is simply the mean longevity for the group, varies from a high of over 16 for the younger women to a low of 9 for the older men. This simply demonstrates the generally true principle that being younger and female is associated with living longer. The second term shows the factor to be applied to a person's deviation from the average life expectancy for his group. This factor is lowest for Negroes, which shows that life expectancy has less effect in predicting longevity among Negroes than among the other groups. The third term for the total group, for the younger women and for Negroes, shows the factor for the person's deviation from average physical functioning. Among the younger women and Negroes, this factor is twice that of the total group, which reveals again the relatively great importance of general health for these groups. The fourth term for the total group (and the third term for the younger men and whites) shows the factor to be used for a person's deviation from average work satisfaction. This factor is highest for the younger men, which again demonstrates the importance of work satisfaction for the younger men. The last term for the total group, for the older men and women and whites, shows the factor to be applied to a person's deviation from average performance intelligence. This factor is much higher among the older men than any other group.

The standard error of estimates derived from these equations ranges from 4.3 for the older women to 6.1 for the younger men. This means that if longevity is normally distributed in a specified group, the chances are two out of three that the actual number of years remaining for a person in that group will be within plus or minus 1 standard error of his predicted longevity. For example, the average woman over 70 would have a predicted longevity of 11.7 years remaining and the chances would be two out of three that she would actually live between 7.4 and 16 more years.

Perhaps a case illustration will clarify how this prediction equation can improve on the simple actuarial life expectancy. Case 8075 was a white male aged 81 at the initial study in 1955. His actuarial life expectancy at that time was 5.6 more years. But his health was average ($PFR = 20$ percent or less limitation), his work satisfaction was the highest possible, and his performance intelligence was high. Substituting his weighted deviations from the average in the prediction equation in Table 11–23 for the total group we get $Y = 12.7 -5.1 -.4 +1.6 +.7$, which equals a predicted longevity of 9.5 more years. Case 8075 actually lived 11.6 more years, even more than predicted by the equation. But it is clear that the actuarial life expectancy (5.6) was only half his actual remaining years (11.6), and the predicted longevity (9.5) was much closer, even though it too fell short.

## Discussion

Generalizations based on a sample of 268 volunteers from the central region of North Carolina should, of course, be made only with extreme caution. Also the measure of longevity used is only a best estimate for those who are still living, based on the number of years lived since initial testing plus their present life expectancy. One weakness of this estimate is apparent from the frequency distribution of the longevity measure, which shows a marked dip in the middle caused by the assumption that all those now living will live the additional average number of years shown by their present life expectancy, when in fact some of them will die soon and "fill in" the dip. Thus the distribution of this longevity measure will smooth out and become more normal as more people die and move from the estimated longevity category to the actual longevity category. This in turn should improve the correlations and accuracy of the prediction equations.

An alternative way of controlling for the effect of chronological age was attempted by dividing the present longitudinal measure by the person's actuarial life expectancy at initial testing. This results in a longevity quotient (observed divided by expected longevity) analogous to an intelligence quotient. However, the longevity quotient generally shows results similar to those presented in this paper. Also, use of the simpler method allows study of the relative predictive power of the actuarial life expectancy compared to other factors. Therefore we decided to use the simpler measure of longevity in this presentation. It may be that for certain types of analysis in which the effect of chronological age should be removed or for certain groups with a wider age range the use of the longevity quotient would be preferable.

Our predictions may also be improved by using delta scores (differences between the scores at two points in time) rather than the absolute scores at one point in time. Thus, for example, it may be that a decline in physical functioning is more closely related to shortened longevity than is the absolute level at initial testing. Also, various log transformations of the longevity measure were tested but showed no improvement in distribution or correlations.

Finally, it should be remembered that correlation does not prove causality. However, if we keep all these qualifications in mind, it may be useful to speculate about the meaning and practical implications of these findings. The substantial improvement in predicting longevity that results from adjusting for physical functioning, work satisfaction, and intelligence suggests that life insurance companies and others concerned with longevity could substantially improve the accuracy of their estimates by using not only complete physical examinations but also tests of intelligence and work satisfaction (or a similar rating of social adjustment) to adjust their life expectancy scores. The meaning of the high association between physical functioning and longevity seems obvious: A healthy and well-functioning person has a better chance of surviving the stress and trauma of aging longer than a sick and weak person. The meaning of the association between intelligence and longevity is less clear. Are the more intelligent better able to adapt to the problems of aging and take better care of their health because they are smarter? Or is their higher intelligence just a sign that they are aging slower in general? Or is it mainly an indicator of higher socioeconomic status with its usual advantages in comfort and medical care? This is unlikely because of the low correlations of socioeconomic measures with longevity.

Similarly, is the association of work satisfaction and longevity a spurious one simply due to its association with health? This is unlikely because there is a significant association left even after the variance in longevity explained by physical functioning is taken out. Does it mean that men who stay active in useful roles are better able to maintain high morale and functioning, which in turn increases their longevity? The latter interpretation is consistent with other evidence linking greater activity with greater satisfaction and adjustment (Havens, 1968; Maddox, 1964; Palmore, 1968).

We cannot be sure, but the evidence seems to imply that the most important thing for longevity is to maintain high levels of health and physical functioning (presumably through the standard means such as prompt medical care, balanced diet, adequate exercise). Another implication suggested is that keeping mentally active and alert as well as maintaining or finding satisfying and useful social roles may also contribute to longevity.

## Summary

A longitudinal study of 268 volunteers aged 60 to 94 showed that (*a*) actuarial life expectancy at initial testing, (*b*) physical functioning, (*c*) work satisfaction, and (*d*) performance intelligence were the four best predictors of longevity. While actuarial life expectancy was the best single predictor in general, use of the other three predictors in a multiple regression improved the amount of variance explained by about one-third. Also work satisfaction was the best single predictor among men aged 60 to 69, and physical functioning was the best single predictor among women aged 60 to 69 and among Negroes. Prediction equations for specific age-sex groups are presented with a standard error of about five years. The evidence suggests that maintaining health, mental abilities, and satisfying social roles are the most important factors related to longevity.

## References

Burgess, E. W., Cavin, R. S., Havighurst, R. J., and Goldhamer, H. *Your activities and attitudes.* Chicago: Science Research Associates, 1949.

Busse, E. W. A physiological, psychological, and sociological study of aging. In Palmore, E. B. (Ed.), *Normal aging.* Durham, N.C.: Duke University Press, 1970.

Havens, B. J. An investigation of activity patterns and adjustment in an aging population. *Gerontologist,* 8:201–206, 1968.

Jarvik, L. F., and Falek, A. Intellectual ability and survival in the aged. *Journal of Gerontology,* 18:173–176. 1963.

Maddox, G. L. A longitudinal, multidisciplinary study of human aging. *Proceedings of the Social Statistics Section of the American Statistical Association.* Washington: American Statistical Association, 1962.

Maddox, G. L. Disengagement theory: A critical evaluation. *Gerontologist,* 4:80–83, 1964.

Palmore, E. B. The effects of aging on activities and attitudes. *Gerontologist,* 8:259–263, 1968.

Riegel, K. F., Riegel, R. M., and Meyer, G. A study of the dropout rates in longitudinal research on aging and the prediction of death. *Journal of Personality and Social Psychology,* 5:342–348, 1967.

Wechsler, D. *Manual for the Wechsler Adult Intelligence Scale.* New York: Psychological Corporation, 1955.

# Chapter 12. Summary and the Future

*Erdman Palmore*

The reader may have noticed that certain themes seem to recur in these reports even though the different investigators gathered and analyzed their data in different ways as appropriate to their different specialties. These recurring themes seem to represent the solid core of the findings on normal aging from the Duke Longitudinal Study. A relationship or trend discovered by one investigator becomes more significant and well established when it is also found by another investigator with different methods and a different perspective.

## Themes

An underlying methodological theme is that of the advantages of longitudinal and interdisciplinary study. The longitudinal analysis made possible the discovery of general persistence in activities and attitudes, the substantial numbers with improving health and with increase in sexual activities, the patterns of hypochondriasis and denial of illness over time, the general stability of intelligence, the factors predicting longevity, and so forth. The interdisciplinary teamwork made possible the analysis of such relationships as those between social activities and psychological attitudes; between socioeconomic status and health, neurological symptoms, intelligence, hypochondriasis, activities, and attitudes; among cholesterol, cardiovascular disease, and intelligence; among intellectual functions, EEG, and deafness; and between physicians' evaluation of health and the panelist's own health evaluation.

Another basic theme is that the well-known patterns of declining health and physical functions do apply in general to a majority of the aged. This theme first occurs in the analysis of changes in the physical functioning rating over time and is repeated with variations in the findings of increased neurological symptoms, increased skin lesions, increased alterations in blood vessels, slower reaction times, and decreased sexual activity.

But in contrast to this general theme of declining physical functions, there are several qualifying and contrapuntal themes. One is that there are many exceptions to this pattern. A substantial minority of the panelists actually showed improvements in physical functioning, in skin conditions, in blood vessels, and increases in sexual activity. Thus the process of physical aging is not necessarily an irresistable and irreversible force. Health and functioning can and do improve for some aged persons just as they do for younger persons.

A second contrasting theme is that while physical functioning tends to decline on the average, social and psychological functioning shows little or no overall decline. The average scores on activities and attitudes show no significant decline among the men and only small declines among the women over a 10-year period. The retest of intelligence showed little decline after a 3-year interval. When required to make a choice of risky alternatives, the aged showed no more cautiousness than the young. The aged were able to recall "high arousal" (meaningful) phrases as well as the young. Most panelists showed no particular concern about illness or death, and most had a fairly realistic evaluation of their own health and age category. Most did not feel neglected or lonely even though they tended not to live with their children or relatives.

In fact, it is rather striking that despite substantial impairment of physical functioning, EEG abnormalities, cardiovascular diseases, and impairments in vision and hearing, most of these aged persons remained functioning residents in the community, living fairly mobile and independent lives. This is a significant testimony to the ability of the normal aged to compensate for their various physical ailments and remain socially and psychologically healthy. This theme is a brighter counterpoint to the more somber theme of physical decline.

Finally, there is the theme of individual and group variation among the aged and the attempts to account for this variation on grounds other than simple chronological age. It is pointed out that the aged usually show even more individual variability than the young. And even when there are significant mean differences between the young and old, there is a considerable overlap between the scores of young and old. For example, even though the average aged person tends to have slower reaction times than the average younger person, many of the above-average aged are faster than many of the below-average young. Thus attempts are made to get behind the stereotype of the uniformly and inexorably declining aged person and to account for the great variation in levels of functioning. For example, socioeconomic status is generally found to be related to physical, mental, and social functioning. Persons in upper socioeconomic groups generally have better health, better vision, fewer neurological symptoms, less hypochondriasis, less sexual activity, higher intelligence, more social activity, and more life satisfaction. For another example, the large variation in life satisfaction is partly related to physical functioning and partly to the amount of activity engaged in. The correlation of changes in activity with changes in satisfaction indicates that when activities are curtailed satisfaction tends to decline.

Hypotheses

As a more systematic summary, the major findings of these reports will be stated in the form of 48 tentative hypotheses about normal aged living in the community.

A. Physical Problems
1. About half of the aged surviving any given time period have decreased physical capacities, but the other half have no significant decrease and some have significant improvement in physical functioning.
2. The aged with lower socioeconomic status have more limitations on their physical functioning and more impaired vision, arteriosclerosis, cardiovascular disease, high blood pressure, pulmonary disease, arthritis, and neurologic impairment than the aged with higher socioeconomic status.
3. When matched for age and socioeconomic status, the physical capacity of the normal aged does not differ significantly between the sexes nor between the races.
4. Over a third of the aged have one or more neurologic impairments such as abnormal reflex, gait, tremor, or loss of olfactory function.
5. Most aged have some skin problem such as lax skin, seborrheic keratoses, and dermatophytosis.
6. The conjunctival blood vessels show that most aged have one or more symptoms of vascular problems such as venous sludge or arterial masses.
7. Cholesterol level is less related to cardiovascular disease among the aged than it is among the middle-aged.

B. Mental Illness
1. Over half of the aged have symptoms indicating mental illness, with hypochondriasis and depression being the most common psychoneurotic symptoms.
2. Depression among the aged is primarily related to the loss of self-esteem which results from declining health, declining social roles, declining financial security, or a combination of these factors. There is usually an absence of guilt feeling, self-condemnation, or other evidence of inwardly turned hostility.
3. When depression among aged who are community residents is compared to depression among aged hospitalized patients, the community aged have less severe depression, show less guilt, have less tenacious

depression, involve less suicidal thoughts, and have fewer related physiological changes.

4. Negro aged and aged of lower socioeconomic status have higher rates of disabling depression than whites and upper socioeconomic aged.
5. Most of the aged have some mild impairment of memory or mild intellectual impairment such as difficulty in concentrating and comprehending newspapers or magazines. However, most are able to compensate adequately for these difficulties.

C. Electroencephalographic Patterns
1. About half of the normal aged have some EEG "abnormality" (according to young adult standards), but many of these "abnormalities" have little or no prognostic or diagnostic value among the aged.
2. Diffuse slowing of the EEG is associated with impairment of intellectual functioning, while the occurrence of fast activity is associated with well-preserved learning ability.
3. Diffuse EEG slowing in the aged is often accompanied by circulatory disturbances.

D. Reaction Time
1. Normal aged have slower reactions than younger persons, both in terms of premotor time and motor time.
2. Normal aged can improve their reaction times with practice more than younger persons can.
3. Normal aged have greater individual differences in reaction time than younger persons.
4. Slower responses among many aged are related to their diminished amounts of exercise.

E. Intelligence
1. The usual intelligence score norms for the aged (based on Kansas City subjects) are not applicable to some other regions, such as the Southeast.
2. Intelligence of the normal aged tends to be stable over periods of several years.
3. Rorschach performance is more closely related to intelligence than to chronological age.
4. Even the aged with cardiovascular disease are usually able to maintain their intellectual abilities despite their CVD.

F. Perception and Affect
1. Hearing loss has more serious effects on rigidity of emotions, vocabulary, and perceptual organization than does impaired vision.

2. Normal aged tend to express less emotion and activity than younger persons, but the aged express more emotion and activity than ill persons.
3. Galvanic skin responses show that normal aged perceive normal auditory stimuli as often and as rapidly as younger persons.
4. Normal aged can recall, as well as the young, phrases with strong meaning to them, although overall recall is lower among the aged.

G. Marriage, Family, and Sexual Behavior

1. Happy marriages among the normal aged are characterized by (*a*) husbands several years older than wives, (*b*) absence of mental disturbances, (*c*) more frequent sex relations, (*d*) husbands equal to or superior to wives in mental abilities.
2. Most normal aged with children live in a household separate from the children but maintain close ties with them based on mutual affection and some dependence.
3. About one-half of men aged 72–77 continue to be sexually active.
4. About one-fourth of men 78 or over continue to be sexually active.
5. Aged men continue to have more sexual activity and interest than aged women.
6. The majority of normal aged experience some decline in sexual interest and activity, but a substantial minority maintain stable activity and interest and some even experience increasing activity and interest.

H. Activities and Satisfaction

1. Disability usually causes less activity but usually is unrelated to satisfaction with life.
2. Socioeconomic status, rather than race, is the primary social influence on activities and attitudes of the normal aged.
3. Patterns of activity and attitudes among surviving normal aged tend to remain stable, with little or no overall decline during periods of 10 or more years. The few aged with declines tend to be balanced by a few aged with increases.
4. Declining activity usually causes declining life satisfaction, while stable or increased activity usually sustains stable or increasing satisfaction.

I. Attitudes toward Health and Cautiousness

1. Two-thirds of the aged are fairly realistic in evaluating their health and tend to be consistent over time in their evaluation.
2. The hypochondriac aged tend to be younger, less active, and more

often female and of lower socioeconomic status in comparison to aged who deny their illness.

3. Few of the normal aged have much concern about, or plan for, future illness.

4. Although the normal aged tend to avoid choosing among risky alternatives when possible, their cautiousness is no greater than that of younger persons when they are forced to decide what chances of success they would accept in choosing a risky alternative.

## J. Age and Death

1. About two-thirds of community residents over 65 identify themselves as elderly, old, or aged (rather than young or middle-aged); and the older a person's chronological age, the more likely he is to identify with one of these older categories.

2. Negroes and persons feeling in poor health tend to identify more often with an older age category.

3. Aged Negroes believe there are more advantages to old age than do white aged.

4. The age category in which an aged person identifies himself has no significant relationship to most activities and attitudes.

5. Most normal aged do not have strong fears about death.

6. Fear of death among the aged is mostly associated with (a) less belief in life after death, (b) less Bible reading, (c) depression, and (d) lower intelligence.

7. Health, mental abilities, and satisfying social roles are the most important factors related to longevity.

In considering these hypotheses, one should bear in mind the cautions stated in the first chapter about the limitations of the original sample and of the successive samples following attrition. It should be remembered that while attempts were made in the sample selection to reflect the age, sex, ethnic, and socioeconomic characteristics of the older population in the locale, the sample was not a probability sample in any sense, and the use of volunteers resulted in a somewhat better-than-average group in terms of most variables. And as time went by, the survivors who returned for repeated examinations tended to represent more and more an elite group physically, mentally, and socially. This is one of the inevitable limitations of longitudinal studies which must be recognized. We do not know how well these findings would or would not apply to those below-average aged who did not volunteer in the beginning or who dropped out because of illness, death, or lack of interest.

## The Future

The search for better and more comprehensive explanations of variations in normal aging continues. Now that six complete sets of observations over a 10-year period have been fully coded and entered on electronic tape, we can expect more emphasis on longitudinal analysis from future reports. Now that the basic data in each specialist's own area have been explored, we can expect more emphasis on interdisciplinary analysis of relations between areas of behavior and functioning. The seventh round of examinations and interviews will soon begin, and the plans are to continue repeating these examinations on the survivors in the panel until all are deceased.

Meanwhile, a second longitudinal study has been started to supplement the first and further test the findings and hypotheses generated so far. An important improvement in the second study is that it will have a more representative sample in order to allow more confident generalizations to larger universes. The sample is an age-and-sex-stratified probability sample of all members of the local health insurance association. Demographic and hospitalization information about those who refuse to participate can be compared to information on those who do participate in order to estimate the amount and type of bias introduced by refusals. Furthermore, the sample will be about twice as large in order to allow more precision in analysis and the systematic comparison of five-year cohorts through time. This will also allow the use of such methods as "longitudinal sequences" and "time-lag" analysis (Baltes, 1968; Schaie, 1965).

Another difference is that the second study focuses on aging in the middle years (45–69) and is more concerned with adaptation to the stresses that usually occur in those years, such as children leaving home, retirement, menopause, serious illness, and death of spouse. For this reason it is usually called the "Duke Adaptation Study." In many other respects it is similar to the first study and attempts to extend and test more precisely the hypotheses reported in this volume.

Activities and attitudes are being measured even more precisely to see if they tend to persist in the middle years as in the later years and if changes in the number and type of activities are followed by similar changes in life satisfaction. Intelligence and reaction times are being measured over time to examine the normal pattern of change of stability in the middle years. Sexual activities, physical functioning, and medical problems are all being carefully examined over time for relationships between themselves and with the mental and social variables. The general hypothesis that those with greater physical, mental, and social resources will more successfully adapt to stress will be systematically explored. Other factors not necessarily related to chronological aging will be examined as possible explanations of the wide individual and group variations found in the normal aging process. Most of the other hypotheses listed will be further tested and specified in both the second study and in the continuing analysis of tests that are repeated every two or three years on the survivors of the first study. Undoubtedly, new and unanticipated findings in the future will generate new hypotheses to correct or add to those in this volume.

## References

Baltes, P. B. Longitudinal and cross-sectional sequences in the study of age and generation effects. *Human Development*, 11:145–171, 1968.

Schaie, K. W. A general model for the study of developmental problems. *Psychological Bulletin*, 64:92–107, 1965.

# Index

Activity: and attitudes, 304, 305, 332, 340; change in attitude, 337; compared with morale, 25; disengagement, 318; effects of aging on, 332; interpersonal, 321; noninterpersonal, 321; and physical well being, 304; race and socioeconomic status, 310–318; reduction, 334; satisfaction, 320, 329; socioeconomic group, 310, 312; theory of aging, 337

Activity Inventory, 305, 311, 320, 332, 333; score of Duke panelists, 24; *see also* Activity

Actuarial life expectancy, 407, 410; *see also* Longevity

Acute brain disorders, 110

Adlersberg, D., 65, 71

Affect: and culture and aging, 98, 101; and perception, 232–265; and age, 243, 250; *see also* Depression

Age: concepts, 381; and death, 383; distribution of subjects, 30; identification, 389–395; physical disability capacity, 39; reaction time, 167, 175, 186, 193

Age awareness, 381–388; and chronological age and sex, 383; factors involved in, 381; health and attitudes, 386; and socioeconomic level, 384

Aging: and culture and affect, 98–107; definition of, 39–40; versus illness, 39–47; theory of, 337

Allergic skin, 56

Alpha activity, 147; *see also* Electroencephalogram

Altrocchi, J., 400

American Psychiatric Association (APA), 108, 109

Ames, L. B., 218, 220, 222, 243, 248

Andermann, K., 140

Anderson, J., 319

Appetite, 94

Apter, N. S., 228

Arteriolar red cell masses, 62, 63

Arteriosclerosis, 37, 227–231; and blood pressure, 160; and EEG, 155; and metabolic disturbance, 40

Arthritis, 37

Attitudes: and change in activity, 337; death, 395–401; effects on aging, 332; and physical well being, 304; and race, 310; and socioeconomic group, 310, 320; toward health, 342

Attitude Inventory, 305, 311, 320, 332, 333

Attrition, 5

Auditory defect, 240; and Rorschach rigidity, 233

Auditory reaction time, 171

Avoidance of problems, 372; *see also* Cautiousness

Babcock, I. W., 98, 103

Baer, R. L., 56

Baltes, P. B., 423

Banham, K. M., 247, 248

Barker, N. W., 65, 71

Barker, R. G., 232, 238

Barnes, R. H., 51–65, 116, 119, 122, 133, 139, 148, 153, 154, 251

Basovitz, H., 377

Beard, B. B., 400

Behavioral impairment, 45; *see also* Physical function rating

Behavior in relation to CVD, 227

Bell, A., 215

Berger, H., 152

Beta activity during photic stimulation, 147; *see also* Electroencephalograph

Bevis, W. M., 98, 103

Biasing effects, 20, 23, 27

Birren, J. E., 168, 243, 251

Blalock, H. M., 334

Blaw, Z., 360

Bloch, E. H., 58, 59

Blood pressure, 58, 158, 227–231

Blood vessels, 55, 57–65

Bloor, W. R., 66

Body hair, changes in distribution of, 54

Borsky, P., 19

Bortz, E. L., 251, 364

Botwinick, J., 135, 167–193, 251, 372–379

Brain syndrome, 108–114; acute, 110; chronic, 111

Brazier, Mary A. B., 126

Brinley, J. F., 181

Bromley, D. B., 251

Brown, R. G., 75–83, 84

Bruens, J. H., 120, 157

Bulbar conjunctive, 57

Burch, N. R., 254

Burgess, E. W., 270, 311, 364, 384, 389, 390, 392, 394, 406

Burke, C. J., 334

Stroller, A., 122
Stromgen, E., 99, 106
Studies, basic and peripheral, 16
Subcutaneous tissues, 51
Subjects, selection of, 18; *see also* Methods
Summary of health and vital statistics, 30
Summary of results, 417–422; activities and satisfaction, 421; attitudes toward health and cautiousness, 421; EEG patterns, 420; intelligence, 420; marriage, family, and sexual behavior, 421; mental illness, 419; perception and affect, 420; physical problems, 419; reaction time, 420
Surwillo, W. W., 185
Swanson, P., 65
Syphilis, 49
Systolic blood pressure, 37; *see also* Blood pressure

Team research, 8; *see also* Interdisciplinary
Tenacity, 93; *see also* Depression
"Test wiseness," 209; *see also* Intelligence
Thaler, M. B., 122, 133, 217
Themes of longitudinal and interdisciplinary study, 417
Thompson, L. W., 65–73, 138–151, 167–193, 227–231
Thompson, R. C., 50
Thompson, W. E., 276, 360
Tietze, C., 98, 105
Time lapse on consistency of self health and medical evaluation, 342–350
Tindall, John P., 50–57
Touch, 48
Townsend, P., 276
Turton, E. C., 135, 158

United States Senate, 363
U.S. Department of Health, Education, and Welfare, 363
U.S.N.H.S. (United States National Health Survey), 19, 21

Van der Drift, J. H. A., 120
Vascular lesions, 55; *see also* Cardiovascular disease

Venous sludge, 62
Verdeaux, G., 140
Verwoerdt, A., 282–298, 299–302, 401–406
Visual defect, 232–242
Vitols, M. M., 98, 103, 104
Volunteers: and random sample, 19–22; Duke subjects, 27
Von Mering, O., 363, 365

WAIS (Wechsler Adult Intelligence Scale), 122, 124, 269; among refusals, 23; and electrocortical activity, 141; in relation to CVD, 228; retest, 209–216; standardization, 194–208; *see also* Intelligence
Waisman, M., 50
Walker, A. R. P., 72
Wallach, M. A., 372, 373, 377
Wang, H. S., 282–302
Warner's Index of Status Characteristics, 197, 274
Warner, W. L., 197, 274, 310, 311
Wechsler-Bellevue in relation to EEG, 122, 124; *see also* WAIS
Wechsler, D., 195, 197, 206, 215, 243
Wechsler Memory scale, 228
Weiner, H., 122
Weiss, A. D., 172, 173
Weiss, S., 157, 167, 168
Welford, A. T., 138, 139, 402
Wells, C. E., 139
Welton, D. G., 52
Werner, H., 238
Wilcox, H. H., 251
Williams, R., 319
Wilson, J. L., 53
Wilson, S., 138–151
Winer, B. J., 170, 374
Woodbury, R. M., 39
Woolman, M., 17
Work satisfaction, determination of, 407; *see also* Attitudes

Young, A. W., 50
Young, W., 111, 155, 160

Zakon, S. J., 50, 52
Zeller, K., 58
Zuker, L., 238